The Orange Order

The Orange Order

A Contemporary Northern Irish History

Eric P. Kaufmann

OXFORD
UNIVERSITY PRESS

OXFORD

UNIVERSITY PRESS

Great Clarendon Street, Oxford OX2 6DP

Oxford University Press is a department of the University of Oxford.
It furthers the University's objective of excellence in research, scholarship,
and education by publishing worldwide in

Oxford New York

Auckland Cape Town Dar es Salaam Hong Kong Karachi
Kuala Lumpur Madrid Melbourne Mexico City Nairobi
New Delhi Shanghai Taipei Toronto

With offices in

Argentina Austria Brazil Chile Czech Republic France Greece
Guatemala Hungary Italy Japan Poland Portugal Singapore
South Korea Switzerland Thailand Turkey Ukraine Vietnam

Oxford is a registered trade mark of Oxford University Press
in the UK and in certain other countries

Published in the United States
by Oxford University Press Inc., New York

British Library Cataloguing in Publication Data
Data available

Library of Congress Cataloging in Publication Data
Data available

Typeset by Laserwords Private Limited, Chennai, India
Printed in Great Britain
on acid-free paper by
Biddles Ltd., King's Lynn, Norfolk

ISBN 978–0–19–920848–7

1 3 5 7 9 10 8 6 4 2

For Stuart and Alannah

Acknowledgements

I would like to acknowledge the support of my wife, Frances, and my children, Stuart and Alannah, who have had to put up with my trips to Northern Ireland and enthusiasm for an obscure subject. In terms of time and money, this project could not have been completed without the generous support of the Economic and Social Research Council, which sponsored this research through a two-year fellowship and a grant under its 'Devolution and Constitutional Change' programme. Henry Patterson, my collaborator on a forthcoming co-authored book on the Orange Order and UUP, *Unionism and Orangeism in Northern Ireland since 1945* (Manchester: Manchester University Press, 2007), has been a tremendous source of insight into Northern Ireland society, history, and Unionist politics. Ruth Dudley Edwards started me on my way with an important list of contacts and pearls of wisdom about researching the Order. Chris Lloyd at Queen's University Belfast gave important advice on geographical analysis. Cecil Houston provided encouragement at the very beginning. This research was sparked off years ago by a comment from Philip Buckner of the Institute for Commonwealth Studies ('I wonder whatever happened to the Orange Order in Toronto'), so thanks must go to him. Useful comments and discussion have also come from, among others, Jon Tonge, Dominic Bryan, Don MacRaild, David Fitzpatrick, Jonathan Mattison, William Jenkins, David Wilson, Seamus Smyth, Paul Dixon, Chris Farrington, and the Northern Ireland Politics group of the Political Studies Association.

This book would never have been written without the excellent access and help of Orangemen throughout Northern Ireland. Foremost among them are the former Executive Officer George Patton and the current Executive Officer Dr David Hume. The Rev. Brian Kennaway, former chairman of the Education Committee, was extremely helpful. Orangemen at county level helped to plot lodge halls on Ordnance Survey maps and provided local knowledge and access to county reports and minute books. Here I would like to especially thank Perry Reid, Robert Abernethy, and Henry Reid in Tyrone, Joe Campbell and Trevor Geary in Armagh, Tom Wright in Belfast, Noel McIlfettrick in Fermanagh, David Brewster in Londonderry, Drew Nelson in Down, and William Leathem in Antrim. The former Grand Master of Canada Norm Ritchie has been helpful with advice and contacts.

Acknowledgements

Note that the views expressed in this work are entirely my own and do not reflect those of any of the above individuals. Colour versions of maps and charts from this book, full statistical appendices, articles, and other Orange material can be found on my Orange website: http://www.sneps.net/OO/ book1.html.

Contents

List of Illustrations

List of Figures

List of Tables

Abbreviations and Main Sources

Organizations and Other

COI	Church of Ireland
DUP	Democratic Unionist Party
ECHR	European Convention on Human Rights
GOLI	Grand Orange Lodge of Ireland, membership dominated by Northern Ireland
IOO	Independent Orange Order, breakaway militant Orange organization
IRA	Irish Republican Army, main paramilitary wing of the Republican movement
LOI	Loyal Orange Institution, same as Orange Order
LOL	Loyal Orange Lodge, prefix applied to all lodges
LVF	Loyalist Volunteer Force, paramilitary association
O & P	Orange & Protestant Committee, militant Orange splinter group, c.1954
PC	Parades Commission, set up by British government to adjudicate on parades
PIRA	Provisional Irish Republican Army, Republican paramilitary association
PSNI	Police Service of Northern Ireland, regular police force. Superseded the RUC in 2001
RUC	Royal Ulster Constabulary, regular police force before 2001
SDLP	Social Democratic and Labour Party
SOD	Spirit of Drumcree, militant Orange splinter group, c.1995–8
UDA	Ulster Defence Association, Loyalist paramilitary association
UDR	Ulster Defence Regiment, local part-time police force
UHRW	Ulster Human Rights Watch, non-governmental organization
UPA	Ulster Protestant Action, Paisleyite splinter group
UPNI	Unionist Party of Northern Ireland, short-lived Faulknerite party, c.1975
UUAC	United Unionist Action Council, formed by UUUC
UUC	Ulster Unionist Council, governing body of UUP
UUP	Ulster Unionist Party, previously known as the Official Unionist Party
UUUC	United Ulster Unionist Council, united Unionist political front
UVF	Ulster Volunteer Force, Loyalist paramilitary association

Main Sources

BT	*Belfast Telegraph*
CAIN	Conflict Archive on the Internet: http://cain.ulst.ac.uk/
CC	Central Committee Minutes of the Grand Orange Lodge of Ireland
GL	Reports of Proceedings of the Grand Orange Lodge of Ireland
GOLI	Grand Orange Lodge of Ireland
NI MOSAIC	Northern Ireland Mosaic (Copyright 2002 and 2004. Experian Micromarketing), obtainable from http://www.interface.ie/micro-marketing.html; MOSAIC is a system of postcode classification (for further details, see the website)

CC, GL, and GOLI documents are at the archives of the Grand Orange Lodge of Ireland, Schomberg House, Belfast; other documents are there except where otherwise specified.

1

Introduction

On 10 September 2005, the worst rioting in Northern Ireland in twenty years was sparked by a parade of mysterious bowler-hatted men wearing Orange sashes accompanied by hard-thumping marching bands and throngs of young spectators. Many outsiders know the Orange Order as the incomprehensible organization at the centre of the conflict-ridden July marching season in Northern Ireland. This book presents the first modern history and social analysis of the Orange Order, and is based upon the Orange Order's treasure trove of internal documents—whose contents have never been exposed to a non-Orange audience.

The Orange Order, or Loyal Orange Institution (as it is officially known; LOI), in Northern Ireland is a fraternity dedicated to furthering the aims of Protestantism and maintaining the British connection.[1] Its loyalty to the Crown is an inheritance which is conditional upon the support of the British Crown for Protestantism and the continued political connection between the British government and Northern Ireland.[2] The Order is an extremely multifaceted organization which must be considered in all its manifestations: cultural, religious, convivial, and political. It also has economic functions as a benevolent association, property holder, and charity. It is an organization located between the private sphere of individuals and the Protestant community as a whole. We can go further and specify that—at least in its main outlines—it is more of a cultural than an economic or political association.

Francis Fukuyama famously predicted that liberalism, democracy, and capitalism would spell the 'End of History' as twenty-first-century man came to appreciate that his cultural inheritance was merely one among many rather than a treasured tradition. Nationalism, in this view, was merely a growing pain which underdeveloped societies would pass through on their way to the cosmopolitan, individualist 'End of History'.[3] Anthony Giddens's sociology of high modernity sounds a similar note: globalization and fragmented identities are leading to de-traditionalization.[4] The twentieth-century decline of sectarianism in North America, Australia, and northern England reinforces the instinctive belief that conservative traditionalism naturally gives way to modern liberalism.

But what has occurred within Northern Ireland in the past thirty years turns conventional theories on their head. Society there has modernized and grown wealthy, but history continues to live in the hearts of men. The economy has developed and global pop culture flourishes, but underneath this surface, younger generations are more wedded to their ethnic past than their parents. Like youth everywhere in the West, young Unionists and Nationalists in Northern Ireland have rejected many of the traditions of their elders. But in common with the youth of the Muslim world, the rejection of established hierarchies has paved the way for militant communalism rather than cosmopolitan liberalism. Orangeism is an old tradition which is nonetheless geared towards communal solidarity. It thus finds its sails caught in the conflicting crosswinds of historical deference and youthful defiance.

The Order as an Ethnic Association

In its official statements, the Order stresses its religious basis. It takes great care to repudiate those who use the term 'Protestant' in a secular fashion, and the recent (1997) LOI Commission avers that 'Ulster-Scot', 'Unionist', or 'Plantation' is better suited than 'Protestant' to describing the Order's *culture*.[5] The Order's 'Constitution'—*The Qualifications of an Orangeman*—makes reference to only ethical and religious obligations. Nevertheless, while its religious mission is central to its being, the Orange Order is not an evangelical religious organization like the Christian Coalition in the United States. Though it shares some features with the Coalition's anti-Catholic predecessors like the National Association of Evangelicals or the nineteenth-century Evangelical Alliance, it is an entirely different creature.[6]

Here we come to what is perhaps the crux of Orangeism's *raison d'être*: that of an *ethnic* association representing the Ulster-Protestant people. In addition, the Order has adopted a this-worldly, ethno-cultural orientation in virtually every part of the world where it has taken root, thereby alienating religious fundamentalists. For instance, in the strongest Canadian Orange province, Newfoundland, evangelicals like the early Methodists, Salvation Army, and now Pentecostalists have long discouraged their members from joining the Order.[7] In Northern Ireland, a similar pattern can be discerned in the significant number of Orange apostates who leave the organization because of their 'born-again' rediscovery of Christ. As the Grand Master of the Orange Order, Martin Smyth, found out in 1995 when he participated in a prayer breakfast sponsored by American evangelicals, Ulster-Protestant ethnic boundaries do not take kindly to being stretched by religious proselytizers.[8]

In Canada and Australia, the Order was rooted in British-Protestant dominant-group ethnicity. Dominant ethnic groups are communities of shared ancestry which dominate particular nations or states.[9] The composite British-Protestant group which holds sway in Canada and Australia is similar to that of the mixed Anglo-Scots 'British' group in Northern Ireland. These mixed ethnic groups were avid participants in what Douglas Cole refers to as Britannic nationalism: the feeling of shared 'British' (as opposed to English) descent, Protestant faith, and imperial destiny.[10] Outside these locales, things were slightly different. In Scotland, England, and the United States, the Order identified with the broader Protestant ethnic majority, though it never became accepted as 'native'. As a result, Scottish, English, and American Orangeism relied mainly on immigrants and their descendants from Ulster (in Scotland and England) or Canada (in the USA). In other locations, Orangeism was aligned with a minority ethnic group. In West Africa, the Order is linked to the Ewe minority, which straddles the Ghana–Togo boundary, and in Eire, it is part of the fabric of the small Irish-Protestant minority. In places where the religious division between Protestant and Catholic is non-ethnic (as in Continental Europe or the Western Isles of Scotland), Orangeism has never taken root.[11]

The ethno-cultural dimension of Orangeism was confirmed in a straw poll taken at a conference on the future of the Order in 2003, attended by 250 selected delegates, the vast majority from the six counties of Northern Ireland. Of those voting, just 3 per cent referred to the Order as a purely religious organization and fewer still spoke of it as a social, welfare, or charitable organization. On the other hand, 46 per cent considered the Institution to be 'a cultural organisation with its basis in the reformed faith', 36 per cent saw it as a 'religious organisation with cultural characteristics', and 14 per cent felt that no one aspect was paramount.[12]

Scholars of ethnicity and nationalism emphasize that ethnic groups are demarcated by cultural features like religion, language, or race. Groups need not possess the full range of cultural markers—Ulster Protestants and Catholics have the same accent—but at least one significant difference is needed.[13] In Ulster, religion serves as an ethnic boundary marker between Catholic-Irish and Protestant-British ethnic groups. This reinforces Brendan O'Leary's and John McGarry's contention that the conflict is an ethno-national one, but does not invalidate Steve Bruce's hypothesis that religious narration helps to reinforce Ulster-Protestant ethnicity. Indeed, it seems to me that the two positions are compatible.[14] Religion, for instance, helps Protestants frame their communal story as one of divine election and religious mission. The Old Testament, which Ulster-Protestants hold dear, is packed with references to Israel as a chosen people, and provides a template for Ulster-Protestants' religious nationalism.[15] A similar process occurs elsewhere in the world.

Around the Mediterranean or Balkans, for example, many groups, whether Christian or Muslim, define themselves as 'defenders of the faith', and their glorious past typically invokes battles against the infidel (e.g. Serbs against Turks at the Battle of Kosovo in 1389).[16]

The Social and Geographical Anatomy of the Order

In 1997, an Orange Order Commission which received responses from 41 per cent of Orange lodges found that just 22 per cent of the membership could be described as even broadly 'white collar'. Fully 40 per cent were manual workers, 20 per cent farmers, and 5–10 per cent retirees. The Order is also younger than some imagine: 20 per cent of members are under thirty and just 25 per cent are over sixty.[17] Orangeism has always drawn its principal strength from the working and rural masses, but encompassed all ranks of society in its lodges until the twentieth century. In 1900, as we shall see later in the book, those in the top several hundred positions (i.e. in the district, county, and grand lodges) in the Order were disproportionately drawn from the middle and professional classes of Ulster-Protestant society. Those at the pinnacle of the Orange pyramid, Grand Lodge, had the same social origins as the province's landed and mercantile elite until the 1960s. Orangemen from the mass base of local lodges, by contrast, contained very few non-manual members. Fifty years on, things had changed completely: Orange leaders came from the same social background as their followers and were no longer drawn from the higher social strata of the population. This has been accompanied by a wider anti-elitist cultural shift from 'deference to defiance' within the Orange rank and file, who are no longer prepared to tip their hat to their social betters.[18]

In 1950, roughly a fifth of adult Protestant men wore the Orange sash, though a much larger number, perhaps another 10 to 20 per cent of Protestant males, had been initiated at some point in their lives but let their membership lapse. When we add junior and female Orangemen to the total and consider Orange families and sympathizers, we begin to see that Orangeism is a major cultural force whose power vastly exceeds the number of paid-up members at any given point in time. This influence is not uniform, but geographically variable. No two points in Northern Ireland are much more than two hours' drive apart, but the degree of local diversity is impressive. Arguably the most important engine of local Protestant variation is religion. Antrim, for instance, has a strong Scottish-Presbyterian strain in its population. Fermanagh Protestants, on the other hand, are largely Church of Ireland (COI). The local Catholic population is not evenly spread either, but is more heavily concentrated in the western half of the province, in West Belfast and along the southern boundary with Eire. On the other hand, Antrim, North

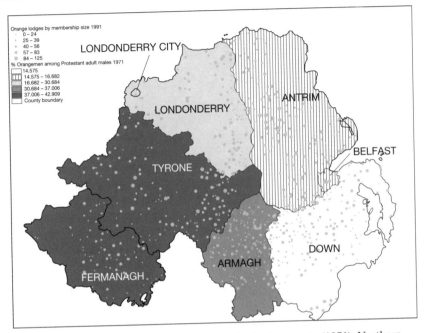

Figure 1.1 Orange lodges (1991) and Orange density by county (1971), Northern Ireland

Sources: Northern Ireland Census 1971; GOLI returns, 1971, 1991; based upon Ordnance Survey of Northern Ireland (OSNI) digital boundaries. © Crown copyright.

Down, and Belfast county borough (until recently) have solid Protestant majorities.

The map in Figure 1.1 shows the proportion of Orangemen within the Protestant male adult population ('Orange density') of the six counties and two cities of Northern Ireland in 1971. The map also plots the more than 800 lodges, adjusted by membership size, in the province in 1991. With the exception of Lough Neagh in central Northern Ireland, areas without lodges represent sections of the province which are almost free of Protestants. Though Orange density has fallen sharply in the cities, the basic county-level differences remain much as they were. Notice that Orangeism is strongest among Protestants in the western counties of Northern Ireland, (darker shades) where there are more Catholics and a higher COI population. What this level of geography cannot show is the disproportionate strength of Orangeism along the entire southern border, where the proportion of Catholics is very high. It will later become clear that Orangeism thrives best when local Protestants feel under siege, but not defeated. This explains its social power in the border counties and its relative weakness both in the Republic of Ireland and in Protestant-majority counties in the north.

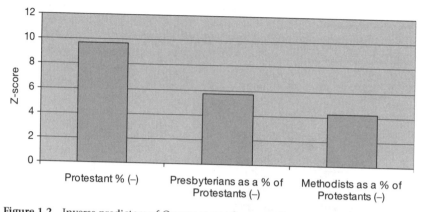

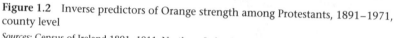

Figure 1.2 Inverse predictors of Orange strength among Protestants, 1891–1971, county level

Sources: Census of Ireland 1891–1911; Northern Ireland Census 1926–71; Orange county reports, 1891–1971.

These trends are confirmed through statistical analysis of membership at county level for the years 1891–1971. The strongest trend is that Orangeism is weakest in Protestant and Presbyterian counties in eastern Ulster. The inverse of this is that a higher Catholic and COI population boosts Orange participation in a county. Occupational distribution, migration, and total buildings (a proxy for area wealth) had no effect on Orange membership density (Orangemen per Protestant population) in these years. On the other hand, the denominational mix in each county predicted almost three-quarters of the variation in Orange density over place and time (see Figure 1.2).[19]

In the glare of the headlines, people sometimes forget that Orangeism is a fraternity like any other, with an important convivial function. In many communities in the nineteenth century, there were few sources of entertainment beyond that provided in the lodge hall.[20] Halls are not only used for meetings, which allow friends to get together outside a church setting, but also host community social events. Even today, lodge halls are often among the most prominent recreational buildings in many small communities. Rational-choice theories of resource mobilization argue that political organizations which provide their members with 'selective incentives' like sociability perform better in the long run than those which simply emphasize political ideology and action.[21] Orangeism is a community tradition, and memories of Orange events are handed down across the generations. For many Orangemen, the political aspirations and theology of the Orange movement are less real than local memories, events, and parades. Membership, especially in rural areas, is often inherited via family connections rather than chosen by those seeking a distinct Orange ideology.[22]

The Political Activities of the Orange Order in Twentieth-Century Northern Ireland

Political activity has always been a key ingredient in the Orange repertoire, and I would argue that the Order has served as both a cultural association—what Robert Putnam calls an agent of 'bonding' social capital—and a political interest group. In the evolving political context of the twentieth century, it has shifted from being a political insider ('protective' interest) in a corporatist system to an outsider, or 'promotional' lobby group, in a pluralistic polity.[23] In the process, it has lost the elitist, consensus-building quality which characterizes groups at the very centre of state policy, and has instead become more independent of the state and party politics.[24] Cosy backroom meetings with friendly politicians have been replaced by adversarial meetings with hostile officials. The Order is also conditioned by its political environment in an ethnically divided society. In divided societies, parties try to outflank each other as the best defenders of their particular ethnic group's interests.[25] The Grand Orange Lodge was caught up in this struggle, and constantly had to watch out for challenges from Ian Paisley and other Independent Unionists on its right flank.

The variegated role of the Orange Order among Ulster Protestants finds expression in its Grand Lodge committee system, which has developed over the past century in response to changes in Northern Ireland's socio-political environment. Grand Lodge may be viewed as the Orange 'parliament' where delegates from the counties gather to discuss and vote on policy and Orange laws (see Figure 1.3). Yet Grand Lodge is an unwieldy body of more than 100 people which met only twice per year until 2000 and now meets just four times per year. This raises the issue of who exercises Orange power between the Grand Lodge sessions. Originally, policy was executed by Grand Lodge through ad hoc committees such as those charged with setting up a new headquarters (1922) or erecting the obelisk at the Battle of the Diamond (1927). Repeated functional requirements have since led to broad lines of organization which reflect the stimuli to which the Order has responded.[26]

Committees of the Order after the creation of Northern Ireland in 1922 were originally less numerous than they are today, but many of the basic functions have persisted (see Figure 1.4). For example, there existed a Historical Committee, reconstituted after 1922, to oversee the Order's ethno-historical role of maintaining an Ulster-Protestant collective memory. This broad 'historical' category encompassed archiving of documents, constructing memorials, re-enacting events, producing pamphlets, and lecturing to the rank and file. The Historical Committee is the ancestor of today's Education Committee, though

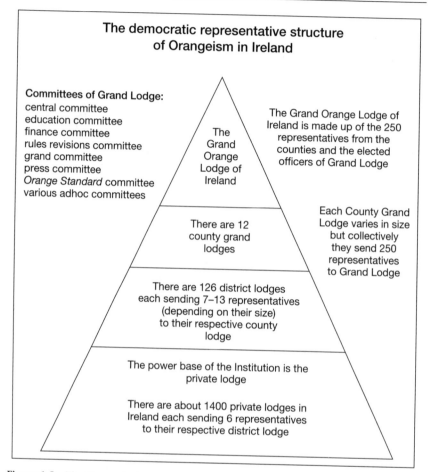

Figure 1.3 The Orange lodge structure

Source: GOLI policy document in response to the SOD, 1997.

the latter incorporates legislative concerns arising from the 1947 Education Act (N.I.).[27]

In 1922, two new committees were formed, the Press Committee, dedicated to rebutting 'slanderous' accusations in the radio and printed media of the day, and the Parliamentary Committee—formed to oversee new legislation and to 'take whatever [political] action they consider necessary' in response.[28] The Press Committee survived until the 1990s, when technical advances allowed Grand Lodge and its public relations officer to reappropriate this function and communicate directly with the public. Needless to say, there would be few in the Order today who wouldn't sympathize with the sentiments of the Press Committee's founders! The work of the Parliamentary Committee was largely devolved to the Central Committee in the years after partition as well as to specialist committees like that for education, which could focus its fire on appropriate specialist agencies of government. In addition, the Grand Lodge's Finance Committee (which survives today) helped to oversee budgetary matters.

Most important of all is the Central Committee. The Central Committee acts as the nerve centre of the institution and may be considered the Orange 'cabinet'. Contrary to the assertions of the splinter group Spirit of Drumcree (SOD) in 1997, the Central Committee is not a recent invention, and proved a decisive actor soon after Partition in 1921, forming a kind of Orange 'cabinet' by 1926.[29] Here the Grand Master ('president'), Grand Secretary ('vice-president'), and other top-ranking Orange officers—mostly county masters and secretaries as well as conveners of committees—discuss major policy initiatives and decide which items of business to forward to the periodic Grand Lodge sessions. They are also empowered to issue press releases and, since they meet more frequently than the Grand Lodge, have the important role of managing the intersessional affairs of the Institution.[30]

The Central Committee, Elitism, and Executive Power

The Central Committee of Grand Lodge gives the Orange elite considerable latitude in managing the flow of grassroots private, district, and county lodge resolutions, executing policy, and making public statements. It thus exercises a degree of elite control in an otherwise highly democratic institution, though there are good reasons for believing that the Central Committee is less of a socially elite body than it was in previous years. How is control achieved? On the surface, the structure of the Central Committee is relatively open: three members are sent by each county Grand Lodge in Northern Ireland and two apiece from the county lodges in the Republic. In principle, there is no reason why this should not ensure a strong grassroots democratic flow up to Grand Lodge (see Figure 1.3).

In practice, however, several 'intangible' forces allow for a stronger dose of executive power. First of all, as we move from the private level through intermediate tiers up to Grand Lodge, each lodge level possesses emergent properties (i.e. not just a sum of lower-level actors) and places greater value upon the 'qualities' of the men it puts forward to higher levels. Thus men of means, influence, ambition, and political talent find their way up the lodge structure. In two American labour movements of the early twentieth century, the Congress of Industrial Organizations and the Industrial Workers of the World, union leaders of white Anglo-Saxon Protestant ('WASP') descent led a predominantly southern-eastern European workforce because the latter 'pushed' WASPs to the top of the union hierarchy, where it was felt they could

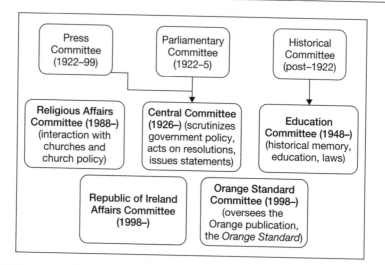

Figure 1.4 Evolution of major policy committees, Grand Orange Lodge of Ireland

better fit in with American political culture.[31] Likewise, in the Order, up until the 1960s, the strongly deferential Loyalist culture—especially in southern and western parts of the province—resulted in a higher socio-economic profile at Grand Lodge level than at private lodge level. For instance, Fintona District in Tyrone, in view of the vacancy caused by Sir George Clark's departure as Grand Master, recommended the Marquess of Hamilton, MP. It would be an 'honor for County Tyrone to have such a worthy brother in this high office . . . [he] would bring "grace and dignity" to this office [and] would mean much goodwill for the Orange Institution in Ireland'.[32]

Add to this the cost of subscriptions and the time demands placed on individuals as they ascend the Orange ladder, and we can see how higher levels helped nominate (until recently) individuals of middle-class or aristocratic background to positions of leadership within Grand Lodge. Whereas class no longer divides Grand Lodge from the rank and file, two other factors allow for some concentration of power at Central Committee and Grand Lodge. The first is the low degree of participation at Grand Lodge meetings, where scarcely more than half typically attend.[33] This facilitates the emergence of committed 'leaders' who dominate discussion at Central Committee and Grand Lodge and are the most active in Grand Lodge affairs. To some extent, this is necessitated by the fact that time for discussion is limited, the need for action is often urgent, and Grand Lodge rarely meets. In reading minutes of the Central Committee since 1945, it becomes apparent that the Grand Master is often, but not always, the dominant figure, with particular others wielding significant influence. For instance, Sir George Clark and James (Jim) Molyneaux are two individuals whose experience and clout gave them a great deal of legitimacy within the Central Committee in the late 1960s and early 1970s during a period of relatively weak Grand Mastership. In most Central Committee meetings, policy is decided by discussion among just a handful of key individuals. Though individuals frequently disagree, a consensus usually emerges quite quickly—often in support of respected 'leaders'.

The format of discussion at Central Committee typically involves a list of business items (including lodge resolutions) and reports from committee conveners. Debate then follows on various policy items, often beginning with the election of officers and grand chaplains. There is a high degree of accord on many issues, and many votes have a consensual ring to them, with little dissent from the Grand Lodge 'back benches'. Resolutions from lodge, district, and county levels can be sent back to the counties or merely taken as read, thereby allowing the Central Committee to contain grassroots tendencies. To take but a few examples: in 1935, a resolution from Ballymoney district 'on a variety of subjects, several of which would require government legislation to be passed', was simply referred back to the County Antrim Grand Lodge.[34]

In 1968, when a County Londonderry private lodge resolved to censure its county lodge for taking no action against Robin Chichester-Clark, M.P., for attending a Roman Catholic service for Colonel McCausland, the Grand Secretary pointed out that proper procedure had not been followed, so the resolution could only 'possibly' be considered at a subsequent meeting.[35] Even as late as 1971, at the height of the Troubles, Central Committee power was strongly reaffirmed by those present. As one member bluntly put it: 'all [district and county] secretaries must accept all instructions given by all leaders.'[36] However, the momentum of power had begun to swing away from Grand Lodge in line with general Unionist disenchantment with the traditional Unionist elite and the UK government. This later manifested itself in catcalls from the platform on the Twelfth of July in 1971.[37] After this date, rumblings of discontent from the Orange masses were voiced with increasing alacrity.

Rebels and Traditionalists: the Great Divide Within Orangeism

One of the most salient divisions in the Unionist community is between what I term 'rebels' and 'traditionalists' (see Table 1.1). Protestantism was originally a dissenting religious movement, and its populist, fissiparous spirit still animates Protestant Ulster.[38] However, there is a great difference between the COI, with its establishment status and links to tradition, and low-church dissenting sects like the Presbyterians and Methodists. The latter have a history of conflict with the established Anglo-Irish elite over the right to worship freely and many supported radical movements like the United Irishmen and, later, the Ulster labour movement. This tension foregrounds the multifaceted divide within Unionism, which is represented in the form of 'rebel' and 'traditionalist' ideal types in Table 1.1. These categories nest within the 'Ulster-Loyalist' vs 'Ulster-British' dichotomy developed by Jennifer Todd, and may also be seen to complement Todd's work by dissecting the 'Ulster-Loyalist' category. The liberal, civic 'Ulster-British' tradition is a minor chord in Orange and popular Unionist life. Instead, I look at the majority 'Ulster-Loyalist' strand and the differing traditions therein. The 'rebel vs traditional' schema attempts to root its competing idioms in distinct regional-historical locations and sketch out the difference in fundamental principle between the two. One could go even further and dissect 'rebel Unionism' into Steve Bruce's categories of evangelical (sectarian) and secular (ethno-nationalist). Some prefer to throw up their hands and speak of Unionism as an irreducibly diverse babble

Table 1.1 Rebel and Traditionalist Modes of Ulster Unionism

	Rebels	'Loyal' traditionalists
Denomination	Presbyterian, Methodist	Church of Ireland
Plantation origin	Scots-Irish	Anglo-Irish
Mass base	Industrial labour, small freeholders	Rural tenants
North American exemplars	'Scotch-Irish' patriots in USA, c.1776	Orange Loyalists in Canada, c.1837
Interpretation of Orangeism	Uphold militant Protestantism	Uphold traditional British-Protestant values
View of Grand Lodge and Unionist leaders	Sceptical	Respectful
Preferred political expression	Direct public protest	Informal elite channels
Preferred Orange principle	Ulster-Protestant ethnic interest and reformed faith—as embodied in abstract principle and the sentiments of the mass membership	Orange tradition—as embodied in Orange laws, ordinances, customs, and history
Leadership	Evangelical clergy, petit bourgeoisie	Aristocracy, large local businessmen
Political philosophy	Lockean radical change, populism	Burkean evolution, deference to elite consensus
Attitudes to alcohol, band discipline, and traditional social mores	Secularists more permissive, evangelicals more conservative than even traditionalists	Conservative
Stance towards paramilitaries and political violence	More permissive, especially secular rebels	Antagonistic
Attitude towards British Crown	Conditionality	Loyalty
Interpretation of Protestantism	Protestantism as dissent	Protestantism as tradition
National identity	Ulstermen	British
Favoured Northern Ireland party	DUP	UUP
Regional base	Antrim, North Down, Belfast	South and west

held together only by a commitment to the Union.[39] What the study of Orangeism reveals, however, is that there is a definite clustering of positions within Unionism. Unbundled, the individual strands of Unionist diversity (i.e. class, region, denomination) remain relatively latent and unimportant. Meanwhile, many seem to think that rural traditionalism equates to militant Protestantism, but the Orange Order—a deeply conservative association which has spurned militancy and street politics in all locations—confounds this easy equation.[40]

In the underground museum at Franklin court in Philadelphia, one exhibit relates how the Presbyterian 'Scotch-Irish' of the Pennsylvania back country endorsed the frontier populism of the anti-Indian Paxton Boys prior to the Revolution. Later, these 'Scotch-Irishers' strongly supported the Revolution of 1776–83 against the one-third of Americans who remained loyal to the British. The children and grandchildren of the 'Scotch-Irish' Patriots gave birth to Jacksonian populism in the 1830s and were prominent among the pioneers of Texas. They may be identified as the archetypal Ulster-Protestant 'rebels'. The Ulster-Protestant 'traditionalist' alter ego could be found north of the American border, where Irish Protestants (the largest ethnic group in English Canada by 1867) from more Anglican counties like Cavan, Monaghan, and Leitrim established Orangeism as the backbone of the Canadian Tory Party.[41] Canadian Orangemen, few of whom were Presbyterian, fitted in well with Canada's counter-revolutionary loyalism and served as the shock troops of popular toryism. They supported the established church and political elite, helping to suppress the liberal rebellions of 1837–8, 1870, and 1885, and were distinguished by their enthusiasm for Empire and the British connection into the 1970s.[42]

Counties Antrim and Belfast have generally been the most rebellious in the province, with their high Methodist and Presbyterian populations and significant working-class and dissenting histories. The roots of this originated with the United Irishmen, with their strong Antrim base, whose struggle for religious freedom for dissenters and land rights for tenants had a long pedigree. Meanwhile, in growing, rapidly industrializing Belfast, a class element was added to the mix. This began no later than the 1860s, when William Johnston of Ballykilbeg became the spokesman for a new, Belfast-based popular Orangeism. In a period when Orange marches were officially banned, Johnston's movement challenged the Anglo-Irish Ascendancy who dominated the Order, with their penchant for loyalty and hierarchy. Less concerned with protecting the land rights of the aristocracy and the established status of the COI, this new brand of Orangeism focused on attaining the right to parade and galvanizing the Protestant working class. Though conservative forces managed to oust Johnston from the leadership, he gained the support of many proletarian Orangemen in Belfast. Dominic Bryan ascribes Johnston's rise to working men's more independent economic status (as compared with the traditional tenantry), which made them less dependent on traditional forms of landlord–tenant loyalty.[43]

Antrim advocates of tenants' rights, Belfast working-class agitators, and militant Protestants coalesced to form the basis of the breakaway Independent Orange Order (IOO) in 1903. The movement's beginnings can be traced to heckling at the Orange platform during a Twelfth gathering at Castlereagh in 1901. Thomas Sloan, who became an IOO leader, challenged the Belfast Grand Master Colonel Thomas Saunderson over remarks he made that supposedly defended the government's position in banning the 1901 Rostrevor parade. Sloan's appearance on the platform, and his challenge to an individual of Saunderson's class, were unprecedented. Sloan's subsequent successful decision to run against a Conservative Association candidate in South Belfast sealed the rift between Sloan and established Unionism.[44]

Sloan's suspension laid the groundwork for the rise of the IOO, which blossomed during 1903–8 and maintains an active following today—particularly in North Antrim, where the Rev. Ian Paisley is a prominent supporter.[45] What is not appreciated is that mainstream Orangeism, especially in Antrim, shares an 'independentist' streak, manifested through support for the Democratic Unionist Party (DUP) and through a cherishing of the Presbyterian–United Irishmen tradition of rebellious, contingent Unionism. For instance, though the Antrim Grand Officer the Rev. John Brown occasionally warned of Paisleyite tendencies in particular lodges like LOL 159 Magheragall, he also tried to speak sympathetically to their concerns and bring about a rapprochement with the IOO. In 1967, for instance, he accepted an invitation to preach at an Independent Orange service in Ballymoney, County Antrim, in an attempt to build bridges.[46]

Rebel Unionism has been a recessive trait through much of the nineteenth and twentieth centuries because of mainland Britain's Unionism and the paternal mediating role of the Ulster-Protestant elite. As the end of the millennium approached, things began to change. Brian Faulkner, the last Unionist Party leader to speak with a patrician pseudo-English accent, symbolized the demise of the old Ulster 'squirearchy'. In his wake came men such as James Molyneaux, William (Billy) Douglas, and Martin Smyth: self-made populists chafing against the domination of the traditional elites. The new breed were in better tune with the Protestant masses who were losing their deferential traditionalism. Modernizing impulses led to flattened status hierarchies and a search for a fundamental ethnic Unionism, freed from the cake of custom, ritual, restraint, and compromise. In this way, modernization, far from heralding a new spirit of liberalism and 'civic' Unionism, helped instead to recharge a recessive rebel Unionism, bringing it to prominence. In contrast to 1914, when a temporary emergency united the elites and masses of Ulster against Britain leaving the class structure intact, rebel Unionism in the twenty-first century represented a root-and-branch overhaul of the system, a return to a spirit unseen since 1798.

Structure of the Book

The first two chapters of this book consider Orangeism's political influence towards the end of the Stormont period (1922–72). During this phase of its existence, Orangeism saturated the Official Unionist Party, which controlled the Northern Ireland parliament at Stormont on behalf of the Protestant majority.[47] Though Michael Farrell's apellation, 'the Orange State', is often fitting, none has demonstrated how the Order managed to hold state officials to account. Before the mid-1960s, an elite of mostly patrician and mercantile grandees with Unionist Party connections captained the Order. Their stature combined loyalty to the Unionist Party with a defence of Protestant interests, and in this period they successfully contained grassroots discontent against the government. Then things began to change.

Chapter 2 examines the turbulent years under the new Prime Minister, Terence O'Neill. Under O'Neill's leadership, Catholic civil rights campaigners and a British government sensitized to Protestant discrimination began to pressure the Unionist government to reform. O'Neill's Unionist government attempted to comply, but the Unionist grassroots were outraged. This put the old UUP–Orange corporatist system under intolerable strain. The ascent of James Chichester-Clark as Prime Minister of Northern Ireland in 1969 made little difference, as we shall see in Chapter 3. During 1969–72, the entry of the Irish Republican Army (IRA) onto the scene prompted the peak of the violent conflict between Catholics and Protestants known as the 'Troubles'. The Orange response to the chaos and violence, and its unwillingness to bend even in the face of danger, forms the centrepiece of this chapter.

In 1972, the British government abolished the Northern Ireland parliament at Stormont. British direct rule was soon accompanied by a reduction in the level of IRA violence. Chapter 4 probes the Orange response to the British–Irish search for a new constitutional arrangement for Northern Ireland based on power-sharing and a role for the Irish government in the running of the province. During 1972–7, the Order resisted these measures, coming into open confrontation with Faulkner's Unionist Party and landing itself outside the official circles of power. The Order's attempt to unite anti-Sunningdale forces under the umbrella of United Unionism held for some time, but also exposed the fissures between the Order's 'respectable' traditionalism and the rebel Unionism of Ian Paisley and the Protestant paramilitaries.

In Chapter 5, the story of Orange policy responses to British initiatives after 1978 continues as the Orange Deputy Grand Master James Molyneaux assumed the leadership of the UUP. The close relationship between

Molyneaux and Grand Master Martin Smyth ensured a stable axis of anti-power-sharing rejectionism which encompassed the entire 1979–94 period. With the help of survey and mass membership data, this chapter also turns our attention to some of the sociological and geographic currents moving within the wider Unionist electorate in this period. The Orange Order lost 500 men to the Troubles, and its reaction to this violence is interrogated in greater detail. We find that the Order was politically more conservative than the Unionist electorate, but steered its membership away from militancy and paramilitary violence.

Chapters 6 to 10 are concerned with the recent period of Orange history from 1995 to 2005. Changes in Republican strategy since the 1995 ceasefire brought about the rise of Nationalist 'residents,' groups which began to contest the right of the Order to parade contentious routes. In Chapters 6 and 7, the book concentrates on the battle between the Orange Order and Nationalist residents over the Drumcree parade route in Portadown. During 1995–7, the Order successfully paraded, but the ensuing violence proved a public relations disaster which split its membership. Social changes since the 1960s, documented here, radically altered the class composition of the Order and led to falling membership, fuelling populism. Out of the violence at Drumcree rose the aggressive SOD, a populist movement within the Order which supported the antics of the paramilitaries at Drumcree. This led to a reaction among traditionalist Orangemen, encompassing much of the leadership, clerical Orangemen, and the Education Committee. This battle for the soul of Orangeism is the main theme of these chapters.

In Chapter 8, the book changes direction to examine the troubled links between the UUP and the Order in the Trimble era. David Trimble's willingness to consider the unthinkable and sign up to executive power-sharing with Sinn Fein cost him the support of a majority of the Unionist community. The Orange response was predictably fiercer, and began with opposition to the Good Friday Agreement in 1998. This chapter also uses survey and Ulster Unionist Council (UUC) data to show the impact of Orangeism on successive UUC votes and the role of the Order in emasculating Trimble and the modernizers within the UUP. Finally, the chapter examines Orange opinion data to politically locate the Orange voter, and reveals the discussions which led to a fracturing of the century-old link to the UUP. After a fifty-year cold war, much of the Order's leadership and many members finally reconciled themselves to Ian Paisley and his Free Presbyterians, the outlaws of Unionism who came to power in late 2003.

The Whiterock parade riot in 2005 showed that parading conflicts remain as fraught as ever. Chapter 9 returns to the battle lines to continue the story of Drumcree. The Parades Commission (PC) was set up in 1998, and its determi-nations—which coincided with a period of increased parade restriction—are bitterly resented by the Orange Order. This chapter examines the Order's efforts to have the PC abolished, and the Grand Lodge's decision to employ a legal and public relations strategy based on secular civil rights to defeat its opponent. This saga continues to this day, but has split the Order between affected districts like Portadown, who wish to put their case to the PC, and the majority of the Order, which feels that legitimacy should be withheld from this body.

In Chapter 10 we take a hard look at two deep social problems which bedevil the Order at the dawn of the twenty-first century: falling membership and violence. An array of data sources is used to diagnose the cause of the Order's 40–50-year membership slide, which has reached crisis levels, especially in the cities. The chapter uses postcode profiling and statistical techniques to examine membership, resignation, and suspension data. It asks whether there really has been a middle-class exodus in response to the violence of Drumcree and the Troubles. It scrutinizes expulsion and suspension data to address the vexed issue of violence recently raised by the Orange writer Brian Kennaway. The conclusion pulls it all together and poses normative questions about the validity of Orangeism and 'ethnic' Unionism as identity choices in contemporary Northern Ireland.

Part I

From Insider to Outsider, 1963–1995

2

Cracks in the Establishment: Orange Opposition to O'Neill, 1963–1969

James Craig, John Andrews, and Basil Brooke (Lord Brookeborough) were the only three individuals to serve as Prime Minister of Northern Ireland between 1921 and 1963, reflecting the high degree of stability of the Stormont regime. The Ulster Protestant political elite was organically linked with the Order, from which it had built its stock of political capital and learned its communal traditions. Hence Craig remarked in 1934, 'I am an Orangeman first and a politician . . . afterwards.'[1] After leading Northern Ireland, Andrews captained the Order as Grand Master from 1948 until 1954, and Brookeborough served as Fermanagh County Grand Master.

Dominic Bryan suggests that Orangeism was an inherently volatile political tool for the Unionist elite, which was always susceptible to 'independent' militant Protestants or labour leaders, many hailing from Antrim and Belfast. This is particularly true of periods of quiescence (i.e. the 1930s, post-1945) when few pressing issues were available to unify elites and masses around a common Protestant political project. At times such as these, notes Bryan, the economic interests of the Protestant elite and the expressive desires of the Protestant urban masses pulled in opposite directions. The result was a rise in 'rough' parading, a decline in support for the UUP and Grand Lodge elite, and heightened expressions of populist political dissent.[2]

The Orange Establishment, 1950–1963

Bryan's remarks are broadly correct. They must, however, be qualified by the fact that there has been an important post-1950s trend towards greater tolerance of dissent by the Order's leadership. Grand Lodge reports show few rebellious resolutions from private and district level until the 1950s. Where the Order opposed the government, as in the 1946 Grand Lodge debates surrounding the new education bill, it did so as a united body. Moreover, the tone adopted was generally one of respectful disagreement with the government since virtually all government ministers were Orangemen. The Prime Minister's attendance at the 1946 Grand Lodge sessions was symbolic of the strong link between Orangeism and the state, and successive speakers stressed that while they wished to see policy change, they did not wish to tarnish or 'hurt the Prime Minister'.[3]

In 1953, the Northern Ireland government's decision to prevent an Orange band from parading in the Nationalist town of Dungiven, County Londonderry, led to widespread ructions within the Orange and Unionist community. A vocal group of Dungiven Orangemen led by the outspoken former flight lieutenant Billy Douglas of County Londonderry challenged the government's decision (and by extension Grand Lodge's acquiescence) and accused Grand Lodge of complicity and weakness in the face of IRA assertiveness. On balance, the Orange Order's grassroots supported the band's right to parade despite the opposition of most local Protestants. Douglas and others formed a rebellious splinter group known as the Orange & Protestant Committee (O & P) to press for reform, and held a mass rally of 1,400 people at Belfast's Wellington Hall, where the main grievances were aired.[4]

The O & P demands called for a reform of the elitist Central Committee and an end to formal Orange–Unionist Party ties. However, the Order was at a peak of membership and influence, and the Orange establishment in Grand Lodge felt secure enough to quash the O & P movement and drag its members in front of a disciplinary tribunal, and openly called for the membership to support the governing Unionist Party against Independents and the Northern Ireland Labour Party in the coming elections.[5] They also paid scant attention to the noises coming from the young firebrand preacher Ian Paisley. The Orange Order first moved to censure Paisley's breakaway Free Presbyterian Church in October 1951, when, at the urging of clerical Orangemen, it formed county committees to vet the credentials of clerical brethren from non-mainstream denominations. Several months later, a resolution went out advising that Orange halls were not to be used by non-approved denominations such as the Free Presbyterians.[6]

Paisley's bombastic response thirsted after controversy, accusing the Order of ecumenism and moral lassitude:

Are we to take it that those who stand outside both the [ecumenical] World and British Council's [sic] are not recognised as religious bodies by Grand Lodge? Perhaps the Grand Lodge feel that the cause of Protestantism is better served when their halls are used for the consumption of alcoholic liquors than for preaching the pure gospel of Jesus Christ . . . if we receive nothing further from you, we will not hesitate to make known [our] position in this matter.

The Central Committee incorrectly felt that Paisley's challenge would ultimately abate and saw no reason to change its policy.[7] During the Dungiven controversy, Paisley piled into the fray, seeking to capitalize on grassroots disquiet with the Orange and Unionist elite.

Ill. 1 John Millar Andrews, second Prime Minister of Northern Ireland (1940–3) and Grand Master during 1948–54. During Andrews' tenure, Grand Lodge openly urged its members to vote for the Official Unionists.

During the late fifties, Grand Lodge continued to act as a brake on grassroots militancy, brushing rebellious resolutions under the carpet or sending them back to the county and district levels whence they came. In 1959, a second Dungiven parade ban reignited the conflict between Grand Lodge and rebel Orangemen. A special Orange commission discovered that Protestant clergy and merchants, as well as most Protestant parishioners in the Dungiven area, supported the government's parade ban. The Orange commission thereby endorsed the government's actions. The response from militant Protestant populists was swift. Billy Douglas and a slim majority of County Londonderry Orangemen, as well as many Orange fellow travellers from eastern Ulster, rose up against Grand Lodge once again. Ian Paisley's Ulster Protestant Action (UPA) movement had come of age, and, together with the leading Independent Unionist Norman Porter, was ready to cause trouble for the Orange–Unionist establishment.[8] This was first expressed at a parade and rally at a Belfast shipyard and forcefully emerged at the Twelfth platform at Finaghy in Belfast, where the Minister of Home Affairs was heckled by UPA supporters who handed out leaflets. Meanwhile, on the Orange platform in Coleraine, there was an attempt to submit a resolution protesting the government's actions.[9]

Grand Lodge now viewed Paisley and the UPA as a major threat. Information on the UPA suggested that this was a new group with four branches, three in Belfast and one in Coleraine, underlining the north-eastern character of rebel Unionism. At Central Committee, Belfast County officers, including John Bryans, the County Grand Master, pinned the blame for the Finaghy Twelfth disturbances squarely on Paisley's UPA, who had been present in the field from an early point and had coordinated the agitation. Alfred Lee, Grand Secretary of County Londonderry, made similar points with respect to Dungiven, contending that the Bovevagh band leader Douglas was obviously receiving his instructions from Belfast and had no idea a week before the parade that his band was going through Dungiven.

Discussion turned next to Ian Paisley. The Antrim Grand Master James Baillie, while acknowledging Paisley's theological background, showed sympathy for Paisley's rebel position by reiterating the Order's religious, non-political basis. However, Baillie and County Antrim were the only sponsors of rebel Unionism on Central Committee. Aside from the Labourite Sam Campbell of Belfast, most others backed the leadership, and dissenting voices in other counties were repressed at lower lodge levels. Grand Master Sir George Clark now stepped in to refocus the meeting on troublemakers such as Douglas and Paisley and emphasized the need to deal firmly with lack of discipline in the lodges. Harry Maguire, JP, continued by attacking Paisley's attendance record in Antrim, claiming that he had never once attended his lodge in District 9 (Magheragall) after transferring in from District 6 (Lisburn). Maguire concluded by arguing forcefully for penalties against such defaulters. The Grand Master now solicited comments from 'provincial brethren', perhaps aware that border Unionists would back a tough line against the Dungiven rebels. He was not disappointed: the Fermanagh representatives Archdale Porter and Edwin Liddle favoured the expulsion of troublemakers and thought it the primary duty of Central Committee to express its support for Topping, the Minister for Home Affairs. Though Baillie counselled caution, this groundswell resulted in a resolution, proposed by Robert Webb (Down) and seconded by John Bryans and Senator Cunningham, in which:

The Central Committee of the Grand Orange Lodge of Ireland, at a special meeting held in Belfast, unanimously desire to place on record their highest appreciation and warmest thanks for the outstanding service the Rt. Hon. W.W.B. Topping, Minister of Home Affairs has rendered, and continues to render in connection with the defence of our Imperial Province. We warmly endorse his recent action, whereby he approved a decision of the police authorities in ensuring that no breach of the peace occurred in Dungiven.[10]

This caused consternation among Douglas, Paisley, and other rebel Unionists, but Grand Lodge was more than capable of containing their fissiparous energies in this era. Yet Paisley's increasingly high-profile militancy had raised the stakes for Grand Lodge, and the Rev. John Brown of County Antrim stated that while 'we [Orangemen] wish to disassociate ourselves from "Paisleyites"', he felt that the Prime Minister's recent remarks regarding incidents on the Orange platform at Dunloy, Antrim had 'caused some disquiet and unsatisfaction in the community'.[11] This agitation proved a prelude for further divisions occasioned by the ascent of Captain Terence O'Neill as Prime Minister in 1963.

Things began well enough between O'Neill and the Order. Ian Paisley's threat to seize a tricolour from the Divis Street headquarters of the Republican Party in West Belfast prompted the Minister for Home Affairs, Brian McConnell, to sanction the removal of the tricolour on 28 September 1964 in defence of the Flags and Emblems Act. This undercut Paisley's challenge and brought written congratulations from Central Committee (which the minister later acknowledged), but led to some of the worst rioting in years in the city and clashes between police and Republican crowds in West Belfast.[12]

Despite O'Neill's initial toughness, Clark was soon forced to defend the Prime Minister's administration in October 1964 against internal naysayers. Led by the Rev. John Brown and the newly appointed Belfast Orange representative, the Rev. Martin Smyth,[13] Orange critics claimed that McConnell was soft on security. With the onset of the IRA border campaign in 1956 came the first mention of the security issue (from Tyrone lodges) that would loom so large in the following decade. Then, Lord Brookeborough assured the Grand Lodge that any steps necessary would be taken to deal with this threat, but with more violence in 1959, Tyrone lodges like LOL 178 in Dungannon (backed by the Tyrone County Lodge) demanded the immediate apprehension of the IRA 'murder gangs'.[14] This marked the beginning of what would become a running sore as the government repeatedly failed to satisfy Unionist security concerns during the Troubles.

Border Orangemen first aired their criticism when the government introduced mobile patrols and centralized RUC detachments in 1963. The Orangemen argued that these would reduce the effectiveness of border security. McConnell replied that the new moves would not jeopardize security, but Smyth, along with Brown and several others, alleged that the reply was inadequate. Clark, in summing up, steered clear of these troublemakers by using his moral stature to defend the government. He stressed that the ministry, along with the Inspector General of the RUC, had considered this issue carefully and Clark was satisfied. This temporarily ended discussion on the matter.[15]

The Belfast riots of 1964 helped nurture O'Neill's liberalism, but traces of his contrarian politics were evident much earlier. An MP for Bannside since 1946, O'Neill applied for membership in a lodge in his constituency, LOL 231 (Ahoghill District, Antrim), in 1952—perhaps unaware of the radical streak of Antrim's Orangemen. Lodge members rejected O'Neill's application on the grounds that 'it was alleged' that he had once remarked that 'he was as good a Protestant out of the Institution as he would be were he in it'. Senator Cunningham urged that further enquiry be made into the matter and left things with Grand Master Andrews.[16] With Andrews's assistance, O'Neill subsequently joined LOL 504 in Ahoghill, and was elected master of his lodge in 1965.[17] Later, he joined the cosier confines of Clark's Eldon LOL 7 in Belfast, the establishment lodge, where O'Neill's picture still hangs alongside those of other luminaries that have met in its private, oak-panelled room in Clifton Street Orange Hall. O'Neill had evidently paid his Orange dues, as he was enthusiastically welcomed by Grand Lodge at the December 1965 meeting, and Clark referred to the fact that despite the Prime Minister's workload, 'hardly a week passed during the summer months without the Prime Minister taking part in Orange functions'. O'Neill responded by thanking the Grand Master and the Order for their loyalty and support, and received rapturous applause after his speech.[18]

The O'Neill–Lemass talks of 1965 exhausted O'Neill's stock of Orange capital and made Clark's matter-of-fact defence of the Prime Minister at Central Committee increasingly difficult. Clark, no doubt mindful of the populist discontent that emerged in the wake of Dungiven, met the Prime Minister and sent him a letter asking for an assurance that the constitutional position of Northern Ireland would remain unaffected and would not be discussed with either Lemass of Eire or Britain's Harold Wilson. The Prime Minister responded with an unqualified reply that bent over backwards to reassure Clark that the constitutional question was settled. Despite this, many at Central Committee expressed concern that the press was conveying a different message to the rank and file. The ease with which the suspicions of segments of popular Orangeism could be aroused is illustrated by the case of two members of the troublesome[19] Ballymacarett LOL 1310 in Belfast. These two—one of whom was a local councillor—charged Clark and Terence O'Neill with 'conduct unbecoming an Orangeman' and made statements to the press. Naturally, Central Committee deemed such charges unacceptable and agreed to discipline the brethren involved.[20] Later, Grand Lodge rushed to the Grand Master's defence, moving a resolution of confidence in both the Prime Minister and the Grand Master and repudiating 'all charges and rumours'.[21]

1966 was another test year for a nascent O'Neillism and the Orange elite, owing to the fiftieth anniversary of the Easter Rising. On 26 March, Fermanagh, arguably the most loyal county, came out strongly against the government's decision to permit Easter Rising celebrations to take place, citing a groundswell of private and district level resolutions.[22] In Tyrone, outrage was expressed at the flying of this 'provocative flag causing offence to loyal citizens'.[23] Several days later, after a Central Committee meeting at which Martin Smyth, the Rev. Brown, Billy Douglas (of Dungiven fame), and several other populists demanded tough action, Clark wrote to the Prime Minister, attaching the Fermanagh resolution and asking him to 'Do all that is in your power to curtail such Demonstrations as in our opinion they are provocative in origin, and at best must put the good name of Ulster in jeopardy since they create situations which could easily result in public disorder.'[24] The Prime Minister evidently took Clark's concerns very seriously, responding just four days later with a lengthy letter. In it, he mentioned that discussions had taken place with Fermanagh County Lodge representatives and 'having heard the reasons behind the Government's attitude, they fully understand and accept it'. O'Neill then attempted to justify his position as follows: 'Let me say at the outset that the sentiments behind the 1916 celebrations are repugnant to me and my colleagues in the Government—as indeed they are to the majority of our citizens. The Government will deal firmly with any attempt to organise offensive or provocative displays likely to lead to disorder'. O'Neill first attempted to argue that the new position changed little. 'Ceremonies commemorating the Easter Rising have taken place in Northern Ireland for many years,' he wrote, 'the policy being followed this year is consistent with what has been done in the past.' However, he must have realized that things had changed, for he proceeded to adopt the only tactic available to Protestant liberals in danger of being outflanked: externalizing the source of liberalism and invoking Protestant 'unity':

This year the Government have had to take account of some other factors. These are first the effect on public opinion in Great Britain and indeed throughout the world if, as a result of the banning of all individual celebrations, outbreaks of disorder were to occur when the ban is enforced; such outbreaks would be attributed by Ulster's enemies to repressive police action and however much we might attempt to justify our actions our reputation and standing would, undoubtedly, suffer. The Government have also had to bear in mind the general security of the province in the face of the danger of I.R.A. attacks—a danger which still exists—have had to ensure that the police are not over-committed in enforcing a number of bans in different parts of the country at a time when their supreme task is to maintain the highest possible state of readiness against the I.R.A. There can be little doubt that the I.R.A. would welcome an opportunity to involve the police in civil strife, and/or to draw off their forces, and then to exploit the position on the Border or elsewhere. All of us feel most strongly that the best interests of Northern Ireland will be served by ensuring that the peace is kept.[25]

Clark, mindful of exposure on his right, quickly moved to undercut popular Orange criticism by immediately copying his letter and O'Neill's reply to all county and district lodges as well as all private lodges that had issued resolutions.[26]

Clark's behaviour partly reflected the changed reality of Central Committee in the wake of the Dungiven challenges of the fifties. Already, the composition of this committee had begun to alter in subtle but decisive ways. For instance, James Baillie of Antrim had become a trustee of Central Committee, and he was no longer one of the few populist voices in the upper reaches of the Order. The Rev. John Brown and the newly appointed James Molyneaux gave increased weight to the concerns of Antrim Orangemen. Martin Smyth of Belfast added another relatively reformist voice to the equation, and William Douglas, the leader of the Dungiven revolt of 1959, was now a Central Committee representative for County Londonderry. The other side of this equation was that the alliance of the Belfast elite and west Ulster patricians which had so dominated proceedings in the past was beginning to lose influence.

The renewed political activity of Ian Paisley did not go unnoticed by Central Committee. Paisley, who had left the Order in 1962, criticized it in his newspaper, the *Protestant Telegraph*, over the Prime Minister's letter to Clark.[27] Senator James Baillie was now 'concerned by the inroads being made by Mr. Paisley'. The Grand Master felt a clash with Paisley should be avoided at this point, but William Douglas, the Dungiven hardliner, seized this moment to advocate that Grand Lodge steal Paisley's thunder. 'We should make a statement of our stand. The July resolutions should be so firm and strong that the Institution in particular should know where we stood on all these matters. Action was needed. The Rank and File members had to be considered.' Captain Michael Armstrong, a leading Armagh City UUP activist, supported Douglas and added that this was a time when the Grand Master should be strongly backed. Others complained that Paisley's rise owed much to the failure of the Protestant clergy to 'do their jobs' (i.e. practise the pure Reformed faith). Even so, some, like the Rev. Crossley, were optimistic, contending that 'men like Paisley had failed before'.[28] The evident distaste that the Order had for Paisley does not mean that he lacked support in certain Orange quarters: a number of resolutions were received in late 1966 deploring Paisley's incarceration.[29]

In the June 1966 reports of proceedings, strongly worded resolutions from the grassroots which once would never have seen the light of day, ran for page after page as a result of democratizing reforms introduced by County Antrim in the wake of the second Dungiven crisis. The Easter Rising parades had shocked many in the grassroots, whose mindset had not adjusted to the new political climate. Four district lodges in Antrim tendered resolutions criticizing the Easter Rising celebrations and Grand Lodge's lack of response to the 'concessions' that had been granted to Nationalists. Overall, some twenty-four resolutions were received from all levels of the Order in relation to the parades. A further ten concerned the visit of the Archbishop of Canterbury to Rome and the trend towards ecumenism within the Anglican Church.

Belfast, with just a fifth of total Orange membership, accounted for half of the resolutions on the Easter Rising issue. A typical response was that of Prince Albert Temperance LOL 1892 of Clifton Street District, Belfast:

That this Lodge views with grave concern the present arrangements being made in the City of Belfast to celebrate the acts of treachery and violence which took place in Dublin fifty years ago; We are of the opinion that the Orange Institution should exert the most extreme pressure on the Northern Ireland Government not only to curb these activities, but to ban them completely. This Lodge thinks these Republican celebrations will lead to outbreaks of violence in the City of Belfast, and as they have nothing in common with our way of life they should not be allowed to take place here. We know very well what would happen if the Orangemen of Dublin decided to hold demonstrations in that City. On the basis of these facts we urge No. 3 District L.O.L. and the County Grand Lodge of Belfast to take action immediately and impress on the Grand Lodge of Ireland the urgency of the situation.

A number of resolutions made the threat of violence either implicit or explicit.[30] Defending Grand Lodge against this outpouring of grassroots anger, Clark reiterated that the government 'would deal firmly with any attempt' to organize offensive or provocative displays likely to lead to disorder.[31]

The Grand Master was obviously influenced by the depth of popular feeling on this issue. He remarked that 'it was the first time he could recall that the Resolutions, which in the past had been the Grand Master's prerogative to draft, were being awaited on with such interest by the Order in general, and indeed by outside bodies'. Clark went on to say that his second resolution (on ecumenism) was drafted explicitly in response to grassroots concerns of the past three years. This represented some concession to mass sentiment, but at this point relations were still good enough between O'Neill and the Order that the third resolution for that July was an expression of gratitude to the Prime Minister. In view of O'Neill's mastership of LOL 504, the Grand Lodge even unanimously agreed to refer to him as 'W.M. Bro. O'Neill'.[32]

The cheery reception which O'Neill had received at Grand Lodge in 1965, and Clark's readiness to defend him during 1964–6, proved to be among the last notes of government–Orange harmony and arguably represent the end of an era. At the Twelfth platform in 1966, hecklers—no doubt of the Paisleyite variety—greeted O'Neill's name with cries of 'traitor'. Although Clark attacked Paisley, he was cognizant of the broader Orange mood. By 1966, he began slowly to question his relationship with O'Neill, relating to Central Committee the details of a chat he had with the Prime Minister regarding the question of 'better relations' between Protestants and Catholics. 'We as an Order could not go any further in this apparent one way traffic,' Clark objected. This statement gained Clark the plaudits of one of the more radical members of Central Committee. Clark continued to win the support of populists by setting up two new committees, one to look into ways of challenging ecumenism, and the other to examine the means of resisting the attacks on Northern Ireland's constitutional position.[33]

An early example of the newly defiant mood in Central Committee appears in Martin Smyth's remark, after reading a letter from the Minister for Home Affairs which noted a rise in crime, that the minister hoped that the Orangemen would be 'fobbed off' with a 'simple acknowledgment'. This remark passed without comment, and led to a renewed call to press the minister on the question at hand. This is a small piece of language, otherwise insignificant, but represents the kind of flippant attitude towards the government which would not have been found even five years earlier but would become increasingly common in the coming decade. When the government was still considered part of 'us', such remarks could be contested. Once the Order became alienated and detached from the government, the ministers of government became outsiders to the institution and would receive little loyalty from the elites of the Order.

The Order's July 1966 resolution on the ecumenical drift of the Protestant churches was said, by a number of Orange chaplains, to have had major repercussions within the churches.[34] Leaders of both the Presbyterian and Methodist churches responded by underlining their commitment to the principles of the Reformation. However, the Grand Lodge singled out the Lord Archbishop of Armagh, the Rev. James McCann, as being the only major leader not to reply to the resolution. This action was not without its consequences: the Orange resolution may have led to the exit of more liberal-minded ministers, such as the Rev. C. S. Lowry and W. M. Beamish, both of whom requested that their names be removed from the list of Grand Lodge officers in 1967.[35] Further proof that there were liberal dissenters within Orange ranks comes from letters sent to Tyrone County Lodge from a district lodge and a private lodge which asked what action Grand Lodge would take against 'those defaulting brethren who refused to read this resolution at the July demonstrations'. This was aimed at individuals like the Rev. R. Elliott, Lord Bishop of Connor, whose re-election as a Grand Chaplain, in the eyes of the lodge, made 'a mockery of the Orange Order' since Elliott 'has publicly denounced us by refusing to participate on a public platform . . . because Grand Lodge would not withdraw one of the [anti-ecumenical] Resolutions'.[36]

Notwithstanding this limited degree of dissent, the Order was generally able to call to account liberal churchmen who were members of the Order, such as the Rev. Archdeacon Mercer, who wrote an article in a church magazine critical of the Order's resolution. A number of Belfast representatives felt that Mercer should be suspended or expelled. Clark, however, counselled caution, emphasizing the need to limit divisions between the church and the Order.[37] At a subsequent meeting, Mercer and his colleague Elliott apologized to Belfast County officers for their statements and the matter was laid to rest despite the misgivings of the Rev. John Brown and Billy Douglas.[38] Mercer subsequently raised the matter of attending Roman Catholic services now that Catholics were permitted to attend Protestant services. In reply, Clark left Mercer in no doubt that deviation from traditional Orange laws would not be tolerated and that Mercer's ecumenical conduct was less than satisfactory:

[It] has been generally accepted throughout the Institution that Orangemen [do] not attend Roman Catholic places of worship. Recently considerable public opinion has been brought to bear on this subject, and the Orange Institution has been under severe criticism for intolerance . . . The Obligations have withstood the test of time, and I understand there is no record of any Resolution asking for an Amendment. We are primarily an Organisation for the defence and expansion of Protestantism...Historic background...has given rise to the sharp divisions...that must separate the two Churches...I believe this is a question of individual conscience, and I feel that those who are unable to abide by the long established Rules of the Institution should have considered more carefully the problems in relation to their private and public life that membership would entail, and having done so if they are not prepared to abide by the code of conduct as an Orangeman would have been better to have withdrawn their application for membership. At the same time those who are in the Institution and are not satisfied with its Laws should use machinery at their disposal of having their problems discussed rather than causing adverse publicity to an Organisation to which they belong through using outside sources to criticise the working of the Institution rather than to confine their criticisms to where they belong, within the Lodge Room of the Institution.

Clark's reprimand of Mercer received the rousing applause of those gathered. Brian Faulkner, MP, the Minister of Commerce, was in attendance and 'strongly supported the Grand Master's remarks', stating that in his opinion there should be no change in the laws of the institution. This, too, was greeted with applause.[39] In late 1966 and early 1967, sensing the changing mood at the top of the Orange pyramid, the Rev. Brown of Antrim spearheaded a Grand Lodge resolution to the Minister of Home Affairs and the Prime Minister demanding that the proposed Fenian Rising celebrations be banned.[40]

Meanwhile, along the south-western frontier, Fermanagh County Lodge's concerns lay with the security situation, especially the closure of local police stations. These concerns were a portent of things to come, and won the support of Lord Brookeborough and Harry West, the local MP. Responding to these concerns, the Grand Master and Martin Smyth spoke in favour of using 'our M.P'.s' instead of Grand Lodge as the vehicle for their lobbying efforts. Smyth pointed out that 'not enough was made of our M.P'.s' in this respect.[41] This indicates that the Order served as a surrogate avenue for political participation, probably being a more instinctive channel for protest than that which connected constituents to their local Stormont MP.

1967 was a transition year in Northern Ireland politics. The Queen's speech for the year gave Orangemen the first hint of what was to come. The Rev. Brown presented the main points. First of all, legislation was on the books that would provide grant funding for the Roman Catholic maternity hospital, known as the 'Mater Hospital'. Second, and more worrying, the government was contemplating electoral reform. Brown warned that 'electoral reform had its dangers with regard to the Minority. We could be put in a very difficult position.' Brown continued that pressure for reform was coming from Harold Wilson in London. There were challenges afoot in housing and education as well: Brown commented that the housing trust allocation in Derry City offered some 198 houses to Catholics and just twenty to Protestants. 'There was a danger here that we would lose area control,' he related gravely.[42]

Matters had evidently reached crisis point. Brown now questioned the ability of Stormont to manage the flow of events in the face of British pressure to reform: 'We should ask the Government, what is your position? What are you really going to do? Where do we stand on all these urgent and important matters? Where exactly are we going?' Brown moved that Grand Lodge send a deputation to the Prime Minister, which was passed unanimously. In review, the Grand Master cautioned those present not to repeat what was said. 'The interest of Ulster is at stake. We must be discreet.' He also explained that pressure was coming from Westminster and that those in attendance needed to appreciate the situation between London and Stormont.[43]

A month later, the Orange delegation met the Prime Minister and his ministers of Health, Home Affairs, Education, and Development at Stormont Castle. Grand Master Clark began by laying out what he termed the 'growing concern' in the country over government policy. 'Change was inevitable in any community, but tradition died hard in Ulster', Clark continued. The changes being made were too rapid and were causing discontent in the Orange Institution. For the 'Government [to] continue to have the support of the Orange Order', an honest talk was necessary. Clark complimented William Craig, the Home Affairs Minister, on banning the Fenian 100th-anniversary demonstrations, but proceeded to outline Orange concerns over local government reform and the Mater Hospital issues. The Health Minister, William Morgan, assured Clark that no concessions would be forthcoming on the Mater Hospital issue.

However, on the local government issue, O'Neill stressed the 'considerable subsidies' that Ulster received from England and how Wilson had prevented his backbenchers from requesting a royal commission of enquiry into the running of Ulster in exchange for an honest meeting between London and Stormont. 'There is no doubt that the Irish Vote is much sought after . . . by both Labour and the Conservatives,' O'Neill complained, 'and the support that we have had in the past is now much more a matter of economics and [political calculation] than traditional loyalties.' Clark concluded the meeting in a deferential manner, pronouncing his wish to avoid abusing 'the privileges which they enjoyed in meeting the Prime Minister on these subjects'.[44] This last flourish, to which comments were added about the aim being the health of the 'entire community' (i.e. including Catholics), allowed all parties to the discussion to maintain an outward fiction of impartiality while ensuring that the Order retained its influence at the highest levels.

At the following meeting, the issue of housing came up again. Housing development in the City of Derry was leading to a situation where the Protestants were at risk of losing parliamentary seats, complained the Orange delegation. The recent balance of housing allocations was 250 to Catholics and just twenty to Protestants, declared the Rev. Brown. Clark complained that the Unionist population was too apathetic to act on its own through its MPs. Brown then turned to the recent meeting with the Prime Minister. He suggested that the Prime Minister was under financial pressure from Westminster to reform. However, in the opinion of Captain Armstrong, who had attended the meeting with O'Neill, the government had mishandled small problems already on the local government issue, so how could it be expected to deal with the bigger ones to come? H. F. Young worried that the government had lost control of the housing trust. Sam Magowan concurred, claiming that local governments should take over the housing trust. At this point, it was stressed that nothing of this discussion should be included in the Grand Lodge reports but that the Grand Master would take a personal message to the Prime Minister relaying these concerns.[45]

The itinerary for the meetings of the Imperial Grand Orange Council of the World for 1967 included a visit to Stormont and a banquet for delegates at Ulster Hall, attended by Belfast city councillors, O'Neill, and William Morgan, Minister of Health and Social Services. Clearly, the July Resolutions of 1967 continued—at least on the surface—to trace a narrative of Orange–government unity. The resolution began by paying 'tribute to our Brother, Captain The Rt. Hon. Terence M. O'Neill, Prime Minister, for the policy of his Government, whereby Ulster's position has remained strong and viable within the United Kingdom'. But the resolution ended with some policy pressure as well, urging 'that the approaching 50th anniversary of the Constitution of Northern Ireland will be marked by a suitable occasion'.[46] More importantly, the Twelfth platforms in 1967 resounded with tension between populist and pro-UUP elements. Whereas not long ago the speeches were the 'dullest part of the proceedings', wrote the *Belfast Telegraph*, they now bore witness to a 'struggle for the possession of Northern Ireland's soul'. Speeches by MPs were heckled and the resolution in favour of O'Neill jeered. At Coagh, the Westminster MP for Mid-Ulster, George Forrest, was 'pulled from the platform, kicked and left unconscious after he threatened demonstrators with his chair when they jeered O'Neill's name'. Forrest died the following year, receiving an honourable mention over and above the usual obituaries from the recently installed Grand Master, John Bryans.[47]

Bryans assumed the leadership when George Clark tendered his resignation in October 1967 citing 'ill-health'. Within a year, Clark would leave a ship whose prow was bound for increasingly stormy seas. For the moment, though, the Order remained in the political driver's seat. Right through 1967 and into 1968, the Orange association managed to keep up the pressure on the government and major institutions of Northern Ireland society like the churches and the BBC. As Martin Smyth noted, the Order maintained 'close contact' with Stormont on key matters.[48] The anti-ecumenical resolution read at the Twelfth platform served as a warning to the main churches; letters to the BBC threatened Orange non-cooperation with future Twelfth broadcasts unless coverage improved, and communications with Stormont left ministers in no doubt that the Order would not tolerate concessions on the Mater Hospital issue. In all cases, the targeted parties responded courteously and promptly.[49]

A major issue for 1968 concerned the government's new White Paper with its proposals for education reform. These proposals retained local council involvement on the 'Four [school representative] and Two [council representative]' school committees and a local council veto on changes proposed by particular schools. However, fears were raised by some—including Martin Smyth—that loopholes could be exploited by Catholic schools and that new grant-maintained schools might be used for 'parochial purposes'. Others worried that new Catholic schools might be able to opt out of local government oversight. After a detailed presentation on this issue by the Rev. James Johnston, Central Committee mulled over the issues. Clark summed up the mood: 'we [cannot] . . . agree to any further concessions'.[50] Subsequently, the Grand Lodge Education Committee tabled a report highlighting what it saw as a government concession which gave schools undiluted authority over the appointment of teachers. The Education Committee therefore demanded a meeting with the minister 'at his earliest convenience' to 'clarify' the proposals.[51]

Early 1967 was a time of great ferment in the Nationalist community. In early 1967, the Northern Ireland Civil Rights Association (NICRA) was formed, followed by the Derry Housing Action Committee (DHAC) later in the year. Together, they were to engage in rallies and direct action which brought long-simmering Catholic grievances over local government, education, and health into the open. Organized Nationalist action in Northern Ireland would rapidly remove any breathing space for the government as the triangular noose of popular Unionists, Nationalists, and the British government began to tighten around its neck.

The Orange Order formed the bulwark of popular Unionist resistance to concessions, though it was being outflanked by the noisier street politics of Ian Paisley and his Ulster Protestant Volunteers. Negative resolutions from the Orange rank and file over Clark's talks with Senator Lennon in 1962–3 (as with the O'Neill–Lemass talks of 1965) had established the principle that any Unionist figure who negotiated with Nationalists—however moderate—would suffer politically. A similar attitude existed with respect to attendance at Catholic church services. Recall that George Clark, under duress from the Central Committee's right wing, made clear to the Rev. Archdeacon Mercer in 1966 that no matter what Catholics might allow their members to do, no Orangemen could be permitted to attend Catholic services. This decree ruffled the feathers of more moderate Orange churchmen who wanted to initiate goodwill initiatives for community reconciliation. It also affected Orange MPs, who felt that they could not discharge their representative functions properly without attending Catholic functions. This issue shows how secular demands grated against ethno-religious boundary maintenance and is illustrated well by the saga of Phelim O'Neill, a North Antrim Unionist MP who sympathized with many of the demands of the civil rights movement.

In 1966–7, the County Antrim Grand Lodge expelled Phelim O'Neill and Colonel Henry Cramsie for attending a Catholic funeral in O'Neill's constituency. The background to the expulsions was read out by the Antrim leadership, notably John Brown and James Molyneaux, and unanimously confirmed by Grand Lodge Central Committee. The issue was not at this time viewed as a critical one by many Central Committee 'backbenchers': Clark bemoaned the fact that few committee members had bothered to return from lunch to discuss what he felt was this 'important' issue.[52] However, he grasped the urgency of the situation and probably sought to rally traditionalist forces in time for the upcoming Grand Lodge sessions, which were to decide the ultimate fate of the two accused Antrim men.

The February sessions of Grand Lodge hosted a much longer debate on this issue. The Rev. John Brown, seconded by his fellow Antrim committee member Molyneaux, tabled the expulsion resolution. At this point, Clark intervened, expressing his concern that the expulsion might be illegal under Orange laws and revealing that he had asked for a legal opinion on this matter. The opinion of the Orangeman the Rt Hon. Anthony Babington, QC, was that there was legal ambiguity on the question of whether the two had violated Orange law against 'countenancing and attending' Catholic church services. To some degree, this foregrounds the clash between traditionalist legitimation (i.e. Orange laws and ordinances interpreted by elites) and fundamentalist legitimation based on the Orange 'principle' of expelling those deemed traitors to Protestantism. Clark took care to stress that he was not motivated by any affinity for the accused (though he later spoke well of Cramsie, as opposed to O'Neill), but rather did not wish to see legal action from the accused tarnish the good name of the Order.[53]

Clark's intervention in the meeting prepared the ground for moderates under Senator Kinghan (County Grand Master of Down) to press their case. Kinghan issued a resolution asking that, in view of Clark's statement and the legal ramifications, the expulsion of O'Neill and Cramsie be rescinded and the whole initiative sent back to Antrim County Lodge for further consideration. This led to heated discussion. John Brown sought leave to withdraw with his Antrim delegation to discuss strategy. He returned, and expressed surprise at the whole legal issue, claiming that nothing of this matter had been mentioned to him and thus he had been unable to take any other course of action than to propose his resolution. Brown then proposed that the matter be referred to Central Committee. Kinghan accepted, withdrawing his anti-Antrim resolution as a quid pro quo.[54] The elite traditionalists had temporarily checked the advance of the populists, but the Grand Master and his elite supporters could no longer dictate to the populists on this major issue, and the battle was postponed for another day.

The next meeting at Central Committee promised a clash between traditionalist and rebel forces. The rebels (Brown, Smyth, and Molyneaux, as well as Londonderry's infamous William Douglas) began by accusing traditionalist elements within Central Committee of leaking details of the O'Neill affair to the press. George Clark, Senator Kinghan, and Sam Magowan 'categorically stated' that they had not mentioned details of the case to the press, and that this kind of leakage was 'nothing new', having occurred as far back as they could remember. Later, the discussion of the expulsions began in earnest. Brown argued that there 'was nothing to be gained by further discussion. Justice must be done.' He condemned the decision taken at the February Grand Lodge meeting and urged immediate expulsion. Martin Smyth from Belfast next added his opinion, stating that if legal counsel's view was that O'Neill and Cramsie could not be expelled, then previous expulsions—such as that of a certain Bro. Graham who had angrily returned his collarette to a past Grand Master and swore that he would vote Republican in the next election—also needed to be rescinded. To this charge, Grand Secretary Walter Williams replied that Graham had been properly expelled under Orange law by his own private and district lodge. An expulsion coming directly from Grand Lodge did not carry the same legality.

George Clark then interjected, claiming his 'surprise' at the 'tone' of Brown's and Smyth's remarks. There was a good deal of ambiguity in the Orange ordinance which spoke of 'countenancing by your presence or otherwise at a form of Roman Worship', claimed Clark, no doubt mindful of the fact that public duty made it virtually impossible for certain Orangemen not to violate a strict interpretation of this principle. He was supported in his caution by Captain Armstrong of Armagh, who instead recommended the lighter sentence of a seven-year suspension.[55]

This did not satisfy Brown, who strenuously pushed for expulsion. He underlined the grassroots pressure he would face at the Antrim County Lodge if he did not give a 'full account' of actions taken by Grand Lodge. In response, Sam Magowan from Down backed the stance taken by Clark and Armstrong, claiming that Phelim O'Neill and the press both wanted to see the Order eject O'Neill. Given the delicacy of these matters, Magowan urged that the matter be sent back to Antrim. Brown, though acknowledging that the press wanted to see O'Neill expelled (so as to vilify the Order), rejected Magowan's suggestion outright. Smyth then reiterated his fundamentalist claim that 'we should stand firm for our Faith and our Principles' and expel the two brethren. This was backed by his fellow Belfast County representative, Robert McMullan. At this point, Senator Cole of Cavan raised the objection that as a senator in the Republic and a County Grand Master, he often had to attend Roman Catholic funerals at the request of the President of the Republic. Dr Johnston of Londonderry also asked for clarification on this matter.

Clark now moved that a decision be taken. He proposed an intermediate solution of a seven-year suspension, and this was seconded by Armstrong. The matter was so divisive that the vote was taken by ballot rather than by a show of hands. The results were a blow to the traditionalists: twenty-two of those present backed expulsion, and only thirteen favoured suspension. This vote showed a divided Central Committee, albeit one with a clear majority now in favour of the populist position. This landmark vote represents a watershed moment in which rebel Unionism first came to dominate over the traditional Orange elite. As if to underline the short-sightedness of his fellow delegates, Clark informed those present that Robin Chichester-Clark, an Orangeman, senator and MP, had informed Clark that he intended to be present at the Catholic funeral of Lieutenant-Colonel McCausland. Those present agreed that this was a private matter between Clark and Chichester-Clark and that the final decision on rules concerning attendance at Catholic funerals would need to be made by the Rules Committee.[56]

The symbolic victory over O'Neill clearly mattered more to the populists than the enforcement of a general principle which in practice was often breached. For example, a resolution from the radical LOL 1310 concerning the proper stance of Orange MPs if a priest should say prayers at Stormont was killed by the Rules Committee, who merely claimed that they would keep the matter 'under review'. Later, members who served on local government school management committees asked whether they could attend the opening of new Catholic schools where some reading of Scripture and a prayer would be said. It was privately determined that brethren could attend such services without suffering expulsion.[57] In December of that year, when a County Londonderry private lodge resolved to censure the county lodge for taking no action against Chichester-Clark for attending McCausland's funeral, the Grand Secretary pointed out that proper procedure had not been followed and so the resolution could only 'possibly' be considered at a subsequent meeting.[58]

The O'Neill and Cramsie expulsions were next considered at the June session of Grand Lodge. Reports of this had reached the press, partly through O'Neill's public statements. The 'Protestant' press was strongly opposed to any expulsion. If Phelim O'Neill were expelled from the Orange Order for his attendance at a Catholic function, it would 'raise searching questions about the role of a Unionist public representative in fulfilling his duty as he sees fit', claimed the *Belfast Telegraph*.[59] The Belfast *News Letter* added that the two should not be expelled and that Grand Lodge should 'take cognisance of the contribution such occasional public and private attendances at Roman Catholic functions make to better community relations'.[60] Press opinion had been raised as a factor by moderates in discussions on Central Committee and no doubt was raised again at Grand Lodge. However, despite Clark's and Magowan's renewed attempt to make their case for suspension instead of expulsion, Grand Lodge voted by a 'large majority' to expel Phelim O'Neill and Colonel Cramsie. Some indication of the depth of grassroots feeling is provided by the private lodge resolutions demanding expulsion. Interestingly, all came from Antrim (four districts and five private lodges, representing almost a hundred lodges) and Belfast (one district and five lodges).[61]

Ill. 2 Senator Samuel Kinghan, c. 1967 —A high-ranking Unionist Party man and Deputy Grand Master of County Down, Kinghan's traditionalist faction unsuccessfully battled populists like Martin Smyth, James Molyneaux and John Brown to prevent the expulsion of two Unionist politicians for attending a Catholic funeral in 1967.

The political fallout was immediate. The Nationalist leader and Republican Labour Party MP Gerry Fitt said that he would raise his concern at the Order's 'unhealthy influence' over the Northern Ireland government at Westminster.[62] The *Belfast Telegraph* warned that many Unionist MPs were uneasy with the ruling, viewing it as 'an open challenge to one of the main objectives of government policy—improvement of community relations by involvement at local level'. Further expulsions, claimed the *Telegraph*, would lead to a split between the Order and the Unionist Party. For his part, O'Neill exclaimed that the Order had 'far too much political power as a pressure group'. Though William Craig, Minister of Home Affairs, defended the Order as not being anti-Catholic, an editorial in the *Telegraph* claimed that the Order had damaged the Prime Minister's efforts at improving community relations. The paper proposed that a choice needed to be made: 'either the Order alters its out-dated rules or surrenders its influence in party affairs'.[63]

George Clark had officially handed over the reins of the Grand Mastership to John Bryans back in February and was thus already seen as a 'lame duck' leader by the April meeting. Clark, mindful of the new mood on Central Committee, was probably only too pleased to hand power over to his successor. His defeat over the O'Neill affair exemplified the trend towards populist assertion that had begun under John Andrews's tenure and grown after the second Dungiven crisis in 1959–60. The Orange grassroots had evidently begun to challenge their established leaders, and many of the delegates they sent to Central Committee were willing to give voice to their populist views rather than those of the establishment. In this respect, Bryans was a compromise candidate—a Belfast County Master, but also a JP and not a populist like many of his fellow county men.[64] How is one to explain this resurgent Unionist populism? Part of the answer lies in a growing sense of threat from a resurgent Nationalism as well as British reforms. However, we should not discount the 'modernizing' social pressures which had begun to flatten the social hierarchy within the Order from top to bottom.[65]

Orange brashness clearly did not go unnoticed by the UUP. A letter from Norman Porter of the Evangelical Protestant Society pertaining to a meeting on Orange–UUP relations noted 'rising unrest in Orange circles over recent anti-orange statements by Unionist Branch Leaders'. The letter went on to ask if the Order could trust the UUP any longer. In response, Martin Smyth supported the UUP–Orange connection, citing Roy Bradford's recent defence of the link. Captain Armstrong seconded Smyth's remarks, displaying a rare moment of traditionalist–populist unity. However, this did not satisfy two Londonderry hardliners, William Douglas and Henry Young, who complained that the UUP was not vigilant enough in rebutting 'slanderous remarks' made against the province. At this, Senator Kinghan retorted that the UUP would meet any deputation. Clark remarked that Norman Porter was a 'great worker' for both Orangeism and Protestantism and suggested that a meeting take place between the UUP and Orange Order. This was seconded by both traditionalists and hardliners, though Clark reiterated that this should be low-key since 'any suggestion of a conference between the two bodies would be disastrous'.[66]

At this time, Ulster was being portrayed in the British and world media as a Protestant-dominated statelet denying Catholics their civil rights. The meeting between the UUP and the Order took place in October to address this development. James Baillie, speaking for the government rather than as an Orangeman, addressed Orange allegations that it had not done enough to counter negative press from England about Ulster. Baillie countered that the government had in fact sent replies to the press in both England and Northern Ireland. In reply to questions from John Brown and Martin Smyth regarding poor television coverage, Roy Bradford, the Chief Whip who would later die at the hands of the IRA, claimed that the government had been in touch with the BBC about all the 'bad coverage' of recent weeks. In reply to Norman Porter's observation that Unionist branch leaders had criticized the Orange Order, Bradford said that 'odd people' spoke out against the Order and that the Order should ensure that members attend Unionist branch meetings to put their case. He hinted that many Orangemen had 'opted out' of branch meetings and said that the 'Party and Order should be closely interwoven in order to safeguard the vital interests of our Ulster and British Heritage'. This was seconded by Baillie, who opined that all Unionist Party leaders wanted to see Orange and Unionist ties strengthened. Bradford added that the Unionist government would not give away anything on the local government franchise, though he suggested there would be some concessions on housing and social policy.

The cosiness which had obtained up to this point, and which suggests that the Orange Order was successfully holding the UUP to account, appeared to crack when Brown pressed Bradford on specifics. He referred to a March 1967 meeting at which 'it was agreed' that the Grand Lodge would be 'kept in touch' about any major changes in government policy. Bradford, however, rebutted this statement, claiming that he was not aware of this arrangement. This was a direct challenge to Orange power which did not go unnoticed. Though Baillie put a positive spin on the meeting by saying that 'there was no doubt the Unionist Party and the Government always had the support of the Order' all was clearly not well.

After the meeting, there was concern at Bradford's attitude and a 'feeling that certain ties between the Orange Order and the Unionist Party will be severed'. Members of the Orange delegation reassured themselves that the Order was a powerful force within the Unionist Party with representation at all levels.[67] Subsequently, Molyneaux voiced his opinion that Bradford did not have the confidence of a number of UUP backbenchers. Clark added that the Chief Whip 'had not a good enough Ulster background' to make the statements he did. He dismissed talk of severing ties between the party and the Order and also referred to 'silly talk' regarding an Ulster declaration of independence. 'This [is] out of the question,' Clark continued, not least because 'our financial grants [are] from the United Kingdom'. In the end, he called on Orange delegates on the UUC to use their voice to greater effect.[68]

The social pressures which were to burst into flame during the Troubles the following year were building during 1968, and both the Order and the O'Neill government were attempting to come to grips with the new assertiveness of the Catholic community and reformist pressures from politicians and the media in mainland Britain. Local government reform was high on the agenda of both the Nationalists and the British. The government of Northern Ireland attempted to address these concerns in its White Paper presented to Parliament in December 1967, which invited concerned citizens to respond to its proposals. The paper contended that the present system of local government based on nineteenth-century boundaries had outlived its usefulness, and argued in functional, economistic language for a reshaping of local government.[69] A special Orange committee had been set up to deal with this issue in February 1968.[70] Its four aims included ensuring (1) that control of education 'remain in the right hands'; (2) that as few Orangemen as possible be unwillingly included in areas under Nationalist control; (3) that

Ill. 3   Rev. Martin Smyth and Sir George Clark, 1967 —(l to r): Grand Secretary Walter Williams, L.P.S. Orr (MP and Imperial Grand Master), Sir George Clark, Martin Smyth and Rev W. S. K.Crossley (Grand Chaplain and Convenor of the Education Committee). Clark was one of the last representatives of patrician Stormont Orangeism. Smyth, by contrast, represented the new breed of grassroots populist leader.

the new boundary-drawing be kept out of Nationalist control; and (4) 'That we should watch the Local Government Franchise'. The committee's radicalism was further enhanced by the subsequent inclusion of William Douglas and James Molyneaux.[71] At the next Central Committee meeting in April, the special committee proffered that it could not design a scheme appropriate to all counties, but that different solutions would be most appropriate for different counties.[72]

In September, members of the Black and Orange institutions agreed to work together on both the housing and local government issues. The Grand Black Chapter—an organization whose membership was restricted to Orangemen who had attained the highest ritual degree—would look into the issue of a bias towards Catholics in housing permits while the Orange would focus its efforts on the local government issue. Harold Cushnie of the Black suggested a joint deputation to see the Prime Minister and relevant ministers. Captain Armstrong averred that this was not the best idea. Instead, he preferred to go to the government the following spring. This was agreed, though John Brown and Martin Smyth added that they looked forward to getting rid of the housing trust as soon as possible. Others like Tom McClay of Tyrone warned that any new proposals had to be carefully thought out, or 'the good work [i.e. gerrymandering] done for over 50 years with regard to the present system of franchise' would be lost and a third of Tyrone could fall to Nationalists.[73]

Events soon threatened to overtake the Order. On 24 August, the Campaign for Social Justice (CSJ), the Northern Ireland Civil Rights Association (NICRA), and a number of other Nationalist groups held the first 'civil rights march' in Northern Ireland from Coalisland to Dungannon. Under Loyalist pressure, the planned rally was banned. This garnered the subsequent approval of Orange hardliners such as Brown, who moved that a letter of congratulation be sent to the Minister of Home Affairs which also called upon him to similarly ban the fateful civil rights march planned for Derry on 5 October.[74] Though the march was banned and halted by RUC baton charges, it resulted in a great deal of adverse publicity for Ulster Unionism, not least owing to the presence of three sympathetic British Labour MPs and foreign film crews. Immediately after the march there were two days of serious rioting in Derry between the Catholic residents of the city and the RUC.[75]

At this early stage, a number of members of the government seemed clearly on the Order's side. Brian Faulkner (then Minister of Commerce), for instance, had appeared at Grand Lodge sessions in 1968 and had written a letter supporting the Orange Order in its bid to retain the current local government franchise. As late as November 1968, Sam Magowan defended the government, claiming that the Prime Minister, the Minister for Home Affairs, Craig, and the Minister of Commerce had 'stood up' to Harold Wilson in London. The record of that meeting shows a much more mixed picture, however, with Wilson doing most of the lecturing and the Stormont delegation attempting to exercise damage control.[76] Meanwhile, resolutions of support for Craig came in from Fermanagh and Armagh. Even so, the events at Derry persuaded Central Committee to press for a meeting with the Prime Minister 'without delay', no doubt to ensure that government resolve held firm.[77]

The Orange deputation met O'Neill on 14 November. John Brown first presented evidence of Nationalist marchers using 'strong arm tactics' against members of the Loyalist public, causing them to be 'disgusted and humiliated', but congratulated the Prime Minister for banning all subsequent marches in the City of Londonderry the day before. William Douglas referred to Ian Paisley's counter-demonstration of 9 October and, in an apparent alignment with Orangeism's bitter foe, warned of serious repercussions if 'rebel elements' continued to 'flout the law'. Douglas called on the government to ensure firmer RUC action, claiming that this had been effective in restoring 'confidence' after the Dungiven controversies. In reply, Craig injected a note of realism into the discussion, 'emphatically' stressing that the use of baton charges would be a police decision, that the situation in Derry was in chaos, and that no one could tell what would happen in Derry on 16 November. He emphasized that the matter was no longer a Derry affair, but now involved outside elements. Later he mentioned that the worldwide student movement was 'rubbing off' on the civil rights marchers in Northern Ireland.

Brown, while reiterating support for the police, continued to press, venturing that the police attitude had 'softened' since 5 October owing to adverse publicity. In an interesting—and arguably rehearsed[78]—intervention, George Clark asked him whether violence might ensue if the Nationalist-led Citizens' Action Committee marched in defiance of a ban. Brown tendered evidence that 'many of the Loyalist people would not stand idly by' should marchers defy the ban. This subtle threat of violence was intended to prevail on the government to resist foreign media and political pressure and to give police a freer hand to enforce the law. Brown then raised concerns about liberal trends in the public education system, citing the fact that pupils such as his daughter were being 'brainwashed' by teachers who asked them to answer questions about the civil rights movement and police activities. Captain Armstrong next put the question of local government franchise reform to the minister in the context of pressures from Northern Ireland newspapers and the British government for change. He stressed that any concessions would cause 'deep resentment'.

In reply, the Prime Minister spoke of the dependence of Northern Ireland upon the British treasury, indicating that there might be limitations on the government's freedom of movement. At this, Martin Smyth and James Molyneaux stressed that concessions would lead to a 'slippery slope', and Billy Douglas declared that 'money or no money. . . motorways or no motorways, we would be prepared to tighten our belts in order to retain our particular way of life'. This statement suggests that symbolic considerations certainly eclipsed material ones in the eyes of many Orangemen. In conclusion, George Clark thanked the ministers for their time (nearly two hours) and reiterated a previous promise made to the Order to consult them on any possible changes which could seriously affect their lives, so as to aid in explaining policy to the members.[79]

Though Grand Lodge pledged its support to the Government and several county and district lodges did the same, some lodge resolutions expressed opposition to any alteration of the local government franchise. This was particularly true of the respectfully worded resolutions from Fermanagh and Tyrone, which warned that should 'one man, one vote' win the day, a number of key committees such as Welfare and Education would be lost to Nationalists. Here we see that border Orangemen tended to become politically active only on moral issues or when their basic socioeconomic interests were threatened. In reply to Tyrone, Grand Master John Bryans held that an Orange Special Committee was keeping a watching brief on the franchise reform question and urged Orange representatives on the UUC to submit the Tyrone resolution to the UUC executive committee for adoption.[80]

Though O'Neill had agreed to a reform package with the British and made his plea for moderation with his 'Ulster at a Crossroads' speech, this was still a period of relative unity in which Orangemen (conditionally) backed the government. Support also poured in from other Orange jurisdictions, including Canada, the USA, and Australasia. On 27 November, the Grand Lodge issued a statement in defence of the government, calling on it to stand firm:

The Government of Northern Ireland has been presented by Rt. Hon. Harold Wilson with what amounts to an ultimatum backed up by financial threats. The Ultimatum is an attempt to dictate by economic sanctions what is to be done on matters within the responsibility of the Parliament and people of Northern Ireland. To yield to these threats would undermine the authority of the Government . . . and expose the Country to continued outbursts of violence by those whose aim it is to destroy the peace and prosperity of the people of Northern Ireland and to take away the Civil and Religious Liberties which all its citizens enjoy.[81]

A special meeting of the Central Committee was convened in early January 1969 and attended by three MPs, Robin Chichester-Clark, Nathaniel Minford, and Albert Anderson. The main subject was the civil rights marches, and the meeting ended with a press statement in support of the government and RUC, despite calling for stronger measures to be taken to enforce law and order. The issue of local government reform also loomed on the agenda, but Chichester-Clark refused to commit to anything ahead of the upcoming White Paper.[82]

The government was rapidly losing popularity among the Orange rank and file and with it the pro-O'Neill Orange elite. A microcosm of the shift towards populist Orangeism took place within the walls of the large Clifton Street Orange Hall, in which most Belfast lodges now meet. Eldon Lodge 7 was the traditional elite lodge, favoured by many Stormont MPs.[83] In March 1969, Eldon placed a resolution on the floor of Belfast County Lodge which read: 'This lodge deplores the fact that the public at large both at home and abroad associates our Order with the violence and intolerance inconsistent with our religious principles. This lodge considers our Institution to be in a state of emergency, demanding immediate and positive action by the Grand Lodge of Ireland.' One of Eldon's eighty-five members was Captain O. W. J. Henderson, director of Ulster Television, proprietor of the Belfast *News Letter*, and UUP modernizer, who spoke to the resolution.[84]

Henderson knew that his paper's rival, the *Belfast Telegraph*, had steadily criticized the Order, leading Cliftonville District (Belfast) to impose an unofficial one-week boycott on the purchase of the paper by its members.[85] Henderson, as a 'newspaper man dealing with business people from all parts of the world', expressed concern about safeguarding the 'good name' of the Orange Order. Among the sources of shame were the laws regarding attendance by Order members at Catholic services. Recall that Henderson's *News Letter* had editorialized in vain against the O'Neill and Cramsie expulsions. Henderson now sought to reintroduce the issue to underline what a public relations disaster it was.

Henderson, pronouncing himself a Christian, observed that Orangemen were already attending Catholic funerals and weddings without causing problems. Referring to Colonel McCausland's recent funeral, Henderson stated that if he had been in the province, he would have 'felt duty bound as an ex-officer who had served under the Lt. Col. to attend as a matter of respect'. Henderson added that while he would do everything he could to discourage his three daughters from marrying Catholics, 'if unsuccessful he would have no alternative but to stand by his child'. Though he might be expelled, Henderson felt that in his conscience he would have done nothing wrong. 'By attending the service [I] would be none the worse for it,' he said. On the other hand, 'the persons who wore Orange regalia in unauthorised parades were guilty of as great a crime and they were dragging our Institution into disrepute and this. . . should be forcibly condemned.' In a thinly veiled jibe at the antics of Paisley and the paramilitaries, Henderson reminded those Orangemen present that Order members had a duty to obey the civil authorities. Roman Catholics, he continued, were entitled to be termed 'brethren' and deserved full civil rights. In a foreshadowing of events that would take place some thirty years later, Henderson concluded by calling for a 'small, powerful' clerical committee to investigate the greater use of public communications—undoubtedly for the purpose of improving the Order's image. He concluded on a conciliatory note, deploring the reporting of Orange business to the press.

Smyth returned fire for the populist majority by disclosing that he had been approached by two *News Letter* reporters recently seeking information about lodge proceedings. Smyth was followed by Hugh Peden, District 9 secretary, who retorted that he had 'never heard so much brain washing' as he had from Henderson and that Henderson should instead be using his paper to refute the slanderous remarks being made against the Order. If an Orangeman 'was free to attend a [sic] R.C. funeral and still be doing his duty as. . . an Orangeman [then] in his opinion Brother Henderson was the greatest liability we ever had'.

The Rev. Cecil Mills, District 10 chaplain, agreed with Peden, adding that while he had attended Catholic funerals, he had not attended the services themselves. 'If our rules were ever changed to suit those who were not prepared to abide by them then [my] collarette would come off for good,' he declaimed, adding that he didn't care what others called him so long as he was loyal to his God. A distinct line of anti-elitist criticism was then levelled by Councillor Charles McCullough, who accused Henderson of introducing class distinctions within the Order (probably a reference to terms such as 'businessmen'). Smyth continued the attack by accusing Henderson of having 'not given the lead' since local papers like the *News Letter* fed world opinion. He added that, as a clergyman, he could find nothing in the Orange Rules that he was ashamed of.[86]

The populists had the upper hand, but the Eldon elite weren't finished. Senator David McClelland, master of District 7/8, weighed in at this point, commending Henderson for his 'challenging address' and drawing attention to two related items of concern for the Order: he asked, 'how many schoolteachers were members of the Order' and second, 'how many boys going to university ever joined the Institution or were even sympathetic to us'. Alexander Hill replied with incomprehension at this apparent fifth column within the organization: 'the press [is] biased against us and they [have] the means to publish the true facts'. Jack Galbraith accepted that the Order could be criticized, but objected to being slandered. In summary, Henderson concurred with the desire to defend the Order from slander, accepted that he had learned a lot, and stressed that he would 'remain a friend of the Institution'. Henderson's private thoughts must remain a mystery, but his words illustrate the kind of identity crisis that many middle-class, 'liberal' Orangemen faced.[87]

Subsequent meetings in Belfast contained other aspects of controversy, demonstrating the split between the rising populist cadre and a significant middle-class wing of liberals. For example, Cliftonville District brethren were divided over the sermon preached at an Orange church service by a certain Rev. Gillies, a militant Presbyterian and non-Orangeman. More serious divisions emerged over the political direction of the province. One speaker raised the question of the behaviour of Orange delegates to the recent UUC meeting that had reaffirmed O'Neill's position on a 338–263 vote.[88] In reply, a delegate named Garland expressed his regret that Grand Master Bryans had supported O'Neill in the UUC vote. The Rev. John Lockington, in what would become a recurrent pattern among anti-establishment Orangemen, thereby called for a breaking of the link between the Unionist Party and the Order. This triggered a defensive reply from the district secretary, William Murdie, who asked, 'what position [would] the Order be in if we had not a Unionist Government?' Lockington replied that as a religious institution, the Order should not be linked to a particular party. 'If this [is] the case this meeting should not be discussing politics,' retorted Murdie.[89]

Murdie's position was backed by McClelland, a UUC delegate and probably an O'Neill supporter, who stressed that the Order was 'highly valued at Unionist H.Q'. At this point, another participant promptly interjected that politics should be kept for the ballot-box.[90] A similar division emerged when a private lodge submitted a resolution of no confidence in O'Neill. Edward Meneely feared that this resolution could cause a split in the Order 'as there were pro and anti O'Neill supporters in our ranks'. On another occasion, the same resolution produced 'heated discussion' among participants.[91]

Throughout these debates at Clifton Street, one senses that the likes of McClelland and Henderson were giving way to the voices of a new generation of 'self-made' anti-elitist leaders like Smyth and the Rev. Lockington. Certainly the controversy between populists and traditionalists which characterized Cliftonville and Belfast County meetings in 1969 faded in the 1970s as the populist wing rose to prominence. Ironically, thirty years later the ground had shifted so much that Smyth had become a defender of traditionalist Orangeism against hardliners while Lockington resigned from an Order he believed had become too militant.[92]

In these first months of 1969, the Central Committee was particularly active in responding to rapidly unfolding events. The Orange leadership needed to be seen to be 'doing something' so as to project itself as the leader of the Unionist people. This was particularly acute given the growing spate of resolutions from the grassroots criticizing the inactivity of Grand Lodge in the face of mounting disorder. Grand Lodge responded immediately by reporting its activity in both its reports of proceedings (read by many members) and private correspondence. The Orange leadership claimed its activity had directly led to shifts in government policy.

For example, Grand Lodge officers met Terence O'Neill on 21 January 1969, and 'expressed their views strongly'. On 18 April 1969, the Grand Master and secretary issued a 'serious warning' to the government. This was no idle threat, for elements of the Order in Belfast had previously threatened to take up arms if the civil rights movement paraded from Burntollet—though the Order appears not to have actually stored any weapons in Orange halls.[93] A similar message was conveyed by an Orange deputation that saw the Prime Minister on 6 May, stressing the danger of permitting a proposed civil rights demonstration in Derry the next day. Grand Lodge credited the resulting ban to its own pressure on the Prime Minister.[94] At this point, the general feeling was that the status quo ante could be salvaged given an appropriate government security response. However, it was becoming increasingly clear that the Catholic minority was determined not only to gain socio-economic and political equality, but to express its nationalism by parading and flying the tricolour.[95]

The reforms which O'Neill promised in November 1968 after meeting Harold Wilson sought to redress some of the inequalities between Protestants and Catholics in housing and to tackle the issue of local government reform. O'Neill's initial policies and moderate appeals merely led to mild Orange discontent since they dodged the issue of local franchise reform. This only delayed the inevitable, however, since Unionist government thinking had come around to accepting franchise reform. The UUP leadership thus steeled itself for the task of persuading Unionist party backbenchers of the need for change in order to pre-empt more drastic British measures.[96]

But the grassroots were not ready to accept this medicine. O'Neill's dramatic attempt to get his party to back 'one person one vote' franchise reform and his sacking of William Craig as Minister for Home Affairs in mid 1969 broke the dam of Orange restraint. No fewer than sixteen resolutions came in to Grand Lodge in June expressing non-confidence in Terence O'Neill and/or deploring the dismissal of William Craig.[97] This symbolized the mood among many Unionists in the province. Though Official Unionists had defeated the anti-reform 'Unofficials' in the February election by 27–12, there was an important groundswell of anti-O'Neill opinion which continued to build. A number of Loyalist bombs planted by paramilitaries helped engender a mood of crisis which eventually led the UUP to express its non-confidence in O'Neill. He in turn became the first in a line of Unionist reformers to meet their fate by the same Orange hand which had brought them to power.[98]

3

Orangeism under Fire: Negotiating the Troubles, 1969–1972

The Order wasted no time in meeting the new Prime Minister, James Chichester-Clark, to press its views for two hours on issues such as law and order, the reshaping of local government and the franchise, funding for the Catholic Mater Hospital, and plans for the fiftieth anniversary of Northern Ireland. Orange–UUP unity was symbolized by Chichester-Clark's Minister of Development, Brian Faulkner. Faulkner at this point maintained a hardline reputation based on his resignation from O'Neill's cabinet in January 1969. He served on the Orange Grand Committee and attended the June 1969 Grand Lodge sessions, where he was warmly welcomed. Nevertheless, the honeymoon would not last long. Chichester-Clark was summoned to a meeting with Wilson in London in May, and his team was compelled to commit to reforms.[1]

On the ground, the first deaths of what came to be termed the Troubles occurred in July. On 15 August came the first Protestant fatalities. The security situation now took on a measure of added urgency, even though this theme had already become established as a major area of Orange concern. In response to these events and the continued advance of reforms, the Orange leadership pursued a busy round of press statements and meetings with Government. The tone was supportive of Chichester-Clark and backed his calls for law and order. In September, Martin Smyth's booklet 'In Defence of Ulster' was launched and 45,000 copies distributed. In order to demonstrate resolve, Orange officers met to consider launching a new Covenant similar to the 1912 mass petition against Ulster's inclusion in an all-Irish state. At no point, however, did the Order countenance violence or civil disobedience of the Paisleyite variety. In four public statements during September and October, Orange leaders expressed support for the Prime Minister and called upon the 'Orange and Protestant people' to dismantle barricades. On 11 September, an Orange statement called upon Protestants 'to accept the assurances of adequate protection by the security forces' and to cooperate in the removal of barricades.[2]

All the while, of course, the issue of local government reshaping bubbled in the background. A set of further proposals on the reshaping of local government had been drafted by O'Neill's government, no doubt accelerated by British pressure. The new cabinet had already made up its mind to pursue 'one person one vote', and the trick was going to be selling it to the Order and the Unionist grassroots.[3] The government's 1969 White Paper on local government reshaping suggested a seventeen-area plan.[4] At the Orange end, Harold Cushnie's Grand Black chapter committee charged with overseeing developments in this area was despondent, and one has a sense that it was losing control over UUP policy to London. The committee feared that the proposals, when combined with the 'now almost unavoidable universal franchise', would cost Unionists control of over half of the councils. Cushnie next contacted William Craig, MP, and noted his alternative plan for either three or five constituencies, both of which excluded Belfast. The combined Orange–Black committee set a date for an emergency meeting of 23 August. Clearly it pinned its hopes on Craig's plan.[5]

At the 23 August meeting, Captain Armstrong expressed pessimism about the government altering its proposed seventeen-council plan given the recent publication of its White Paper, suggesting that the government had lost power to Whitehall. For Armstrong, the focus now had to be on effecting 'minor' changes in the government's plan and on using 'all power at our disposal' to achieve marginal changes. Armstrong's mood represented a decided shift from the formerly self-confident tones displayed at other meetings. For the first time in many years, one gets a sense from the responses of Orange leaders that matters were beginning to slip out of their control. No doubt they were mindful of Paisley's challenge and would have liked to press a hard line on the government, but it is clear that they sensed that British intervention had changed the rules of the game.

Fatalism had not yet set in, though. Smyth struck a defiant tone by arguing that since the Nationalists criticized the White Paper, the Order should be doing the same. This can be labelled Orange intransigence, but it is equally true that a hardline strategy, as translated through to the government and then on to London, might be seen as bearing more fruit than an accommodationist one. In such circumstances, it is difficult to be certain what the most rational short-term course of action was, though the British government threat to prorogue Stormont, and the wider battle for the moral high ground against the civil rights movement, might have suggested a more conciliatory strategy. Though there appeared to be some opposition to Craig's five-area plan, a majority agreed to endorse his proposal and to pursue a meeting with Chichester-Clark.[6]

The meeting with the Prime Minister was surprisingly cordial. The Orange deputation expressed its confidence in Chichester-Clark and his government. The Prime Minister tried to reassure his Orange guests that the Unionist interest would be protected by Unionist-controlled councils. We 'have got to be fair,' responded Chichester-Clark, 'it is not realistic to give Unionists control everywhere'. He noted that few councils would fall into Nationalist hands. At this point, William Douglas broke the ice by challenging his interpretation of 'Unionist-controlled' councils. Captain Armstrong added that the present proposals were seen to be appeasing the opposition. Would three or five areas be acceptable to the British government? The Prime Minister feigned interest in this proposal, asking for a more detailed plan from Armstrong. Given Chichester-Clark's appraisal of the situation between London and Belfast, it is doubtful that this was anything more than a delaying tactic.[7]

The grassroots remained defiant, and considerably behind the curve of political developments. A Tyrone lodge, for example, embraced the logic that Northern Ireland councils should be of similar size as mainland British ones in order to press for the five-area plan and called for the complete withdrawal of the White Paper.[8] Yet the reality of London's power was beginning to percolate downwards, especially in 'Loyal' border counties. In Armagh, for example, Richhill District 2 Lodge called for an immediate county meeting, but was rebuffed by the county secretary, W. C. Moody, who described the meeting at Stormont Castle of 19 September in relatively accommodationist terms. 'We were left in no doubt about the seriousness of the situation, particularly the constitutional position . . . [and] we gave the Prime Minister a unanimous vote of confidence . . . our County Grand Master considers all has been done that can be and cannot see that a special meeting is necessary at this time.'[9]

In a meeting with the Prime Minister on 21 October, the second in just over a week, a number of subjects were discussed. Chichester-Clark spoke of his meeting with the British Home Secretary, Callaghan, and his meeting at Downing Street with the British Prime Minister, Harold Wilson. He spoke of 'the real threat to suspend the Parliament' and mentioned that the first item on the agenda of the British government was the 'immediate disbandment of the 'B' Special Constabulary'. Chichester-Clark claimed that, he, along with Brian Faulkner and John Andrews, 'fought this point out and decided to accept the last course', namely the establishment of a Special Reserve Force along the lines of the 'B' Specials, only better trained and equipped. He stated that he aimed to have the new force remain under Stormont's control, but he stressed that it was only 'with the greatest difficulty' that the British approved of a paramilitary force operating outside the remit of the British armed forces. He tried to impress upon the Orangemen that constitutional relations were strained and the British could have simply abolished the 'B' Specials over the heads of Stormont. The Prime Minister added that the new civil servant from Britain who would help to oversee the working party that would construct the new special constabulary 'seemed to be most co-operative'. Captain Armstrong, a member of Grand Lodge and an officer in the

'B' Specials, was co-opted onto this working party, he noted. Chichester-Clark also mentioned that he received a number of security guarantees from the British government.

The Prime Minister had attempted to mollify the Order and elicit some sympathy for the UUP's worsening bargaining position with the British, but while Grand Master John Bryans expressed appreciation for being received by the Prime Minister, the Order felt 'greatly perturbed' by the Northern Ireland government's acceptance of the Cameron and Hunt reports (on civil rights disturbances and police restructuring) and was anxious about the outcome of the Scarman tribunal (to look into civil disturbances). Most of all, the Grand Master declared the Order to be 'very angry about the banning of all parades, particularly the Church Service Parades... the brethren could not take much more and should there be any threat or question of banning the 12th July (or 13th) Demonstrations, all the British Troops in the Country will not keep the Orangemen off the streets.' This was accompanied by laughter from all those present.

In reply, the Prime Minister said that the reports were accepted because they 'were there' but that he did not personally agree with all they contained. He said that as a former serving soldier, he appreciated that troops were shot at and had this not happened, they would not 'have got into this ugly mood'. Of the rioting in the Bogside and Falls Road, the Prime Minister was at pains to stress that any forced entry of troops would have started a 'shooting match'. Nevertheless he had every intention of implementing law and order in these areas, he said. Martin Smyth then intervened, and claimed that 'many people had lost confidence in the government' as a result of the death of Constable Arbuckle of the RUC and the West Belfast rioting. James Molyneaux referred to the 'grassroots' of Orangeism and the fact that people felt that the government approved of the Cameron report. To these remarks, the Prime Minister said that Northern Ireland was a place where there were no easy answers and that it was difficult to define 'loss of confidence'.

The former Northern Ireland Prime Minister Lord Brookeborough next spoke for Fermanagh Orangemen and mentioned that people were becoming suspicious about policy. He asked what might happen if the UK government decided to 'solve the Irish question' by breaking the constitutional link. In his trademark style, Smyth directly challenged the Prime Minister, arguing that many felt the Northern Ireland government to be a mere 'rubber stamp' for British policy and declaring that 'we may as well not have a Parliament'. He suggested that the minority was being allowed to dictate to the majority. Robert McMullan, another Belfast hardliner, pressed the Prime Minister on RUC reform, to which the Prime Minister responded that a change in the colour of the RUC uniform would not discredit the organization. For Henry Young, the key issue was why the 'B' Specials had not been mobilized when Troubles started in the Falls and Bogside. To this, the Prime Minister replied that they were not trained for riot duty. After these hard questions, the Grand Master, Grand Secretary, and junior secretary enquired about the possible extension of the current parade ban.

The Prime Minister did not entirely cave in to this and tried to toe an intermediate course, claiming that the last thing the government wanted was to ban an Orange parade but that an 'element' on the pavements (i.e. Orange spectators) could create trouble. He said that while he hoped that 31 December would mark the end of the parade ban (imposed in August), this depended 'entirely on the people' and on the situation.[10] Though always feisty in defence of its position, the Order seems to have broadly accepted his assurances. This relative goodwill towards the Prime Minister reappears in an Orange statement of 9 December responding to a Stormont debate in which the government was attacked for its connections to the 'sectarian' Orange Order. The Grand Lodge praised the Prime Minister's 'demolishing' of this suggestion.[11]

At grassroots level, the parade ban proved a bigger concern than the security situation, which suggests that symbolic concerns played a vitally important role for the rank and file. This is attested to by the twenty-six private and district parading resolutions from the three eastern counties as well as two county-level resolutions from Fermanagh and Tyrone. This was a larger groundswell of resentment than the nonetheless impressive twenty lower-level lodge resolutions on the security question.[12] During late 1969, there was relative calm on the marching front, but a quiet process of communal conflict was heating up as intimidation and house-wrecking sharpened communal boundaries—especially in Belfast. The handful of Protestant deaths in September and October and the rise of no-go areas indicated that a dormant IRA was a rising force. Dominic Bryan suggests that this prompted increasing involvement from the British government which undermined the state's monopoly on the use of force. This undermined the basis for traditional Orange–UUP hegemony, fraying the compact between the Unionist elite and the working class and leading to the growth of inner-city Protestant paramilitaries.[13]

The security situation was a concern, but most events continued to be attributed by Orangemen to a lack of a forthright security response by the government. If only there could be a clampdown and an end to the appeasement of the disloyal civil rights movement, many Orangemen felt the Republicans would flee from the streets and shrink from making demands on the state. Arguably deceived by the relative success of the 'Orange state' in putting down disturbances in 1935, 1953, and 1956-62, many in the grassroots sincerely believed that strength would be vindicated and weakness punished. There is no hint of fear among lodge resolutions, nor any willingness to suspend parading activity in the interests of safety. This could be attributed to a dogged determination related to Ulster Protestants' ascetic temper and Old Testament 'siege mentality' (also displayed by their spiritual cousins on the frontier in South Africa, Texas, or Israel), or it might have been due to a rational expectation that strength would deliver as it had in the past.[14]

On 11 December, true to form, Bryans complimented the Prime Minister's (half-hearted) agreement to lift the parades ban and reminded him that Orange walks were not demonstrations but traditional events whose prevention would be 'most damaging to the Order's highly-respected and commendable charitable works'. Bryans ended by legitimating Orange claims on the ground that they had been 'loyal' to the state and government and also warned of a 'disastrous conflict of opinion' should parades be banned.[15] On 20 December, the Prime Minister replied, and began by correcting Bryans's perception that a relaxation of the ban was in the offing:

The right to hold traditional parades is something I personally regard as important, but at the same time the peace of the country cannot easily be put at risk... I appreciate the cooperation which the Orange Order has given during this period... For the present, despite the improvement in the atmosphere in recent weeks, we do not feel that the time has come for a full relaxation of the ban.... I am sure that the Orange Order will continue to lend its support to the Government in its endeavours to restore normality.[16]

Unionists who sought to make policy against the Orange grain, as we have seen, could be legitimated only by an invocation of external constraints. Here, Chichester-Clark is invoking the security situation, a response which in the past largely failed to placate Orange disquiet. It was no different this time. At the local level, parading rather than security was the key issue, and resolutions poured into district and county lodges. In Armagh, four district lodge resolutions had been received by 17 November. For the secretary of Richhill District Lodge, the parade ban was denounced with reference to hard-won liberties: 'we reaffirm our right, won ferociously at the Boyne and the Diamond, to walk the roads of Ulster peaceably'. The letter from the county to Grand Lodge demanded that the Grand Lodge 'warn the Government that [bans on] future parades and demonstrations in connection with our organisations would not be tolerated'.[17]

In the report to members in June 1970, the Grand Lodge put a gloss on the Prime Minister's words, contending that the government was anxious that traditional parades be allowed to proceed in 1970 but the ban would need to stand for a further four weeks. Nevertheless, the Order seems to have sensed that it would not be defied. In a reply to the Prime Minister in January 1970, Grand Secretary Walter Williams expressed Orange understanding for the Prime Minister's difficult position and gave him the Orangemen's sympathy and support. But, in view of the upcoming review of parades at the end of the month, they asked him to meet a deputation ahead of this date (no doubt to influence the outcome of the review). The Prime Minister acceded to this, and the parades issue was discussed on 28 January.[18]

What is interesting to note in correspondence and meetings between Orange leaders and the prime ministers of the 1960s and 1970s is the lack of an overtly shared sense of identity. In 1966, O'Neill had been welcomed as 'Brother' at Grand Lodge meetings, but in correspondence, the Order never referred to Chichester-Clark as 'Brother' even though Chichester-Clark addressed his letters to 'Brother Williams'. Nonetheless, the tone of meetings and correspondence is relatively detached, and one has the impression that the Order and the government are two distinct political actors with their own separate, clashing, agendas. Rarely does the professional tone drop, and never is an overtly sectarian language of 'us' (Protestants) and 'them' (Catholics) used. There are references to 'Ulster' or 'Northern Ireland' and its opponents, but it is never so much as hinted that 'Ulster' is anything other than a politico-territorial, as opposed to ethnic, designation.

This sense of separateness appears in a set of correspondence between Belfast County Lodge and the Prime Minister. A Belfast County resolution accused the government of a 'serious slanting against Protestant Officers and preferment of Roman Catholics for senior posts' in the civil service. It continued, averring that being a 'Protestant and/or Orangeman, is an automatic disqualification' for top posts. After expressing fears that Catholic promotion into senior ranks would lead to a similar infiltration into lower ranks, the Belfast statement noted that while 'as Orangemen, we are conscious of the need for tolerance in Public Affairs', tolerance and even-handedness in hiring and promotion 'is not a quality noticeably present in Roman Catholic dealings'. State loyalty oaths apparently did not satisfy the Belfast Country Grand Lodge, which suggested that Catholic civil servants would cynically take the oaths 'as an exercise in public relations' despite a lifetime of disloyalty to the state.

The resolution was duly forwarded by Williams to the Prime Minister on behalf of Belfast County Lodge. In reply, the Prime Minister stoutly defended the government, first mentioning that it was not involved in such appointments and that in any case there was no question of any 'slanting' in favour of either Catholics or Protestants. Chichester-Clark strenuously defended the government's record on appointments to public boards, which he insisted 'should be representative of the whole community'. His letter also expressed surprise that such a resolution should be issued by a county lodge, illustrating how far Orange grassroots assertiveness had progressed over the past decade.[19]

The Order ultimately won the right to parade in 1970, which suggests that Orange pressure prevailed over the Prime Minister. As Dominic Bryan remarks, 'banning them [parades] would be political suicide'.[20] On 14 May, Orange leaders from Grand Lodge and Belfast met the Prime Minister to discuss upcoming parades. The Prime Minister opened the discussion by explaining the seriousness of the security burden imposed on the army and police by parades when security resources were strained to the limit already. A follow-up letter from his secretary urged the Order to redirect banner-moving parades in Belfast along more direct routes. Though he was overruled by the Order, the Prime Minister had clawed back some minor concessions from Grand Lodge in the form of re-routed Belfast parades.[21]

Ill. 4 Clifton Street Orange Hall, c. 1970. At the time, the hall was busy every night of the week. Today, less than a third as many men meet within its now faded, mesh-covered facade.

This was not the end of the story, though. The British government now became directly involved. At short notice, a pre-parades meeting was called by the British for 7 July and was attended by Bryans, Smyth (for Belfast County), and two British MPs: the Home Secretary, Reginald Maudling, and the Minister of State (Home Office), Richard Sharples. The presence of the British delegation symbolized the growing powerlessness of the Unionist government, and, fittingly, the main tête-à-tête pitted the Home Secretary against the Orange deputation. The British delegation appealed to the Order to abandon its parades. The Order's leaders 'felt unable to agree to this'. Upon hearing this, the Home Secretary 'suggested that if Orange Leaders could not agree to call off the parades altogether, there might be a token march, as there had been during the war, or that church parades...should be given increased emphasis'. In reply, the Orange leaders said 'they did not feel these suggestions afforded a practicable alternative', but gave assurances that they would do their best to meet requests for re-routing or regulation of marches and stood ready to meet security authorities. One wonders what the British delegation felt after their first encounter with Orange resolve.[22]

The Belfast County Lodge and Grand Lodge had stood firm, but reciprocated by taking a definitive stand in favour of decorum and non-violence. The county repeated its appeal

to all citizens to show calmness and restraint. They [the county] congratulate Lodges who have rearranged their routes to avoid undue strain on the security forces, and urge any Lodge contemplating Banner movements to exercise the utmost restraint. In particular they ask the General populace not to parade the streets but to watch the marches and not to give opponents of the Order any apparent grounds for complaint.[23]

What is interesting here is the Order's ranking of priorities. Its utmost concern was—and arguably remains—to protect its right to parade rather than to fight for a more general right for its onlookers to sound a triumphalist note. This is in keeping with the 'respectable' ethos which the Orange leadership has generally always sought to advance within its ranks even though this has often been resisted by a 'rough' sentiment among actual participants, be they private lodges, bands, or supporters.[24]

Policy victories tended to be taken in their stride by the Orange grassroots, so concerns in other areas continued to fester. Police reform—then as now—was a major irritant. The disbandment of the 'B' Specials and attempts to change their uniform had prompted an angry response from the grassroots in late 1969. The Hunt and Cameron reports, claimed some, 'badly let down' the RUC and 'B' Specials despite their 'loyal service to the state for nearly 50 years'.[25] Some watering down of reforms occurred, but the general mood remained vigilant rather than accommodationist. Thus Belfast District 1 issued a resolution requesting the government to rescind its decision (as per the Hunt Commission report) to disband the 'B' Specials. It added that failure to do so would lead to the organization of a 'demonstration in strength to Stormont'.[26] On the Twelfth platforms, government ministers were generally absent, and speeches like those of the deputy master of Belfast District Lodge 9 (Shankill) were critical of the government.[27]

Cracks also appeared in the facade of Orange–UUP unity. Chichester-Clark had attempted to build bridges to Catholics by inviting them to join his party and by appointing a Minister for Community Relations, Robert Simpson, who resigned from the Orange Order upon taking up his post. Later, in early 1970, Roy Bradford, Minister of Commerce, publicly questioned the Orange–UUP link.[28] This flurry of activity was interpreted by some Orangemen as tantamount to disloyalty. At Central Committee, one speaker urged that the Committee 'take note that three non-Orange MPs have spoken against a member of this Central Committee (and also an executive of the UUP) and accused him of disloyalty to the leader of the party'.[29] The Order also passed a resolution urging 'upon the Government, caution, lest it drives a wedge between its traditional supporters and itself'. Though 'appreciative of the problems facing the Government', the Order asked it to hold firm and not to implement policies that 'appear to be contrary to the democratically expressed wishes of the majority'.[30]

The Order had reinforced its traditional role as guarantor of Protestant unity, but had also leaned on the government to stiffen its back against reform. In reply to Williams, the Prime Minister seized the sliver of common ground offered by the Orange resolution by responding to the first concern about unity rather than to criticism of the government's policy direction. He inveighed against dissenting Unionists, declaring that while the majority of the party and UUC had endorsed government policy, 'unfortunately we have an element in our Party who have consistently ignored this principle'.[31] The Prime Minister's response did not impress many Orangemen, with the Rev. John Brown of Antrim complaining that he was 'pulling wool over our eyes' and making policy without adequate debate. Martin Smyth of Belfast declared that the Order should not go further towards accommodating re-routing of parades and suggested that the hand of Harold Wilson lay behind the Government's policies. On the other hand, George Cathcart, a more traditional Unionist from Fermanagh, defended the Prime Minister, arguing that the fault did not rest with him. Once again, divisions between 'rebellious' north-east Ulster and the more 'loyal' border counties are highlighted in these discussions.[32]

The Prime Minister's attack on Paisleyism in his letter to the Orange leadership underlined the government's sense of powerlessness as British reform and Paisleyite radicalism encroached on the UUP's political real estate. The Bannside and South Antrim by-elections of April 1970 confirmed his worst fears. These seats, vacated by the retiring liberal-minded Unionists Terence O'Neill and William Ferguson, fell to Paisley and his Free Presbyterian clerical comrade the Rev. William Beattie. UUP figures, including John Andrews and Brian Faulkner, campaigned hard against the Paisleyites, emphasizing a forward-looking 'civic Unionism' based on the British connection. In so doing, they tried to depict Paisleyism and its related Ulster independentism as narrow-minded and sectarian in contrast with the broader-minded, inclusive Unionism once championed by Sir Edward Carson. However, as Graham Walker points out, Official Unionists such as Carson had traded, since the Home Rule crises of the 1880s, on their dual identity as both 'ethnic' Ulstermen and 'civic' British Loyalists.[33] This balancing of 'rebel' and 'loyal' aspects was a key to Unionist unity, and the abandoning of the 'rebel' Ulster alter ego proved too liberal by half for many Unionist voters.[34]

Walker writes that the 1970 by-elections foreshadowed future difficulties which liberal Unionist projects continue to face up to the present. In this he is largely correct, but one point is worth noting—namely that both Bannside and South Antrim were seats in a traditionally upstart county, Antrim, which may not have been as representative of Northern Ireland as Walker suggests. Indeed, it is unlikely that Paisley would have triumphed in border counties of Ulster where traditional loyalty to the party ran stronger. In Antrim and Belfast, though, this was manifestly not the case, with some Belfast Orangemen sporting 'I'm Supporting Paisley' badges at the 1970 Twelfth parade.[35] This was no isolated sentiment: fully ten resolutions had poured into Grand Lodge from Belfast lodges (three of them district lodges) protesting against the UUP partisanship of the Imperial Grand Master, Captain L. Orr, during the Bannside election campaign. Orr responded by writing to the Belfast Grand Secretary saying that he had been misquoted and that he was merely expressing a personal opinion that 'Orangemen should support Orangemen', adding that he was not purporting to speak for the Order when he endorsed the UUP.[36] Whereas the Grand Lodge brazenly supported UUP candidates against the NILP and Independents in the 1950s, its leaders now had to tread very carefully for fear of upsetting Paisleyites within its ranks.

At this time, in early 1970, there was an upsurge in Catholic rioting in Belfast and Londonderry. This was also the period of the so-called 'Arms Trial' of Charles Haughey and Neil Blaney, two ministers in the Irish Republic accused of being party to arms trafficking across the border to the IRA.[37] During 1970, the Grand Lodge was keen to show its membership that it was highly active, responding to the rapidly unfolding events on the ground. This it did by citing twelve separate statements or actions that it had taken between January and June 1970.[38] Some concerned the worsening security situation. Belfast County's recommended policy medicine (issued to the press) was for the government to get tough by (1) initiating searches in Nationalist areas where weapons stockpiling 'is known' to have taken place; (2) releasing the security forces from their 'political stranglehold', which was preventing them from doing their duty; and (3) embarking on an information campaign in England to reveal the 'true nature of the conspiracy against Northern Ireland' and the 'handicap imposed' on the security forces by the British cabinet.[39] Statements like these, calling for swifter security measures, were to become commonplace in Orange publications in the bloody years ahead. Belfast County Lodge's concerns were taken seriously by the government, and Brian Faulkner attended the June 1970 Central Committee meeting, where he praised Grand Lodge for its leadership. Martin Smyth thanked him for his remarks, but warned that the people of Belfast would 'blow their safety valve' if security was not improved. At this, Faulkner reassured Smyth that security was in good hands, with 1,000 troops and 700 RUC men at the ready.[40]

Much of what we have seen thus far consisted of a partly successful Orange rearguard action against British-driven policy reforms. The emphasis in Orange thought and action was on tactics and resolve rather than on any major policy rethink. Yet there were small areas where the Order partially liberalized its views. One such realm was that of social and political contact with Catholics. Orange laws at this stage read, 'Any member dishonouring the Institution by marrying a Roman Catholic or attending any of the unscriptural, superstitious and idolatrous worship of the Church of Rome shall be expelled.' In recognition of the reality of secular politics, the Orange Rules Committee unanimously agreed that attendance at a Roman Catholic service be deemed a *serious offence* rather than grounds for immediate expulsion. This rule change led to a number of appeals and reinstatements of high-profile suspended Orangemen such Robin Kinahan (of Eldon Lodge), Senator John Drennan, and Robin Chichester-Clark, MP.[41]

In discussion of this matter, even Martin Smyth and John Brown agreed, albeit haltingly. Many Orange clergymen appeared to be in the van of this more liberal stance. When the Grand Master, Bryans, opined that the clergy should avoid ecumenism and 'stick to the word of God', the Rev. Johnston defended the clerics' position by charging that many Orangemen were not fulfilling their obligation to attend church on Sunday.[42] The tension between many clerical Orangemen and the 'secular' Orange leadership would continue in the years ahead, with Northern Ireland clergymen pulled in an ecumenical direction by their British parent churches and in the opposite direction by the Order and grassroots Unionism. As in 1966–7, some high-profile churchmen resigned from the Order, with the *Church of Ireland Gazette* praising the new Bishop of Derry and Raphoe for his decision to leave the Orange Institution. Significantly, the Orange Grand Chaplain, R. C. G. Elliott, Lord Bishop of Connor, who had previously been reprimanded by George Clark for criticizing the famous 1966 Orange resolution against ecumenism, in turn censured the *Church of Ireland Gazette* for its stance. This led to a resolution of praise for Elliott from a County Antrim private lodge.[43]

Liberalizing sentiments were hardly in evidence in the aftermath of the Twelfth, however. Though the Order had won the first round against British reform by staging a successful and trouble-free Twelfth, the government imposed a parade ban on 23 July at the behest of the new British Prime Minister, Edward (Ted) Heath.[44] This was partly in response to a worsening security situation. The strategy of the PIRA to radicalize the Catholic community and provoke the security forces appeared to be bearing fruit, and the civil rights rationale of anti-discrimination began to fade as nationalist objectives rose to the fore.[45] The Prime Minister justified his decision to Bryans on security grounds, and tried to mollify the Order by hinting that a period of peace might lead to a relaxation of parade bans. He also tried to underline that the 'new developments [i.e. tougher security measures] in the Bogside should be extremely welcome to loyalist opinion in Londonderry'. Chichester-Clark added that the government had not in any way been influenced in its decision by the Irish government or its taoiseach (president), Jack Lynch, 'in whose opinion we are not the least interested'.[46]

The parade ban, despite the Prime Minister's assurances, met with fury and indignation within Orange ranks. At the next Central Committee meeting, Bryans spoke of 'how shocked we all were' at learning of the ban. James Molyneaux added that those close the Prime Minister were equally shocked and that the Orange and other Loyal Orders must now make their influence felt. The Rev. Brown, after providing a run-down of troop strength in various parts of the province and events in Londonderry, warned that if anything happened during the Apprentice Boys' parade on 13 August, the government would be held responsible.

Smyth opined that the government's intent after six months would likely be to extend the ban for another six months, thereby endangering the Twelfth of 1971. He urged immediate action and sought to bring the Royal Black preceptory, Apprentice Boys, and Orange Order together to talk about strategy. Smyth's concerns were not entirely tactical, though, for in his next breath he referred to a Catholic vigil outside a Protestant house where a Mr O'Hagan was killed, where 'nothing was done' to protect these Protestants. Captain Armstrong urged that the Order 'do something now', but Canon S. E. Long counselled restraint, averring that it was tragic that there should be a confrontation between the Loyalist community and the government. Once again, traditionalist moderation seemed to come from a senior clerical figure within the organization. At this juncture, though, the Rev. John Brown from Antrim rapidly changed the atmosphere. He interjected that the Prime Minister was 'at heart an Englishman' and was keen to 'obey the Generals' since he had spent a good deal of time in the Army. 'From good sources', Brown purported to be aware of those members of the cabinet who were keen on the ban. His words elicited no counter-comment, graphically demonstrating how alienated the Orange Order had become from the UUP leadership over the course of the past five years.[47]

Yet this did not mean that the Order was ready to embrace its arch-enemy Paisley, whom it was determined to outflank. Thus Brown cautioned that the actions of Ian Paisley at Enniskillen were designed to show that Paisley was 'the only one doing something—where the Orange and Black institutions were seemingly doing nothing—which was sheer bunkum'. Smyth picked up Brown's cue and suggested that something had to be done to give guidance to the members, even as attempts to gain support from the churches for a 1912-style Covenant had come to nought. 'The ban cannot be enforced,' asserted Smyth, but he feared that a disorganized defiance of the ban would play into the hands of the Republicans. This concern was related to the rising influence of paramilitaries like the resurgent UVF. Captain Armstrong also expressed worry about the infiltration of 'undesirable people' and their 'unorganised parades'. Clearly the Order wanted to parade, but it wanted to sideline paramilitary elements which might prompt violence and blacken the image of the Orange Institution. This 'tough but clean' template would continue to define the Orange world-view on the security question in the decades ahead.[48]

The pressing concern was how to respond to the government, and here the Order's leadership was uncompromising. Joseph Anderson of Armagh suggested that the Prime Minister's letter to Bryans be ignored and a strongly worded statement issued to the press to satisfy the Orange brethren. Joseph Smallwood and Brown voiced a similar concern that 'something be done' for the membership and cited the decisive action of Belfast Orangemen, led by Joseph Davison, in overcoming a parade ban during disturbances in 1935.[49] No doubt the leadership was sensitive to rumblings from an increasingly demanding membership who would issue resolutions against Grand Lodge with little inhibition. LOL 338 from Tyrone's Killyman District, for example, in reference to the prospective 1970 parade ban, 'deplored [the] apparent inactivity of Grand Lodge to give a lead at this time'.[50]

Republican terrorists targeted Smyth in July, but he narrowly escaped the bomb blast at his home. Perhaps influenced by this narrow escape, Smyth concluded the meeting by invoking other-worldly direction. While suggesting that the Order make its protest as strong as possible, he had his moments of doubt. 'Are we simply going to parade' in defiance of a ban, he openly contemplated, and 'what would the Almighty God think if our decision [is] to break the ban?' Such ethical questions clearly mattered to Rev. Smyth, who was aware of being in the vortex of major historical currents. Referring to the biblical decisions taken by Daniel, and the more secular decision of William Johnston of Ballykilbeg to parade in defiance of a decades-long ban, he admitted that 'decisions . . . are not always right'. In intertwining the this-worldly Johnston with the biblical Daniel—a visionary who must fortify his chosen people for a 'testing time' of great war between the north and the south—Smyth clearly enunciated a classical Old Testament nationalism steeped in motifs of divine election.[51] Needless to say, the Order's response to Chichester-Clark warned that a parade ban might endanger the 'close liaison between the Order, the Unionist Party, and the Government'.[52]

The British government was becoming a more active player in Northern Ireland at this time. An increase in house-to-house searches for arms in Nationalist areas was matched by growing involvement in the affairs of the troubled province. The Order had already met British ministers and General Ian Freeland, the chief commanding officer of the British Army in Northern Ireland. In both cases, Grand Lodge officers pressed their case for improved security for Orange processions and the suppression of 'subversive' forces. It seems that the Order sincerely believed that its 'loyalty' would influence the army's delicate political calculations.[53] This appears to have been neither a major policy driver nor a convincing rationale for the British, but it would continue to be used by the Order in its dealings with the Direct Rule administration.

Responding to the Order, the Prime Minister bent over backwards to plead his case that 'there has been an improvement in the law and order situation since August'. He pointed to over 1,200 arrests and 1,000 convictions in the year ending 26 August, and highlighted the growing strength of the RUC—even in the Falls and Bogside. His three-page letter outlined in detail the nine guns, nineteen grenades, and 3,150 rounds of ammunition seized in the Falls Road–Springfield Road area of West Belfast. He ended by indicating a general 'willingness to discuss these problems with members of the Grand Orange Lodge if they so wish'.[54] The letter was, however, deemed 'unsatisfactory' by Martin Smyth, and a further deputation was soon arranged for 23 November.[55]

A number of key figures excused themselves from the 23 November meeting. Sir George Clark was among those tendering their apologies—perhaps sensing that he would find himself in the uncomfortable position of having to back Orange populists against the governing elite. The Rev. John Brown abstained for a different reason. Brown was a realist who was becoming disillusioned with the usual Orange–UUP channels. 'The PM's word cannot be taken,' he caustically remarked. In a subsequent letter to Grand Secretary Walter Williams, Brown claimed that meeting the Prime Minister was a waste of time. The 'man is stupid, unreliable, and depends on his blind acceptance of the "advice" of his "professional advisers"', said Brown. Brown ended by suggesting that George Morrison take his place since 'it would be an interesting experience for him to see J.C.C. doodling and pretending to take people's remarks seriously'.[56] William Douglas, the Limavady hardliner, was less willing to succumb to such fatalism, insisting that the Order had to take an interest in politics since the UUP would prefer to have it out.[57]

The security issue was a mounting concern, and the resolutions at the December 1970 meeting show that security was almost as important a concern as the right to parade. In all, twenty resolutions were received protesting the parade ban, eighteen voiced non-confidence in the Prime Minister, and twelve complained of the security situation. There was no obvious regional pattern, though Fermanagh was involved in only the security resolution, Tyrone was involved in just two resolutions and Armagh in only three, while Antrim, Down, and Belfast accounted for the bulk of the remainder. The Order's leadership responded to grassroots pressure by flagging over ten instances of where it issued a statement or met government officials between June and December. These included several deputations to the Prime Minister.[58] The two camps had drifted apart so badly that Orangemen were prepared to defy Chichester-Clark's regime. On the recommendation of the Rev. Brown and Smyth, Central Committee agreed to inform all districts that they were legally entitled to parade on 8 November, despite the ban! The Grand Lodge would stand by Orange brethren by paying their fines or appealing their sentences.[59]

Harry West's West Ulster Unionist Council (WUUC) had backed the security resolution of Fermanagh County Lodge, and was a consistent thorn in the side of Chichester-Clark's cabinet, which could not ignore the WUUC's hardline demands.[60] Tensions between the Order and UUP openly surfaced in an Orange press statement on 4 December which condemned as divisive the 'ill-advised attempt [by government supporters at a UUC standing committee the following Monday] . . . to interfere with the useful work of the sincere loyalists of the West Ulster Unionist Council'.[61] The WUUC was also praised by the City of Derry Orange Lodge, which mourned the 'surrender' of Derry (through electoral reform) to the Catholic 'enemies' of loyalty and poured contempt on the Prime Minister, holding the UUP responsible for yielding the sacred soil of its 'ancient' city to the control of a Nationalist community which local Orangemen claim was defeated in 1689.[62]

The presence of John Taylor, the UUP MP, at Central Committee was a foil for Orange grievances such as police restrictions on the Apprentice Boys' right to burn the legendary traitor Lundy in effigy. Meanwhile, several in Central Committee called for a William Johnston-like defiance of the parade ban. On the other hand, the Fermanagh traditionalists Lord Brookeborough and George Cathcart urged caution given the risk of a British takeover of the province. Sir George Clark was another elder statesman who advised moderation and remarked that threats should not be used. But these pleas from the older generation seemed quaint in 1970 and distinctly out of phase with the defiant new mood. Despite Taylor's plea that 'it was most damaging to suggest that the government was trying to hurt its own supporters', few took heed as a motion of non-confidence in the government easily passed.[63]

In late 1970, the Order formed an amalgamated committee with other Loyal Orders to help rescind the ban. At a meeting with the Prime Minister on 21 December, the Prime Minister made it clear that his government wanted the ban lifted, but saw trouble ahead in 1971. Citing figures which showed 1,342 Loyalist parades in 1968, he stressed the large number of parades in any given year, which 'give some people the chance to create trouble'. Such events imposed considerable financial burden on the RUC and Army, he continued, and government policy would seek to allow processions in peaceful 'country areas' outside Derry and Belfast. In the cities, the Prime Minister urged the Order to reduce the number of small parades and re-route parades around flashpoint areas. He specifically asked for the Apprentice Boys to hold their annual 12 August parade in Protestant Waterside rather than Catholic Cityside. He urged the Order to curtail its marches in Nationalist areas such as Newry and called for new band licences to be introduced and authorized by the RUC. The Prime Minister added that the government was considering broadening the scope of parade ban legislation (beyond the threat to public order) to include cases likely to lead to severe financial and troop burdens on the RUC, Army, and local businesses. He followed his demands with a list of flashpoint areas.

This added up to a tall order for an Orange deputation accustomed to symbolic—even if not legislative—acquiescence from the government. Smyth began by questioning the definition of 'flashpoint' areas, claiming that many, like the Glenard Estate, were actually Protestant, and that in other cases, it was Republican agitation that drove the process. Smyth said that 'if the present principle was adopted . . . every time a complaint came from Nationalists/Republicans then the main Belfast Parade to Finaghy would be stopped'. Other Orangemen present pointed to instances of Republican pressure and the lack of police presence around 'flashpoints', claiming that Orange marchers were not 'coat-trailing' but were instead responding to RUC security concerns by re-routing. The amalgamated committee impressed on the Prime Minister that it spoke with one voice and that its support was conditional: 'we will support the Prime Minister if we have the support of the Prime Minister'.

In response, the Prime Minister tried to emphasize the 'guerrilla war' that was being fought. 'We were trying to stop a conspiracy in Northern Ireland by the Republicans and I.R.A,' he painfully explained. 'If we want to succeed we cannot continually take away Army and R.U.C. in large numbers to look after parades.' This cut little ice with Smyth, who asked what steps would be taken to prevent Republicans making trouble at parades and 'unavoidable' flashpoints. Captain Armstrong tried to inform the Prime Minister of the shift in the Loyalist mood after the July 1970 parading season. After 'the success' of 13 July, said Armstrong, 'the Protestant people had thought the corner had been turned, because action had at last taken place in the Falls and we had exercised our rights to march again'. But, he continued, the new ban left the Loyalist community feeling as though it was back at square one, and a mood of 'I told you so' had taken hold which discredited not only the government but the leadership of the Loyal associations. Bans might make life easy for the Army and RUC, but this would tag the Orders as responsible for disorder.

Undaunted, the Prime Minister continued to defend his actions as unpopular but necessary. Changing tack, Sir George Clark raised the spectre of Paisleyism with Chichester-Clark. The ban, claimed Clark, endangered Unionist unity by splitting the Official Unionist Party. The government should take firmer steps to root out Republican troublemakers and protestors rather than ban organized lawful parades. The Prime Minister said that he welcomed counter-proposals, but reiterated the need for the parade ban. This led Smyth to threaten the possibility of counter-demonstrations: 'If ever the tricolour were to be carried through Belfast, we will come out also and march to stop it,' he declared, 'because Orangeism is still on the increase in Belfast.' Smyth then hinted that improved security could lead to a Unionist politico-demographic victory in contested areas: 'When the Security Forces give adequate protection in certain areas of Belfast, our Brethren and loyalist people will remain and take over these completely.'[64] Wedged between the Unionist grassroots (Orange and Paisleyite) and the British—who had already begun to look beyond the lame-duck Prime Minister to explore the option of Direct Rule—the besieged Chichester-Clark seemed to have no relief from any direction.[65]

Once again, Smyth's statements showcase the Orange Order's role as defender of the Protestant ethnic interest, albeit within the confines of traditional institutions such as the mainline churches and UUP. This kind of anti-Paisleyite Loyalism proved a robust template which bound the Order in a conditional relationship to the UUP much as Ulster Protestants were conditionally loyal to Britain. This did not of course rule out significant reservoirs of Paisleyism in Antrim and Belfast lodges. Was the Order ready to overcome its prejudice towards the great rebel? Lodge 1310, 'Banner of the Cross', certainly thought so. This rebellious and politically active Belfast lodge was founded after World War II and contained over sixty members by this time.[66] In 1969, it tried to get permission to hold its own independent service on the Twelfth platform after the county service was finished, but was refused.[67] Later, it issued a resolution calling for the Free Presbyterian Church to be included among the denominations from which chaplains of the Order could be drawn.[68]

In June 1971, the Free Presbyterian motion was considered. Bryans spoke of this as a serious matter, but the Rev. Cecil Mills asked Orangemen to look beyond 'personalities' (i.e. Paisley) and see the Free Presbyterians as Protestants and Christians who should be considered for Orange chaplaincy positions. Most clerics within the Order were decidedly cool about this. The Rev. Blackstock, for example, referred to a Free Presbyterian paper's criticisms of Martin Smyth and Warren Porter as being 'not of our Christian faith'. The Rev. Coulter related a recent anecdote whereby he, as a Presbyterian minister, was barred from taking part in a Free Presbyterian wedding. The Rev. Thompson spoke of the Free Presbyterians' 'unbiblical' doctrine. Porter asked whether they were prepared to accept 'our clerical brethren'. The Rev. Griffiths found the resolution unreasonable since the Free Presbyterians 'were opposed to the Order'. W. J. Hamilton of Tyrone said that this would be a serious change to existing practice that would cause dissent in the ranks. The Rev. Johnston agreed, arguing that Law 81 'was a fundamental' of the Order and that 'we must not make a decision through fear'. The Rev. Crossley, chair of the Education Committee, acerbically noted that 'we would make an ass of ourselves if we started communicating with the Free Presbyterian Church' and that District 6 of Belfast was wrong to bring the matter up. John Brown, Smyth, and James Molyneaux agreed that the resolution should be sent back to the Belfast district (6) which had passed it on.

What clearly emerges from these discussions is that the Order, while rejecting government reforms, perceived Paisley, his church, and his party as a threat. Here Orange traditionalism clearly trumped rebel Unionism. Or at least it mostly trumped it, for there were those willing to speak up for Paisley even within the Order. John Brown, Grand Master of Antrim, despite assenting to the majority view, asked if a Free Presbyterian minister who was a lodge member could become chaplain. George Morrison, the Grand Secretary of Antrim, from Lisburn District, later answered that in his district, 'we were not depriving the Free Presbyterian ministers from becoming chaplains', and, in a barb directed at the 'ecumenism' of those mainline clergy present, challenged: 'would they [Free Presbyterian ministers] not be better than our existing clerical chaplains?'[69] These unpopular interventions made little impression, and it was decided that the Free Presbyterians would have to provide satisfactory answers to three questions before they could be considered. These asked whether Free Presbyterian ministers (1) 'would follow the rules of brotherliness in our Order which precludes unfair public attacks [on Order members or beliefs]; (2) 'could accept as Christians' ministers from other denominations; and (3) could have 'fraternal fellowship' with the latter.[70] The matter did not come to a vote again until 1977, when it likewise failed to pass, demonstrating the power of traditional Orange antipathy against Paisley and his upstart Free Presbyterians.[71]

Internecine squabbles within Unionism were a luxury the Order could ill afford, since the Institution was finding it ever harder to get satisfaction from Stormont. The Order's letter to the health minister requesting an update on the issue of government funding for the Catholic Mater Hospital in Belfast had not been answered, and another chasing letter had to be sent.[72] When the reply eventually was read in June, it was deemed highly unsatisfactory. Martin Smyth suggested informing the minister that 'we are not a third party and are tired of the government sidestepping issues' concerning the Roman Catholic Church. Evidently the Order was not willing to accept the status of an 'outsider' lobby group, though it would soon become precisely that.[73] One Orange-approved policy which did eventually succeed was internment. Smyth remarked that certain members of the security forces favoured this policy of holding suspected terrorists without trial. He recommended that these 'rumours . . . be conveyed to the outgoing Minister of Information' in the hope of influencing policy. Internment was considered in March and opposed by Chichester-Clark, but implemented in August by the new Faulkner administration.[74]

Grassroots Unionism's resistance to reform and the British government's equally adamant desire for change derailed Chichester-Clark's government. The British were well aware of the Prime Minister's flagging popularity and lack of grassroots support. They feared that he would be replaced by a hardliner, but continued to withhold permission for tougher security measures and to press for reforms in the knowledge that they could always suspend Stormont. After being refused additional troops in March, Chichester-Clark resigned. Brian Faulkner easily defeated the more hardline William Craig by 26–4 to gain the leadership of the UUP and won overwhelming support from the Ulster Unionist Council.[75]

The response from the Order to the new Prime Minister was much more guarded than on previous occasions, when congratulations greeted new Unionist leaders as a matter of course. George Cathcart, the Fermanagh traditionalist, began the proceedings by proposing that the usual letter of congratulation be sent to Faulkner. Faulkner had kept his Orange connections watered throughout 1969 and 1970 and had opposed O'Neill's reforms, and Cathcart opined that he was a member of Grand Lodge and 'the only man' who could carry out what the country demanded. Sir George Clark seconded Cathcart, but Smyth said that the Order should be 'very loath to send a letter which would give the PM the impression that we are 100 percent behind him. The Order should not be committed.' Henry Young agreed that the Order should withhold support since 'many brethren were not supporters of Faulkner'. In response, Captain Armstrong of Armagh made the traditionalist claim that Faulkner deserved Orange praise since there was no harm in congratulating 'a member of our Order who had received such a high honour'. Clark, a leading figure in both the UUP and the Orange Order who seems to have successfully kept both balls in the air,[76] agreed, and cordial and fraternal greetings were sent. The old guard had won a small victory for loyalty, though Faulkner's reputation within the Order would eventually succumb to the same fate as that of his predecessors.[77]

Dissension within the ranks was also apparent over preparations for the fiftieth anniversary of Northern Ireland, planned for 26 June. On a 17–14 vote by the Jubilee Committee, the decision to parade was mothballed. The Belfast hardliner Robert McMullan evinced disappointment at this, condemning those counties 'who were frightened' to go to Belfast for the demonstration. Bryans spoke of his 'bitter disappointment'. Brown of Antrim spoke of 'certain undercurrents' leading to the cancellation of the parade and said his county 'condemned the taking of a ballot' and the secrecy of many Jubilee Committee meetings. Billy Douglas called the cancellation a 'bungle'.

Border Orangemen were undoubtedly behind the cancellation, with Richard Thornton of Fermanagh regretting that the date and time of the parade were unsuitable but stating that his county would be ready by March. At Grand Lodge a few days later, a Coleraine man expressed relief that the parade would not take place in June as the date was not suitable. Ostensibly, the reason many gave for failing to parade on 26 June had to do with transport and logistics. In reality, the decision may also have been linked to fears that violence might break out, which could endanger both human life and, perhaps more importantly, the Twelfth. This was the theory propounded by the *Belfast Telegraph*, though members of Grand Lodge vigorously denied this. What is clear is that only five lodges responded affirmatively to a parade call sent to over 100 lodges. Once again, the division between the more radical counties of the north-east and the more traditional, locally orientated lodges of the countryside was manifest.[78]

One parade on which there was unanimity was the Dungiven Church parade of 1971. In a rehearsal of the events of 1959, Douglas stated that the police had vetoed a parade. The Prime Minister, though denying knowledge of the event, said that he would have to ban it, though the Grand Lodge reports put a more optimistic spin on things to the membership, suggesting that 'no request had been made by the Prime Minister to call off the parade'.[79] At Grand Lodge, the Rev. Dickinson prayed that the service would go ahead and said that 'if we do not carry out our parades this year then we are finished. The PM is the person responsible for banning of parades.' The Belfast Grand Master Martin Smyth and the Antrim Grand Master John Brown intimated that the 'time had come to "call a halt" to the policy of "where there is a republican stronghold" no Orange parade will take place'. Others agreed, and a resolution was issued to the media citing 'threats to the constitutional rights and liberties of the people of Northern Ireland'.[80]

Though Faulkner banned the Dungiven parade, Douglas seized the initiative and announced that he would parade in this Nationalist town in defiance of the ban. For Douglas, the Order had desisted from parading in the town on 12 July 1971 and felt that it had earned the right to this parade, which had otherwise taken place uninterruptedly since 1960.[81] However, the parade was blocked by police, an Orangeman named William McCrea was arrested, and Orange officials were unable to control the ensuing riot, which had to be quelled with tear gas and rubber bullets.[82] Divisions between the Orange leadership and local Protestant militants were clear, with the former urging the crowd to disperse and the latter asking their leaders, 'What did you bring us here for?' The pro-Unionist Belfast *News Letter* suggested that the Order had given a confusing signal by allowing Douglas to call for support and then changing its mind at the eleventh hour. At the post-mortem meeting, George Clark called for unity. Douglas was unrepentant: '*Our country* has been pushed down,' he thundered, using Ulster nationalist language. 'The next attack is on the Orange Institution . . . if the Order was destroyed *our country* would not survive long.'[83]

Douglas went on to describe the events of that fateful day. Noting the presence of Catholic troublemakers on the sidelines, he instructed his men to go to the field by car. But before they could do so, the crowd surged forwards and the riot began. Blame was placed on police, who he claimed had advance notice but did little to provide security. Clark then put his Orange loyalty above his party, saying that 'we [either] change our obligations or change the Government . . . do we openly want a break with the Unionist party?' Internment, he lamented, would take place only 'when the army suffers a disaster. Our people are being conditioned to accept change. Change when we entered the Common Market and [change when] General Turzso [said] that we are being contained while politicians sort out a solution. We should never lose the opportunity we have of being able to approach our Prime Minister.'

Smyth took heart from the bloody events, saying that 'many were of the opinion our Order had risen'. Douglas argued that if it was impossible to parade, 'our Protestant people [should] be used to form a body of Militant Protestants to defend our heritage'.[84]

Even at the height of this conflict, the Order never counselled violence, illustrating the importance of the admirable Orange tradition of 'respectability' which nonetheless coexisted with the 'rougher' tradition of popular deviance expressed by bands, onlookers and some working-class brethren.[85] Clark implored his audience to keep parades respectable, and other traditionalists on Central Committee spoke of troublemakers on both the Protestant and Catholic sides. Finally, the resolution adopted at the June sessions drew on the covenantal language of religious Nationalism to commend

The self-discipline and restraint shown by the Orange brotherhood in the face of great provocation. In the interests of peace and order in the community, we recommend all brethren to *observe the rules and traditions* of the Institution, to obey the orders and keep the arrangements made for them by our own leaders. Only by unity, *self-discipline* and active cooperation in maintaining law and order, can our people overcome those evils by which we are now encompassed. Proud of Ulster's progress over fifty years in the face of arson, sedition and murder, we acknowledge our thanksgiving to Almighty God for His mercies, and reaffirm our trust in Him for the future, pledging ourselves to do all that we can to promote the peace and prosperity of the Province.[86]

The Dungiven saga reveals several things. First, by this point, few Unionists could imagine halting Nationalist displays (of say, the tricolour) within Catholic areas, but they at least wished for the authorities to possess a monopoly on the use of force in such areas. Second, the Order was fighting to preserve its right to march in strongly Nationalist areas as a symbol of control over the province's public space and thus its national territory.[87] But were the Order's motives solely based on the desire to maintain ethnic hegemony over the land? A counter-explanation is that the desire to parade could also be justified for reasons of local cultural tradition and freedom of expression. Indeed, from a liberal perspective, one could argue that local Catholics had no more right to halt a peaceful march than did the 1,000 Ku Klux Klansmen and their supporters in all-white Forsyth County, Georgia, in 1987. Police presence ensured that the civil rights activists in the USA were able to pass in Forsyth, so why not the Orangemen at Dungiven or Apprentice Boys in the Bogside?

There was a strong civil rights case here, but unfortunately this was undermined by the nearly-as-vigorous Orange insistence that Republicans should not be allowed to parade the tricolour into Unionist areas. Thus the Grand Lodge inveighed against the authorities' failure to 'enforce the ban on a Republican parade in Dungiven on Easter Sunday'.[88] To invoke civil liberties in one instance and disloyalty in the other is not a consistent approach. 'Traditional' parades may be more dear to Orange hearts than a new Loyalist marching band route, and this should count for something, but it is also true that Unionist parades vastly outnumber Nationalist ones, and that this partly reflects the unequal power relations of the past. All of this necessitates a common standard that balances considerations of freedom of expression with that of public order.[89] Were Unionists to assent to Nationalist parades full stop, then it seems logical that Republican arguments that Orange parades simply constitute 'coat-trailing' would not hold water.

Meanwhile, dealings with the British in 1971 continued to be difficult for the Order. Though James Molyneaux described discussions with British Minister for Northern Ireland, Reginald Maudling, as 'not wholly unfruitful', the Home Secretary, James Callaghan, was viewed as a different animal. Callaghan, it was noted, had refused to speak to the Order on previous visits, citing lack of time. Clark asked why, if this was the case, had he spent so much time in Dublin. 'Federal Government? United Ireland? Common Market? He was no friend of ours and a man to be despised for the policies he has forced upon us.'[90] Smyth stated that the reason for Callaghan refusing to meet was that Callaghan 'was here to take sectarianism out of our politics' and should thus be avoided unless he came to meet the Order. Whether this amounted to an endorsement of sectarianism is unclear from this passage.[91]

Brian Faulkner's subsequent Stormont administration was no kinder to the Orangemen than that of Chichester-Clark. Widely viewed as Unionism's last chance before the British intervened, Faulkner sought to move ahead with reforms which brought Gerry Fitt's moderate Nationalist SDLP closer to the heart of government.[92] Faulkner's reforms included forming shared committees with the SDLP which would have real policy-making clout. Faulkner could also point to reforms in housing and local government, though these had been delayed somewhat by the violence. In December 1970, the Chichester-Clark government had accepted the Macrory report, which advocated a major reshaping of local government in Northern Ireland. This report called for the abolition of the existing two-tier system of eight counties or county boroughs and their panoply of local government subunits, to be replaced by a rationalized system of twenty-six elected district councils rather than the five favoured by the Order and William Craig. Two new area boards for overseeing health, education, and social services were also proposed.[93] Many of the new administrative units would fall under Nationalist control, breaking Unionist hegemony in many areas.[94] In effect, many services delivered by the largely Unionist-dominated county councils came under central government control.

At the Grand Lodge sessions in June, County Londonderry spearheaded the opposition to local government reorganization. The Rev. Dr James Johnston from that county proposed a resolution which was adopted and released to the press and Prime Minister. Orange criticism focused on the 'loss of democratic rights' occasioned by the fact that Stormont was centralizing power over services in housing, health, and education. The setting up of mixed-faith appointments committees for principals and vice-principals for state (i.e. Protestant) schools, but not for Catholic-maintained schools, was seen as especially discriminatory. In mainland Britain, the resolution pointed out, local government reorganization devolved power to the people, but in Northern Ireland, the opposite occurred. The Order thus resolved to 'organise the strength of the Order to defend the full British Democratic rights' of the people of Northern Ireland.[95]

Roy Bradford, a Unionist MP who was no friend of the Order, wrote the reply to the Grand Lodge resolution. Bradford made no attempt to soft-pedal his message, stating matter-of-factly that reconsideration of local government reshaping was 'no longer possible'. He outlined a flow of events which included decisions taken by Chichester-Clark's administration, 'fully endorsed by the present [Faulkner] Government and now settled policy'. The Local Government (Boundaries) Act, he added, was approved by Parliament, and the recommendations of the boundaries commissioner, Harrison, were 'being published this week'. Democratic control, argued Bradford, would be expressed through departmental ministers answerable to Stormont. A measure of local control would be retained through local government representatives on the area boards.

Meanwhile, Bradford claimed that the twenty-six district councils were both large enough to be viable administrative units and small enough to ensure local involvement. Only in the field of education did he answer to Orange concerns, arguing that a local aspect would be retained, with local interests making up a majority of those on school management committees. Bradford ended with a customary statement that appears facetious given what he knew of the Order: 'I trust that the Grand Orange Lodge of Ireland will reconsider its stand on the issue and exert its influence in support of the course of action on which the Government has embarked.'[96]

Bradford's letter stressed functional imperatives, but glossed over the fact that power was being taken away from the local level. Here the Order clearly had the advantage in the argument. The Orange response to Bradford, as with its original resolution, thus comes across as professional and well written, focusing heavily on the loss of significant local power to Stormont. Less persuasive was the argument against geographical reshaping. Here the Order rested its case on the fact that the new areas made little geographic sense (in one case because a district included territory on both sides of the Sperrin mountains) and because the new districts destroyed logical existing catchment areas for various public services. The letter ended by contrasting the democratizing devolution of power in mainland Britain with its usurpation in Northern Ireland. 'Northern Ireland is British. Northern Ireland policy hitherto has been step by step with Britain . . . . Why this basic departure from past policy in Northern Ireland and from present British policy?'[97]

The Order had a point, but neither it nor Bradford was prepared to acknowledge openly that the crux of the matter was that power was being removed from local Unionists and handed to a central Faulkner-run administration bent on reform in the interests of both communities. Privately, the reforms had been subjected to a thorough ethno-religious analysis by Dr James Johnston, the brains behind the Order's sophisticated response. Johnston quickly realized the implications:

Of the four country regions for Education, and of the three country regions for Health and Hospital, two will have an R.C. [Catholic] majority. Limavady, City of Derry, West Tyrone and Fermanagh, that is, the Western Region, will be overwhelmingly R.C. The Southern Region . . . will also have an inbuilt R.C. majority. The minority have a right to $1/3$ of the regions, but they have no right to 2 out of 4 and less right to 2 out of 3. No matter how one looks at the reorganisation scheme it is a complete sell out of Democratic Rights and the constitutional position of the loyal majority'.[98]

The Order possessed a dwindling influence on the state of affairs and was functioning almost completely as a lobby on government rather than one of its constituent pillars. Unfazed, it dutifully drew up a thirteen-point platform replying to the government's reforms which an Orange deputation brought to Faulkner's attention. The Order also complained that the centralization of housing was not even mentioned by Bradford (it being presented by the latter as a *fait accompli*). Finally, the long-festering Mater Hospital issue appeared to have been decided in Catholics' favour without forcing the facility to come under the Unionist government's administrative rubric. Here was another straight loss for the Order, which viewed the government as having 'sold out' yet again. The Rev. Long, a traditionalist, called for a study of the links with Faulkner and the Official Unionists (UUP).

Within Central Committee, discontent from the right with the elderly John Bryans's leadership burst into the open. William Douglas brusquely condemned the Grand Master's leadership and suggested a 'younger man'. Traditionalists like the Rev. Crossley, the Education Committee chairman, and Sam Magowan, the County Down MP, were shocked, springing to Bryans's defence. Belfast's Hugh Radcliffe backed Douglas's call for Bryans to go, but Colonel Edwin Liddle, CBE, of Fermanagh and Joseph Twyble of Armagh supported the Grand Master. Douglas, backed by Alfie Lee of Londonderry, put Brown's name forward as deputy, and Molyneaux and Brown proposed Smyth as the new Grand Master. Once again, the largely north-east Ulster rebels were opposed by the rump of border Unionist grandees. Though both populist candidates were withdrawn, they were harbingers of a further erosion of the Loyalist traditionalism within the Grand Lodge as the Order's elite came to resemble its popular base in both social and ideological terms.[99]

On the ground, a battle between increasingly restive populist elements and the traditional Orange hierarchy in border counties was being played out.

County Armagh's officers, including Twyble and Armstrong, remained loyal to Grand Lodge and the government. They thus resolved to discipline those who had heckled county officers and UUP politicians on the platform at the Twelfth. At Armagh County Lodge, the motion to suspend the hecklers was passed unanimously, suggesting that traditionalist elements still remained in control. Among those expelled by the county was an anti-Faulkner local councillor, Douglas Hutchison.[100] This split the Order in Armagh. In the militant Protestant newspaper, the *Protestant*, a headline spoke derisively of County Armagh Lodge and its 'Kangaroo Court'. A correspondent wrote a letter to the *Protestant* condemning Armagh County Lodge, thundering that several 'loyal Orangemen faced the O'Neillite and Ecumenical Inquisition to be sentenced for the legitimate protest they made against the speakers who disgraced the platform'. Deputy Grand Secretary Whitten was referred to as 'Brian [Faulkner]'s Yes Man', and other county officers were simply labelled 'O'Neillite'. Grand Chaplain Crooks earned the moniker 'Ecumenical Apostate'.[101]

Hutchison, the expelled anti-Faulkner councillor, had accused Whitten of caving in to 'certain [O'Neillite] delegates' of the Central Armagh Unionist Association, thereby reinforcing the impression that the UUP and Order hierarchies remained strongly linked at the local level in border areas.[102] He also referred derisively to James Stronge, who had run in Mid-Armagh on an anti-O'Neill ticket, but subsequently deceived the voters, who supported him by backing the government.[103] Hutchison and Stothers appealed their expulsions to Grand Lodge, where they found a more sympathetic ear. During the hearing, it emerged that the accused had hissed and booed at the resolution of loyalty to HM the Queen, underlining the clash between traditional Orange loyalty to the Crown and its 'rebel' alter ego. Armagh officers such as Whitten stressed the damage done to the institution and said they could never remember this kind of trouble. When asked by the Grand Master if he was sorry about what he had done, Hutchison retorted, 'Not one bit'. When asked why he did not use the machinery of the rule book, Stothers remained silently defiant. At a number of points, George Little (Tyrone) and George Watson of Belfast suggested that Armagh's decision of expulsion be upheld, but they withdrew their motion and, though the appellants' attitude was condemned, their expulsions were ultimately commuted to three-to-seven-year suspensions.[104]

A similar dynamic was taking place in the government, and Edward Heath realized that if Faulkner's leadership was to be saved, Faulkner needed to be able to show something to his grassroots. As a result, Faulkner was able to persuade the British to back off from their demand that the Twelfth be banned because this would unduly alienate Protestant opinion ahead of a political settlement. Luckily, the Twelfth passed off without incident despite a spate of IRA bombs in Belfast the day before.[105] Just as importantly, internment was adopted in August partly to keep militant Protestants from rebelling. The rise of these militants was in some measure attributed by the British to 'the demoralisation of the "squirearchy" in Ulster...Chichester-Clark's resignation was clearly viewed as signalling the political collapse of this brand of Ulster Unionism'. The same process was clearly at work in the Order as the old guard of border Unionist elites gave way to a rising cadre of Young Turks.[106]

Security became an increasingly important issue for the Order, but fear never governed Orange strategy. Republican paramilitaries increased the number they killed from seventeen in 1970 to ninety-eight in 1971. The number of Ulster-Protestant dead jumped from ten in 1970 to forty-five in 1971, including a rising number of RUC and UDR men. A large number of British soldiers were also among those killed and symbolically counted towards the 'Protestant' total.[107] In the midst of these fatalities, Grand Lodge issued a statement to its members and the press which commended 'the patience, restraint and commonsense of the Protestant majority in the face of continuing provocative violence of savage terrorists'. The statement criticized the British government for its failure to protect the 'peace-loving people of Ulster' and warned that 'any talk of a political settlement of the Northern Ireland problem is wrong-headed while the murderer, bomber and arsonist is running loose'. Though eschewing paramilitary violence, the Order urged 'all Orangemen, in addition to measures already taken, to safeguard households and neighbourhoods, to accept the challenge of the call for the build-up of the [UDR] defence forces...Further, we commend service in the [RUC] Police Reserve, provided that the Government reorganises it as a properly equipped force'.[108]

Not all Ulster-Protestants agreed to act through legal means. The newly formed Ulster Defence Association (UDA), a paramilitary organization, took matters into its own hands, and Loyalist paramilitaries killed twenty-one people in 1971; the total rose to well over 100 in 1972. These street thugs should be seen as largely independent of the generally law-abiding Order, though some paramilitary men were also lodge members. Meanwhile, Martin Smyth, though committed to non-violence, succumbed to an increasingly alarmist attitude at the next Central Committee meeting, which underlined the Order's degree of estrangement from 'its' Government. After stating that he was withdrawing from any future deputations to the Prime Minister, Smyth called for the Order to act independently. 'All lodges must be told that all members must be prepared at this time for an emergency,' he stressed, 'We must...act for Ulster'. Action was focused on mobilizing the Protestant community. Thus sanction was given to Belfast County to 'prosecute the signing of the Covenant in which ever way is fit'. There were also references to Loyalist meetings organized by William Hull of the Loyalist Association of Workers, who urged Smyth to use his influence with Liverpool and Glasgow Orangemen to gain their financial support for rallies.[109]

A resolution passed by Grand Lodge called on the membership to steady themselves for an IRA siege:

1. 'Prepare to defend households and communities';
2. 'Render active support to the Security Forces in their efforts to destroy the enemy';
3. Blow up all 'unapproved' roads along the border to prevent gunmen from escaping;
4. 'Defend with all our strength and whatever the cost the Constitution of the Land we love for which our forefathers fought and died'.

The resolution also called on the government to rearm the RUC and set up another local defence force, extend curfews in 'troublesome' areas, and withhold social benefits from those participating in the civil disobedience campaign against internment. While the Order threatened that 'the patience of the Loyalist people is near to breaking point', it reaffirmed its vows to remain loyal to the Queen.[110] Though the Order often threatened violence, it never really took steps to amass weapons, and the views of the Rev. John Lockington that 'our greatest weapon is the truth' represented the sentiments of the overwhelming majority of Orangemen.[111]

Though the Order reaffirmed its loyalty to the Crown and refrained from violence, it still reserved the ultimate right to take up arms and disobey Britain in the spirit of 1912 (when the fear of being forced into a United Ireland by a British-Nationalist deal led to the mass Unionist mobilization of weapons and men). In a Grand Lodge statement of 8 December 'for the guidance of its members and loyalists of Ulster', it called on its members to 'join the R.U.C., the Police Reserves, and the UDR' and take 'all steps' to defend persons and property against the IRA. Significantly, the Order threatened that 'Should the democratic process be ignored or avoided, the loyalist population should prepare for a programme of disobedience against *any power* which usurps the rightful Government.'[112] It also initiated a mysterious 'eyes and ears' intelligence operation, replete with local units, though this appears to have come to little.[113] On 30 December, Central Committee reiterated its stance in a press statement, declaring that the Order and Loyalist community would not 'be a party to any agreement made without its consent. It pledges itself to a policy of disobedience should the Powers at Stormont be further diminished or the Constitution changed.'[114] The Order's attitude here, as in many other matters, was defensive rather than offensive. To the degree that this ruled out violence, it is to be applauded, though significant numbers of more militant-minded recruits left after 1972, frustrated by the lack of armed action.[115]

The Rev. Dickinson suggested that the Order was being sold out by its government and that this was affecting lodge attendance, but an increase in total membership was noted by Central Committee.[116] This is interesting since the Order in Northern Ireland had been in steady membership decline since attaining a peak strength of almost 70,000 in Northern Ireland in the late 1950s. This slide was reversed after 1969, partly because Protestants re-entered the Order for mutual protection.[117] Some no doubt expected to acquire weapons, but were disappointed and left the Order after its membership peak (since unequalled) in 1972. Who were the new recruits? In Belfast in 1971, 1,625 men joined the Order, with an average age of almost twenty-five years—nearly five years older than those recruited in 1965. Their denominational profile roughly matched that of Belfast Protestants as a whole, including over forty Free Presbyterians and a handful of Pentecostalists and Salvation Army men. In class terms, one is struck by the fact that there were virtually no professionals or white-collar employees among the inductees. A few English-born Anglicans from HM Forces, nine policemen, and roughly ten 'civil servants' were oddities among the fitters, plumbers, drivers, postmen, machinists, clerks, and electricians. Surprisingly, fifty were foreign-born, most of them English and Scottish but including one German student and one Tasmanian-born 'student apprentice'.[118]

The new Orangemen entered an organization preparing for a showdown with Stormont and the British over proposed constitutional changes. Proportional Representation (PR), which would greatly reduce the dominance of Unionists at Stormont, had been opposed by Belfast County Lodge since late 1970. Despite this, the Order formed a committee to study PR in more detail, signifying a willingness to consider PR on its merits.[119] Though the Rev. Dickinson understood that Protestants in Catholic-majority areas felt that PR might benefit them, he ultimately came down against it, stating that even in Londonderry and the west, PR was against the 'loyalist cause' and that the Order should emphasize its opposition to the government's Green Paper on electoral reform.[120] The government and the British, of course, were in no mood to concede ground back to the Loyalists, since internment—a policy marred by poor intelligence which saw innocent Catholics jailed while IRA gunmen slipped away—was proving a public relations disaster with the Nationalist community. On the other hand, Faulkner had the sense to realize that Nationalist participation in cabinet and the introduction of PR were non-starters for the Loyalist electorate.[121]

The events of 'Bloody Sunday', 30 January 1972, when thirteen Nationalist demonstrators in Derry were killed by the British Army, failed to merit a mention at the next Central Committee meeting, though an alarmed Rev. Dickinson announced that 'Londonderry is taken over by the I.R.A. . . . Protestant people are living in fear'. This period arguably represented the pinnacle of unrest in the province, and the death toll of nearly 500 for 1972 made 1971 seem like a picnic. In the midst of this tense atmosphere, Harold Wilson, then British Labour Party leader, remarked that a United Ireland was the only solution to the conflict in Northern Ireland, while the Home Affairs Minister suggested that the west bank area of Derry should be ceded to the Republic of Ireland. Orange deputations were hastily arranged to see both Lord Carrington and Faulkner over security and other matters.[122]

IRA retaliation for Bloody Sunday worsened the situation, and Faulkner was asked by the British Prime Minister to consider a number of emergency reforms. These included involving Nationalists in government, transferring control over law and order to London, ceding border areas to the Republic, conducting a referendum on the border question, and easing internment. Faulkner was prepared to consider only the last two, no doubt mindful of the force of grassroots Unionist opposition to the first three proposals—including the Order's characterization of proportionality in government appointments as 'religious discrimination' in a meeting with British officials.[123] Judging by Orange scepticism, even Faulkner's preferred Green Paper, a kind of 'third way' between reform and the status quo, would have had a hard run. Orange reaction to the Green Paper, circulated in a six-page statement to the press and Unionist politicians, softened somewhat at the eleventh hour, but was not enthusiastic.[124]

On 3 March, Faulkner addressed the annual UUC meeting. He began by praising John Taylor, and giving thanks for Taylor's 'miraculous escape from the bullets of the assassin'. His courage, glowed Faulkner, symbolized the 'spirit of Ulster which will never be defeated'. Faulkner defended internment by claiming that the situation had begun to worsen before internment and would worsen if the detainees were freed. He praised the 'loyal and brave men' of the security forces, both Protestant and Catholic, and inveighed against the brutality of the IRA and their campaign of terror, murder, and propaganda. He singled out the government of the Republic as irresponsible and soaked in blood, opining that 'it is in the South that the whole, romantic, violent, blood-stained "physical force" tradition . . . has its home. Too many of their political leaders have been nurtured in that tradition to break free of it; too many have honoured the graves of yesterday's assassins to be wholly resistant to today's.'

The results of these policies could be seen in the 'empty and silent stands at Lansdowne Road [racetrack in Dublin] or the deserted hotels once full of British tourists'. At this point, Faulkner hinted that Unionists were part of the Irish family by remarking that the IRA campaign was a 'strange form of fellowship' and that the Republic was unable to sympathize with 'a million of what they themselves claim to be their fellow Irishmen'. Nevertheless, in the next breath, he quickly jettisoned his Irish identity to defend stoutly the idea of Ulster as an inseparable part of Britain, linking Ulster's fate to that of the British nation and its struggle for democracy. He displayed his national identity as British rather than Ulsterite by asserting that though the main battle lines were in Ulster, 'the whole British people' and its democratic values were at stake. The solution, claimed Faulkner, was to accept the partition of

Ireland agreed by Lord Craigavon and the Irish president, Cosgrave, in 1925 that was derailed only by De Valera's subsequent irredentism.[125]

Though Unionists are often viewed as doggedly pessimistic, Faulkner expressed a belief that a 'truth-telling' campaign would bring public opinion in the UK and USA towards the Unionist point of view. He praised the efforts of Unionists who had made their case in Washington, despite the fact that, once again, 'Senator [Ted] Kennedy has revealed the depth of his prejudice and ignorance about our affairs'.[126] This Unionist optimism had been repeatedly expressed by Orangemen in the previous decade ever since the reconstruction of the Press Committee in 1964.[127] It was felt that if only Unionists could get as organized as the Nationalists and tell their side of the story, they would win the hearts and minds of the American and British public. Grand Lodge was regularly pressed to make a better case for Unionism to the world, and responded with occasional trips to the United States, such as Martin Smyth's excursion to New York in 1971, which was viewed as a success by the Order.[128]

In the midst of growing British discussion of Direct Rule, the Order was anxious to press the government not to give in. 'Will we accept anything . . . Can we get an assurance that our government will not be abolished? What is our role in the event of interference?' These questions haunted a special meeting of Central Committee on 10 March. The consensus was that there was no plan to abolish Stormont, though George Clark cautioned his audience that there was a 'screen in the Unionist party' that prevented backbenchers from knowing what the British had in mind. Even so, Clark staked out a defiant claim that 'we should inform the P.M. that the "Order" would not tolerate any interference with our "Government"'. Captain Armstrong was more sanguine, maintaining that since the British had effectively controlled security since 1969 there was no harm in control passing from Stormont to Whitehall. What was needed was a defence not of the government, he said, but of Northern Ireland's constitutional position and parliament. In the end, those present settled on a programme of 'passive resistance' but sought to express this resistance through William Craig's new Vanguard movement.[129]

Late 1971 saw a major polarization in Northern Ireland's community relations, almost to the point of civil war. Internment, and the SDLP's civil disobedience campaign against it, made it impossible for the centre of moderate Unionists and Nationalists to hold.[130] On the fringes of Unionism, Ian Paisley had formed the DUP in 1971, and Craig, flanked by UDA paramilitary men and those from William Hull's Loyalist Association of Workers (LAW), launched Ulster Vanguard in February 1972.[131] The Orange Order, though formally connected to the UUP, was clearly exasperated by the government of the day. Orange connections to Hull and his Orange-funded LAW were robust, and the Order came in on the ground floor of Craig's Vanguard movement.

Brethren should be asked to support the Vanguard movement directly, suggested one delegate at a special meeting of Central Committee in March 1972. Captain Armstrong, reflecting the traditionalist concern that the Order should not involve itself in politics, argued against any 'wholehearted . . . directive', though he felt that the Order should support the upcoming Vanguard rally in Belfast. William Douglas then suggested that a statement be issued in support of the rally, a proposal which was seconded by Armstrong.[132] The Vanguard rally, which took place soon afterwards in Belfast's Ormeau Park, brought together leading figures within Orangeism and the UUP. Their battle cry was that Britain should honour its long-standing practice of not withdrawing powers that had been devolved to provincial tiers of government. Craig spoke of the UK's 1949 'guarantee' of Stormont's powers. Though Faulkner derided the Vanguard rally as a 'comic opera', Craig had the last laugh as Britain's Ted Heath informed Faulkner in late March that Stormont's fifty-year rule was officially over.[133]

As its ties to the government frayed, the Order's leading priority was to be seen to be responding to the concerns of its membership, and its June report to the members outlined page after page of resolutions, meetings, and statements by the leadership. These included Smyth's handing over to the British Home Secretary, Reginald Maudling, of the New Ulster Covenant, which contained over 334,000 signatures, and a letter for the British Prime Minister, presented to Maudling at 10 Downing Street. The proposed parade ban of 1972 was also condemned at the meeting with Maudling.[134] The suspension of Stormont by the British in late March was deemed 'treacherous', and the Order swore to build upon the mandate provided by the Covenant to restore a local parliament to Northern Ireland.

The Order was not without some sympathizers in Britain, though, and spoke of a good meeting with fourteen Conservative MPs, including Enoch Powell, who would later emerge as a leading Unionist MP.[135] In the final analysis, the Order, despite losing clout to the British, had stiffened the Unionist government's back against reform beyond what the British could stand. Orange intransigence may have produced a sub-optimal result for Unionism, leading to the collapse of the very institutions that might have safeguarded the Protestant constitutional position while opening the door to militant Republicanism. On the other hand, it may well be the case that many Unionists preferred Direct Rule to the humiliation of allowing Nationalists to touch any levers of executive power. On this reading, the Orange watchword 'No Surrender' was both an emotional and a rational guide to policy.

4

Unity in the Face of Treachery, 1972–1977

The turbulent period 1968–72 saw the Orange Order's membership partly recover from its modest post-1961 decline. Some of the new working-class and rural recruits were drawn to the Order as a self-defence organization, but if they expected to join a paramilitary organization, these hopes were soon dashed by an Institution still wedded to traditional principles of respect for law and order. By 1974–5, membership had sunk to its 1968 level and a new pattern of slow but steady numerical decline had set in. This slide did not necessarily lead to a reduction in political efficacy. True, the Order's ties to the Stormont establishment—social and political—were strained throughout the late 1960s, and finally ruptured with Direct Rule in 1972. But its release from establishment constraints also endowed it with greater room to manoeuvre. No longer did it have to moderate the populist conservatism of its base, but it could now wholeheartedly throw its weight behind a distinct brand of 'no' Unionism. This Unionism rejected British-initiated reforms and their progressive UUP fellow travellers and sought a restoration of the pre-1972 Stormont regime. However, the traditionalism of the Order—rooted in its historic ties to the Official Unionists and mainstream churches—ensured that Orange rejectionism continued to flow within established Unionist institutions.

In the midst of the turmoil of 1972 following the imposition of Direct Rule, the Order began to see itself as the locus of unity for the beleaguered Protestant cause. To be sure, there was the question of whether to back integration (i.e. Direct Rule) or press for a return to devolved government. But integration was to be a 'last resort', and all speakers at a special session of Central Committee emphasized the need for 'local N.I. government'. The sense of crisis engendered by the anarchy in the streets and the sense of British constitutional 'betrayal' formed a heady cocktail. If Britain betrayed Ulster, then it was time to resist authority and abandon loyalty. It was thus agreed that all Orangemen should 'hold on to their private arms...by all means delay handing over arms'.[1] At Grand Lodge, the matter was raised again, and a call was made by George Watson of Belfast for Grand Lodge to give its approval to the Orange Volunteers (OV), a Loyalist paramilitary group headed by an ex-serviceman, Bob Marno, which was the second largest Loyalist paramilitary group after the UDA and was associated with the Ulster Volunteer Force (UVF).[2]

This was the closest the Order would come to endorsing armed struggle, but even in the midst of this chaos, there were voices counselling restraint. One such figure was Martin Smyth. Smyth was already acknowledged as a charismatic leader within Orangeism, but the strains of 1972 prompted him to tender his resignation as chairman of Central Committee in early June. Urged to reconsider by all those present, he returned to the chair.[3] At the next meeting, George Watson called for support for the OV, but Smyth replied that 'we should not be termed subversive'. He did however call upon all counties and districts to tighten their coordination. The Order would not yet take up arms, but it was willing to threaten violence if anarchy continued to reign. A military-style telegram was drafted to be forwarded to William Whitelaw, who was now the British Secretary of State for Northern Ireland: 'The Grand Lodge of Ireland assembled at Bushmills. Restore Law and Order at once or the Grand Lodge of Ireland will call its members to action in support of Loyalist Organisations acting together for this purpose.'[4]

There was also division and confusion in the highest Orange circles concerning the now toothless Unionist Party. Antrim predictably criticized the Unionist Party, but went further, chastising Grand Lodge reports of proceedings as being 'of no value'. Belfast announced that it was breaking with the local Unionist association, and a local lodge spearheaded a resolution requesting that the Order sever the link with the UUP. However, the motion was merely taken as read and, interestingly, Belfast District 6 (Ballymacarett) issued a resolution in support of Faulkner and his protest against the prorogation of Stormont. The resolution was sent back, but a heated discussion ensued, with Captain Armstrong urging caution.[5]

What all could agree on was support for Vanguard and William Craig. The Vanguard rally in March demonstrated that a powerful Ulster-Protestant nationalism could emerge vis-à-vis Westminster. This was anchored in the post-partition belief that Ireland's Protestants had already made a supreme concession by ceding the South to Catholics, and that the least that 'Ulster' (i.e. the six-county Ulster-Protestant nation) could expect was that there would be no further encroachment on its political powers or territory. Craig had flamboyantly declared that he would not accept Direct Rule, and threatened violence if Britain attempted to transfer Ulster to an all-Ireland republic. This was backed up by appearances alongside paramilitary escorts. Dominion status was Craig's preferred constitutional solution, even if it meant a loss of British financial assistance. 'We'd have to tighten our belts initially,' suggested Craig, 'but I think the loyalist worker would be prepared to make the sacrifice. The Protestant has dignity and would rather eat grass than be humiliated.'[6]

At the Grand Lodge sessions in June, Billy Douglas announced a resolution in support of Vanguard and its attempt to restore the constitution and parliament of Northern Ireland. This passed, but only once a revised version 'without names' was drafted after Sir George Clark and George Watson expressed concern about Vanguard–UDA links.[7] The devolutionary position of Craig accurately reflected grassroots sentiment; Craig was emerging as the 'messiah figure' of choice for the Unionist community at this difficult time, and his Vanguard movement received the backing of the Unionist party, Faulkner, and the Order, despite its flirtation with the UDA.[8]

The Order and the UUP, in opposing integration, wrong-footed Paisley, whose call for further integration in the direction of Direct Rule went down badly with the grassroots and cost the DUP dearly in electoral terms. Craig's Vanguard, with its strong call for Ulster self-determination, was more in tune with the public mood, as was shown by its successful demonstrations and strikes against Direct Rule in late March.[9] Though both the Order and the UUP embraced Vanguard, it cannot be said that Vanguard effected a 'takeover' of either of these established Unionist institutions, and the paramilitaries which formed part of Vanguard's support base were effectively sidelined by both the Order and the UUP. On the UUP side, Faulkner managed to co-opt Craig to support the UUP document *Towards the Future*, which advocated reformist measures like an American-style committee system for Stormont and a north–south intergovernmental council.[10]

The case of the Order is somewhat similar. With the demise of Stormont, the Order had begun to think of itself as the institutional nucleus of a Unionist government-in-exile. Pressure for the Order to take the lead in unifying the disparate elements of political Unionism reflected the yearnings of grassroots Protestants for unity in the face of adversity. As we shall see, this was offset by the equally strong determination of Unionist figures (notably Ian Paisley) to advance their power during a period ripe with political opportunity. Grassroots Orangemen mainly focused on what they felt was the division amongst their elites in the face of a united enemy. In April 1972, for example, a private lodge in Killylea, Armagh, wrote to its district leaders: 'Our opponents are united . . . If we remain divided in our policy and stand idly by we will . . . only hasten the downfall of our state. We would suggest that the leaders of the Orange Order act as an umbrella under which a united common policy could be engineered for the safety of our future.'[11] A month later, the members of Omagh LOL 71 expressed their concern at 'the number of Protestant political parties . . . and request it [Grand Lodge] to take immediate steps to call the spokesmen of all these various splinter parties and the official Unionist Party together . . . United we stand, divided we . . . fall.' Should no unity be forthcoming, the Omagh brethren wanted 'a clear directive from the Grand Lodge as to what party we should support in the event of elections'.[12]

One of the lodges which took the lead in promoting unity was Cross of St Patrick LOL 688 of Clifton Street, Belfast. It is an interesting lodge with a middle-class social composition, something borne out by its two initiates of 1971, a student and a medical practitioner.[13] In a remarkable display of grass-roots political activism, this local lodge issued its own 'Synopsis' and 'Outline Proposals & Programme' to Brian Faulkner as well as Craig, Paisley, and others. In pleading its case to Grand Lodge, the lodge secretary Lindsay Smith spoke of his lodge's work as 'a final effort to achieve what has so far eluded us' and spoke of Nationalists as deliberately fostering Unionist divisions.[14]

The lodge's position paper is drafted to a high standard, and appears to endorse the London *Times* columnist Julian Critchley, who decried the passing of Unionist leadership from moderate middle-class Unionists to successively harder-line and more working-class leaders like Craig and the UDA. LOL 688 asked all Loyalist leaders to draft a 'declaration of intent' that asked the British to make a clear proposal for the future of Ulster (even if this be a United Ireland) and to put the matter to the people of the province and be prepared to heed the wishes of the majority. Should the British government try and act against the wishes of the majority, the lodge made it clear that 'we will take any action which we deem necessary', including forming a pan-Loyalist coalition government to lead the people 'in the struggle to come'.[15]

The popular yearning for unity made it imperative that the leaders of all loyalist parties at least speak the language of comity. On 4 July, Ian Paisley called for Loyalist parties and associations to unite—partly influenced by his party's weak position following its disastrous endorsement of integration. However, Paisley's strategy was hardly conducive to goodwill, as was evident in his challenge to the Order and Official Unionists: 'Do you really want unity, or is it power which you seek?' Perhaps Paisley was transposing his own latent desires onto the Orangemen, but the Order responded with magnanimity and agreed to host pan-Loyalist talks between Paisley, Faulkner, and Craig. A preliminary meeting between the Order and the DUP leaders Paisley and Beattie managed to agree on the basic principles of maintaining loyalty to the Crown and constitution and the link between Ulster and the UK.[16] The call then went out to all leaders to meet at Sandy Row Orange Hall on 23 August.[17] This met with applause from sections of the Orange rank and file.[18]

Paisley had always maintained an adversarial, obstructionist stance towards the Order and UUP, and must have bristled at having to sit down with his establishment adversaries. Paisley's reply to Williams reflected Paisley's desire to see 'fringe' organizations invited:

Further to our conversation by telephone I was rather surprised that the invitations . . . did not include all the groups I specifically mentioned in my Larne speech. To convene only representatives of the Ulster Unionist Party, the Ulster Democratic Unionist Party, Vanguard and L.A.W., and to leave out the other organisations originally proposed, namely the Royal Black Institution, the Apprentice Boys of Derry, the Independent Orange Institution, the Ulster Defence Association and the Ulster Protestant Volunteers would defeat the whole purpose of the exercise. I certainly could not, if these organisations were not invited, take part in such a conference.

After providing contact details for the omitted organizations, Paisley continued to press on Orange sensibilities by impudently demanding 'an immediate response to this request'.[19] There is no question that the Order maintained a consistent position: it intended to convene the main political players in Loyalist politics and not all comers.[20] For instance, it received requests from smaller splinter organizations such as the Ulster Loyalist Association to attend the conference. The latter tried to convince the Order of its importance despite its 'not being in the picture as of late'![21] The Order had direct links with the Black and was on friendly terms with the Apprentice Boys but was obviously not enamoured of the IOO or the paramilitaries. Paisley knew this and included these organizations in a cynical ploy designed to torpedo Orange attempts at unity which might swallow up the DUP's hard-won brand.

The Orange response to Paisley reflected an exasperation born of decades of conflict. Despite the Order's opposition to the reforms of the Official Unionists, it had never embraced Paisley:

I wish to clarify that the Grand Orange Lodge of Ireland's offer to convene a Conference is not subject to conditions made by anyone else . . . The Grand Orange Lodge of Ireland considers this to be essentially an exploratory meeting, concerning the bodies most intimately involved in the political situation. This does not exclude the possibility that under certain circumstances others, including those you mention, may wish to be represented at later meetings . . . On receiving this clarification, I am sure you will feel very willing to take part, and look forward to a happy issue for our loyalist people from this Conference.[22]

On 22 August, the day before the proposed conference, Paisley made it clear that he was in no mood for conciliation:

It is now quite evident that without informing me or my party, the Orange officers took it upon themselves to change the terms of reference already agreed on . . . The gross inconsistency of the behaviour of the Orange officers is to be deplored . . . My party has sought in these critical days to put the country and not the party interests first, and I can only express the hope that after Wednesday the Grand Orange Lodge officers will honour their original promise and call a real unity conference.[23]

At the same time, it must be acknowledged that the Order was reluctant to include the paramilitaries. The reciprocal hostility of the UVF was palpable as it accused the Order of cowardice in a year when 122 Ulster-Protestants and over 117 non-Catholic 'others' (mostly security forces) were killed by Republican guns and bombs:

There are people on the Loyalist side who in their hypocrisy would deny us the right to sit at a Loyalist Conference Table. But we would ask those people what have they done to defend the Loyalist population? It is not enough to depend on the forces of Law and Order, as the explosion at the Standard Bar fully illustrated. The men and women of our Organisation have laid and shall lay their lives on the line in defence of our people, and though we are banned in law, this shall not deter us in our pursuance of our duty. The long established Institutions in our midst [i.e. Orange, UUP] have failed our people and consequently made themselves whipping bags for an appeasing Government and proved Republican Curs. The disillusionment . . . has been assuaged by the emergence of genuine Loyalist Militant bodies, prepared to back up every word that they utter . . . Never again shall shallow men hold the confidence of our people, never again shall Ulster be degraded and maligned and never again attacked without swift and terrible retribution . . . We demand a seat at the Loyalist conference table.[24]

The conference itself took place the following day *sans* the paramilitaries, Paisley, and his entourage. Along with Craig, Vanguard was represented by the Rev. Dickinson (showing the intimate connections between the Orange and Vanguard elites), Austin Ardill, MC, Stanley M. Morgan, MBE, and Louis Gardner, Esq.[25] Their participation had been in question a week earlier, when Craig queried the wisdom of meeting those (e.g. Paisley) who would not 'commit themselves to the re-establishment of a strong Ulster government'.[26] Five Official Unionists were also in attendance, including Faulkner, along with two observers from the Grand Orange Lodge of Scotland. The composition of the meeting, therefore, did not depart significantly from the control of the Ulster-Protestant establishment.

Faulkner and Craig took the lead at the conference, and both shared the view that an Ulster Parliament should be restored. Craig's language was especially to the point. He asked for 'some straight talking in public' and little compromise with the British government, adding that 'we must give our people a sense of destiny' and a future. If no reasonable terms were forthcoming from the British, 'we should seek them outside'. Faulkner called for an election and reiterated Craig's call to stand up to the British at Westminster. Martin Smyth added that any new initiative must not be on the terms of the British government. Faulkner closed by defiantly claiming that the Unionists would not consider citizenship outside the UK and that all were agreed on the necessity of a Northern Ireland parliament.[27]

Meanwhile, tensions continued to simmer between Paisley and the Order. Williams had publicly criticized Paisley for releasing his rejection letter to the press. Paisley responded by claiming that since Williams had requested a comment in writing, he, Paisley, was free to reveal it to the press. Next, Paisley accused the Grand Lodge of not reading his correspondence at the Unity conference meeting: 'The concealment . . . of my correspondence is a grave matter, and I await your explanation which I believe I am entitled to have.'[28] Williams responded that he had in fact mentioned Paisley's correspondence

(Williams mentioned it but did not go into detail). He rebutted Paisley's contentions, and his words graphically signal the degree to which the Order distrusted Paisley. 'My reasons for asking you to put in writing your comments made by telephone, on matters relating to the conference, were solely to ensure, that I could not be held responsible for any possible misrepresentation. Your correspondence was not for the conference, but for the Grand Lodge . . . I was [therefore] surprised when the Press telephoned to advise that you had released the contents of your letter.'[29]

There were still some who felt that all was not lost, notably the Grand Lodge of Scotland. The estrangement between the Irish and Scottish Grand Lodges had healed since the departure of its mercurial embezzler of a Grand Master, Alan Hasson. Ulster Orangemen had been impressed by the vitality of Orangeism among young Scots and appreciated the generous donations from Scotland towards Orange social causes in Northern Ireland.[30] Scottish Orangemen were looking to play a more high-profile role in Ulster, and the unity talks offered them an opportunity. Accordingly, the Scots envisaged inviting all shades of Loyalist opinion over to Scotland for a conference. Failing to understand the depth of Orange–DUP schism, the Scottish Grand Secretary, John Adam, insisted that 'there ARE points of unity which MUST be common to all [including the UVF, UDA, or UPV] . . . otherwise Ulster is fighting a losing battle'.[31]

Adam received a courteous reply and a promise to consider the matter at Grand Lodge. This was not enough for Adam, who pointed out that 'the meeting, having represented only three bodies—no matter how influential—did not produce the effect of solidarity'. Once again, Adam offered his lodge's services to bring all parties together. After a month went by with no response from Northern Ireland, a follow-up letter was sent.[32] At Central Committee, the Scottish proposal was rebuffed, with some concerned about the influence of Paisley.[33] The eventual response to the Scots was cordial and thanked the Scottish Order for its rallies and its donation of hundreds of pounds to the Orange distress fund, but stressed that the Ulster Order 'unanimously agreed' that a unity conference 'would not be the answer to our many problems'. The letter concluded with an acknowledgement of Scottish–Ulster solidarity, which it was felt might extend to the military sphere: 'We know, that in certain ways, you will continue to prepare yourselves to support the Loyalists of Ulster should the present dangers increase.'[34]

At the next meeting of Central Committee, the Rev. Dickinson reported that the unity conference had 'got nowhere'. Smyth felt that the time for round-table conferences had passed, and Dickinson agreed that the Order should proceed on its own. Sir George Clark averred that the conference had brought people together and that what was missing was a Christian attitude—hence the Order would have to lead Unionists to a 'better spirit'. Other speakers endorsed the idea that the Order would have to supply the leadership and unity that the conference could not bring. John Brown mentioned that he was conferring with the Independent Order in Antrim, and both he and Dickinson supported the idea of an intra-Orange conference, though the latter warned that 'bad spirit' also existed within the Order (between different factions). The first action to be endorsed therefore was a meeting of Orange chaplains.

Ill. 5   Past Grand Master John Bryans turns sod for House of Orange, Dublin Road, 1974. Others in the photo include (l to r): Grand Master Martin Smyth, Antrim Grand Master Rev. John Brown and Grand Secretary Walter Williams.

The chaplains' conference brought together some fifty leading Orange clerics, who put their heads together to fashion an intricate statement of 'respectable' Orangeism. They argued that a series of measures was necessary to improve the 'quality' of the Order and bring it into line with its respectable Christian principles. These measures are fascinating in that they sketch the lineaments of 'traditional' Orangeism as against its rising 'rebel' alter ego. Measures included:

- Tightening admission procedures for new initiates, with coordination between local chaplains and district lodges to vet candidates
- Improving lodge meetings

- Attracting business and professional candidates. 'Could we find ways and means of improving the character of the Order', the chaplains mused. 'Could we put it on a higher plane?'
- The necessity of disciplining brethren who wore Orange regalia in non-Orange parades
- The need for Grand Chaplains to be more proactive in setting the agenda at private and district lodge level
- The need to advance the 'spiritual life of the Country'
- The need to stem the advance of immorality, 'bigotry, malice and intolerance' in Northern Ireland
- Improvement in the public display on Twelfth platforms, including upgrading the 'amateurish' public address system and bringing better decorum to platform proceedings
- Using the influence of the chaplains to improve the Order's public image
- Restricting Orange support for 'outside Loyalist Organisations' and their parades and rallies
- Encouraging the membership to join the UDR
- Imploring the media not to use the words 'Protestant' and 'Catholic' so frequently.[35]

The chaplains largely steered clear of politics, believing in the Order's traditional mission as a Christian organization standing above the affairs of Caesar. Nonetheless, other leading clerical figures on Central Committee took a much more 'this-worldly view' of things at the October Central Committee meeting. 'We ought to be thinking politically,' offered the Rev. Long, 'We may have to take over.' The Rev. Dickinson asked whether the Order could accept a United Ireland. 'We should be thinking within the next two weeks what we are going to do,' he pressed. This was deemed urgent in view of the British government's White Paper on constitutional reform, and some at the meeting openly worried about a system being 'imposed on us' by the British. It was agreed to send a deputation to see William Whitelaw and Ted Heath, which would involve James Molyneaux and brethren from the Scottish and English Grand Lodges.[36]

Whitelaw 'gladly' accepted the Grand Lodge's offer of a meeting, and an Orange committee was appointed for the purpose. The British at this point mistakenly believed that there was no anti-White Paper consensus on the Unionist side and felt that it could achieve support from the population for its constitutional initiatives. These included a regional assembly for Northern Ireland to replace Stormont and a permanent transfer of law and order functions to Westminster. More importantly, the document envisioned the use of power-sharing (crystallized through a proportional representation electoral system) and a North-South 'Irish' institutional dimension.[37]

At the behest of Tyrone representatives, one of the subjects to be taken up with the Secretary of State would be security. Another was power-sharing and proportional representation (PR). Though there had been some consideration of the latter's merits by the Order in the past, the consensus at this meeting, well summed up by Bryans, was that PR was 'objectionable' since it was not used elsewhere in the UK and was based on religious discrimination. PR, he claimed, 'was being imposed to beat the monolithic built-in [Unionist] system of loyalty'. The security guarantees of the White Paper were viewed as hollow in the light of past experience, and its constitutional proposals viewed as a threat to democracy and the Orange slogan of 'civil and religious liberty'. Whitelaw would therefore be asked to 'reconsider'.

The preferred alternative to the White Paper was set out at Grand Lodge in April by the new Grand Master, Martin Smyth: (1) total defeat of the IRA; (2) no Council of Ireland; (3) proper representation at Westminster for Northern Ireland; (4) control of internal security by the Ulster parliament and retention of British heritage including the restoration of the office of governor. These views chimed with the stance of William Craig's breakaway Vanguard Unionist Progressive Party (VUPP), which had left the Unionist Party when the UUC voted by 281–131 to accept the White Paper. Clearly the Order was in no mood for compromise, and it continued with a rejectionist stance which reflected the instincts of its base and the tactical preferences of the leadership. Though Orange figures like Smyth, Molyneaux, John Taylor, and Willie Ross stayed within the UUP, they consistently resisted liberal currents. In this manner they reinforced a distinct 'Orange' brand of politics which combined loyalty to traditional Unionist institutions with opposition to reform.[38]

Opposition did not mean idleness, however. Warren Porter insisted that whatever the views of Protestants, 'if we failed to vote [in the elections for the proposed Assembly] we would commit political suicide'. Bryans agreed that a massive turnout at the polls could beat this 'un-British' system. The Grand Lodge needed to give guidance to the membership by asking them to vote against the proposed constitutional changes and discouraging abstention. This was duly accepted, and a more exacting directive went out to the membership in April 1973.[39] Throughout this period, numerous references were made to the need to give 'leadership' and 'guidance' to the membership. Central Committee saw itself as charged with the responsibility to lead the Protestant community and saw its political role as a voice for the Protestant interest in a confusing period of change.

The April 1973 report of proceedings and accompanying public statements provided clear instructions to the membership. In terms of specifics, the Grand Lodge reminded members to vote for 'loyalist candidates' and to encourage friends and family to do the same. The report also explained the single transferable vote system of voting: 'It is unnecessary to vote for every Candidate in order of preference. Limited voting is wiser. Vote only for thoroughly loyalist Candidates.' The leadership went on to urge loyalist political organizers to field only candidates who commanded wide support (i.e. not militant candidates) so as not to fragment the Unionist vote. It stressed that care must be taken in selecting candidates to the Assembly and local government, restricting their number to 'enthusiastic Ulster men and women... who are proud patriots... Now is time for quiet thoughtfulness... The head must control the heart. Sentimentality is a luxury Ulster cannot afford at such time as this.'[40] This message was circularized among the lodges, through the press, through the 16,000-circulation *Orange Standard*, and through printed reports.

This is not to say that the entire membership simply followed suit. County Armagh Lodge 'commended' Grand Lodge's statements on the White Paper to its district lodges, but asked that it be 'carefully studied' by the districts. Moreover, it was recommended that district lodges 'neither accept [nor] reject the White Paper entirely', but rather 'use it to the best advantage'. This was a more nuanced picture than that provided by Grand Lodge of 'an ingenious document competent to deceive the unwary and a surrender'. Nonetheless, many districts came to the conclusion of Bessbrook District, which unanimously 'decided to support the line' of Grand Lodge and criticized Brian Faulkner. At Grand Lodge, several private and district lodge resolutions congratulated the stand taken by Grand Lodge and none opposed it.[41]

Smyth had taken up the reins of the Institution with little fanfare after Bryans's retirement in late 1972. His leadership is symbolic of the changes that the Order had undergone in the previous decade, from being a pillar of the establishment to being a rebellious working-class lobby group. Smyth himself had no connection to the Unionist social elite and came from middling Belfast origins. Though he was involved on the UUC executive, with spells as chairman and vice-president, his views diverged sharply from the reformist tendencies of the UUP elite.[42] On the other hand, in what was to prove a robust template for Orange politics, Smyth and other senior Orangemen remained faithful to their traditional party, the UUP, and failed to follow Craig's breakaway movement with its increasingly shrill calls for independence. This saved the UUP, though Craig's movement took a toll in more 'rebellious' areas such as North Antrim and parts of Belfast.[43] Orange support for Craig at this time was not seriously discussed, and the Grand Lodge's voting instructions to the membership clearly favoured larger parties such as the UUP.

On the other hand, elements of the membership were acutely aware that the UUP had acted against the wishes of the Order in supporting the White Paper. Though the creeping hand of ecumenism was often a bigger concern than political issues for many grassroots lodges, others, like Castlecaulfield and Killyman district lodges (Tyrone), called on their County Grand Lodge to disaffiliate from the Official Unionists in retaliation for the UUP's support of the White Paper. Though a discussion took place on this matter, County Tyrone Grand Lodge managed to neutralize this challenge and convince those present that no action should be taken. Evidently Faulkner still had some support within the Order.[44] In Armagh, strains between party and

Order were reflected at the local level. The local UUP party branch and the County Orange Lodge had been haggling over the £50 annual fee since 1972. Armagh County Lodge had refused to pay this 'exorbitant' sum, and the local Unionist association appeared unwilling to press Armagh County Lodge to pay promptly. Here we see how local UUP structures played a key role in co-opting the Order and ensuring that its rejectionist politics did not translate into disaffiliation—which would have been fatal for the party.[45]

The UUP itself was being torn apart by rifts over the proposed White Paper, and fielded both pro- and anti-White Paper candidates. The divide also ran through the Assembly and parliamentary wings of the UUP. The parliamentary UUP representatives at Westminster in the Direct Rule era, notes Walker, were much more representative of the grassroots than Assembly candidates. Not only were their views closer to those of the masses, but their social origins in the working and rural population more closely matched those of their constituents.[46] James Molyneaux was one such Westminster MP and also Deputy Grand Master of Ireland. Molyneaux crafted a statement which was released in the June reports of proceedings, welcoming the amendments tabled by the UUP's parliamentary party as consonant with the Order's stated 'restorationist' position on constitutional reform: 'These amendments would have the effect of restoring a system of majority Government; of returning . . . control over internal security; of removing the power of an Ulster Executive to move into a Council of Ireland . . . for restoring the Oath of Allegiance for membership of the Assembly.' Molyneaux concluded that 'we consider that in the forthcoming elections for the Assembly, only those candidates who support these principles are worthy of wholehearted support'.[47]

Despite the strength of grassroots opposition, twenty-two of Faulkner's pro-White Paper candidates were elected on 28 June, as against just ten anti-White Paper Official Unionists. In combination with eighteen anti-White Paper Unionists from the DUP, VUPP, and other parties, this gave the rejectionists a majority of Unionist support. Whitelaw and the British nevertheless believed that they could cobble together a deal between pro-White Paper Unionists, the Alliance Party, the Northern Ireland Labour Party, and the SDLP which would carry cross-community support. Talks began fitfully in October, with some progress made on less contentious issues. At the UUP Standing Committee in October (132–105), and again at the UUC in November (379–369), delegates voted narrowly to support power-sharing and endorse the idea of allowing UUP members to take part in a new power-sharing executive.[48] This paved the way for the Sunningdale Agreement of December 1973.

This historic agreement provided for power-sharing between Nationalist and Unionist parties in both the executive and the Assembly. Significantly, there was to be a substantial north-south dimension in the form of the Council of Ireland, which provided for regular ministerial meetings between the new Northern Ireland executive and the government of the Republic on issues such as cross-border security and economic cooperation. The moderate SDLP tried to sell the deal to Nationalists as a step towards a United Ireland. For instance, the SDLP MLA Hugh Logue gave a speech at Trinity College, Dublin, in which he said that the Council of Ireland was 'the vehicle that would trundle Unionists into a united Ireland'. Noises from the Irish government did little to dispel this conception, which led Ted Heath to excoriate his Irish counterpart, Liam Cosgrave. Faulkner had the tougher job of convincing Unionists that the deal would improve security and spell the end to the Republic's irredentist claims. In the event, the high court in the Republic failed to repudiate the irredentist articles 2 and 3 of the Republic's constitution.[49]

As in the past, attempts by UUP moderates to compromise with Nationalists prompted Grand Lodge and the Orange grassroots alienation from the party. The first notes were struck with the July Twelfth resolutions calling for a restoration of Stormont.[50] At the same time, a series of press releases made it clear that the Order was sticking to its four restorationist principles, including 'no Council of Ireland'. It also began meetings with Enoch Powell and other sympathetic Tory parliamentarians and businessmen as part of a 'keeping in touch' operation. On 28 September, an Orange rally was held at Ulster Hall in Belfast to keep up the pressure on the UUP. Minutes record that numbers were 'adequate' and included Unionist professionals.[51]

At the October 1973 Central Committee meeting, a deputation was organized to meet the officers of the Unionist Party and 'make the [Orange] position on power-sharing quite plain'.[52] Two weeks later, Grand Lodge officers met Faulkner and officers of the Ulster Unionist Council. No minutes have survived, but one can imagine that—despite Faulkner's paid-up Orange membership—this was no occasion for brotherly love. A week later, Central Committee condemned the power-sharing agreement and congratulated those who voted against it at the Standing Committee of the UUC. On 8 November, the Order abandoned its principle of non-intervention in electoral affairs, and Smyth warned Orange delegates to the UUC to vote against the agreement:

Normally we are left to use our judgment in an ad hoc situation, but I would draw your attention to the four requisites of Grand Lodge [including 'No Council of Ireland'] . . . our solemn covenant signed by about 350,000 people pledged us to work for the restoration of our constitution without tie or bond should it be abrogated without the consent of the majority. That consent has not been sought much less given. Now is the time to go forward to achieve our object. I would ask you therefore to use your best endeavours to this end and exercise your vote accordingly.[53]

Smyth also asked delegates to 'influence others' and, if they could not attend, to send along a substitute with written Grand Lodge authority.[54]

Meanwhile, at a meeting of the newly formed Public Affairs Advisory Subcommittee of the Order, chaired by Jim Molyneaux, those present stated their opposition to the Unionist Party's stance. It was suggested that 'pledged' (pro-White Paper) candidates did not represent the party, but only Faulkner's wishes. This set the stage for a discussion of whether the Order should disaffiliate. While the subcommittee felt that breaking the link would 'free the Order from any implied responsibility' for Sunningdale and Faulkner's policies, it was unwilling to cut the cord. The reasons are instructive. Molyneaux and his subcommittee argued that severing the historic ties would prompt many Orangemen simply to opt out of politics and the party, with the result that the Order would (1) lose the prospect of changing the leadership and direction within the UUP and (2) undercut the power base of anti-Sunningdale Unionist Assembly members 'who have consistently supported Grand Lodge of Ireland policies'. This hints at two separate dimensions of Orange power in the Direct Rule period: (1) the ability to mobilize grassroots members for political action more effectively than if the Order's 'social capital' with the UUP no longer functioned; and (2) the capacity to exercise power over UUP policy through Orange delegates to the UUC, who largely supported the Grand Lodge line.[55]

Smyth and Grand Lodge were also highly effective in helping to set up the United Ulster Unionist Council (UUUC). In a rare display of Loyalist ecumenism, this included the anti-Sunningdale UUP, the DUP (having recently jettisoned its unpopular integrationism), and Craig's Vanguard Unionist Party as well as representatives of the Apprentice Boys, Royal Black Institution, and Independent Orange Order. At a meeting in Ulster Hall, all parties agreed to three resolutions. These pledged to restore the status quo ante of 1972 and dedicated the UUUC to making the Sunningdale institutions 'unworkable'. The press statement which followed the Ulster Hall meeting also criticized police reform and described the Council of Ireland as 'so obvious[ly] a preparation for a United Ireland that to deny it is to deny the meaning of truth'.[56] Its policy paper envisioned Northern Ireland becoming an integral part of a devolving United Kingdom along the lines suggested by the Kilbrandon report and demanded an enhanced security role for the UDR.[57]

On 4 January, Faulkner suffered the fate of all Unionist reformers since O'Neill as the UUC voted by 427–374 to reject the 'Council of Ireland' proposal contained within the Sunningdale Agreement. He resigned soon afterwards.[58] What needs to be understood is that Orange mobilization arguably played the most significant role in undermining UUP support for Sunningdale. This continued into January as the Order hosted signings of the anti-Sunningdale petition at lodges throughout the province.[59] Another big blow to the process was the February Westminster election, where UUUC-backed candidates took eleven of twelve seats, including just over half the popular vote as against just 13 per cent for Faulkner's liberal rump party, the UPNI.[60] Curiously, Faulkner appears to have underestimated the tenacity of his grassroots Unionist opponents, lamenting that 'everyone was shattered by the extent of the feeling against a Council of Ireland (even amongst the most moderate opinion which had gone over to the Loyalists [UUUC] in large numbers)'.[61]

The final nail in the coffin proved to be the Ulster Workers Council (UWC) strike, which began on 14 May 1974. This paralysed the province, including many key services. However, Merlyn Rees, the new Secretary of State for Northern Ireland, did not attempt to break the strike, despite Nationalist and Irish government calls to do so, since he knew full well that it commanded widespread Unionist support. Meanwhile, Harold Wilson, the new British Labour Prime Minister, scored few points with Unionists by describing the UWC strikers as 'spongers'—a remark widely interpreted as an attack on the entire Unionist community. The strike helped to defeat Sunningdale, and a broad united front of Loyalist politicians celebrated as Faulkner and the rest of the Sunningdale executive resigned on 28 May.[62]

Within the Order, there were resolutions commending the 'successful' UWC strike and lots of support for the stand against Sunningdale taken by Grand Lodge. One lodge from near Portadown spoke for the majority when it declared that 'any Government which shared power with Republicans was indeed a traitorous Administration' and accused Faulkner of 'conduct unbecoming an Orangeman'.[63] Support from farmers and Scottish brethren for the strike was applauded. There is no direct evidence that the Order helped to organize the strike, though it certainly gave strong direct support to the UWC's predecessor, the LAW. The Order also hinted at its ambiguous role in the strike when George Clark cautioned his Central Committee members about issuing a triumphant press release after the strike had led to the collapse of Sunningdale. In Clark's words, 'the less said about the organisation of the strike, the better'.[64]

The Unionist victory over the Sunningdale agreement is a suitable juncture at which to take stock of the main trends in Orange politics in the Direct Rule period. During this era, the IRA continued its campaign of violence, with Protestant and British Army fatalities in the 100–200 range during 1974–6 and in the 50–100 bracket through 1977–84.[65] This reinforced the Order's pastoral and defensive role. The lack of any obligation among the Orange elite to mollify the government allowed the Order to align its policies squarely with those of the rank and file. Alongside this change, the social composition of Grand Lodge was becoming increasingly similar to that of the Orange masses. Let us consider the main features of Orangeism in this period:

Policy coalesced around a number of key principles which were often 'rebellious' in nature and ran counter to the wishes of the UUP establishment:

- Rejection of power-sharing and any north–south dimension
- Demand for devolved government for Northern Ireland—effectively a restoration of the Stormont regime and an end to Direct Rule

- Calls for tighter security on the border and control over Nationalist no-go areas, as well as 'total defeat' of the IRA. These to be facilitated by empowering the UDR and RUC as well as increasing the army presence
- Demand that all Northern Ireland citizens and civil servants swear allegiance to the Crown and its emblems
- The right to march along traditional parade routes, but a ban on non-traditional or 'disloyal' Nationalist parades
- Resistance to police reform
- Calls for the Irish Republic to cooperate on security matters and rescind irredentist articles 2 and 3
- Resistance to talks with Nationalists.

Institutionally, the Order functioned as an ethnic lobby group in a manner which favoured the idea of Protestantism as tradition rather than as rebellious dissent through:

- Maintenance of the link to the UUP, where the Order served to buttress 'no' forces
- Maintenance of the link (through lodge chaplains at every level) to mainstream denominations, excluding the Free Presbyterians
- Attempting to serve as an ecumenical bridge between supporters of the UUP, DUP, and Independents to reach consensus and maximize Unionist political clout. Note that this was not seen to contradict the UUP–Orange link
- As a result of its traditional stance of being a Christian organization 'above politics' in which members could vote according to their consciences, an unwillingness to instruct members blatantly as to which party to vote for, but rather, like most lobby groups, to support individual candidates or policy positions
- Hostility to paramilitarism and violent street politics, as well as rowdy or drunken displays by Orangemen or their independent Loyalist sympathizers.

In terms of *mobilization*, the Order employed:

- Expert committees to scrutinize legislation, constitutional proposals, education policy, and press statements, and to recommend action
- Circulation of petitions and instructions to lodges, raised at lodge meetings
- *Orange Standard* editorials and stories to the membership
- Reports of proceedings to members
- Conveying of Grand Lodge policy through Orange networks connecting Grand lodge to counties, districts, and private lodges, typically as letters or in the form of items discussed at lodge meetings.

In terms of *political action*, the Orange Institution could no longer rely on back-room pressure within elite Unionist networks and thus largely favoured more modern 'rebel' tactics:

- Use of 'monster' demonstrations, with corresponding media coverage and statements
- Helping with strikes and other pan-Loyalist protests
- Press releases from Grand Lodge or Central Committee as well as television and radio appearances
- Deputations and letters to British and Northern Ireland politicians as well as the media and churches.

Some contend that Loyalist paramilitary violence was key to limiting the British government's ambition to cede Northern Ireland to Republicans.[66] However, one should not discount the democratic strategy of strikes and protests within the law. The Orange Order and much of popular Unionism were repulsed by paramilitarism (even Craig's symbolic variety) and sincerely believed that protest and a demonstration of democratic will would ensure that they were not forced into any deal. Naturally Grand Lodge's policy stance did not receive unanimous assent from members, since a small minority backed a more liberal stance. The leadership's traditionalist support for established institutions and decorum caused friction with more militant members, some of whom supported violence. Finally, Grand Lodge's political activity did not always receive the approval of traditionally minded brethren, who saw the Order as a purely religious or social institution which should not become embroiled in political matters. In the section to follow, I focus on the rejectionist politics of the Order, but take care not to neglect the stresses and strains which occasionally led to departures from the rule.

The Order's traditionalist ideology can be seen to have shaped its approach to a series of political initiatives in the 1970s. In 1974, Central Committee took a wary approach to the reform-minded New Unionist Movement (NUM). Orange leaders agreed that the Order should maintain its distance from the movement so as to maximize its influence in time-honoured fashion.[67] The fact that the Order was willing to meet leaders of the movement is partly due to the moderating influence of James Molyneaux, in whom, Captain Armstrong commented, 'we have so much confidence'. Molyneaux felt that the Order should speak with the NUM despite its backing for PR and some north–south institutions, and the fact that it was not 'altogether on the other side of the fence'.[68] The Order also deepened its links with the UUP, increasing its total representation on the UUC and its representation on the UUP Executive Committee.[69]

Politically, the Order continued to press its case when and where it could. The Northern Ireland Office minister Roland Moyle, for instance, received a deputation from Grand Lodge which raised issues from security against the IRA to the confiscation of 'legally held' arms from Loyalists and the subsidizing of denominational teaching. Another Orange deputation met the

Chief Constable later in 1974 to plead its cause on security and marching. In terms of tactics, the Order possessed the capability to moderate its views for prudential reasons, as in late 1974 when the Rev. Robert Bradford successfully argued that it 'must not call for the release of [Loyalist] detainees at the moment . . . we have to keep a balanced view'.[70] Overall, though, it remained 'on message' and did not appreciably alter its defensive policy.

Some things had changed. For one thing, the doors to the corridors of power were not nearly as open to Orangemen as they had been under Stormont. Thus in late 1975, Central Committee reported on its request to meet Harold Wilson, the British Prime Minister. Wilson sent a message saying he was unable to attend and suggesting that the Order arrange a meeting with the Home Office. A letter was subsequently received from the Home Secretary saying that his responsibilities lay in England. Faced with this multiple snub, the Order was relatively powerless, and Smyth could do little more than write to the Home Secretary regretting the latter's failure to attend.[71]

Likewise, on the marching front, the Order now had to deal with a Chief Constable whose terms of reference were set by the British and not a Unionist government. Thus the Chief Constable, backed by the Secretary of State, Merlyn Rees, banned the Order's controversial Dungiven parade in June 1975. Unlike in 1953, 1959, and 1971, there was little that William Douglas could do other than rail against the 'nonsensical ruling', 'double standards', and 'absolute foolishness' of Rees.[72] The same thing happened in 1976, when Derry City Grand Lodge failed to agree a parade route with the RUC divisional commander. All the Grand Lodge could do was pen a letter to the Chief Constable asking for more sympathy and understanding.[73] In reply, the Chief Constable thanked the Order for its cooperation with the security forces but supported his divisional commander.[74] In private, Central Committee members bemoaned that fact that Derry brethren were often simply told that they 'must' accept RUC decisions.[75]

Meanwhile, the Order was active on other fronts, such as its traditional 'ecumenical' role of healing intra-Protestant divisions. The UUUC strategy had worked well for anti-Sunningdale Unionists, and the UUUC won 54.8 per cent of the vote in the 1975 Constitution Convention Election.[76] Prompted by a County Antrim call for DUP–UUP union, Grand Lodge pressed for political unity, saying that the Vanguard party had already agreed to amalgamation.[77] However, upon closer inspection, the Vanguard and DUP were loath to give up their independence. 'Dr Paisley's party' was especially reluctant. Smyth used Paisley's recalcitrance to press his opinion that the only hope for the Order was to retract 'into the old UUP with the Orange Order taking an active part. Vanguard and the DUP are not happy to have Orange Order representation. There is no point in becoming like the Grand Lodge of Scotland or England with little or no political influence.' Antrim's John Brown, ever scornful of the UUP elite, dissented, arguing that unity lay in Ulster, not in parties. Henry Young disclosed that Londonderry had withdrawn its UUC representatives. Smyth, accustomed to sharing the insurgent backbenches with Brown in the 1960s, was now deeply involved at the highest levels of the UUP and now found himself in the uncomfortable position of defending the moderate view![78]

The issue of the Orange–UUP link continued to fester through late 1975 when Robert Overend of Londonderry tabled a resolution supporting candidates for the UUC. This was deemed 'dangerous' by Edwin Liddle, and Cecil Harvey called for a completely new Unionist party. This was countered by the traditionalism of a delegate named MacFarland, who said that 'we cannot go outside the Unionist Party which was formed by the Institution'. Captain Armstrong disagreed, claiming that any pro-UUP motion would be divisive, and his views prevailed by 56–6. John Brown said that the discussion proved that there was in fact division and bemoaned 'undignified. . . name-calling in public' among Loyalists.[79] Meanwhile, William Craig, in a stunning volte-face, argued during a UUUC meeting in late 1975 that the Unionists should enter a coalition government with the SDLP. This proved too radical a step for Unionist opinion, and Craig was expelled from the UUUC, splitting his Vanguard Unionist Party. His ideological trajectory, from hardliner to radical reformer, was not unknown among Unionist politicians, but few had travelled quite so winding a road as the Vanguard leader. Craig eventually lost his seat in the 1979 election to a DUP challenger and never returned to politics.[80]

Latent divisions within the Order soon burst to the surface over the issue of affiliation with the United Unionist Action Council (UUAC). The context for its emergence was the very real belief among many that the British were secretly planning to withdraw troops from the province. Known as the 'Algeria' strategy, this was seriously considered by the British government and was sincerely believed by IRA leaders until early 1976. In such an atmosphere, militant Unionists felt they had to prepare for war.[81] The Orange Order, however, took a much more sceptical line, and Belfast County Grand Lodge commissioned a report which debunked such allegations.[82] The UUAC was formed by the UUUC in 1976, and was later to organize an unsuccessful strike. Paisleyites took a leading role on the UUAC from the beginning. It appears that the formation of the UUAC occurred without a proper meeting being convened, and no Orange representatives were able to attend the initial meeting. Smyth also expressed concern 'that members of our Order did not speak and defend the actions of our Institution when under attack [from Paisleyites] at these meetings'.[83] This discussion then led to a split between pro- and anti-Paisley (or at least traditionalist and hardline) wings of the Order. George Watson and Thomas Passmore, both of Belfast, agreed with Smyth's scepticism towards the UUAC. However, George Morrison (Antrim) and Overend expressed disappointment at the lack of Orange support for the

UUAC by these Belfast brethren even though he acknowledged that there were some undesirable people on it.

Once again, others were sceptical. Watson remarked that he was 'afraid of the men on the committee' and feared that they would use the Order and then take over the UUAC. Even Brown was non-committal. 'What action is proposed by the [UUAC]?' he asked. Smyth replied that the UUAC vowed to 'take all necessary action' to achieve its aims and expressed concern at the ability of the UUAC to achieve these goals. Brown agreed that the UUAC had not been effective thus far. Passmore added, in reply to Overend's earlier remarks, that he had little confidence in the members of the UUAC.

At this point, Overend defended the committee men and insisted that 'all the grassroots Orangemen are for action', and that the Order could help to shape the UUAC if it joined. William Douglas argued that the Action Committee might help to defeat the IRA. Brown then interjected that before the Order committed itself, it must 'deal with the loudmouths' on the UUAC (who were critical of the Order). The Rev. Crossley agreed with Brown. Action was needed, but 'proper action' and not action from the UUAC. George Clark, acting as peacemaker, tried to postpone the decision pending further information, but Smyth replied that the Order already knew most of the men on the UUAC. He agreed that the Order was divided and that there might be a protest on the Twelfth from certain quarters. In concluding, Smyth referred to the UUAC as a forty-one-member 'talking shop' which had attacked the Order, and said that the Order was unlikely to win control of the committee. It was agreed that three observers would be sent to the committee but the Order would not commit itself.[84]

The issue of joining the UUAC continued at the next Central Committee session. Douglas said that the Order's influence would help the UUAC and that the Order could withdraw at any time if it did not like what was happening. On the other hand, Smyth argued that the UUAC would do its work anyway regardless of whether the Order joined. The Rev. Long was unhappy with joining and was displeased with the implied equivalence between the Order and the Independent Orange Order. At this, Overend once again stepped in to propose that the Order join the UUAC. Douglas seconded him. But few followed. In addition to the Belfast troika of Smyth, Watson, and Passmore, Captain Armstrong (Armagh) and Samuel Foster (Fermanagh) expressed disquiet with the UUAC. Foster, a UDR man and UUP stalwart, said that membership of the UUAC could make patrols in border areas more difficult. On a vote, Overend's motion fell by 16–4.[85]

At the following meeting, a report was read regarding the UUAC meeting attended by Orange observers. It was revealed that Smyth had taken 'stick' from some UUAC men—probably over his attendance at UUP–SDLP talks that spring—and that the Independent Orange Order and a full range of other Loyalist institutions (presumably including paramilitaries) had attended. Some expressed concern at this, with Watson querying whether the issue of guns had been raised. Douglas, however, stressed once more that the Order was not bound and could pull out at any time.[86] When the matter was put to a ballot at Grand Lodge, the hardline faction lost, with more than two-thirds of those present voting against the motion to join the UUAC.[87]

Institutional loyalty to the UUP was in keeping with Orange practice, but the Order seldom followed where 'liberal' UUP initiatives led. Despite this, some softening around the edges was evident within the Order. Loyalist opposition, as organized by the UUUC, managed to kill off the Constitutional Convention of 1975–6, and the SDLP and Unionists remained as far apart as ever. Yet Martin Smyth related to Grand Lodge that the UUP had held four meetings with the SDLP since the closing of the convention. Though there had not been substantial progress, he noted 'a glimmer of hope' and received a round of applause for his efforts.[88] Furthermore, most of those present at Central Committee agreed that the Order should not be bound by a directive from the UUAC not to talk with government representatives from Eire. This may have had to do with squabbles over power, but most of those present recognized that they needed to meet representatives from the Republic to 'work on behalf of our people', notably Orangemen from Eire.[89]

The Order had already agreed that its members could take part in services where Catholic priests were present so long as worship was not 'of an RC nature'.[90] Meanwhile, Smyth took the daring step of appearing on television in the Republic with Catholic priests.[91] Later, he attended a diplomatic meeting in Dublin, citing the need for the Order to 'accept [our] public responsibilities'.[92] Smyth subsequently commented in an Orange report to members that in attending a seminar on human rights convened by the Irish School of Ecumenics, it was

useful for helping people of diverse views to know one another and to face one another in civilised conversation and debate. Perhaps this is profit enough in the present situation. It is never easy to assess what future effect friendship will have on people who hold opposite views now. It must be advantageous to know that we are not ignorant of the views and the personalities of those who disagree with us.[93]

In the 1960s, any contact with the 'other side' would have been treated as a violation of the boundary between the sacred and the profane. The modest breach of this boundary indicates some (albeit limited) erosion of the rigid segregationist principle, though as yet there was no willingness to accept power-sharing. This was despite some evidence from contemporary polls suggesting that a majority of the Protestant public—around 60 per cent—was willing to countenance power-sharing.[94] On the other hand, these polls must be taken with a large dose of caution given the political imperatives which may have shaped their methodology and the ambiguity attached to the term 'power-sharing' in the minds of the Unionist public.

The Order was no longer allergic to Catholics, but in constitutional terms its ideology remained unchanged. For instance, Grand Lodge's Twelfth resolutions of 1976 reiterated the need to maintain the British connection, 'but equally, the Institution is convinced that the proper way to administer Northern Ireland is by devolved Government'.[95] Walker rightly draws attention to the integrationist influence of Enoch Powell, who became an Ulster Unionist MP for South Down in 1976. Walker argues that Powell's integrationist vision clashed with the Ulster ethno-nationalism of Bill Craig and Harry West. He adds that despite Molyneaux's paying lip-service to devolution, he was more willing than Craig or West to accommodate Powell's vision.[96] If so, Molyneaux was truly playing a double game, since devolutionist assumptions were strongly held by Grand Lodge, and Molyneaux had to appear tough on Direct Rule. 'We're pledged to a return of Stormont in Westminster,' Molyneaux told those present at Central Committee in March 1976, 'We support the stand of the Grand Master (Smyth) and the others who stand in the Convention'.[97]

Molyneaux could not have stated otherwise, since scepticism of the UUP's intentions ran high within the Institution. For instance, the Rev. Brown criticised British civil servants and called for more powers for local government, while Captain Armstrong stated that the Home Office was seeking to divide the Loyalist community and that Direct Rule must be discredited. At this, Molyneaux reiterated that his party was dissatisfied with Direct Rule. Next, Clark—ever the unifying voice—commended the efforts of Smyth and Molyneaux and urged that the door be kept open to negotiation so as to secure the Unionists' place in the UK. Here we see something of a reprise of pre-1972 politics, with high-level Orange figures with UUP links pushing a moderate agenda at Grand Lodge. The difference this time is that the 'moderates' were largely drawn from the ranks of ex-populists, and were thus unlikely to bend to the same extent as the old Ulster 'squirerarchy'.[98]

The devolution–integration debate continued at subsequent meetings. Smyth was initially hesitant to broach political subjects for fear of dividing the Order, but both Brown and Douglas assured him that no one in their jurisdictions had any problem with Smyth's UUP connections. With this settled, Smyth described the political scene in September 1976 as 'fairly open' but in typically dramatic fashion added that 'anarchy might prevail'. In reply to a question from the Rev. Dickinson on progress towards devolved government, Smyth related that the SDLP was pressing for this—which suggests that at least on the issue of devolution, Unionists and Nationalists were singing from the same hymn sheet. Dickinson accused the British government of taking its cue from the SDLP and ignoring the Unionists, but Smyth took care to correct him, stating that Unionists' views were being considered, but that they were divided. Molyneaux added that Unionists had benefited from the appointment of Roy Mason as the new Secretary of State as opposed to Roy Hattersley, who was the SDLP's first choice.[99]

Smyth and Molyneaux were senior UUP men, yet, in contrast to the likes of O'Neill, Chichester-Clark, and Faulkner, both had time-tested histories of Orange activism. Their positive appraisal of the UUP thus did not elicit the same populist reaction that it might have done in the Stormont or Sunningdale period. The discussion then moved on to specifics. Captain Armstrong pointed out that 'acceptance of power-sharing' was the crux of the issue between Unionists and the SDLP. He suggested that the departure of Faulkner from the scene meant that the UUUC was freer to reach a deal. However, the Rev. Dickinson felt that the SDLP wanted things its way only. Armstrong, though more moderate, largely concurred, claiming that the SDLP had to decide whether it wanted devolved government with no power-sharing in cabinet or would push for power-sharing at the risk of no devolved government.[100]

What is important is what was going unsaid. The Order opposed power-sharing in cabinet, but its more realistic elements may have been softening their stance on the use of PR at the Assembly level. Thus at the next Central Committee meeting, Smyth matter-of-factly reported that Mason would use PR in the upcoming European elections. There was little comment on the matter.[101] At a subsequent meeting with Mason, Thomas Passmore (Belfast) supported the Secretary of State's call for political movement towards devolved government, and it was recorded that 'deep consideration will have to be given to our voting system'.[102] Again, in early 1977, the matter of PR was raised. It was noted that the system 'should be looked at', though some called for a recovery of the 'United Unionist mentality' which opposed PR. Jim Molyneaux, however, argued that the Order's policy of encouraging its members to use PR to their best voting advantage was a success.[103] For his part, Smyth, despite moderating his views by the mid 1970s, was still given to dire predictions, such as his conviction that the IRA would be mounting an intense campaign to 'show their strength and establish a military junta'.[104]

Roy Mason's tenure as Secretary of State represented a period of relative calm on the constitutional front, and the period 1976–9 was a less fraught one for Unionists. Conservative government policy seemed to shift in an integrationist direction at Westminster. During this interlude, the UUP became solidly entrenched as the leading Unionist party, partly because of Paisley's tactical blunders.[105] The UUAC, now even more firmly in the grip of Paisley, announced plans for a second workers' strike to press the British to implement the convention report, which would restore a Stormont-style majoritarian system. This call was greeted with derision by the UUP, Orange Order, and Vanguard Unionist Party. Thomas Passmore, County Grand Master of Belfast, attacked the UUAC strike plans. He also alleged that a member of the UUAC had been involved in discussions with the IRA.[106] Here we may need to revise

Walker's remark that UUP opposition to the strike was tactical, conditioned by the strike's poor chance of succeeding.[107] Orange evidence suggests that, quite apart from differences over tactics and ideology, turf wars between Orange and DUP forces for control of the UUAC lay behind Orange opposition to the strike. By early 1977, Smyth was openly deriding the 'immaturity' of the media appearances of Jim Craig's deputy, Ernest Baird.[108]

The souring relations between the Paisley-dominated UUAC and mainstream Unionism of the UUP, Vanguard, and Orange Order led to a rupturing of the three-year-old UUUC in May 1977. The Order and mainstream Unionist parties had never embraced the UUAC (a UUUC steering group initiative) as they had the UUUC itself. The strike's violent repercussions and paramilitary links, coupled with its limited success, were enough to reopen a wedge between Paisley and the mainstream Unionists. With Unionist unity in tatters the Unionist parties were free to contest elections and squared off against each other in the 1977 local elections. The UUP came off best with almost 30 per cent of the vote, as against just 13 per cent for the DUP.[109]

The security issue featured strongly in the later stages of the UUAC strike, and here the Order attempted to directly influence the course of events. During 1976, the British government took steps to 'Ulsterize' the conflict by placing the RUC and UDR in leading security roles so as to reduce the risk to British troops. The Order appears to have concurred with this approach in the hope of Unionists gaining more control over security in the province through their disproportionate involvement in the UDR and RUC. First, Smyth encouraged rank-and-file Orange members to join these organizations.[110] A year later, he again played a signal role in encouraging the 'Ulsterization' of the conflict. Noting that defence estimates allowed for a British force of 14,500 men, he urged that 'we should endeavour to have this reduced to garrison strength [i.e.] 7,500. For Ulster's sake we must discourage the thoughts [among Orange members] that it is unmanly to join the reserves or UDR.'[111]

Of course, UDR and RUC service was far from an 'unmanly' walk in the park for those young Orangemen who eventually heeded the call in significant numbers. Among Protestants, 300 RUC men and 200 UDR men lost their lives in the conflict, and over 100 of these 500 during 1976–9.[112] At one Grand Lodge meeting, a Tyrone member was acknowledged by those present to be under attack by the IRA for his participation in the UDR.[113] Roy Kells, a former Fermanagh Grand Master, recounts that two-thirds of his lodge joined the UDR Reserve or RUC Reserve, most of them around 1970. This made them legitimate targets for IRA hit squads. Kells adds that three of the forty members of his lodge were killed and that he himself only narrowly escaped assassination, surviving three separate attempts on his life.[114] In the short term, though, 'Ulsterization' successfully reduced security problems. Molyneaux expressed satisfaction with the turn of events, ironically remarking that at a House of Commons debate on security, some who had first urged 'Ulsterization' now 'complained bitterly' when the RUC took over.[115]

The Ulster Service Corps (USC) was linked with the UUAC and operated as a vigilante-paramilitary organization undertaking patrols in rural Northern Ireland. Ian Paisley even admitted that he had gone on patrol with the USC. One of its trademarks was the illegal roadblock, and this was used repeatedly during the UUAC strike.[116] The USC was granted use of the House of Orange for a meeting—likely through connections with William Douglas—which suggests that some of its members may also have been Order members.[117] The Order certainly agreed in private to 'help [the USC] where possible'.[118] On the other hand, in mid 1977, Smyth and Grand Secretary Walter Williams met representatives of the USC. The USC men attempted to justify their tactic of conducting 'spot-checks' and 'mobile patrols' to the Orange officers. Here the Order was noncommittal but not critical. Members of the USC were entitled to their own views on how to improve security, noted Smyth and Williams, but Smyth stressed that Grand Lodge's position was to encourage its membership to join the 'proper and legal forces of the Crown'. Predictably, Douglas demurred, contending that the USC men had a great love for Ulster and that there was a lack of communication between the Orange and the USC. In the end, the Grand Lodge agreed only to keep the matter 'under review'.[119]

With constitutional issues stuck in neutral, security questions rose to prominence. This was despite the fact that the number of Protestant and British Army fatalities had halved since 1976 to around seventy-five per year.[120] A security resolution from Lower Iveagh District (Co. Down) prompted Smyth to call for a major demonstration on the issue. He wanted brethren of the Order mobilized within the week. For Smyth, there was no point in demonstrating at Stormont unless 'we take it over'.[121] At a meeting with Mason, Orange representatives harangued the minister over security deficiencies in their respective counties. Besides the defeat of the IRA, other matters discussed included UDR recruitment and constitutional questions such as PR and devolved government. Mason responded that he was as determined to defeat terrorists as the Order, and the Order reported that all expected to see a marked improvement in security by the beginning of July.[122]

These occasional meetings with Mason were about as close as the Order would get to the levers of power during Direct Rule, and were a far cry from the Stormont days when the Stormont Prime Minister would sometimes see several deputations of Orangemen per month. But the 'Ulsterization' strategy—to which the Order and British were unwitting dance partners—appears to have borne fruit. At the September meeting of Central Committee, most counties reported significant improvements in security as a result of greater UDR and RUC control. Antrim cited 'more help from RUC', and Belfast approvingly commented on the increase in the number of brethren joining the RUC

Reserve and UDR. In Belfast, South Down, and Fermanagh, it was reported that the RUC and UDR were gaining ground even in hostile areas, with the UDR local commanders having 'local power'. Only in Derry, where the RUC and local district masters had failed to agree on parade routes, was the situation deemed problematic. Not content to rest on his laurels, Smyth warned that despite the favourable security trends, the Order was not over the 'hump' yet and could ill afford to 'sit back'.[123]

Matters were going well on the security front largely because of IRA disarray after its temporary ceasefire. Half a year later, the IRA returned to violence, claiming twelve Protestant victims in a bomb attack on a hotel in Castlereagh on 17 February 1978. Molyneaux, who had proclaimed the success of his pressure on Mason, now declared that the Secretary of State had encouraged a false picture of the security situation, and Captain Michael Armstrong warned of the IRA 'paving the way for the intervention of the Eire Army or the UN'.[124]

There was also evidence of Paisleyite dissension in the ranks. Reports from various county Twelfth demonstrations were satisfactory, but heckling was not uncommon. In Fermanagh, it was considered a success that there was only one heckler during a speech on the platform by the UUP leader Harry West. In other cases, platform speakers were critical of Grand Lodge policy. Robert Overend (Londonderry), a hardline member of Central Committee and elected Vanguard politician, did not participate on the platform, having disagreed with the leadership, and Ernest Baird's name was also mentioned among the list of troublemakers. Alfie Lee of County Londonderry Lodge described the behaviour of his fellow county representative Overend as 'embarrassing'.[125]

Overend subsequently claimed that he did not breach Orange laws but simply failed to appear on the platform.[126] This seems to have been accepted by Smyth and the others, and no disciplinary action was taken against Overend or other brethren despite their apparent breach of Orange Law 28. Rather, those present seem to have preferred vague pronouncements and a desire to let things take care of themselves. Here it seems that the will of the Order's elite to enforce Orange law and custom against populist upstarts was limited. This tolerance for a diversity of views in such a decentralized organization was both its strength—in that it minimized the conflict between individual identities and Order membership[127]—and its weakness, because it impaired coordinated action and unity.

The issue of integrated schooling also emerged around this time. Initial proposals were made by the Ministry of Education in 1974. These were greeted with scepticism by the Order since the state (i.e. Protestant) sector was deemed to be open to all. While acknowledging the success of integrated education in the technical colleges, the Order was anxious to 'preserve the right of denominational teaching in the schools as allowed for in the 1948 Education Act'. The safeguarding of Christian worship and the 'rights of parents and teachers' was deemed paramount.[128] Later in 1977, a more circumspect attitude prevailed. 'Integrated education has worked in the past in some areas,' remarked a delegate, and integrated education proposals should be considered on a case-by-case basis.[129] The Order's attitude towards another non-sectarian movement, the Peace People (who won a Nobel prize in 1977 for their work), was also sceptical, albeit with some justification. The Peace People had claimed that the Order was redirecting money raised in Canada and the USA for Orange widows to purchase weapons. The Order solicited advice on whether to pursue a libel action but dropped the case because it was unable to show that it had suffered clear damages.[130] Later, it focused its attention on educating the membership about the 'detrimental' influence of the Peace People and kindred organizations.[131]

The first five years of Direct Rule had seen the Orange Order vigorously oppose the UUP's attempt to share power with Nationalists. The Order arguably played the leading role in mobilizing a pan-Unionist front which could defeat the Sunningdale Agreement. Though Unionist political unity had collapsed by 1977, the Orange Order had effectively steered the UUP away from its flirtation with power-sharing. At the helm of the Orange ship was Martin Smyth, whose resistance to power-sharing was matched by his rejection of the independent Unionism of Paisley and the paramilitaries and his loyalty to the traditional institutions of Ulster Protestantism: the Orange Order, the mainstream churches, and the UUP.

5

Stable Rejectionism: The Smyth–Molyneaux Axis, 1978–1995

Politically, as mentioned, the late 1970s proved a quiet period. James Molyneaux, the UUP Westminster MP, had increasingly emerged as Unionist leader along with his confederate Enoch Powell. Martin Smyth, as a leading UUP Convention member (1975–7) and in 1982 a new Westminster MP, was in close contact with Molyneaux. Molyneaux knew that the return of Stormont was—for the moment—a dead letter but remained the long-term goal. Realizing that devolution and power-sharing were irrevocably yoked, Molyneaux charted a cautious course. He accepted Direct Rule as a temporary expedient and emphasized 'administrative devolution' as an alternative to legislative devolution. Talk of devolution pleased the Unionist rank and file without forcing the UUP to share power with the SDLP and hence lose support to the DUP.[1]

During his Grand Master's address, Smyth continued to bemoan the lack of progress towards a devolved administration for Northern Ireland. The same UUUC logic—based on the idea that Northern Ireland should be governed the same way as the rest of the UK—informed the speech, which was greeted with a round of applause:

We regret the injudicious words of the Secretary of State in declining to give proper local democracy to Ulster...basic electoral rights no longer exist for over one million people in the United Kingdom...false claims [have been made] that we look for a Protestant dominated Stormont. Remember it was the Westminster Government, at the behest of Nationalist Terrorists, which imposed Stormont upon Ulster. Further, Craigavon's 'A Protestant Parliament for a Protestant People' was in reply to a Southern Cabinet Minister's cry 'A Catholic Parliament for a Catholic People'. Perhaps it was because Craigavon's alliteration was better, that people remember it. Nevertheless, the fact is, that the Protestant people in the South...have been clearly crowded out from political power. One member elected in the Dail is scarcely a proportional return...Ulster will not surrender its cherished place within a larger family, nor will it pay the price for pseudo democracy by power sharing.[2]

Was the Orange Order reflecting the sentiments of the Unionist population and its mass base? A major academic survey of political attitudes undertaken in 1978 helps us answer this question. The survey included over 800 Protestant respondents and revealed the following preferences for the 'most workable or acceptable' constitutional solution (see Table 5.1).

The first thing to note is that only a minority (under 40 per cent) of Protestants in 1978 backed the Grand Lodge's restorationist position on the constitutional future of Northern Ireland. Collating the options under the 'pro' or 'anti' power-sharing label yields some interesting findings. 54 per cent of Protestants wanted to restore Stormont or favoured Direct Rule, but fully 43 per cent polled expressed a willingness to share power to some degree[3] with either Catholics or the Irish government. Nor can the answer be found in the opinions of those who supported parties the Order backed, namely the UUP and Vanguard, which Grand Lodge had endorsed ever since Faulkner's UPNI seceded from the UUP. For instance, Table 5.2 shows that roughly 40 per cent of UUP and Vanguard supporters approved of power-sharing.

Table 5.1 Protestant Constitutional Attitudes, 1978 ('Most Workable or Acceptable')

Constitutional option	Proportion in favour
Stormont-style majority-rule (devolution)	38%
Sunningdale-style power-sharing (devolution)	35%
London Direct Rule	16%
United Ireland	1%
Federal Ireland	4%
Independent Northern Ireland	3%
Joint authority	2%
Survey sample (Protestants)	816

Source: E. Moxon-Browne, *Northern Ireland Attitude Survey, 1978* [computer file], Colchester: UK Data Archive, SN 1347 (1980).

Table 5.2 Protestant Opposition to Power-Sharing, 1978, by Party of Support

Party supported	Proportion opposed to power-sharing
DUP	86.4%
Official Unionist Party	61.1%
Vanguard	60.0%
Northern Ireland Labour Party	51.9%
UPNI	35.7%
Alliance	22.3%

Source: Moxon-Browne, *Northern Ireland Attitude Survey, 1978*.

Clearly, there was a marked difference between supporters of various political parties on this issue, with DUP identifiers least willing to compromise with Nationalists and both Vanguard and UUP supporters less radical. 57 per cent of the Protestant sample were UUP supporters, and they opposed power sharing only by 60–40. In contrast, the 17 per cent of Protestants sampled who voted DUP opposed power-sharing more decisively, by 83–17. Anti-power-sharing DUP sympathizers were twice as devolutionist in orientation as their anti-power-sharing UUP counterparts. This makes it all the more incredible that Paisley once considered playing the integrationist card against Vanguard and the UUP when the latter supported restoring Stormont in 1972.

Could it be that the Order was reflecting its working-class base? Even excluding the top two classes of respondent (professionals, managers, and technicians—representing 18 per cent of the Protestant population) so as to approximate better the Orange class profile, only 57 per cent of Protestants opposed power-sharing. Why then, was there such a limited representation within the Orange leadership of the more than 40 per cent of Protestants who supported power-sharing?

One answer is that, on the majoritarian principle, the Grand Lodge should have opposed power-sharing since 61 per cent of UUP and Vanguard supporters did so. Also, support for some degree of majority rule was strong even among Unionists who supported power-sharing. The Moxon-Browne survey of 1978, for instance, asked a question which tapped the issue of whether Protestants should be allowed to express their constitutional preferences through majoritarian democracy. Roughly 65 per cent of Protestants agreed (slightly or strongly) with the statement that: 'Since they are the majority, it is only right that Protestants should have the last word in how Northern Ireland is governed.' A summary of responses by constitutional position appears in Table 5.3. Note that even among those favouring power-sharing, a majority agreed with this statement.

Yet the majoritarian explanation does not explain why grassroots Orange resolutions almost invariably came from the right and almost never from pro-power-sharing lodges. Perhaps supporters of power-sharing failed to form a majority in any lodge and had their support spread too thinly? For this to

Table 5.3 Protestants should have 'Last Word' since they Form the Majority: Protestant responses, 1978

	Agree	Disagree
Support power-sharing	51%	49%
Oppose power-sharing	76%	23%

Source: Moxon-Browne, *Northern Ireland Attitude Survey, 1978.*

obtain, a more resounding degree of opposition had to exist within the Orange mass. Let us examine whether this may have been the case. Returning to the wider Unionist public support for power-sharing, statistical tests using logistic regression (see Figure 5.1) show that the key background factors predicting an 'anti' response are, in order of strength: low level of education, region (Antrim or border counties), and being unmarried (see Figures 5.2, 5.3, and 5.4).

Class,[4] age, urban/rural residence, strength of belief, and denomination play no significant role once education, region, and conjugal status are accounted for. It is also the case that the correlation between class and education is not strong enough for us to assume education and class to be tapping the same underlying construct. Indeed, only at the very top and bottom of the six-point class scale (professionals who favour power-sharing versus the unskilled who strongly oppose it) can we see much difference in attitudes. But these are

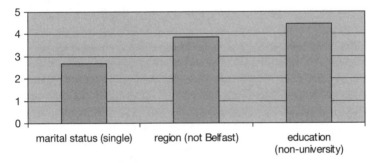

Figure 5.1 Predictors of opposition to power-sharing (by z-score significance)

Sources: Moxon-Browne, *Northern Ireland Attitude Survey, 1978*; statistical analysis using STATA Intercooled 7.0. Detailed results available at <http://www.sneps.net/OO/bk1stats.htm>.

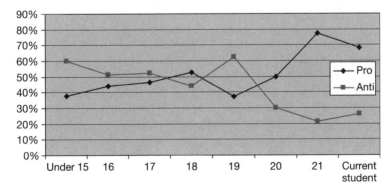

Figure 5.2 Attitude to power-sharing, Protestants, by age of completing education, 1978

Source: Moxon-Browne, *Northern Ireland Attitude Survey, 1978*.

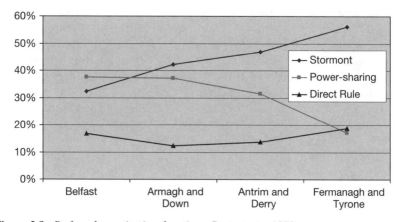

Figure 5.3 Preferred constitutional options, Protestants, 1978
Source: Moxon-Browne, *Northern Ireland Attitude Survey, 1978*.

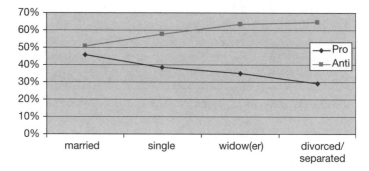

Figure 5.4 Attitudes to power-sharing, Protestants, by conjugal status, 1978
Source: Moxon-Browne, *Northern Ireland Attitude Survey, 1978*.

very small categories. The vast majority of Protestants from managers and technicians through to partially skilled manual workers tended to be mildly against power-sharing in 1978.[5]

The map in Figure 5.5 shows that region was particularly important, with those in mid Antrim and the west (shaded darker on the map) strongly against power-sharing. More positive views on power-sharing were expressed by those in greater Belfast and parts of the north (lighter shades). Evidently border Unionists had yet to make the transition from being the most obstructionist to the most accommodationist of their tribe.

The same regions (west and north) which opposed power-sharing also seemed to feel closer to the DUP than the Official Unionists. Those from the Loyalist working class were also more likely to back the DUP and, disturbingly for Smyth and Molyneaux, younger respondents were significantly more

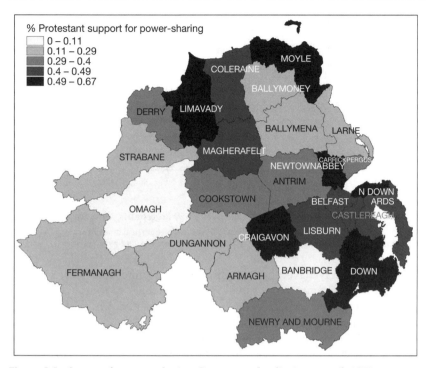

Figure 5.5 Support for power-sharing, Protestants, by district council, 1978

Sources: Moxon-Browne, *Northern Ireland Attitude Survey, 1978*; based upon Ordnance Survey of Northern Ireland (OSNI) digital boundaries. © Crown copyright.

likely to warm to the DUP than older Unionists (see Figure 5.6). A statistical model which ranks Unionist parties from the most radical (DUP) to the least (Alliance) found the same relationship between youth and the DUP, though education also played a role in bolstering the anti-DUP vote. Overall, it seems that in 1978, political liberalism was linked to being from greater Belfast and possessing a higher level of formal education while resistance to reform flourished among the less educated and those from outside metropolitan Belfast. Older and higher-status respondents backed the UUP, but did not necessarily support power-sharing.

Since few Orangemen possessed a university education and the balance of the membership is weighted outside the Belfast area, we would expect Orangemen to be less inclined towards power-sharing with Catholics. Yet even in combination, these effects are not strong enough to explain the almost complete silence from pro-power-sharing Orangemen. At the very least, we would expect to see more evidence of local divisions on constitutional issues and to see some lodges backing power-sharing. The same divisions might be expected vis-à-vis support for the 'Orange party', the UUP.

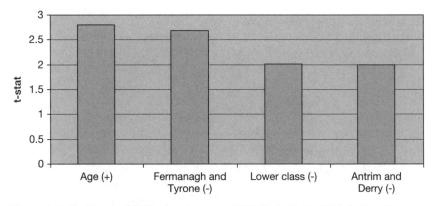

Figure 5.6 Predictors of UUP advantage over DUP, Protestants, 1978 (by t-stat)

Sources: Moxon-Browne, *Northern Ireland Attitude Survey, 1978*; statistical analysis using STATA Intercooled 7.0. Detailed results available at <http://www.sneps.net/OO/bk1stats.htm>.

Orangemen may have opposed power-sharing more than their Unionist neighbours, but recent Orange survey work shows that Orange views and political preferences do not radically differ from those of other Unionists—though of course it is possible that a slightly different picture existed in 1978.[6] A more likely possibility is that there was a 'silent minority' of pro-power-sharing Orangemen who dared not or cared not to speak their name. This Orange minority may have been attracted to the Institution for cultural, social, or family reasons and thus failed to become politically active within it. As we shall see, this is particularly likely in rural communities and small towns west of the Bann River, where Protestants are the most Orange in the province. In this context, it is extremely important to remember that many members' primary experience of Orangeism lay in the conviviality provided by their lodge and with the pageantry of the Twelfth.[7] Some support for this comes from the 1997 Loyal Orange Commission, which found that 65 per cent of members[8] wanted the Order not to be associated with any political party.[8]

The existence of a silent minority is far from problematic since a very great degree of apathy and decentralization existed within the Order. We can see the disjunction between a 'politicized' Grand Lodge (and selected politicized lodges such as Belfast's LOL 1310) and a far more apathetic membership by examining the response to certain Grand Lodge initiatives. One was the Orange in-house newspaper, the *Orange Standard*. This initially sold 27,000 copies in early 1973, but the sales fell to 16,000 in mid 1973 and just 4,000 by mid 1978. Subsidies, diktats, reorganizations, and promotion efforts managed to nudge this figure only to around 5,500 by 1980. The paper was £2,000 in deficit by 1982, and its content and distribution were routinely criticized at Central Committee. On several occasions, it barely managed to survive motions to cease publication.[9] Likewise, a Queen's Jubilee Twelfth booklet of

1977 sold just 2,500 of the 20,000 copies produced, which resulted in a loss for Grand Lodge of £2,500. To add insult to injury, Orangemen purchased just 15 per cent of the booklets sold, compared with 85 per cent which were sold to onlookers! This was despite an aggressive sales plan on the Twelfth including over sixty sales staff. 'As the day progressed and sales staff were constantly refused,' lamented Grand Lodge, 'enthusiasm started to fade. . . All methods of sale were used and each proved similar in result.'[10]

Other Grand Lodge crusades faced identical barriers. For instance, Grand Lodge was beginning to lose the battle against alcohol in the lodges. In 1974, a temperance watch committee was set up to monitor drinking in Orange halls.[11] At this time, a growing number of Orange lodges were setting up separate rooms for alcohol consumption so as to circumvent Orange Law 5, which banned the consumption within the lodge room, but not in rooms adjacent to the lodge room in the same building.[12] In 1978, Hillsborough District in County Down cited 'divisions' over the issue of licensed halls within its district. There were calls for a referendum at Grand Lodge on the issue of liquor sales in Orange halls. Only an uncompromising stance on the part of George Watson, John Brown, and Captain Armstrong ensured that the traditional line held. Watson bemoaned the fact that he had to fight against the advance of drink in his hall, and Armstrong suggested that lodges meeting in licensed premises should have to hand in their warrants.[13] In June 1978, a protracted debate over a temperance motion found many again counselling tolerance of drink in lodges. Sir George Clark—who as Grand Master in 1962 had referred to luncheon drinks as 'a little warm refreshment'—warned of the difficult position that many members would find themselves in if those who served liquor were penalized. 'Consideration must be given to the effect this will have upon our Order', he pleaded.[14]

Notwithstanding 'wets' like Clark, Brown's motion to alter Orange law to prohibit lodges expressly from meeting in lodge halls in which 'any portion' was licensed was tabled in 1978. It was reintroduced in 1979 and prevailed by 68–28, though this was far from the end of the matter since a final reading was required at the December Grand Lodge sessions.[15] By December, the 'wet' forces had regrouped. Smyth, leader of the 'dry' forces, began the proceedings by circumscribing the temperance motion, telling those assembled that drink could still be brought to a hall for a social occasion, but that no lodge could meet in licensed premises. Clark, however, spoke against the temperance motion, fearing that implementing such a law would have devastating practical consequences such as adversely affecting lodges that met in licensed Apprentice Boys' halls. In the end, the temperance motion failed, but by only the narrowest of margins, 45–47.[16]

Many of the pro-temperance supporters hailed from Antrim, with 'wet' forces distributed more widely around the province but strongly represented in Belfast. Accordingly, a Ballymena District lodge (endorsed unanimously by

Antrim County Lodge) sent a further resolution in 1980 asking Grand Lodge to reconsider its defeat of the temperance motion. This sparked yet another debate in Central Committee, and led to an amendment seeking to delay judgment on the matter. This stalling tactic was defeated only after strenuous arguments by Watson and Brown in favour of temperance which cited the sacred verses of the 'Obligations of an Orangeman'. In the end, a resolution was adopted which merely called for all members to strenuously promote 'true Religion and Temperance principles' but did not prohibit meetings in licensed halls.[17] Nearly a decade later, a reprise of the 1978–80 debate took place. An initial prohibitionist amendment of 1987 won 60–27 approval at Grand Lodge, but, as in 1979, the second reading in 1988 saw a rallying of the 'wet' troops who defeated the bill by 60–33.[18]

The liquor debate, like the debate over attendance at Catholic funerals, showed that the Order could moderate its puritanical stance where it was prudent to do so. This moderation was often driven by a realization that a significant section of the membership 'silently' opposed the stance of Grand Lodge. Silent opposition and apathy could thereby blunt the easy transmission of Grand Lodge initiatives downwards to the membership. For example, we have seen how County Armagh only 'commended' Grand Lodge's anti-Sunningdale statements to its members in 1973 and took care to allow each district to form its own view. Ironically, Grand Lodge impotence had a desirable effect: resource mobilization theory argues that successful social movements allow for different—often contradictory—views to hold at the local branch and lodge level, thereby managing internal conflict.[19]

Moral improvement and ecumenism, like the perennial issues of dues, parade organization, and the rating of Orange halls, were and are the unsung staples of Orange discourse. These enthusiasms tend to take centre stage during periods of political quiescence, as exemplified by the 1978 county and Grand Lodge resolutions seeking to discipline Protestant clerics who supported the ecumenical World Council of Churches.[20] Resolutions against ecumenism from all levels are a non-controversial part of Orange discourse and a stable feature of the post-1960s period and remain so to this day. For example, ecumenical gestures like the presence of a Pope's representative at the installation of the Archbishop of Canterbury or dialogue between Protestant clergy and the IRA were roundly condemned in the mid 1970s.[21]

The planned papal visit to the UK in 1982, which had the blessing of Margaret Thatcher, led to considerable consternation in Orange circles and generated twenty hostile resolutions.[22] The Order immediately let it be known that the pontiff visited Northern Ireland at his own risk. The Secretary of State, Roy Mason, was warned of the 'serious implications that may arise should such a visit take place'. In reply, Grand Lodge was assured by Mason that the Vatican would not push for a visit. Smyth informed the membership of this in a public statement, and a number of replies from local lodges congratulated him on this policy victory.[23]

Grand Lodge kept up the pressure throughout 1980–2, turning its attention to the Scottish and English visits and coordinating its efforts with the Scottish and English Grand Lodges.[24] Smyth even wrote to Margaret Thatcher requesting a meeting, but was rebuffed and told to contact the new Secretary of State for Northern Ireland, Humphrey Atkins.[25] Unfortunately for Grand Lodge, the effort to obstruct the papal visit did not succeed as well on the UK mainland. The lack of effective Orange mobilization was particularly glaring in the Orange stronghold of Glasgow, and some observers see this failure as marking a turning point for Scottish Orangeism. Namely, that Scottish Orange membership achieved its post-1861 membership peak just after the papal visit of 1982 and went into steady decline from 1987.[26]

In terms of moral crusades, Smyth had railed against the 'prevailing moral climate' in his installation address of 1977. Though he understood the frailties of those 'with strong homosexual tendencies', he cautioned that a lax moral climate would merely encourage the development of these deviant tendencies. 'The next stage', intoned Smyth, 'has already been seen in the rearing of the monster of paedophyllia [sic]'. History, Smyth remarked, showed that nations which indulge such conduct soon succumb to decay. The Bible, he claimed, 'forbids it [homosexuality]' and reveals God's judgement on it. In terms of divorce, Smyth contended that the Grand Lodge favoured divorce laws which gave a 'better deal to women', but was wary of any move towards easy divorce and a lowering of marriage standards.[27] Teaching about gay 'facts' was also a concern for Brian Kennaway, a newly appointed Deputy Grand Chaplain from Belfast who would later gain notoriety as an outspoken defender of traditionalist Orangeism, as well as other members of the Education Committee.[28]

In the meantime, Smyth's evangelical moralism was deeply offended by the victory of the 'wet' forces within Orangeism. After losing the initial temperance vote in late 1979, Smyth gave notice that 'Grand Lodge should look for a new Grand Master as he could not lead now that this course of action had been taken'. This was not Smyth's first attempt at retirement (nor his last) and suggests that it may have been partly used as a tactical ploy. For example, the pressures on him at the peak of the Troubles prompted him to tender his resignation as chair of Central Committee, but he was persuaded back by those who asked that less be 'pushed on him' and that he take it easy.[29] Likewise, in 1979, John Brown, George Clark, and others reacted to Smyth's retirement notice by showering him with compliments. Clark remarked that the Order had 'never been led as well as at present' while Brown expressed his sadness that Smyth's services would be lost. Smyth was persuaded back to the chair, but only on condition that two basic matters be resolved. The first target were the 'wet' forces in Belfast County, which informed their members attending Grand Lodge to vote against temperance; and second, 'Was the Orange Order in the future going to depend on "drink" for its survival?'[30]

Politically, 1978 proved a reasonably calm year, though the Orange leadership cautioned that pressure on the government to tighten security must remain strong. Security concerns formed the substance of a meeting with the Secretary of State held on 15 December.[31] Others worried that the decline in fatalities was but the calm before the storm, with Captain Armstrong fearing that the IRA might pave the way for Eire or United Nations intervention.[32] Constitutionally, PR was dawning as a reality in some Orange quarters. Richard Thornton (Fermanagh) advanced his opinion that PR was in fact suitable for the west of the province, where Nationalists were often in the majority. The Belfast County master Thomas Passmore, by contrast, expressed the more popular view, maintaining that Northern Ireland should not have a different electoral system from the rest of the UK. Despite its use in the upcoming EEC elections, Passmore wanted Grand Lodge to continue to press for a uniform franchise. Kennaway did not disagree, but pragmatically sought guidance as to how to use the system to Unionists' best advantage, cautioning Unionists to avoid abstention.[33]

In a statement to the members entitled 'The Union and the Institution', Grand Lodge attempted to summarize the Orange position. The Order commended the public influence of Belfast County Lodge's 1976 report debunking some loosely floating UUAC-influenced allegations that the British would withdraw from Northern Ireland. It reiterated the findings of the investigating committee that withdrawal was not on the cards, claimed that 'power sharing is no longer a major issue', and assured its Orange audience that there was growing acceptance of Unionist claims on all sides of the House of Commons.[34] The statement, perhaps influenced by Molyneaux's integrationism, urged its members to be more optimistic and not to indulge in negativism, recrimination, or self-pity. The IRA, claimed Grand Lodge, had misinterpreted the intentions of the British, and the intransigence of the SDLP had pushed Ulster further along the road to Union. Now was the time not for an ambiguous embrace of the UK, a 'luxury' that the Unionist community could no longer enjoy, but for actively working to rebuild the province as part of the UK.[35]

In 1979, Ian Paisley was elected to the European Parliament as the most popular Unionist candidate, despite the UUP's 37–10 trouncing of the DUP in the popular vote in the Westminster elections a month earlier. This turnaround is partly explicable by the DUP's anti-EEC stand and its decision not to contest certain seats, as Walker rightly notes. But most of the difference is attributable to intra-UUP leadership divisions between John Taylor, Jim Kilfedder, and Harry West (who collectively polled far more votes than Paisley) as well as the system of PR with single transferable vote used in the European elections.[36]

This ironically meant that the anti-EEC Paisley would, in the future, tend to win European elections while losing most others. Reasoning aside, the UUP was shocked by the loss: the disarray sowed by the UUP's European defeat of 1979 prompted it to examine its own disorganized state and, from this turmoil, James Molyneaux was elected as UUP leader in September 1979.

For the UUP to have elected Molyneaux—Deputy Grand Master of the Order—as its leader is significant. Unlike nominal Orangemen such as O'Neill and Faulkner, or even elite Orange power brokers like Brookeborough, Clark, or John Andrews, Molyneaux was not an establishment man. He had paid his Orange dues and established a solid reputation as a defender of grassroots Orange 'No' Unionism in the sixties and seventies. Likewise, Martin Smyth, another self-made 'No' Unionist who cut his teeth on Central Committee in the sixties, achieved a high position in the UUP executive. Unlike figures such as Clark or Brookeborough, Smyth made it plain to his Orange audience that he owed his rise to the Order and that the Order's priorities took pride of place over those of his party.[37] The ascent of Smyth and Molyneaux meant that the Order was poised to press its case within the UUP with particular vigour, and to constrain the freedom of Molyneaux to compromise with Nationalists and the British. Even if Molyneaux's sympathies were integrationist, as Graham Walker claims, then he needed to tread carefully, for he was answerable to an Orange network which could exert considerable moral suasion on him.[38]

Molyneaux did not disappoint his Orange flock and generally held the line against power-sharing and the north–south dimension until he stepped down from the party leadership in 1995.[39] Molyneaux was the first UUP leader to emerge from the ranks of the newer generation of populist Orangemen, and there can be little doubt that his grassroots Orange connections and beliefs served as an important 'generalised other', to use George Herbert Mead's psychology, which travelled with him to 10 Downing Street.[40] Like Smyth, but unlike O'Neill, Chichester-Clark, Faulkner, or, later, Trimble, Molyneaux was an Orangeman first and a politician second. This cognitive make-up helped to staunch the temptation to reach an accommodation with Nationalists and the British. Despite outward appearances, for example his speech to the annual general meeting of the UUC where he told his audience that the days when a return to Stormont-style devolved government had 'passed away', real compromise was out of the question.[41]

Molyneaux, like Smyth, had simply invested too much psychic and social capital in his brand of popular Orangeism. For the two men to turn their backs on these sunk costs would be to exact a punishing existential and social toll on themselves. Orange links would need to be cut and ethno-religious values ditched—in favour of what? Certainly not the elite or extra-Northern Ireland circles which absorbed O'Neill, Faulkner, and later Trimble. Smyth and Molyneaux rose within the Order precisely because they were part of an anti-elitist wave that eschewed politics-as-usual. This made it difficult for them to perform a *volte-face* and identify with the elite they spurned. Ian Paisley is another individual who has invested—in a different way—in a populist identity, and observers who suggest he may easily cooperate with Sinn Fein as part of a power-sharing administration should take heed from the fifteen to twenty years of Smyth–Molyneaux rejectionism. Despite the new Assembly, Paisley will not readily work together with Unionism's antichrist.

The Molyneaux–Smyth axis was instrumental in reversing the pattern of compromise delivered by the 'nominal' Orangemen who led the Official Unionists from 1965 until 1974. In the period from 1980 to 1995, the Order strayed very little from its established post-1960s platform. This involved rejecting reforms, but doing so from within traditional—as opposed to independent—institutions. The Order's clear opposition to power-sharing, and even PR, tore a path through a succession of constitutional initiatives. These included Humphrey Atkins's all-party conference (1980), James Prior's new Assembly based on 'rolling devolution' (1982–6), the Anglo-Irish Agreement (AIA, post-1985), the Downing Street Declaration (1993), and the Framework Document (1995).[42]

In 1980, responding to a question on the Unionist Party from his Orange audience, Smyth said he was 'amazed' that anyone was asking for meetings with the SDLP or Alliance concerning power-sharing. 'True Ulstermen say what they mean and do it. It was clear from the constitutional stoppage of 1974 that the power sharing government was not on. We know where we are going and will get there. Newtownbutler [site of a planned rally protesting security] will be our next salvo.'[43] In June, the third Twelfth resolution optimistically interpreted Thatcher's endorsement of the consent principle as a rebuff to those who favoured the Republic's having a say in Northern Ireland's affairs.[44] In December, Orange officers 'made clear' their refusenik position on power-sharing in a meeting lasting an hour and a half with the Secretary of State, Atkins.[45]

In 1981, Martin Smyth had this to say about the constitutional initiatives of the new Secretary of State, James Prior:

They say 'rolling devolution' is on the way. May I issue this warning...If a Unionist like Margaret [Thatcher] can fall into the trap and follow the Sunningdale policies of Dr Fitzgerald; beware...I want to put on record my confidence in the steadfastness, resolution and perspicacity of our Deputy Grand Master, James Molyneaux. When others might panic, thresh in frenzy, or lose sight both of enemy and objective, he does not...I have to report to you that though proposed as a member of the team to meet Mr. Prior, I refused to go. I did so in the context of a debate in which a [UUP] member of the so-called devolution group urged that we needed to compromise. I am not given to...change. I am happy that Bro. Molyneaux is not prepared either to compromise on fundamental issues. As an Institution we will examine carefully all proposals, but will not support any which would 'roll us' or in the words of Hugh Logue 'trundle us' into the Irish Republic.[46]

The hunger strike had shaken the Northern Ireland political scene during 1981 and led to the emergence of Sinn Fein as an electoral force with its slogan of 'armalite and ballot box'.[47] Needless to say, this politicization of the IRA did not endear the Order to power-sharing, though it may have begun to introduce a slow thaw in attitudes towards the SDLP.

In the meantime, there would be no change in the Order's constitutional outlook. In preparing for a meeting with the UUP under the United Unionist Forum (UUF) banner, Smyth sounded out the members of Central Committee on their constitutional views by asking a few rhetorical questions. 'Do we want PR voting? Are we prepared to have relations with the South . . . Mr. [Enoch] Powell described Mr Prior's proposals as a squalid deal.' The respondents at the meeting outdid each other in their affirmation of the traditional Orange position, though one delegate asked what those assembled thought of 'total integration'. S. Hamilton responded that the UUF was resolved to pursue devolution. In the end, it was proposed 'that we state our position for the return of Stormont which has always been our call'.[48] In the meantime, Molyneaux boasted of the UUP MPs' collective role in killing off power-sharing. At a UUP executive meeting, Molyneaux endorsed the UUP hardliner Willie Ross, who when asked by the media 'Are you really saying that if you don't get devolved government you won't have anything?' replied 'That is exactly what I am saying.'[49]

The UUF meetings were far from satisfactory for all Orangemen. Hamilton remarked that differences of opinion between the various constituencies within the UUP was so marked that it was impossible to agree on any policy document. He added that the Orange representatives helped to stop any pledge being published. Though the Order recognized that the UUF lacked de facto unity, many felt that it was important for the Order to continue to participate. Two reasons were given: first, to make a show of unity to the members, many of whom wanted to see the Order unite the squabbling factions within Unionism, and second, to keep a conservative check on policy since 'many important matters which would have been detrimental to N.I. would have been pushed through' had it not been for the conservative Orange presence.[50]

In 1984, the Grand Lodge's July Twelfth resolution derided Prior's New Ireland Forum report: 'despite tremendous efforts to present [the report] . . . as a fresh approach, its real interest is the old all Ireland Republic'.[51] A year later, in the calm before the AIA, Grand Master Smyth addressed his Institution. He lamented the 'politicisation' of the IRA by former Secretary of State Merlyn Rees and asked what Rees's successor James Prior and the future Secretary of State Douglas Hurd would do if Sinn Fein replaced the SDLP as the leading Nationalist force. 'If fascists were banned in England and English footballers are banned in Europe then Sinn Fein as long as it grows on violence cannot be given credibility by the abuse of the ballot box . . . will they also support Unionist parties if they [Unionists] take up the armalite?' Smyth warned that if 30 per cent of the Catholic population continued to support the IRA, 'we have no choice but to recognise their implacable hatred and assure them that their efforts will not succeed in defeating us. Rather they will only stimulate a greater resolve to resist them. The watch cry is still "No Surrender".'[52]

Orange and Unionist snubbing of successive constitutional initiatives, in combination with the electoral rise of Sinn Fein, had convinced the Thatcher government of the need to focus on winning a deal with the moderate SDLP. Accordingly, the AIA announced in November 1985 was reached between the British and Irish governments in consultation with the SDLP. The exclusion of Unionists from the process guaranteed their opposition, though it must be said that no Unionist politician with an instinct for self-preservation would have signed up to the document. The signing of the AIA provoked a fresh round of street protests, rallies, strikes, and obstructionist politics among Unionists. On 23 November 1985, over 100,000 people thronged Belfast to hear Ian Paisley and Jim Molyneaux lambast the Agreement. Later, a DUP-organized petition against the AIA to Buckingham Palace garnered 400,000 Unionist signatures. A 'day of action' protest and strike organized on 3 March 1986 by a united coalition of Unionists turned violent, prompting both Paisley and Molyneaux to condemn the Protestant lawbreakers.[53]

Ill. 6 Unionist and Orange protest against the Anglo-Irish Agreement, 23 November 1985 —These protests helped to set limits on the British government's freedom to pursue constitutional reforms but were flagging by the early 1990s.

Importantly, the Agreement catalysed the UUP and DUP into a united front similar to that of the UUUC of the 1974–6 period, leading to another unusual period of Unionist unity—albeit one which masked considerable subterranean fissures.[54] Smyth criticized Unionists who 'previously were hardline' but were now willing to 'accept arrangements worse than those previously rejected'. The July resolution for that year cast a mould which would last more than a decade:

The Anglo-Irish Agreement has changed our status as British citizens. . . . We denounce those who produced by secretive, devious, dishonourable means and without regard to the feelings of the politicians and people most affected, an Agreement to which they will never give consent. We resolve to oppose the Anglo-Irish Agreement by all lawful means . . . We resolve to stand firm against all efforts to make us other than we are, Queen's Men.[55]

In July 1987, a combined UUP–DUP task force produced *An End to Drift*, a Unionist document designed to supersede the AIA. The report was authored by Frank Millar, the UUP General Secretary from 1983 to 1987, and Peter Robinson, deputy leader of the DUP, and voiced the concern that the UUP–DUP–Orange protests against the AIA were losing Unionist mass support.[56] The Order's Policy Committee considered *An End to Drift* and two other key policy documents emanating from within the Unionist community. Its verdict on Millar's and Robinson's document was decidedly negative, criticizing their lack of perseverance, which the biblically inspired Smyth possessed in spades. 'It is regretted that they [Millar and Robinson] have given countenance to the idea that the campaign against the Anglo-Irish Agreement has failed. The Policy Committee would congratulate those who have maintained their opposition.'[57] Even before its release, Paisley had begun to criticize *An End to Drift* for intimating that power-sharing would be a possibility. Molyneaux also cold-shouldered the document, and in the wake of its release, both Millar and Robinson resigned from their posts. This was still a relatively uncompromising document for post-Sunningdale Unionism, but Molyneaux and Paisley were not the best candidates to be sympathetic.[58]

The second document considered by the Order's policy committee was entitled *Common Sense*, and was prepared by the New Ulster Political Research Group (NUPRG), an organization associated with the views of the UDA.[59] A remarkably forward-looking document, it typified a pattern whereby proposals linked to the political wing of Protestant paramilitaries were more moderate than those of the traditional Unionist organizations which opposed street violence.[60] The authors admitted to being 'idealistic', and in a wide-ranging document drawing on academic research and international comparison, they argued in favour of consociationalism:

The acceptance of the practice of proportionality at all levels of government would change the very nature of politics in Northern Ireland. For the first time the people would effectively and directly determine the make-up of the executive by their votes. Coalition is now the practice rather than the exception in modern pluralist societies. We have become so accustomed to equating democracy with majority rule that we tend to forget that majority rule is democratic only when there is alteration in office or when there is broad consensus for it. Majority rule in deeply divided societies is likely to be profoundly undemocratic, and the only democratic system is one that allows participation in government by coalition of all groups, majority and minority, on a more or less permanent basis.[61]

The Orange response was clear and consistent with past practice. The document, though 'well presented', could not be accepted owing to its advocacy of power-sharing. The final paper, from the opposite end of the spectrum, was *The Way Forward*, produced by the Ulster Clubs Movement. The Order's response contained a touch of humour: 'again a well-presented document which would however suggest that it is a blue print for a provisional government and not a very feasible one at that'. The document was also faulted for its infringement of the Order's due political weight: 'On a personal note...it would appear that we [the Orange Order] do not receive the position our numerical strength would suggest.' As an alternative, the Order produced a one-page policy document which endorsed a federation of the British Isles, or, failing this, assemblies for Northern Ireland, Scotland, Wales, and the English regions.[62]

Over the ensuing years, the Order maintained a remarkably consistent anti-Agreement line which undoubtedly fortified the UUP's backbone through the Smyth–Molyneaux axis. In 1987, Smyth pronounced with characteristic wit that 'in the third year of the working of the Anglo Irish Diktat even the most starry eyed romantics cannot say it is working'.[63] In the following year Grand Lodge asked that the British recognize a '*fait accompli*' and consign the 'Anglo Irish Diktat to the waste paper basket'.[64] Though there were occasional voices espousing Ulster independence or integration, the overwhelming sentiment within the Institution—as evident in grassroots resolutions—was devolutionist and resoundingly anti-Agreement through the mid 1990s. This was often backed by Twelfth resolutions against the AIA.[65]

During and after the Brooke–Mayhew all-party talks of 1991, the Order supported the UUP's involvement, though it was critical of Eire's participation. While the Order under Smyth was adamant that 'the Diktat must go', it applauded 'the efforts of the Unionist family during the [Brooke–Mayhew] Talks process to co-operate in the establishment of such structures within Northern Ireland as an integral part of the United Kingdom, and also on matters of mutual interest between Northern Ireland and the Irish Republic'. The Order was not embracing either power-sharing or a north-south dimension, but rather endorsing the established position of Molyneaux that the SDLP could share power only in administrative regional bodies or in toothless ancillary committees of a Unionist-dominated Stormont. North–south cooperation would occur as part of a relationship between sovereign states, and then only on functional matters.[66]

With its ideological exchange rate set, Grand Lodge could focus on action. In late 1987, rallies were organized for Hillsborough, Dungannon, and Londonderry. These were deemed reasonably (but not overwhelmingly) successful.

By contrast, a lobby of fifty Westminster MPs by over 100 Orangemen was deemed a great success.[67] Action could also take the form of eye-catching protests, as with the 1991 Twelfth parade, when all lodge banners were affixed with a 'No Dublin Interference' cover.[68] By 1993, Smyth worried about flagging spirits and endurance, not so much within the Orange as in the ranks of the UUP. Declaring that 'only an ongoing protest campaign can stop the Anglo Irish Diktat', he urged on his troops and proceeded to organize a year of renewed protest against the AIA. Planned activities were to include a second mass lobby of Westminster MPs, a mass mail drop to the Prime Minister, and a protest convention parade.[69]

Grand Lodge could draw on its wealth of experience to mobilize effectively and thus proved a useful pillar of the Unionist 'war effort' against the AIA. The parade was to be executed with military-style efficiency. Grand Lodge was to 'Assemble at the House of Orange at 11:15 A.M. ready to parade to the junction of Great Victoria Street/Hope Street Junction via Dublin Road, Bruce Street to take up the position at the head of the parade which will move off at 11:45 A.M.' For the rank and file, 'County marshals should ensure brethren debus as soon as possible and go straight to county assembly area . . . brethren should march in ranks of five. There should be a band placed at the head of a section of 500 brethren.' An orderly impression was essential, and thus Grand Lodge urged that 'brethren . . . adhere to any request made by the appointed marshals'.[70]

Unfortunately for Grand Lodge, these intricately planned initiatives singularly failed to inspire a response from the mass membership akin to that of 1986–7. First, only about a quarter of districts replied to a summons from Grand Lodge for submissions for the campaign. Then the protest convention parade (above) was cancelled. The mail drop received a 'poor response' and there was a limited presence at the Westminster lobby. Grand Lodge tried again the following year, but Fermanagh's response to its 1994 Anglo-Irish protest call was typical: 'it was discussed [by the County] and it was the general opinion that if this was to take the form of a parade there would be little support'.[71] By 1995, Grand Lodge had given up: 'It was agreed after discussion that Grand Lodge would not organise any form of protest to mark the 10th Anniversary [of the AIA]. County Lodges should again consider lobbying M.P.s.'[72]

Compare this with the enthusiasm of 1986 as expressed by Lurgan District Lodge in Armagh:

The Joint Unionist Leadership, through the Grand Master . . . has requested Orangemen to provide the backbone and organisation of the Anti-Agreement Protest Rally to be held at Belfast City Hall . . . In the past Lurgan was never found wanting when such a call was made . . . It is our firm belief that we will do the same again on 15 November—we want a 100% turnout . . . complete and return the attached slip to your lodge secretary . . . Please encourage other members of your family and non-orangemen to attend.[73]

In the aftermath of the 1993 mobilization failure, Smyth lashed out at an apathetic membership, stating that 'he had no desire to be a Leader of an Institution which carried the veneer of Protestantism and is prepared to continue and carry out ritual... without concern as to what is happening in the community'. He also reminded the brethren that 'when a decision is taken by Grand Lodge, representatives are expected to implement it.'[74] Smyth was more than willing to chastise the rank and file from the vantage point of an evangelical clergyman secure in his position. This degree of legitimacy was reinforced by his apparent willingness to retire and the repeated failure of Grand Lodge to find a successor. In 1979–80, 1982–3, 1988, and 1990, and again in 1995, Smyth attempted to lay down the reins of office but committees (usually led by George Clark) failed to appoint a willing successor.

Smyth generally evinced limited tolerance for the chaotic dissent and perpetual grumbling about Grand Lodge which has characterized the Order for decades. The alcohol issue underlay his resignations of 1979–80 and 1988, and in 1982 he resigned because of criticism of his leadership. He agreed to stay on each time, but urged silent members of Grand Lodge—perhaps temperance-minded clergymen and other 'respectable' Orangemen—to speak their minds. He also wanted to have certain brethren considered who were ineligible because they had not achieved high position (i.e. been elected to county-level office) in the Order. Finally, he warned that he would not agree to hold office 'forever'.[75]

Though Smyth and his Grand Lodge had occasionally adopted a school-teacherly tone towards the membership, this became a more pronounced feature of Grand Lodge reports in this period. Throughout 1993 and 1994, the reports gave cursory responses to some private lodge resolutions (these often being branded as 'counterproductive' or merely 'dealt with') which intimated that those who submitted resolutions had not done their homework or had failed to pay heed to the activities and press releases of Grand Lodge before offering criticism. Though Smyth believed in his anti-Agreement constitutional strategy, he was clearly disillusioned by the often apathetic response of the membership to Grand Lodge initiatives. This was also manifested in a steady membership decline after 1972, coupled with a flat junior Orange programme—both of which seemed remarkably resistant to the flow of events and Grand Lodge exhortations. The amalgamation of districts 7 and 8 in Belfast was indicative of a contraction of total membership by a third in the twenty-three years of Smyth's reign. To be fair, this was hardly Smyth's fault and reflected wider trends of declining 'social capital' (social connectedness) in modern society which also affected other face-to-face organizations like the Masons, unions, and churches.[76] All of this must have done little to lift Smyth's spirits.[77]

There were bright spots in the gloom. The perseverance of Smyth and Molyneaux outdid British politicians with far shorter electoral horizons. In addition, there was some realization among the British by the early 1990s that they could not easily legislate over the heads of the Unionists but needed to redouble their efforts to engage them in the constitutional and peace processes. Thatcher had also become exasperated by the lack of movement from the Irish government on issues like extradition, border security, and the removal of the irredentist Articles 2 and 3 from its constitution. The UUP thereby benefited from a rare glow of positive publicity in the British media.[78]

On the other hand, the lack of ideological ferment under Molyneaux frustrated younger, more restive activists within the UUP, possibly harming the party's longer-term prospects.[79] More damaging was the fact that British government realists seemed willing to abide the sound and fury of Unionist protest, knowing that Unionists would not kill British servicemen. Bowing to Unionist pressure would exacerbate the problem of bombs going off in London, Birmingham, or Manchester or in British Army posts in Ulster. Only a deal with Sinn Fein/IRA would staunch the loss of British men, money, and morale to the troubled province. Only time will tell whether this ethical decision—which can be justified only by a utilitarian philosophy and not a deontological one—was correct.

With British interests in mind, we can see that the Hume–Adams talks, which promised to bring the IRA off the streets and into the 'big tent' of politics, were a more urgent development for no. 10 than the machinations of Molyneaux, the Order, or Paisley. The protests of Unionists over Hume–Adams signally failed to prevent the Downing Street Declaration of 15 December 1993 between the Irish Taoiseach, Albert Reynolds, and the British Prime Minister, John Major. The Joint Declaration was primarily geared towards pacifying militant Republicanism, a strategy which appeared to bear fruit as the IRA announced a historic ceasefire on 31 August 1994. This was attained only as a result of track 2 diplomacy, that is, through a back-channel of communication between the British and Irish governments and Sinn Fein/IRA. From then on, a choreography of role playing unfolded between London, Dublin, and Sinn Fein, with each side helping the others to appear principled in front of their grassroots when in fact compromises were being made.[80]

On 21 October 1994, John Major repealed the exclusion orders on Gerry Adams and Martin McGuinness, the president and vice-president of Sinn Fein. The transition from a period of IRA violence against Unionists and British security forces to a period of relative peace had begun.[81] This was followed by the British government's Framework Document of February 1995, which was roundly rejected by the Order after a meeting between Grand Lodge officers, the Secretary of State, Patrick Mayhew, and Michael Ancram. Though the British delegation tried to convince the Grand Lodge officers that the 'sole purpose of the Document was to get the parties talking and was not an agenda to be imposed', the Orange Delegation 'made it clear to the Secretary of State that the Document offered nothing substantial to Unionism'.

This conclusion was reached after an Orange working party dissected the Document and savaged it as 'unworkable' and not based on 'democratic principles'. The Document's promise that the Irish government accepted the need for Northern Ireland's consent to any constitutional changes was seen by the Orange delegation as irreconcilable with the Dublin High Court's recent defence of articles 2 and 3 of the Irish Constitution, which laid claim to the north.[82] The UUP under Molyneaux also rejected the Document, as did a majority of the Unionist population in opinion polls. John Major's subsequent writings suggest that he accepted the need for concessions to Nationalists in the Framework Documents in order to entrench the recent Republican ceasefire.[83]

The Legacy of the Troubles

The British had temporarily pacified Nationalism, but where did this leave the Unionists? A reduction in IRA violence was welcome and certainly swayed the 'silent minority' of Unionists who had consistently been willing to accept power-sharing. But for the majority of the Unionist population, the predations of the IRA had left a deep legacy of hurt, anger, and mistrust towards Catholics. The British government and its institutions (apart from the Army) also lost a considerable amount of credibility among Unionists during the Troubles. This was partly because the British needed to impose unpopular reforms on the Unionists in order to redress the socioeconomic discrimination and electoral gerrymandering that had characterized the Stormont regime. Yet the bigger factor was the perception of a weak British commitment to security, and a British willingness to draw a moral equivalence between Sinn Fein, which largely supported violence as a political tool, and Unionist parties, most of which eschewed violence. Once again, the British ethical position could be justified in only utilitarian rather than deontological terms, and this makes it difficult for those of deontological bent (such as Kantian liberals or non-violent Unionists) to accept.

We can gauge the depth of Unionist outrage through the Orange Order. As a communal organization with particular strength in border areas and a high enlistment rate in the UDR and RUC, it bore the brunt of IRA violence. Security resolutions dated back to the IRA's border campaign and were a pretty consistent feature of Orange reports through the 1970s, but increased in volume after the peak of violence of 1972–6. In the 1980s, Protestant fatality rates were generally running at half the level of 1972–6, yet security concerns took centre stage for the first time.[84] Why? A major reason was the settling of Unionist fears of a British withdrawal. Parade bans, a feature of 1969–72 UUP–Orange negotiations, also receded as a general issue despite local flashpoints because Orangemen came to accept that certain areas like the Bogside in Derry and Springfield Road or Ardoyne in Belfast were simply no-go zones for Loyalist parades.[85] Finally, Unionist unity had been achieved on constitutional questions post-Faulkner, and security complaints reinforced Unionists' constitutional position that the defeat of the IRA and an end to violence were a *sine qua non* for constitutional talks. Clearly the Order's members did not maintain a limited focus on the saving of Protestant lives, and one may surmise that they valued their political Unionism and right to parade as highly as—if not more highly than—their own security. In effect, many were willing to risk death rather than 'surrender' to the Republican enemy.

This is not to say that the bloodshed had no effect. On the contrary, the killings were sequestered and etched themselves on to the Unionist collective memory, especially at local level. Behind the fatality statistics (albeit reduced over 1972–6) lay unrequited emotions. The depth of grassroots Unionist resentment at both the IRA and government inaction comes across in numerous resolutions. In late 1978, Bessbrook District Lodge 11 wrote a resolution to County Armagh Grand Lodge:

Ill. 7 Tullyvallen Orange Hall —Located in South Armagh near the border, this hall was attacked by PIRA gunmen, who burst through the door beneath the 'exit' sign on 1 September 1975 killing five Orangemen.

I have been instructed by the . . . members of the above District Lodge to express our disgust and protest at the apparent lack of security in our area. Recent murders in the Newry area of members of our Order underline serious breaches in security. The innocent victims singled out for assassination by the Provisional IRA gunmen had strong ties with our District Lodge and their killings revived poignant memories of our great loss at Kingsmills in January, 1976 [when ten Protestants in a minibus were killed at a bogus checkpoint by IRA gunmen]. We are convinced that the latest killings would not have happened had security been maintained at a higher level in the South Armagh-South Down area... We are convinced that these brave men [ordinary policemen and soldiers] are having to act under restraints imposed by Government ministers and security chiefs. We therefore demand the leaders of our Order put pressure on Government ministers and security chiefs to raise the level of activity against Republican terrorists in our midst. This plea is made now so that further murders of good men from within our ranks can be avoided. Trusting our fears will be understood and acted upon, W. Kennedy, secretary.[86]

The Kingsmills killings had a devastating effect at community level in the village of Kingsmills (over 90 per cent Protestant). Questioned by a social scientist in the 1990s, one resident recalled: 'Things were never the same after that [Kingsmills massacre]...how could they be?' A subsequent IRA attack on a local UDR base killed three more local Protestants, and the base never reopened. These killings had a knock-on effect which led to a Protestant exodus: in the early 1990s the post office and local grocery store closed and the commercial core of the village fell into neglect. The local primary school closed in 1995, further repelling young Protestant families from the area. Finally, four of five local Orange halls were attacked in 1994–5. These were perceived locally as attacks on the community, reinforcing the sense in which Orangeism and Unionism are one in border areas. As one local resident noted with alarm, 'this was an attack, not just on a building, but on a people'.[87] Other studies show a similar pattern of UDR deaths leading to a Protestant out-migration, thus underscoring the link between IRA assassinations and 'ethnic cleansing'.[88]

With this much at stake, it is no surprise that calls for action from the Unionist front line reached a fever pitch. In spring 1979, Loughgall District 3 Lodge (Armagh) expressed its view of the IRA's cold-blooded campaign in border areas:

[Loughgall District lodge] Condemns the Dastardly acts committed by the IRA in murdering members of the RUC, RUC Reserve, UDR, Army and Prison Officers and calls upon the Government to pursue vigorously the IRA until it is destroyed. We would further call for the reintroduction of the death penalty for those convicted of terrorist murders. We extend our very deepest sympathy to all who have been bereaved and pray that God will sustain them in their time of grief.[89]

A related resolution from Kildarton LOL 540 in Armagh District criticized the former Secretary of State Roy Mason for making statements and not backing them up: 'It has been apparent for some time that there have always been bombings on an increased scale after statements by the secretary of state and we hope that the Orange Order can convince Mr Mason of his errors in this important matter.'[90] Armagh County passed these resolutions to Grand Lodge and also expressed disappointment to the UUP MP Harold McCusker that Ian Gow, a Tory MP sympathetic to Unionism (later assassinated by the IRA at his home in 1990), was prevented by the British from visiting the victims. Armagh County wanted to show Mr Gow the bereaved and injured, and have him tour devastated frontier areas and towns.[91]

A number of high-profile IRA killings buffeted the Order in 1981. In June 1981, the Order expressed its

dismay and deep revulsion of the murders of our highly esteemed Members, Sir Norman Stronge [former speaker of Stormont] and Mr. James Stronge [his son; both killed at home by IRA gunmen]. It utterly condemns the miscreants who perpetuated these dastardly deeds. The depravity of people who stoop to such criminal acts is beyond the comprehension of all good citizens. Grand Lodge reiterates its demands for greater security for Border Protestants, and for every effort to be made to bring the murderers to justice.[92]

At the next Grand Lodge session, the Order mourned the loss of the Rev. Robert Bradford, a high-profile UUP MP. In addition, the chaplain of the middle-class LOL 688 was 'ruthlessly murdered by the IRA'. This was followed by the minute of silence observed at the start of most Grand Lodge meetings.[93]

The Order did its best, raising the security issue time and again with a succession of home secretaries after 1972.[94] Though it had helped to advance the 'Ulsterization' of security and was successfully getting its members to join the UDR and RUC, it was becoming exasperated by the (politically tactical) restraint of the British authorities as expressed through both the security forces and the Chief Constable of the RUC. The IRA's hunger strike campaign had kicked into high gear and was successfully nudging Thatcher's government toward concessions. Thatcher's administration believed that the best way forward was to walk softly on the security front and push for cooperation with the Republic—a stance which the Tories knew would involve constitutional concessions that would rub against the cherished wishes of most Unionists.

Orange resentment burst into the open at Grand Lodge in December 1982 when a mood of war gripped minds in the period following the hunger strike. Fred King conveyed the view that brethren in his district (Coleraine) felt that the Grand Lodge should be calling for Thatcher to move quickly, as in the Falklands War, 'before it becomes too late'. Nigel Hamilton spoke of his closeness to John Martin, 'murdered three weeks ago'. The Rev. Warren Porter asked when the government would do something and 'stop pushing us off. Our patience is wearing thin—it has come to an end. Has the time not come to tell the secretary of state . . . what we consider must be done?'[95]

Smyth was more realistic about Orange power and cynical about the responsiveness of the British. He said that if 'the brethren wished us to go back to the secretary of state we would go' but seemed unconvinced that anything would happen, lamenting that if Orangemen thought the government would respond, they were fooling themselves. He added that Orangemen must examine their own home and personal security and that in the event of changes in the security situation (perhaps escalation into chaos), 'we must watch our position and [re-evaluate our] restraint'. Despite their pessimism, it was resolved to seek another meeting with the Secretary of State. At this, the Rev. Dickinson again lambasted the Secretary of State for appearing content with the security situation, declaring that the 'Government really want[s] to have us in a United Ireland by fair means or foul'. Rather than another meeting, he favoured an honest message to the Unionist people about the government's hidden agenda: 'Then the People will know if our political and moral position is in danger.'[96] In the event, a meeting with the Secretary of State was arranged, though the Chief Constable refused the Order an audience, countering that meetings were taking up too much time each day. This only served to reinforce the impression within the Order of reduced political clout with Direct Rule administrations, underlining the fact that the British could not be trusted and adding urgency to the need for devolution.[97]

Meanwhile, geo-demographic aspects of the conflict were resurfacing and rising in intensity. Always important, these issues were brought to the fore by PIRA killings. The narrative of 'ethnic cleansing', which was to become a prominent Unionist buzzword, emerged at this time in connection with the IRA's murder campaign in border areas. Smyth thought there was no 'easy answer' on security, though a delegate proffered that the 'B' Specials would have sorted the situation out in six months. Smyth poured cold water on this suggestion, reminding his interlocutor that the IRA's border campaign of 1956–62 in fact lasted six years. He also warned brethren that Protestants should not be

gulled into thinking that those being murdered were in particular UDR and security members. An economic campaign is being waged in the country on bachelor and single business men in the hope of creating an RC takeover of businesses and farms. Bread warfare could be another aspect of this struggle especially those who have indulged in trade with Eire for profit. There are quite a large number of Protestant enclaves where young men will not suffer the discomfort [i.e. risk of death] of joining the RUC or Police Reserve.[98]

The master of Tyrone's District 9 Lodge spoke of local Protestants being 'driven out of town' in Newtownstewart after the IRA blew up the local police barracks.[99] In Fermanagh, Inver Temperance LOL 920 was given permission to circularize the membership as follows:

For the first time in the history of our Lodge we have been compelled to make an appeal to our fellow members . . . During the present terrorist campaign our hall was vandalised by republican elements. Two farmhouses in the area were also attacked by republicans and one farmer was burnt out of his homestead. The Protestant school in the village of Rosslea was destroyed by a large proxy bomb, which was left outside the

RUC station. The school has now been closed and the pupils have been transferred to another school. The last remaining Protestant businessman in the village was shot dead in his Supermarket by the Provos. Fortunately the business was taken over by another loyalist to prevent the enemies of our country buying the property. The few remaining Protestants, who make up about 20% of the population, are endeavouring to hold on in this strife torn part of Ulster.[100]

The appeals and tenacity must have paid off since the lodge had a healthy total of thirty-five members in 1991 and thirty-six in 2001.[101] At this juncture, it is worth noting that land and demography were consistent and interrelated concerns in the post-war period. We can understand this in terms of ethnic conflict, which at the most primordial level is about achieving a congruence between ethnicity (i.e. demography or 'blood') and the maximum amount of land ('soil').[102] The PIRA has been guilty of pursuing this strategy using violence, especially in border areas, while, since the Troubles, Protestant paramilitaries have done the same in greater Belfast. The result has been an increase in residential segregation that has continued since the IRA ceasefire of 1994.[103]

Much of this story is backed up by interview evidence. Henry Reid, the Clogher Valley Orangeman whose invitation sparked Ruth Dudley Edwards's book *The Faithful Tribe*, conveys a strong sense of this to me. A farmer and bed-and-breakfast proprietor, Reid is my age and has many things in common with me, such as a young family, an interest in books, and a facility with technology. Yet he interweaves this with a sense of faith, place, and history which is extremely difficult for the average metropolitan North American or Western European to grasp. This underlines the blend of tradition and modernity which makes Northern Ireland unique and questions any simple 'end of history' modernization thesis. During our drive and subsequent meal, Reid points out that there are many similarities between the tribal conflict in Northern Ireland and the war then raging in the former Yugoslavia, openly referring to Ulster Protestants as 'my tribe'. He speaks of how there is a battle for control of land in these border areas, with the PIRA targeting farmers' sons in order to gain access to properties. He mentions how the PIRA successfully reduced the Protestant population of Newtownbutler from 30–40 per cent pre-Troubles to almost nil at present.

The segmental nature of society (which Emile Durkheim took as the hall-mark of a pre-modern society) is at play here. For example, Reid speaks of 'tribes within tribes' in this area. Free Presbyterians, for instance, tend to marry each other and socialize apart to some extent. There are Orange families whose sons are expected to join the Order and face social ostracism if they 'let the side down', while those from 'non-joining' backgrounds face no such pressure. On the Catholic side, Reid describes most as decent, albeit with a minority from 'provie [i.e. PIRA] families' who possess an ethnic cleansing agenda handed down from their parents.[104] Research shows that border

Catholics are generally more willing to live in mixed areas and countenance intermarriage and inter-communal land sales than Protestants.[105] One explanation for this is that Catholics are demographically growing and therefore self-confident, while Protestants are demographically ageing and thus far more insecure about their ability to retain their demographic position in the face of cross-community mixing. In this regard, the experience of Protestants in the Republic of Ireland is not encouraging.[106]

In border areas, collective memories are long, particularly among Protestants, since most are lifelong residents while more Catholics are in-migrants from nearby areas. Such memories are maintained by local monuments to dead UDR and RUC men, which serve similar functions to wall murals in encoding heroic deeds and memories. Such monuments are ubiquitous among border Protestants in Northern Ireland.[107] Reid shows me how this process ensures that local people inhabit a 'living past' which intertwines present events with those of the past. After a hair-raising drive at breakneck speed at dusk along single-track roads, we reach a black obelisk on a country hilltop. Reid stresses that the memorial—erected only in the 1990s—commemorates the twenty-odd Orangemen (mostly RUC and UDR men) killed within the vantage point of this Clogher lookout. In surreal fashion, he recounts the deaths of various individuals, some shot on their roofs while at work. He underlines that Protestants and Catholics know each other—with Protestants sometimes knowing the Republicans who killed their relatives—in these communities, though interaction is often limited to the economic sphere.[108]

As in South Tyrone, 'ethnic cleansing' of Protestants occurred in South Armagh. Though the Crossmaglen–Slieve Gullion tip of South Armagh is effectively Protestant-free, there is an active Protestant community in the Catholic majority zone just north of this area. During a drive through country roads in this area, a local Orangeman, Trevor Geary, suggests that segregation occurs in patchwork fashion in rural border districts. Thus certain townlands like Aughnagurgan, near Keady, remain overwhelmingly Protestant and local Orangemen maintain links to Protestants living across the porous border in Knockanin, County Monaghan—some of whom attend lodges in Northern Ireland. During the passage over rough valley roads, Geary spoke of 'settler' families of Protestants moving back to the country from 'safer' towns to build homes and raise families in the area. There are echoes in this language of 'settlers' of what things might have been like in the Plantation period. A similar lexicon pervades terms such as 'Indian country', used by one Fermanagh Orangeman I interviewed to describe Catholic upland areas in north Fermanagh.[109]

Geary had driven me through a transition zone between Protestant-dominated North Armagh and Catholic-dominated South Armagh which is just over a quarter Protestant. This takes in all areas south of the towns of Armagh and Tandragee and north of Newry. The zone also formed the basis of a study by Brendan Murtagh in 1999. Murtagh found that the predominant trend in the 1971–91 period was towards increasing segregation of the population. South Armagh Catholics have a considerable fertility advantage over Protestants, and this, combined with IRA 'ethnic cleansing' and Protestants' preference not to be isolated from the bulk of their co-ethnics, led to Protestant decline. Locally, a patchwork of segregation at ward level obtains, with only seven of thirty-two wards being 'mixed' (i.e. with under 70 per cent from a single group). This refracts the growth in Catholic population in different ways. Thus between 1971 and 1991, Keady's Catholic population rose from 79 per cent to 89 per cent while in Tandragee, Catholics declined from 16 to 13 per cent.[110]

In contrast to this narrative of decline is the shining performance of Orangeism. During a period of sharp Protestant decline, the Unionist population has mobilized more strongly behind Orangeism. In fact, the Orange Order has almost held the line on membership in *absolute terms* in border areas and even registered a membership increase in heavily Catholic South Down (see Table 5.4). Fermanagh and South Tyrone are also areas with a high rate of Protestant membership of the Order and have bucked the post-1971 trend of a decline by a third in membership.[111] The performance of border areas is in stark contrast to the big membership declines in the northern, Protestant-majority parts of Armagh and Down. Some of this phenomenon may be accounted for by Protestants who leave the border yet continue to commute to their border lodges, but this cannot explain the trend of northern decline and southern vitality. My impression in South Armagh was of a great deal of local dynamism and mobilization in response to the threat posed by Republicanism.

Figure 5.7 shows the pattern of lodge sizes against a background of Northern Ireland wards shaded by the proportion of Catholics. It is immediately evident that Orange lodges can be found in wards such as Derrynoose (Armagh), Donaghmore (Down), or Derrylin (Fermanagh), which are at least 85–90 per

Table 5.4 Orangeism and the Border: Proportion of Orange Membership in Northern and Southern Districts of Armagh and County Down, 1971–2004

	1961	1971	1981	1991	2001	2004
North Armagh	83%	83%	81%	80%	80%	79%
South Armagh	17%	17%	19%	20%	20%	21%
North Down	73%	71%	70%	71%	68%	62%
South Down	27%	29%	30%	29%	32%	38%

South Armagh districts are Keady, Newtownhamilton, Markethill, and Bessbrook; South Down districts are Rathfriland, Mourne, Newry, Loughbrickland, Castlewellan, and Carlingford Lough.
Source: GOLI membership returns, 1961–2004.

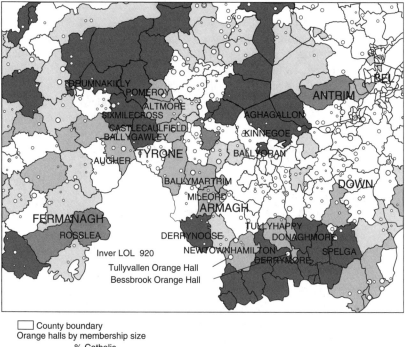

County boundary
Orange halls by membership size
% Catholic

○	0–24	▢	0–0.144
○	25–39	▢	0.144–0.336
○	40–56	▢	0.336–0.552
○	57–83	▢	0.552–0.782
○	84–125	▢	0.782–0.995

Figure 5.7 The Orange 'horseshoe': Catholic population and membership-adjusted Orange halls in the Nationalist borderlands, 1991 (naming strongly Catholic wards with a significant Orange presence)

Sources: GOLI membership returns, 1991; OSNI digital boundaries 1984; Northern Ireland Census 1991.

cent Catholic. South Down is a particularly vibrant Orange area, and it is no exaggeration to characterize border Orangeism as the healthiest in the province. When it comes to Orangeism, adversity certainly brings strength. There are limits to this, however: the fifty-five members of Carlingford Lough District Lodge 16 (which transferred to County Down in 2001) form the only outpost of Orangeism in the 'ethnically cleansed' stretch of Northern Ireland border wards between Newtownhamilton in the west and Lisnacree in the east. The few Protestants in this 'bandit country' are too sparse and weak to combine into lodges. Throughout the border area, the sense of being under siege helps to perpetuate Protestant fears of decline, which often conflate 'ethnic cleansing', demographic decline, and a general alienation from the peace process.[112]

136

Protestants may be losing ground in demographic terms, but if so, they remain reluctant to yield territory to the growing Catholic population. Despite a surfeit of young Catholic farmers (due to their higher birth rate), Protestants have managed to keep a good deal of land out of their hands. Kirk's study of Glenravel ward in County Antrim (with a population around 65 per cent Protestant) suggests why: between 1958 and 1987, only 15 per cent of lands sold by Protestants went to Catholic buyers.[113] On the border, where Protestants lack a comfortable majority, one would expect ethnic closure to be more intense, and Murtagh found that Protestants had a more proprietary attitude to land sales than Catholics, though both indulged in intra-communal practices. This attitude is reinforced by informal sanctions running the gamut from 'friendly advice' to threats, as well as a system of 'gatekeeper' auctioneers, solicitors, and estate agents who withdraw land from sale if a buyer of the correct faith is not found.[114]

Both sides play this game but the Protestant community, which tends to be land-rich but child-poor, has been playing demographic defence for some time and has thus taken more radical steps to protect itself. In times past, Protestant defensiveness was driven more by the perceived fear of 'peaceful penetration' from the south than by demographic reality (which used to be that of Protestant growth). For example, as early as 1938, Grand Lodge approved an Orange Protection (Land) Fund 'to assist orange brethren in . . . Fermanagh to purchase and retain farms and businesses . . . That such fund shall be maintained by a levy of a minimum of one shilling per member, per annum, on private lodge returns.' In 1951, Fermanagh County Lodge expressed its concern that land was 'being bought by the Ministry of Agriculture and sold to RCs in areas where [Protestants] could ill afford to lose property to the other side' since the Protestant 'majority was very slender'. By the 1950s, Protestants felt that their discriminatory practices in housing, electoral boundaries, and the allocation of work permits were leading to demographic victory, though vigilance needed to be maintained. Victory could occur through either Protestant immigration or Catholic emigration—both of which were characteristics of the 1922–61 period. For example, despite a lower birth rate, the Protestant proportion of the population in both Fermanagh and Tyrone increased between 1926 and 1961, slipping only slightly by 1971.[115]

Enormous political pressure was brought to bear by border Unionists on successive Stormont governments to allocate work permits to 'Loyal' immigrants from Eire while denying them to prospective Catholic immigrants from the Republic. A similar attitude characterized Unionists' approach to the supply of public housing. Even new industries were to be discouraged if they altered the ethnic balance in the wrong direction. In this, the Orange Order and local branches of the Unionist Party worked hand in hand. The Lands and Houses Subcommittee of the UUP, set up in 1959, worked to facilitate Protestant property acquisition. Its first move was to vote £40,000 from party coffers to be transferred to five county Protestant defence funds. Of the five, four were run by the Orange Order, and the Derry fund by the local UUP party branch.[116] The results were encouraging for border Unionists. In 1963, the Fermanagh County Lodge noted with pleasure that in twenty-five years 'we have managed to reduce the Nationalist majority [in Enniskillen] and make it a Unionist majority'.[117] In border areas, a traditional subsistence-agriculture view associating demographic increase with land tenure held out despite the fact that demographic dynamics in the border towns owed far more to economic developments.

Tyrone's call for a central Orange land and property fund eventually proved successful.[118] All of this did not prevent Protestants—even Orangemen—from selling land to Catholics. In Fermanagh in 1960, an Orange law against selling and letting property to Catholics was passed by one district and was discussed at county level. At the meeting, one member expressed the view that 'a law like this would interfere with freedom of the subject and that there were already too many bylaws', adding that 'it would be nonsense to commit Protestants to only let to Protestants' and that common sense needed to be used.[119] A quarter of a century later, tolerant views were less commonly aired as battle lines hardened. One Loughgall-area Orangeman who sold property to a Catholic 'knowing well that Protestants were prepared to purchase [the] property' found this out the hard way. He tried to defend himself against all charges, alleging that he had used the proceeds from the sale to buy a more substantial plot of land from a Catholic, and that he had repeatedly tried to sell the land to Protestants at lower rates but they failed to pay as promised. Such economic niceties cut little ice with County Armagh Lodge, which rationalized its decision on the basis that 'it was the feeling in the Diamond area that Protestants support one another and no property be allowed to go over to RC ownership'.[120]

Tyrone had proposed a central land fund in 1964, and in 1992 the idea took flight, leading to the formation of Grand Lodge's Ulster Land Fund out of lodge subscriptions in 1995.[121] The Land Fund merely built upon an acknowledged social reality. By the late 1990s it had amassed almost £150,000, but even this figure was not sufficient to move mountains. 'The Land Fund has given assistance to 5 Districts to hold property in strategic areas and have now purchased a house in a Border town where the few remaining Protestant families are endeavouring to hold out,' reported Grand Lodge. 'This latest acquisition has left our account overdrawn and other requests for assistance are awaiting—Can your district help?'[122]

Ethnic boundaries are strengthened by territorial closure of the soil, but sealed through endogamy of the 'blood'. In this area, as with land sales, Protestants are less likely than Catholics to endorse inter-ethnic contact.[123] Once again, it is difficult to abstract Protestant attitudes from their demographic context. Most offspring of mixed marriages who are brought up with religion are raised as Catholics, and thus a mixed marriage carries a different demographic implication for Protestants from that which it does for Catholics. The Orange Order makes its position very clear on this matter through Orange Law 4: 'Any member dishonouring the Institution by marrying a Roman Catholic or attending any of the unscriptural, superstitious and idolatrous worship of the Church of Rome shall be expelled.' In the period 1964–2002, roughly a third of the 600-odd members expelled from the Order were charged with marrying or cohabiting with a Roman Catholic. This figure rises to 45 per cent if we include those expelled for attendance at Catholic weddings, funerals, or baptisms.[124]

Unlike in Canada, where a split within the Order between liberals and conservatives in the 1990s eventually led to a repeal of the intermarriage law, there has been no recent slackening of communal fervour within the Order in Ireland. This includes Eire, since lodges in the Republic have had to expel only two members for marrying a Catholic in the entire post-1963 period.[125] These data suggest that despite ample evidence of Protestant–Catholic comity, extending from personal friendship to loans of regalia and band instruments between Orangemen and Hibernians in the early 1960s, inter-ethnic contact only goes so far.[126] Murtagh makes a similar point, noting that while individuals will share equipment or help each other, they will not do so if—as with land sales—this compromises group interests.[127]

The Order and Unionist Public Opinion in the Wake of the Anglo-Irish Agreement

Orangeism tapped a deep well of Unionist bitterness over Troubles-related deaths to make its case against power-sharing with Nationalists. Throughout the 1972–95 period, the Order stood by its post-Sunningdale 'United Unionist' logic, which asked that Northern Ireland be treated similarly to other parts of the United Kingdom. This meant a majoritarian, first-past-the-post electoral system and equal citizenship without ethnic power-sharing or employment quotas. One could defend the Order's refusal to countenance any recognition of group rights by invoking an individual human-rights-based political theory. On this theory, only individuals should have votes, not groups, so there is no case for proportional representation. Yet the Order's manifest opposition to human rights conventions ('homosexuality forced on us because of Direct Rule'), cross-community initiatives, and integrated education indicates that individualist logic was used only where convenient.[128] Even when it might have suited the Order's purposes, it refused to play ball with the secular logic of human rights. In reply to a lodge which enquired about how it might combat discrimination against local Protestants in employment, Central Committee advised not to write to the Fair Employment Agency as this would recognize the latter's existence.[129]

Bryan notes that the Order did not defend its right to march through Catholic areas by referring to liberal human rights conventions (or even British liberalism), but through an appeal to tradition.[130] Likewise, the Order did not defend its opposition to the group rights (or consociational) theory of power-sharing through an appeal to universal human rights of 'civil and religious liberty' but rather by invoking the precedent and tradition of British democracy, and seeking to return to a pre-1972 state of affairs. This is not to say that it lacked a vocabulary of liberalism. The notion of 'civil and religious liberty' has a universal import, and was often used. Also, the Order was capable of assimilating the forward-looking logic of devolution and federalism in the early 1990s.[131] But in the final analysis, it largely failed to come to terms with the emerging human rights discourse in the period up to the mid 1990s.

Ill. 8 Bombing of House of Orange, Dublin Road —During the Troubles, numerous Orange halls were burned or targeted by republican terrorists.

More serious was an apparent decline in the willingness of the wider Unionist community to favour a return to Stormont-style majoritarianism. In 1992, the proportion of Protestants who favoured Northern Ireland's 'full integration' into the United Kingdom (40.5 per cent) exceeded the proportion favouring Stormont-style devolution (33.7 per cent), the Grand Lodge's overwhelming preference. And while fewer than a quarter of Protestants expressed a *preference* for power-sharing, 73 per cent said they would 'accept' it. Finally, only 22 per cent of Unionist respondents felt that the AIA would lead them

Table 5.5 Constitutional Preferences, Protestants, 1992

	Power-sharing with Catholics, but within the UK	Integration	Stormont majoritarianism	Direct Rule with Anglo-Irish Agreement
Would prefer	17.9%	40.5%	33.7%	3.3%
Would accept	73.0%	90.4%	83.4%	36.0%

Source: Elliott, Ditch, and Moxon-Browne, *Northern Ireland General Election and Political Attitudes Survey, 1992*.

into a United Ireland, as opposed to 58 per cent who disagreed with this statement (see Table 5.5).[132]

Regionally, there are some similarities with 1978. Acceptance of power-sharing among Unionists varies a good deal by region. In some areas, acceptance is barely 50 per cent, while in others it is close to 100 per cent, as shown in Figure 5.8, where lightly shaded areas are more accepting

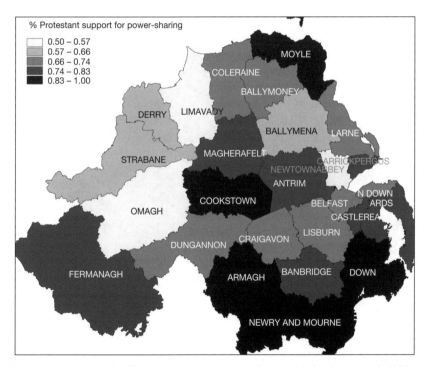

Figure 5.8 Protestant willingness to accept power-sharing, by district council, 1992

Sources: Elliott, Ditch, and Moxon-Browne, *Northern Ireland General Election and Political Attitudes Survey, 1992*; OSNI digital boundaries.

of power-sharing than darker areas. As in 1978, west Tyrone remains a significantly anti-power-sharing area, but by 1992, Protestants along the southern
border from Fermanagh to South Down were no longer in the forefront of
opposition to power-sharing.

Regional factors are less important in determining political attitudes in 1992
than in 1978. Indeed, the overwhelming trend is towards greater province-
wide uniformity. Formerly liberal areas like County Londonderry and greater
Belfast have become more sceptical of power-sharing, while formerly anti-
power-sharing border Unionists (Fermanagh, Tyrone, Armagh) and those
from mid Antrim have become more accepting. Figure 5.9 shows the contrast
in terms of attitudes between 1978 and 1992, with darker areas showing where
opinion has softened (and vice versa) in the intervening period. It also appears
that there is no link between the proportion of Catholics in an area and the
support for power-sharing.

The results of statistical tests shown in Figure 5.10 confirm that regional
differences are still important in 1992 when it comes to determining Protestant

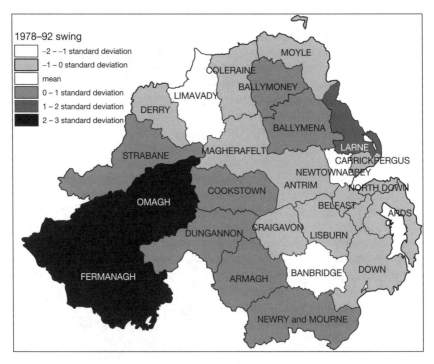

Figure 5.9 Change in Protestant acceptance of power-sharing, 1978–1992, by district
council

Sources: Moxon-Browne, *Northern Ireland Attitude Survey, 1978*; Elliott, Ditch, and Moxon-Browne,
Northern Ireland General Election and Political Attitudes Survey, 1992; OSNI digital boundaries.

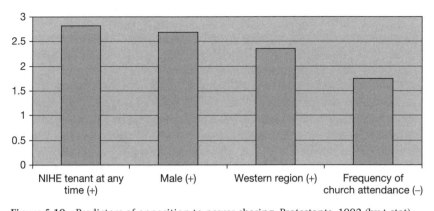

Figure 5.10 Predictors of opposition to power-sharing, Protestants, 1992 (by t-stat)
Source: Elliott, Ditch, and Moxon-Browne, *Northern Ireland General Election and Political Attitudes Survey, 1992.*

attitudes to power-sharing, but less so than in 1978. Education and class are no longer significant, but if respondents were ever a tenant of public housing (Northern Ireland Housing Executive) during their lifetimes, they were more likely to oppose power-sharing than those in private accommodation. Men were now significantly more likely to oppose power-sharing than women, while frequent church attenders were somewhat more likely to accept it. (Though insignificant here, this variable was significant in other models.)

The Order's exhortations and mobilization had obviously failed to stem Unionist acceptance of power-sharing. This does not mean that Molyneaux's UUP suffered from its rejectionist position. Few Unionist respondents favoured power-sharing, despite their willingness to accept it. Good UUP election results also prove that Unionist voters were comfortable with Molyneaux's aversion to power-sharing. Notwithstanding the occasional electoral pacts with the DUP in certain constituencies, Molyneaux generally managed to contain the Paisley factor through the early 1990s.[133] The Order usually did not instruct its members how to vote, though it broke this rule to speak out in favour of the UUP candidate Jim Nicholson in his battle against Paisley in the European elections of 1989: 'The Grand Lodge of Ireland calls on the electorate to give a clear message to Europe on Thursday. Naturally we commend Brother Jim Nicholson representing the resilience of our Armagh brethren to the Province. Three hundred years after William of Orange came to Europe let us send help to Europe in the struggle for democracy.'[134] This shot in the arm failed to prevent Nicholson being eclipsed by Paisley by 30–22 per cent on first-preference votes, though Nicholson was elected in the second round because of vote transfers from Paisley supporters.[135]

The UUP was used to losing to the DUP in European contests. More worrying

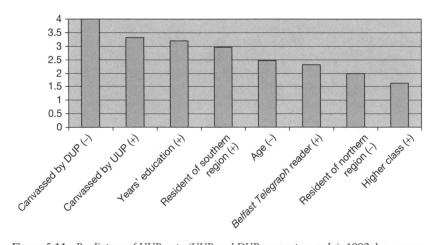

Figure 5.11 Predictors of UUP vote (UUP and DUP supporters only), 1992, by z-score

Sources: Elliott, Ditch, and Moxon-Browne, *Northern Ireland General Election and Political Attitudes Survey, 1992*; detailed statistical output available at <http://www.sneps.net/OO/bk1stats.htm>.

therefore was the continuing trend among the younger generation to drift away from the UUP—Grand Lodge's preferred party—in other elections. Leaving the effects of party canvassing to one side, statistical analysis of the 1992 Northern Ireland social survey data shows that, as in 1978, one of the predictors of a vote for the DUP over the UUP is relative youth. Figure 5.11 shows that party canvassing, higher education level, residence in the southern border region, and *Belfast Telegraph* readership also predict support for the UUP (as opposed to the DUP) in 1992. Class, which was weakly significant in 1978, is mildly insignificant in 1992.

The role of region had shifted 180 degrees since 1978, with southern border Unionists switching their allegiance back to the UUP by 1992. Much of this has to do with the link between the parties and the power-sharing question. In 1978, Protestant respondents' party support was by far the strongest predictor of their view on the power-sharing question, but by 1992, party vote was totally insignificant.[136] Greater acceptance of power-sharing by border Unionists is part of the equation, but the bigger story is the UUP's success in shaking off the accommodationist image it picked up under Faulkner. This suggests that Molyneaux's toughness on the power-sharing question successfully allayed the fears of 'no' Unionists such as many Orangemen and border Protestants, weaning them away from the DUP.

Overall, the Order's political position was a difficult one: it was more hardline than the Unionist population on constitutional issues, but backed an Official Unionist Party which was supported in part by non-Orange, well-educated, Belfast-area 'civic Unionists'. Traditionalists were well represented within the UUP, but civic Unionists remained in the party, backing

UUP modernizers like Robert McCusker, Robert McCartney, and, later, David Trimble.[137] Youth, who were increasingly less likely to join the Order, seemed (as in 1978) to be opting for the more radical tones of the DUP. Like its UUP cousins, the Order was also failing to appeal to younger Unionists, many of whom were joining independent Loyalist marching bands.[138] These are patterns that have accelerated into the present day, causing a series of splits within the Order over policy.

Ill. 9   Martin Smyth and James Molyneaux Making Presentation, 1997 —Both men rose from ordinary backgrounds to high positions in the Order and Ulster Unionist Party. For nearly two decades, they successfully rebuffed all British constitutional reforms.

The Molyneaux–Smyth axis helped mobilize Orangemen and most Unionists in support of a comfortable anti-power-sharing brand of UUP politics from the seventies to the nineties. The UUP's goal was a return to a majoritarian Stormont within the UK.[139] For all its flaws, this strategy kept both reformers and Paisleyites at bay. Yet this balancing act was under great pressure since liberal modernizers in the UUP were beginning to pull one way while younger Unionist 'no' voters, alienated from their established traditions, tugged in the other direction. More and more, the DUP was assuming the mantle of 'no' Unionism and attracting the votes of a new generation. With the arrival of David Trimble on the scene in 1995, modernizing currents would be released within the UUP which would lead to the Order's complete estrangement from the party.

Part II

Orangeism at the Dawn of the Third Millennium, 1995–2005

6

The Battle of Drumcree

In 1995, the Orange Order entered an increasingly turbulent phase of its existence, fraught with danger for the organization. On the face of it, this is a puzzling development. Republican guns had largely fallen silent with the IRA ceasefire negotiated through back-channel diplomacy between Dublin, London, the SDLP, and Sinn Fein. This process may have alienated Unionists from the British, but it should not have threatened the Order. The problem was that the decline of IRA and Protestant paramilitary violence was accompanied by new 'proxy wars' based on local-level conflict. This built upon the familiar Troubles story of 'ethnic cleansing' in urban residential areas or rural tracts, involving Republican or Loyalist intimidation of the local minority, beginning with threats or abuse and escalating through beatings and firebombing of homes to plain murder.

Increasingly, however, conflicts over marching were gaining in prominence. This was partly due to a strategic move on the part of Sinn Fein/IRA to transfer the theatre of conflict with Unionists to the local level. This was to be achieved by mobilizing the residents of Catholic areas into 'residents' groups' to resist Orange marches.[1] Having said this, one must bear in mind the fact that Orange marches had never been popular with Catholics. Though Catholics often watched Orange marches in certain areas during the pre-Troubles period, the history of the province had been marred for over a century by conflicts between marchers (Orange or Republican) and aggrieved residents.[2] As Kennaway notes:

Most thinking people within and without the Institution knew very well that to say that we would 'walk out [sic] traditional routes' was simply nonsense. With demographic changes over the years many routes had been either changed or abandoned. The Orange Order in County Londonderry had not walked in Dungiven since the 1960's . . . Belfast Orangemen had not walked past Holy Cross Roman Catholic Chapel, in Ardoyne, since the early 1970's . . . Sandy Row . . . had not walked down their 'traditional' route of the Grosvenor Road since the early 1970's, when the police told them that they could no longer guarantee their protection. Parades in Coalisland had been long since abandoned. Apart from the megalomania of some Portadown Orange leaders, what was so special about the Garvaghy Road?[3]

Conflicts over Orange parades in such locations as Annalong, County Down, in 1953 or Dungiven, County Londonderry, in 1953, 1959, and 1971 do not fundamentally differ from those which grip Drumcree in Portadown, or which affect the Lower Ormeau Road and Whiterock parades in Belfast. In all cases, Nationalist mobilization against the Order's parades did not occur spontaneously, but required organization. Though the Catholic Church, SDLP, and Gaelic Athletic Association had a presence among Nationalists, the main political actor which was prepared to back up its actions with force was the IRA.

What is clear, though, is the changing balance of power between Protestant and Catholic communities since the incidents in the early 1950s. For, as Jarman and Bryan convincingly argue, parades tend to follow power. In other words, one can parade only if one is safe, and one's protection flows from the willingness of the state to police hostile onlookers. During the Stormont period, the state effectively curtailed Republican parades through acts like the 1951 Public Order (NI) Act or Flags and Emblems Act of 1954. Meanwhile, Orange parades were permitted to proceed along their chosen routes thanks to their status as 'traditional' processions. Yet, as Jarman and Bryan point out, tradition has favoured the expansion of Orange parades since the Order's right to parade was backed up by Stormont state power and the RUC in a way that Republican parades were not. As a result, the number of 'traditional' Orange routes came vastly to exceed that of Nationalists. Since the 1960s, British pressure, Republican agitation, and IRA violence have led to an expansion in Nationalist parading and resistance to Unionist parading through 'Nationalist' areas.

This agitation has not affected the number of Loyalist parades, which has increased steadily since 1985.[4] However, most of these parades are the work of independent marching bands that are not connected to the Orange Order. Some see the upsurge in independent marching band activity as a *surrogate* for participation in the Orange Order. Thus younger Unionists favour the drink, conviviality, and instant gratification of marching over the formality of the quasi-Masonic Orange meetings, laws, lectures, and rituals. Even within those bands that take part in Orange marches, the level of musicianship has declined as the more elaborate silver bands have come to be replaced by the cruder instrumentalism of the so-called 'Blood and Thunder' or 'Kick the Pope' bands. The latter play a narrower repertoire of music focused more intently on Protestant solidarity.[5] The culture of marching bands is shaped by their youthful members rather than the more elderly senior officers of many Orange lodges. Action replaces deliberation and religiosity and thus the Orange tradition is 'translated' into a different realm of practice. All of this may account for the decline of Orangeism at a time of rising marching band activity.[6]

Throughout the long history of Irish marching conflicts, the public authorities have been caught in the crossfire. The police have never been keen on public disorder, and there has also been a third-party state interest in limiting conflicts over parading for reasons of economic and political stability. The authorities strongly played the 'public order' card in the nineteenth and early twentieth centuries as a rationale for restrictions on Orange parading. Though restrictions were muted in the Stormont period because of direct Unionist control, by the 1960s and 1970s, as we have seen, reformist Unionist prime ministers like James Chichester-Clark proposed parade bans, despite their inability to sell these to their recalcitrant flock. Parade re-routings and the cancellation of private lodge parades occasionally occurred during the Troubles. Furthermore, the Unionist leadership and their British Direct Rule heirs could not patrol Republican no-go areas effectively after 1969.[7] As we saw in Chapter 3, the IRA had effectively taken control of Catholic-majority sections of the province like Derry, South Armagh, and much of West Belfast, closing them off to marching routes. This did not affect most Orange parades, though it did impact upon the main Apprentice Boys' route by 1969.[8] In sum, public order has always served as a justification for the state to limit the freedom of expression of marchers, Orange or otherwise.

Demographic change must also be considered. First of all, increase in population led to development—often majority-Catholic—in areas where the Order traditionally marched. More pressingly, the relative Catholic fertility advantage and reversal of Catholic out-migration trends in the post-1950s period led to the growth of Catholic-majority districts through 'tipping' of mixed areas and also through new housing developments such as those bordering the Garvaghy Road in Portadown.[9] Even so, there were limits to the Republicans' success, for they were not able to expand their Easter parading activity into highly self-conscious Loyalist areas. Thus Nationalist parades through Loyalist areas face the same obstacles as Orange parades do in passing through Nationalist areas.[10] In short, a kind of conflict equilibrium has been reached between the competing communities. Though the rule of 'no marches in our area' is now applied more equitably across the board, this hits Unionism harder since Unionists parade at roughly ten times the rate of their Nationalist counterparts.[11] The result of the new equilibrium, therefore, is a disproportionate rise in re-routings or bans of Orange and loyalist band parades.

We can see this graphically in Figure 6.1, where we show the proportion of controlled (ie restricted or re-routed) parades for the pre-Drumcree (1985–94) and post-Drumcree (2001–4) periods. Note that these figures encompass Republican and 'other' parades, and that the proportion of Loyalist parades is always 70–80 per cent of the total. Few parades are contentious, but roughly 55–70 per cent of contentious Loyalist parades are now restricted in some way, many more than in the 1985–94 era. Typically, 80–85 per cent of Loyalist parades are re-routed and the rest face conditions in terms of music, timing, or bands.[12] How does this affect the Order? Jarman and Bryan break Orange

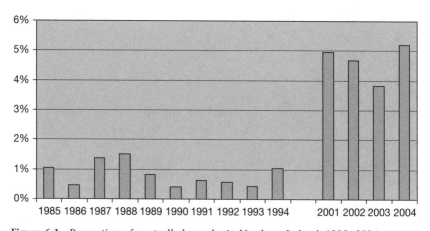

Figure 6.1 Proportion of controlled parades in Northern Ireland, 1985–2004

Sources: Jarman and Bryan, *From Riots to Rights*, 36; Bryan, *Orange Parades*, 182; PC annual reports, 2003 and 2004.

parades into four main varieties, listed in ascending order of importance: feeder, mini-Twelfth, church, and main (Twelfth) parades. Before the Lower Ormeau and Drumcree conflicts, only one (Portadown 1985, 1987) of the roughly twenty annual Twelfth parades had ever been re-routed in Northern Ireland.[13] The more numerous church parades were also largely untouched.

However, this changed during 1995–8 as Nationalist residents' groups challenged the Order's right to march in heavily Nationalist areas such as the Lower Ormeau, Drumcree, Newry (Armagh), Bellaghy (Londonderry), Dunloy (Antrim), Pomeroy (Tyrone), and Derry City. Combined with the North report on processions (1996) and the new parades legislation of 1998 which established the Parades Commission (PC), this led to a step change in the Order's freedom to parade. The PC's decisions were now independent of the police and the political process and fully binding. Instead of re-routing a handful of minor parades, the Order was now facing re-routing decisions on as many as fifty or more events, some of them long-running main or church parades. Even if we exclude the numerous Drumcree applications filed in protest by the Order, restrictions on Loyalist parades have increased fivefold since 1994.[14]

The ebb and flow of power relations, which has recently moved in favour of the Nationalist minority, is the context in which we need to keep the so-called Drumcree parade controversy. Drumcree Church itself is perched atop a hill north of Portadown, in County Armagh. Portadown is known as the 'Orange citadel' for its long-standing association with Orangeism. It is located near to the Dungannon–Diamond area, where Orangeism began, and Portadown District was formed just eleven months after the historic battle of the Diamond of

21 September 1795. In this short period, it already contained twenty-three private lodges and some 2,500 members.[15] Over time, Portadown District developed a strong attachment to two parades which cut through a Catholic enclave on the way to and from Drumcree Church, namely the Twelfth parade and the Drumcree Church parade, which takes place a week or several days earlier.

The town of Portadown sits in a largely Protestant belt that takes in northeastern Armagh and north Tyrone. The eight wards that make up greater Portadown have about 22,000 people, of which three-quarters are Protestant. This area, much of it rural, is highly segregated, even by Northern Irish standards. For instance, no ward contains a minority of more than 20 per cent. Five of the six Protestant wards are less than 5 per cent Catholic. And the two wards north of the city where Drumcree Church sits are over 80 per cent Catholic.[16] Orangeism is not as strong in the city as some might think, since Portadown district represents less than a fifth of County Armagh's membership. Under one in ten of greater Portadown's Protestant males over the age of 16 are now Orangemen, which puts Portadown slightly below the Northern Ireland average.[17] In addition, under a third of Portadown District's members meet in Portadown (Carleton Street) Hall itself. Almost 40 per cent of the membership now come from rural areas well outside Portadown, and these lodges have retained their membership better than the city lodges in the period since 1991. This said, Portadown Protestants have an Orange enlistment rate which is relatively high compared with those of most Ulster towns. Of major towns, only Enniskillen has a comparable Orange density.[18]

Another interesting facet of Portadown is that membership has tended to fluctuate much more rapidly in response to upsurges in ethnic conflict than elsewhere in Northern Ireland. Thus Portadown District contained about 1,600 members in 1968. By 1973, just after the peak of the Troubles, membership had shot up by 23 per cent to almost 1,900. The subsequent halving in the fatality rate which took place in the province during 1973–8 was matched by a sharp decline in Orange membership to its 1968 level. In Northern Ireland as a whole during the same period, Orange membership rose and fell by only about 3 per cent, or about an eighth of the magnitude of Portadown District. In Belfast, the membership fluctuation was about 15 per cent during 1969–72, but only in certain districts (West Belfast, Ballymacarett, and parts of Clifton Street) did the surge in membership rival that in Portadown. Similarly, during the height of the Drumcree conflict of 1995–8, membership in Portadown shot up by 14 per cent while it barely budged in the province as a whole. Within two years after the 'defeat' at Drumcree, membership in Portadown had plummeted to a level well below that of 1995, and the decline continued sharply through 2004 at a much faster rate than in the Institution as a whole. In fact, by 2004, Portadown membership was less than it was at the beginning of the twentieth century. On present trends, Loughgall District will, probably

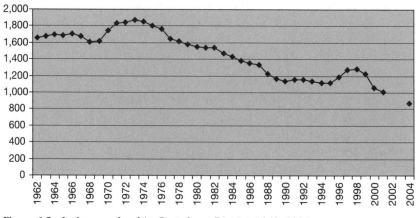

Figure 6.2 Lodge membership, Portadown District, 1962–2004
Sources: Armagh County Lodge reports; GOLI membership returns.

for the first time in the Order's history, overtake Portadown as the largest in Armagh within a decade.[19]

The membership illustrated in Figure 6.2 trends suggest that Portadown Orangemen are among the most politicized in the province, and that their reasons for membership may be more ideological than is the case in most parts of Northern Ireland. Perhaps only parts of Belfast can rival this record. With this in mind, let us consider the emergence of the Drumcree conflict.

A Recent History of The Drumcree Dispute

The recent history of Drumcree parading begins with the advent of the Troubles. Until 1972, Orangemen had followed a parade route through the 'tunnel' under the Portadown railway bridge and onto Obins Street, into the heart of the Catholic district north of the town centre, which they traversed on the way to and from the Drumcree COI church. The return trip brought them to the main Portadown (Carleton Street) Orange Hall. In 1972, Catholic residents mobilized under the banner of the 'Portadown Resistance Council' and issued their first call for a re-routing of the Twelfth parade away from the 'tunnel'. The IRA threatened violence if the parade was allowed to continue, but the local detachment of the UDA, a Protestant paramilitary group, vowed that the parade would proceed and that attempts at interference would have repercussions for local Catholic residents. On the Twelfth, the UDA escorted the Orange parade into the 'tunnel', and the police and military ensured that it went through. Evidently, the ability to parade was governed by the balance of local power, and the UDA was able to face down the IRA on this occasion. Nonetheless, the event was followed by a raft of inter-communal violence and multiple murders.[20]

In the period between 1972 and 1985, the lead-up to the Drumcree Church and Twelfth parades was accompanied by heightened tension and occasional violence, but the parades managed to get through.[21] By the mid 1980s, however, concern at the cost in money and police and security force injuries prompted the RUC Chief Constable, Jack Hermon, to seek to limit or re-route the burgeoning number of parades. He was given the green light from the British to deploy as much force as necessary to enforce re-routing decisions. This was to affect only fifty 'flashpoint' marches out of more than 2,000 parades. In some cases, local lodges acceded to re-routing demands, but in other areas, there was concerted resistance. The goal of the police and security forces was to face down resistance from pro-marching elements, establish a pattern of re-routing, and thereby remove the security problem represented by the marches.[22]

The degree of disobedience—civil and uncivil—thus became crucial. If Protestants can demonstrate a sufficient threat to public order if a march is re-routed, they can persuade the authorities not to re-route traditional parades. On the other side, Nationalists require a similar degree of disobedience to persuade authorities to block a parade. In this numbers game, both sides in the conflict have an incentive to cause as much trouble as possible so as to influence the police cost–benefit calculus over whether to halt or permit a march. Since marches are widely seen as a proxy for symbolic and political power, the stakes are raised. Legal considerations support the need for public order over group expression,[23] and thus the issue of who parades has less to do with an argument over ethics than it does with raw force—in other words, who wins the local numbers war.

Other factors didn't help in the post-1969 period. For instance, the rise in Loyalist 'Kick the Pope' bands and the increasingly aggressive drumming of these bands during Orange parades helped to heighten tension in the Catholic zone through which Portadown Orange marches passed. Growing communal self-confidence meant that Nationalist residents were increasingly unwilling to abide by the double standard which permitted Orangemen to march in the Catholic zone but prohibited Nationalist parades from traversing the Protestant Park Road enclave to complete their circuit. Nationalist residents, led by a local SDLP politician, Brid Rodgers, petitioned the Irish government to redress the situation. Irish pressure led the RUC to sanction a march by St Patrick's Accordion Band in 1985. However, Protestant residents, led by Councillor Arnold Hatch, a former hardliner who has since moderated his views, protested and blocked the route. As a result, the Nationalist march was cancelled by the RUC at the eleventh hour owing to concerns about public safety.[24]

Brid Rodgers sees the St Patrick's stand-off as pivotal in the escalation of the Drumcree parade issue.[25] Sure enough, in 1985, the Order was prevented from marching down the 'tunnel' on the Twelfth of July. In response, a group calling itself the United Ulster Loyalist Front called for concerted action. Its words demonstrate the clear link between the local march and the course of politics in the province. 'The rerouting was a first step towards a United Ireland,' thundered the paper's authors, Philip Black and Alan Wright. 'If we do not register our outright rejection . . . we can be certain that the outcome of the Anglo-Irish Talks will be . . . further steps toward a United Ireland.'[26] As the marching season approached, many Orangemen voiced their disquiet at the 'lack of leadership' from the Portadown District in opposing the 1985 re-routing. Thus in June 1986, members of Portadown's Arch Committee asked whether they should even bother erecting their Orange arches if the leadership failed to stand up for them. In a letter to the Armagh County Grand Master, Norman Hood, the signatories wrote:

We feel the Arches should not be erected if the terms 'No Surrender' and 'In Glorious Memory' mean nothing to the present day leaders of the Orange Order. The grass root [sic] opinion of Orangemen would appear to be that they are prepared to take a stand but there seems to be a distinct absence of leadership from the Orange hierarchy.

The signatories ended with a four-point challenge to Hood. Points 3 and 4 read: '3. Why do you hold the position you are in—is it for prestige or defending the faith and freedom so dear to the hearts of our ancestors; and 4. Do you lack the courage to stand up and be counted with all true loyalists?'[27]

Faced with pressure like this, Armagh could do little but bend to Portadown's wishes and push for the parade—which ultimately went ahead under heavy police protection. This is not to say that moderate voices failed to make themselves heard. On 8 July 1986, Olive Whitten, a member of the Loyal Orange-women of Ireland who would later emerge as a pro-Agreement UUP organizer, wrote to Hood. She urged that the Armagh County master overrule Portadown District's desire to hold the county's annual Twelfth parade in Port-adown. Instead, argued Whitten, the demonstration should take place on its customary rotating basis, and be held in Armagh city. She claimed that many Portadown Orangemen wanted to march in Armagh instead, and expressed 'disgust' at the presence of the Independent Orange Lodge and 'Paisleyites', who were 'mixing freely' with local Orangemen in Portadown. 'They [Pais-leyites] were the ones to blame for the start of the trouble—it was them [sic] who stopped the Roman Catholics from walking Park Road last year on 17th March. As soon as I heard that, I said to Arnold Hatch that the Orangemen would be stopped from walking down the tunnel. He, of course, said never. I never like to say—I told you so'.

'The Brethren [of Portadown] are doing the job that the Roman Catholics have tried to do for years,' warned Whitten, and the actions of Portadown were tantamount to declaring themselves an 'Independent Orange District'. Whitten lamented that Portadown's previous leadership (inc. Bros Brownlee and Toal) were criticized for being weak, declaring Toal and Brownlee 'loyal men [who] never disgraced the Orange Order', unlike the new Portadown leadership. This passage suggests that leadership changes in Portadown resulted in the ascendance of more hardline players, such as the new Portadown District master Harold Gracey.

Finally, Whitten commented on the Drumcree events, showing how divisions were emerging within the Loyalist community, as well as between Portadown and the upper echelons of the Order:

A fellow orangewoman, her father (an orangeman) and myself got into an argument with a man on Sunday morning in Portadown while waiting for the procession to move off for the service in Drumcree. This man objected to the RUC objecting to Bros. George Seawright and Jim Wells [two well-known Belfast militants] walking. Although I agree it is hardly the business of the RUC to decide who walks and who doesn't, I'm afraid I had to agree with them on Sunday morning, those two men should not have been allowed to walk one inch and I know Bro. [Harold] Gracey was told that by senior members of the Order. Portadown District have enough members of their own to put on a good show without any of these undesirables joining in. I have watched 1,000+ Brethren marching to Drumcree before last year and recognised 90% of them, but this year I could almost say I recognised 10%, or 20% at most.[28]

Meanwhile, Grand Lodge had begun to address the mounting problem of drunkenness and hooliganism among spectators and band members. In a communication, Martin Smyth appointed an Orange commission to look into the behaviour of police and spectators at the Portadown Twelfth parade of 1986.[29] These participants tend to dominate the atmosphere at Orange marches to such an extent that the Orangemen often appear to be a sideshow in the spectacle. In mid 1986, a Band Committee of the Order drew up a thirteen-point Band Contract which all bands would be required to sign as of 12 July 1986. This attempted to compel a band to observe codes of behaviour as well as limits on the content of music, style of drumming, dress, and displays of paramilitary insignia.[30] At a subsequent meeting, the United Ulster Bands Association attempted to water down the contract, but the Order remained firmly in the driver's seat, and resisted any attempt to soften the rules.[31] Though enforcement of band discipline has been far less stringent than the text of the contract would suggest, it is also clear that the Order does not desire ill discipline among its bands. For instance, it has recently suspended a series of bands for drunken or undisciplined behaviour.[32]

A related debate raged in Sandy Row District in Belfast, where discussion turned to the question of marshalling and paramilitary intimidation. William Murdie, the district master, proposed that Belfast County Lodge should appoint 'determined marshals to control parades as hooligans are ruining the parades by their actions. We need men to show guts and determination against so called Bully Boys so that the scenes of 15th November of wanton destruction will never be repeated.' This motion was supported by several present, including the Rev. Brian Kennaway, who ventured that, in his opinion, 'many Orangemen did not give support to the leaders who tried to stop the trouble'. After the discussion, those present agreed on regular training for marshals and the need to be prepared.[33]

In 1987, legislation moved decisively against the Orange Order with the Public Order (NI) Order. This eliminated the category of 'customary' parade routes and mandated a seven-day notice period for all parades. Now all parades would be treated as independent events, irrespective of how 'traditional' they were—something which benefited the route-poor Nationalist parading organizations and penalized the route-rich Orange Order.[34] A repeal of the 1954 Flags and Emblems Act also gave Catholics 'parity of expression' and the right to fly the tricolour. Though the Order and Paisley mounted protests against these decisions, these efforts came to nought. In 1987, 1,000 RUC policemen and 3,000 troops of security forces were drafted in to enforce a re-routing of the Portadown parade. This effectively killed any chances of the Order getting through the 'tunnel'. However, the proposed re-routing had the parade return via the Garvaghy Road, an area under redevelopment which would soon become overwhelmingly Catholic, resulting in renewed conflict (see Figure 6.3).[35] The Order saw this decision as a sacrifice of their traditional route (Obins Street) for a guarantee of passage up the Garvaghy Road in the future, hence their consternation when the Garvaghy route came up for dispute in 1995.[36]

Trouble in Belfast: the lower Ormeau Controversy

The Drumcree parade settled down to its new route between 1987 and 1994. By 1995, however, Sinn Fein/IRA's new 'proxy war' strategy had begun to play out with the rise of the residents' groups. Though backed by a majority of Catholic residents in areas like the Lower Ormeau Road (Belfast), Bogside (Derry), and Garvaghy Road (Portadown), intimidation in these areas was an additional factor guaranteeing near-full compliance of the residents.[37] Finally, the appointment of former IRA men such as Gerard Rice (Lower Ormeau) and Brendan McKenna (Garvaghy Road) guaranteed that Orangemen would not speak to the leaders of the residents' groups. According to Ruth Dudley Edwards, this was a strategic move on Sinn Fein's part to divert residents' protests over the heads of the Orangemen and directly to the British government. She cites Gerry Adams's leaked speech to a Sinn Fein party conference in which he spoke of 'three years' work' that went into the 'scene changes' in Derry, Lower Ormeau, Garvaghy Road, and elsewhere. In addition, the Sinn Fein strategy of mobilizing residents' groups was ostensibly designed to pit Orangemen against the RUC.[38]

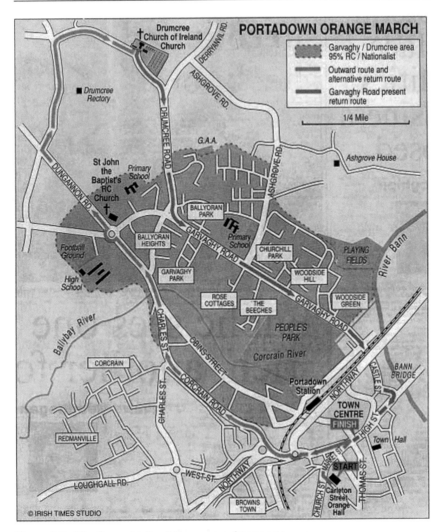

Figure 6.3 The Garvaghy Road Orange marching route
Sources: CAIN, accessed 2005; graphic courtesy of *The Irish Times*.

The mobilization of Lower Ormeau residents in Belfast in April 1995 led to a re-routing of the parade for the first time in recent memory. Citing the memory of five Catholics killed at Sean Graham's bookmakers a few years earlier by Loyalist paramilitaries, the Lower Ormeau Concerned Community (LOCC) residents' group called for the Order to avoid this section of Ormeau Road. Fearing a threat to public order from Nationalist demonstrators, the RUC blocked the path of the Orangemen down the road. Rather than accept re-routing, the Belfast Orange marchers held a service on the Ormeau bridge and sang the National Anthem. The 'dignified' nature of the service, despite the injustice of the situation, was applauded by Grand Lodge.[39] One favourable op-ed piece in the Protestant-leaning Belfast *News Letter* excoriated the RUC for banning the march. 'It would be interesting to be told exactly where the RUC expected the threat to the peace to come from yesterday. A small group of Orangemen on their way to a religious service? Or a mob of Republican demonstrators, many of whom support a party which believes in violence as a viable political weapon?'[40]

The Order's press release spoke of Orangemen being 'denied their civil rights'. Citing the founding of the Order in 1795, it declared that it had been founded because of the 'failure of the Civil authorities' and that, once again, these British authorities 'lack the will to uphold our lawful right to parade the Queen's Highway to attend a Church Service'.[41] Arguments about 'coat-trailing' triumphalism were dismissed since, the Order argued, the parade was following a traditional route that had been in use for years before the deaths at Sean Graham's.[42] By this time, relations between the Order and the Secretary of State, Mayhew, were strained as a result of the Framework Document (which provided for a substantial north–south constitutional dimension). At a meeting on 10 April, policing was discussed, and Mayhew gave assurances to Orange leaders that operational decisions would be above politics. A discussion of demonstrations and protests (presumably Nationalist) ensued and led John McCrea to retort, 'if you want a Demonstration you can have it'. Smyth followed this up by declaring that references to 'non-Catholic' parades were insulting and that 'We are a displaced people.'[43]

After the Lower Ormeau debacle, McCrea wrote to Mayhew, charging that 'mob rule' and Dublin interference had influenced the decision to re-route the parade. This was deemed a betrayal of promises made at the meeting of 10 April, and that 'it is clear that Sinn Fein/I.R.A. intend using the situation for their own ends and purposes'. The letter concluded with a statement from McCrea that the Grand Lodge expected steps to be taken to ensure that the march went ahead in future.[44] Later, the Grand Lodge executive officer George Patton claimed that Dublin's desire for a 'speedy solution to the problem' forced the Secretary of State's hand.[45] Further bad news came in a meeting with the Assistant Chief Constable of the RUC, W. Stewart, on 19 May. Stewart asserted that in his opinion, 'local residents have the right to stop Parades, and that without prejudice, and under prevailing circumstances, the Church Parade on 2 July would not be permitted to go down the Ormeau Road.' Stewart later provocatively added that 'Ballynafeigh District [the lodge that marches down the Ormeau Road] have the *least* right to go through the area'. At this, Smyth told Stewart that the RUC appeared to have given in to mob rule.[46] In the end, the Orangemen did march the Ormeau Road on the Twelfth, but would find it increasingly hard to do so.

Drumcree I

As the Twelfth approached, the centre of activity again shifted west to Portadown, where the newly formed Garvaghy Road Residents Association (GRA) was coordinating resistance to the Drumcree parades. These Portadown-area parades were deemed particularly significant by the Order because they had run for over 150 years and were orchestrated by the fiercely proud Portadown Orangemen. Yet the Garvaghy Road had become increasingly Catholic through development and residential segregation caused by the Troubles. Discontent at Orange marching was certainly there, but Sinn Fein/IRA mobilization was probably required to bring the GRA to life in 1995. The rest of the story is the stuff of legend.

Though the parade had legally been allowed to go through, Nationalist and GRA protests led to the parade being blocked by police. As Brian Kennaway, the moderate Orangeman and Presbyterian cleric, writes, 'What caused the greatest anger, in the hearts of the vast majority of Protestant people, was the fact that firstly, this was a legally approved parade and that the R.U.C. appeared to change their mind because of the threat of physical force. Secondly, this change of direction came while the [Drumcree Church] Service was in progress.'[47] The thousand or so Portadown District marchers refused to comply with the RUC and marched to police lines, led by, among others, David Trimble, the local MP and a County Down Orangeman. A stand-off between Orangemen and the police ensued overnight and into the next day as over 30,000 Orangemen and supporters converged on the site from all over the province and even from adjacent parts of the Republic.[48] Included in the crowd were numerous Loyalist paramilitary men, including Billy 'King Rat' Wright, who would later be killed by Republican inmates in the Maze prison. With this fearsome show of strength, the authorities were persuaded to allow a march without bands and supporters to return via the Garvaghy Road.

The next morning, the Portadown Orangemen walked the short stretch of 'enemy' territory in silence, agreeing to march six abreast so as to pass through more quickly. When they arrived in Protestant territory near Carleton Street Orange Hall, they broke out in spontaneous jubilation and were greeted by the cheers of their supporters. Cameras captured the moment of victory, and David Trimble and Ian Paisley clasped hands and appeared to 'dance a jig' which Nationalists claim was triumphalist and was proof that Trimble could not be trusted.[49] Nationalists vowed not to be fooled (or out-mobilized) again, and the stage was set for an annual cycle of standoffs.

The Orange 'victory' at Drumcree had major ramifications beyond the inevitable protests and rioting which took place in its wake. Most importantly, it made Trimble's political career and broke that of Smyth. Trimble had donned his sash, clashed with police, and stayed up all night and was central to negotiations. Smyth, on the other hand, was absent from Drumcree and claimed that he 'hadn't been asked' by Portadown brethren to make an appearance there and had political duties to attend to in London. Trimble suggests that Smyth failed to turn up because he thought the Orangemen would lose, though Smyth claims it was because he thought they would win.[50]

Wherever the truth lies, the grassroots reacted swiftly and strongly to Smyth's absence. Portadown District expressed the view that it felt 'betrayed' by an 'apparent lack of leadership' from senior officers in County Armagh and Grand Lodge.[51] Yet Portadown's complaint was gracious compared with the avalanche of resolutions from around the province which poured into Grand Lodge protesting against Smyth's absence and calling for him to retire. Only County Monaghan spoke in Smyth's favour.[52]

For many, Smyth's subsequent attendance at an ecumenical 'United Prayer Breakfast' was the straw that broke the camel's back. This event, sponsored by the National Prayer Breakfast movement begun in the USA, was co-hosted by Smyth and the Irish TD (MP) Mary Flaherty. Smyth even signed his name to an invitation extended to many Orangemen. Both Catholics and Protestants were present, and the event was judged to be unacceptably 'ecumenical' by most brethren despite the fact that Grand Lodge reviewed the event and claimed that Smyth had not infringed his 'Obligations of an Orangeman'.[53] Smyth himself defended his actions as evangelism, but the Orange reaction shows the immense difference between the trans-ethnic evangelicalism of the United States and the ethnically bound tradition of its Ulster cousin.[54]

The moderate County Tyrone's resolution against Smyth expressed the sentiments of many in the grassroots and must have struck Smyth particularly hard:

We the Brethren of County Tyrone Grand Orange Lodge . . . view with alarm and dismay the attendance of our Grand Master at the Prayer Breakfast in Drumsill Hotel . . . and also his lack of leadership by his non-attendance at the Stand-Off at Drumcree . . . At this crucial time in our history when strong leadership is so vital, he has failed to set an example to his Brethren and we feel that we can have no confidence in his leadership . . . A quiet departure would be our preferred option and thus save feuds and dissension among our Brethren.[55]

Even in this moderate county, the resolution was carried by 40–10, with 8 abstentions, demonstrating the strength of popular feeling. The contrast with Trimble was marked. As the master of Ballymarlow LOL 637, County Antrim, expressed it: 'Where were the leaders of our institution when all this [Drumcree] was taking place and why were they not in Portadown supporting David Trimble and the Portadown brethren'.[56] Likewise, Ballinlea True Defenders LOL 1511, from Portstewart in County Londonderry, expressed gratitude for 'The Contributions made by Bro. David Trimble, M.P. and Dr. I.R.K. Paisley . . . in helping to ensure that the Protestant traditions weren't going to be trampled underfoot'. On the other hand, they noted 'with dismay and not a little anger that the head of our Institution in Ireland was not present at either Drumcree or the Lower Ormeau to give support to the brethren in taking their stand. It begs the question "where was Bro. Smyth".'[57]

The upshot of Smyth's absence from Drumcree was that his campaign for the UUP leadership was fatally damaged while Trimble's was given a shot in the arm. Many in the UUP had become tired of the long-serving Molyneaux and his inability to stop the Anglo-Irish Agreement, and were open to an inspiring new leader who could put the Unionist case across with more verve.[58] One explanation for Smyth's absence is that he had become immune to the 'noise' of the grassroots and took their frequent complaints with a pinch of salt. This was an unusual sensibility for the leader of a populist Protestant association where the rank and file had acquired the habit of sniping at any hints of elitism from Grand Lodge. Since the 1960s, county and Grand Lodge officers other than Smyth were in the habit of having to justify themselves against charges of being remote from the rank and file and not showing 'leadership' or defending the Order properly against bad publicity. The origins of Smyth's self-confidence lay in his oft-repeated attempts to resign in the 1970s, 1980s, and 1990s and the inability of Orange committees to find a suitable replacement. The problem was that the Order sought to continue its tradition of appointing elite figures, but those approached, like the Rev. John Lockington (who later became Moderator of the Presbyterian General Assembly), declined to take the job.[59] Smyth's cavalier treatment of grassroots concerns was also rooted in his frustration at the membership for its unwillingness to take a stand against drink in lodge halls in the 1980s or to mobilize in support for anti-Anglo-Irish Agreement protests in the early 1990s. All of this resulted, as we saw earlier, in an increasingly parental tone in Grand Master's addresses.

The Drumcree affair was far more serious, yet Smyth's decision to attend the prayer breakfast suggests that—even after Drumcree—he felt a certain latitude to take risks to further his political career. All of this suggests that Smyth had moderated his views somewhat as compared with his populist past. This newly independent attitude was evident as early as 1993 when, in a BBC interview, he suggested that Sinn Fein could take part in talks under certain conditions.[60] Though he was excoriated by Ian Paisley, this does not seem to have affected his stature within the Orange Order. Even the drubbing that Smyth took at the hands of his Orange critics in 1995 left him unbowed. This may have been due, once again, to his attempt to retire and the Order's inability to replace him. Clifford Forsythe, South Down MP, had been proposed to take over from Smyth in 1995, but proved unsuitable because he had divorced and remarried.[61] In his biannual address to Grand Lodge in December 1995, Smyth was unrepentant, invoking the heroes and precedents of Orange tradition to de-legitimate Orange dissent:

1995 has been a remarkable Bicentenary Year for the Orange Institution . . . It has also seen personal attacks upon me as Grand Master. Leaders of our Order have had to face attacks constantly from within and without our ranks . . . The hero [William, of Ballykilbeg] Johnston was pilloried by 'Orange Brothers' because he fought for the right of secret ballot in parliamentary elections. Col. Saunderson knew the wickedness of those who lied about him and divided the Institution with the fragmenting Independents who still snap at our heels without doing much to promote or defend our cause. One expelled from our ranks has the temerity to expect us to reply to his babblings.[62]

Ill. 10 Bicentenary Parade at Loughgall, Co. Armagh, 23 September, 1995 —From left, Rev. Victor Ryan, Fred Stewart (Imperial and American Grand Master), Martin Smyth, Norman Allen (Armagh County Master), Charles Ferrel (New Zealand Grand Master), James Molyneaux and Grand Secretary John McCrea. McCrea was an early and consistent opponent of Orange reformers in Brian Kennaway's Education Committee.

The Orange Social Revolution

Smyth was secure in his standing within the Order's hierarchy, but his approach helped spawn a new force of Orange insurgents, which burst onto the scene after July 1995. Led by the Tyrone Orange rebel Joel Patton, the new Spirit of Drumcree (SOD) splinter group was declared on 14 November

1995 at a noisy rally of over 1,500 rebels at Ulster Hall in Belfast. This was not the first time Orange militants had attempted to mobilize a breakaway faction. Indeed, it is worth recalling the Orange & Protestant Committee (O & P), formed in 1954 (after the 1953 Dungiven parade ban) by sixteen Orange rebels including Londonderry's legendary William Douglas. This group had attracted 1,400 to its rally at Wellington Hall in Belfast and garnered a great deal of media attention. The demands of both the O & P and the SOD were largely identical. These included, in order of importance: (1) the perceived unwillingness of the leadership to take a hardline stance in defence of a particular parade route; (2) the lack of popular accountability on the part of Central Committee and Grand Lodge; (3) the UUP–Orange link, which undermined the Order's religious basis and alienated Paisleyites; and (4) a general perception of being soft on Republicanism. Undoubtedly, the timing of both events was also partly tactical: in both cases, the rebels could count on a groundswell of popular discontent to parlay them into power.

It is important, though, not to lose sight of the major social changes that had taken place within the Orange Order in the forty years that separated the O & P from its SOD populist soulmates. In 1954, when the ex-Prime Minister of Northern Ireland John Andrews was Grand Master, the Ulster squirearchy was still in the driver's seat. Just nine of thirty-five members of Central Committee in that year lacked titles. Indeed, there were sixteen JPs and five OBEs. By 1995, however, Martin Smyth, who unlike Andrews had risen from modest origins, led a Central Committee in which only ten of forty-one Central Committee men were titled. More broadly, the aggregate number of titled members of Grand and County Lodges listed in 1911 was 189. In 1961 it was 175, and by 1981 the figure had dipped to 90.[63] It may be assumed that this figure will continue to drop as elderly members retire.

To look in more depth at the organization, it is clear that a social hierarchy was firmly in place below Grand Lodge level in 1901. At that time, even district officers (masters and secretaries)—to say nothing of county or Grand Lodge elites—were socially superior to private (local) lodge officers. A sample drawn from the 1901 census in Belfast and Tyrone (see Table 6.1) indicates that 54 per cent of Belfast and 40 per cent of Tyrone district officers had non-manual occupations. Most of the Belfast middle-class group were in commerce, while the Tyrone sample consisted of more legal and clerical professionals as well as landlords. In Belfast, just 46 per cent of district officers were in manual work, but fully 80 per cent of private lodge officers were working class. It is also interesting that the proportion of COI adherents among Belfast district officers (53 per cent) slightly exceeded the 49 per cent recorded among private lodge officers, while Methodists occupied the reverse position: 8 per cent among private lodge officers versus 3 per cent among district officers. Notice as well that in both Belfast and Tyrone, Orange district officers had a higher proportion of professional occupations and a more elite religious profile than

165

Table 6.1 Occupations of Private and District Level Orange Officers, 1901

BELFAST 1901	District officers	Master/ secretaries	Belfast mean
Professional	8%	1%	5%
Petit bourgeois	46%	18%	
Skilled worker	38%	49%	
Unskilled worker	8%	31%	
Church of Ireland	53%	49%	39%
N (sample)	39	99	
TYRONE 1901	District officers	Master/ secretaries	Tyrone mean
Professional	23%	no data	3%
Petit bourgeois	17%	no data	
Farmer	57%	no data	57%
Skilled worker	3%	no data	
Church of Ireland	64%	no data	50%
N (sample)	35		

Sources: Census of Ireland 1901; Orange county reports, 1901.

Table 6.2 Postcode Classes of Private and District Level Orange Officers, 2001

BELFAST 2001	District officers	Master/ Secretaries	Northern Ireland mean
Top (A) class	6%	6.6%	9.9%
Top 12 classes (non-rural)	48%	42%	40%
N (sample)	67	166	
TYRONE 2001	District officers	Master/ Secretaries	
Top (A) class	5.2%	6.6%	9.9%
Top 12 classes (non-rural)	63%	70%	40%
N (sample)	77	182	

Sources: GOLI membership returns, 2001; NI MOSAIC 2002, accessed 2005.

the overall population at large. In other words, the Orange district elite was also a social elite within the Unionist community.

The same certainly cannot be said today. 1901 is the last publicly available nominal census, but we can use MOSAIC post code classifications to examine the Order's present-day social composition. Table 6.2 demonstrates two things. First, we can see that the social hierarchy in the Order has collapsed. If anything, the officers of individual lodges live in slightly better postcodes than the 'superior' officers they elect to represent them in their district. The second factor to notice is Orange class 'slippage'. In 1901, Belfast district officers were a social elite, but today they are below the provincial average at the top: 9.9 to 6.6 per cent among 'A' postcodes. Even with regard to the

Table 6.3 The Social Profile of the Orange Order in Comparative Perspective, 2001

	Top 12 MOSAIC postcode classes	Rural 8 MOSAIC postcode classes	Non-rural top 12 MOSAIC postcode classes	Non-rural bottom 7 MOSAIC postcode classes	N
Freemason office-bearers	67.8%	15.5%	80.2%	9.4%	766
Grand Orange Lodge office-bearers	34.7%	44.4%	62.5%	17.5%	144
Northern Ireland population mean	32.5%	18.1%	39.6%	27.9%	1.6m
Orange Order private lodge office-bearers	32.4%	43.9%	57.7%	22.1%	1,429

Sources: Henry Patterson and Eric Kaufmann, *Unionism and Loyalism in Northern Ireland since 1945* (Manchester: Manchester University Press, forthcoming).

top twelve postcode classes, if we take into account the fact that MOSAIC data provide only a Northern Ireland rather than county-level average, and in view of the fact that Belfast has a higher proportion of top postcodes than the province as a whole, Belfast district officers are below the social average. In Tyrone, the picture is different: the county's general population is probably below the Northern Ireland average in terms of top postcodes, and so Tyrone district officers remain above average—certainly with respect to the top twelve postcode classes.

In a survey of all counties, recent work by Henry Patterson and myself using postcode analysis of UUC, Orange, and Masonic members around 2003 is revealing. Table 6.3 shows that in contrast with the Masons, the roughly 1,500 local lodge officers and 144 Grand Lodge officers of the order have a very average social profile. Together with the Northern Ireland population, roughly a third live in the twelve most desirable Northern Ireland postcodes. This reflects the main occupations within the Order: 20 per cent are farmers, 20 per cent are tradesmen, 20 per cent are labourers, and just 5 per cent are professional. In terms of age, the Order is also average, with a quarter of its members over sixty and 20 per cent under thirty.[64] Once again, there is little social difference between the top and bottom layers of the organization, reiterating the tale of a more egalitarian Orange social structure than formerly existed.

The nature of the Northern Ireland valuation rolls makes it difficult to track occupations in the period since 1901 for the mass membership. However, tens of thousands of application forms have survived for Belfast County for the 1961–86 period. These tell a fascinating story about the largely 20–25-year-olds who entered the Order in these years and show that while little more than 8 per cent of recruits were even broadly middle class in these years, the big shift was away from skilled apprentices to the unemployed. The rise of a new Belfast middle class of civil servants and tertiary workers completely passed the Order by, resulting in 'class slippage' against the general Unionist population.[65]

The Spirit of Drumcree

The social changes that flattened the Order's social hierarchy and caused downward mobility may have led to a renewed populism within the organization. Brian Kennaway accuses the Order of an anti-intellectual culture of 'inverted snobbery', remarking that a well-known officer of Derriaghy District damned Robert (Bobby) Saulters soon after his election as Grand Master in 1996 as 'a millionaire from the Malone Road'. Anti-clerical and anti-UUP sentiment were linked with the new populism.[66] Populist sentiment is abundantly evident in the emergence of the SOD. The SOD burst upon the scene after the Drumcree stand-off in July, buoyed by popular dissatisfaction with Martin Smyth's leadership.[67] As Kennaway remarks, 'The Steering Committee, consisting of William Bigger, David Dowey, John McGrath, Joel Patton and Harold Price, had carefully cultivated a relationship with the press and continually fed them information on their demands, so that an air of expectancy surrounded the Ulster Hall Meeting.'[68] The group had met three times—in Antrim, Tyrone, and Craigavon—suggesting that a province-wide rather than local network was operating. The network consisted of like-minded lodges throughout Ulster. Indeed, a letter from William Thompson, a Ballymena-based organizer of the event, asked the SOD confederate Walter Millar to raise the event with his lodge and confirm the numbers who would be participating so that buses could be booked.[69] This, along with the Antrim roots of many key participants, suggests that Antrim played a leading role and that the event was well choreographed.[70]

A subsequent report on the rally for Grand Lodge by Brian Kennaway, though criticized as partly inaccurate by SOD members, remained largely consistent with video evidence. At the Ulster Hall meeting, the Independent-minded Orangemen aired their grievances in cruder terms than their O & P ancestors. After asking the press to leave, Patton, the ringleader, addressed the assembled crowd. He commented on his apt name of Joel, an Old Testament prophet, and emphasized that he was a (born-again) Christian. Patton called for the resignation of Smyth and put forth his group's demands, which were described by Kennaway in the December 1995 Report of Proceedings as follows:

1. Every Orangeman votes for Grand Lodge Officers—'We want direct democracy and will settle for nothing less'

2. Oppose the voluntary re-routing of all traditional parades

3. There must be no negotiation with Community Groups as they are a front for republicanism

4. It is vital for GOLI [Grand Lodge] to compose a strategy to oppose attacks on our culture

5. There must be NO talks with Sinn Féin

6. The link with the UUP. We must take the initiative to break the link NOW. Disaffiliate NOW![71]

He also criticized any suggestion that the UUP (notably Ken Maginnis) should work with the SDLP in local councils. In Patton's words, a Nationalist in any shape or form was a complete anathema to a Unionist.[72]

Patton was followed by David Dowey, an Antrim radical who made Patton seem tame by comparison. After proudly declaring himself a 'sectarian bigot', Dowey went on to contradict Patton and declare that 'The Orange Institution is not a Religious Order—it was set up to defend the Ulster Protestant People...of course the Orange Order has its own self-defence organisation, the Orange Volunteers'.[73] The Orange Volunteers, as we have seen, were rejected by Smyth and the Grand Lodge in 1972 and thus—even if such an organization still existed—were not sanctioned by the Order.

Dowey's remarks grew ever more incendiary. He referred to the Grand Lodge as 'old men' on several occasions. He spoke of Smyth as the 'red hatted weasel' in reference to his participation in the prayer breakfast. He then asked the audience what the Order should do with Smyth. Someone in the front shouted, 'Shoot him!' to which Dowey responded 'Now no violence—not yet!' Dowey also made reference to Central Committee as 'tossers' who were 'Official Unionist to a man' (he later disputed the exact wording). This, claimed Dowey, caused the disaffiliation vote to fail at a Central Committee meeting of 6 October 1995. After warning that compromise on parades would lead to them being 'picked off one by one' by the IRA and the authorities, Dowey tacitly approved of violence as a tool in the struggle against Republicanism: 'I was going to say that I'm glad to see that Orange Halls are not the only type of Halls [i.e. there were Catholic ones as well] being burnt out now,—but I'd better not.' He next demanded a series of reforms, including a mass rally. 'Grand Lodge were scared because a few windows were broken in the City Centre,' he taunted. 'We should have our Mass Rally and go up the Falls [Catholic area in Belfast] and break a few more windows.' At this, someone in the audience responded, 'maybe get cracking Police skulls'.

Dowey spelt out a number of other positions which reveal the complex contours of the psyche of militant young Orangeism. First of all, he wanted to eliminate references to 'Northern Ireland' within Grand Lodge and replace them with 'Ulster', which would refer to the six counties only. As for the 'lost' three counties of Cavan, Monaghan, and Donegal (which had substantial membership and representation at Grand Lodge), Dowey sneered, 'I couldn't care less.' He viewed proscriptions against alcohol as quaint, arguing that Orange Halls should be used for social functions as this got people into the Order. He later opined that 'drink has an important part to play in today's society'. At the end of Dowey's address, the eight ringleaders spelt out their 'Drumcree Initiative' of reforms and warned Grand Lodge that if it did not pass it, 'we will do it for them'. A collection was then taken up among members of the audience to cover the splinter group's expenses.[74] Though the SOD later challenged some of Kennaway's account, much went uncontested.[75]

Dowey's attitude towards alcohol, discipline, religion, and violence is fascinating, and accurately reflects the secular, sectarian wing of the DUP, centred among the working class in Belfast and the major towns as well as among younger Loyalists more broadly. This group sees the Order as an ethnic self-defence association with little real difference from the paramilitaries—a movement in which religion is mere scaffolding. Few such people are in the Orange Order, but an important minority have joined it and sought influence. Patton, by contrast, as a self-proclaimed 'Christian', stands more squarely in the older O & P tradition of wanting the Order to remain religious and detached from politics. That the two planks could coexist on the same platform is testament to the way in which the tensions between religious–Paisleyite and secular–working-class varieties of militant Protestantism are subsumed (as they are in the DUP) in the fight against a common enemy.[76] In any event, though its aims were similar, the tone of the SOD is more impatient, secular, political, and violent than that of its predecessor, the O & P. Here is clear evidence that modernity had induced a shift in sensibility.

The support base for this kind of radicalism should not be overestimated. Among the 1,500 who turned up to Ulster Hall were a variety of malcontents as well as reformers with sincere grievances, but many must have been a bit perturbed by Dowey's performance. For instance, Clifford Smyth, a former convenor of the Education Committee of the Order, was at the meeting handing out leaflets entitled 'Reform the Orange Order'. Yet Smyth, in a subsequent article, wrote that Dowey's language was intemperate and would have resulted in significant damage to the SOD had the words been reported in the press. A video of the event later emerged which led to widespread criticism and caused Dowey to be suspended from his job as a technical officer with the Department of the Environment's planning service in Belfast.[77] This began a series of meetings and correspondence between the SOD and Grand Lodge, with particular personal bitterness between Dowey and Kennaway.

At Grand Lodge, Patton received no succour from Harold Gracey, the Portadown District master, who thanked the Order for its support during Drumcree and urged anyone with influence over the SOD to get it to drop 'Drumcree' from its moniker. Patton's County Tyrone men were similarly at odds with him. The County Tyrone secretary Robert Abernethy related that Patton had raised his views and been told to expand upon them and report back, which he failed to do. The Rev. Warren Porter accused members of the SOD of being 'Sinn Feiners', and others present spoke derisively of them.[78] Finally, the Grand Lodge impaled the SOD on the twin lances of being unchristian and Republican. Thus Grand Lodge resolved that 'Our Order's principal concern is for the maintenance of the Protestant and Reformed Religion and that any political action necessary to be taken must always be subservient to and supportive of its primary evangelical concern.' It added that: 'We totally and unreservedly condemn the unchristian and republican remarks made by those involved and reported to us. Encouragement to violence is unchristian, and calls for "direct democracy" are republican.'[79] The differences between Grand Lodge—despite its more petit-bourgois composition as compared with 1954—and the rebels highlight the distinction between traditionalist and rebel within Unionism. The Grand Lodge officers employed 'traditionalist' legitimation based on religion, precedent, Orange laws, Orange voting traditions, and Orange history. Even Kennaway's reporting of the event homed in on Dowey's violation of his obligations to his brother Orangemen (i.e. to avoid slander) while Sam Foster, a Fermanagh UUP activist, spoke of the violation of Laws 23, 10, and 18. On the other hand, the young Turks of the SOD invoked the Protestant ethnic interest as the paramount concern around which all laws and traditions (including religion) should pivot. They espoused radical change through direct democracy and street politics rather than formal diplomacy or back-room lobbying. These two competing conceptions of Orangeism define the tension within Unionism, but one can arguably see continuity in the winds of change which had been blowing in a rebellious direction since 1954. Indeed, Billy Douglas (who left Central Committee only in 1986) and Smyth were part of the first generation of populist rebels now disparaged by the SOD as 'old men of Grand Lodge'.

The disciplinary response of Grand Lodge to the SOD challenge is just as important as its ideological response. Recall that while some on Central Committee like James Baillie from Antrim defended the O & P rebels in 1954 as representative of the grassroots, there was a consensus that the ringleaders needed to be disciplined and suspended. This time, however, things were different. Forty years of membership decline and grassroots populist challenges combined with a collapsing social hierarchy and twenty-five years of political impotence to take their toll on the Order's leadership. Despite Ruth Dudley Edwards's call for the leadership to 'trample on the SOD's', Smyth and his Grand Lodge lacked the confidence of men like Senator Cunningham or John Andrews, and refrained from disciplining the SOD rebels.[80] This is not necessarily an indictment of Grand Lodge since, realistically, they were more vulnerable to attack than their predecessors. In terms of membership and political influence, the Order was in far worse shape in 1995 than in 1954, and even though Smyth (correctly) diagnosed Orange membership loss as reflecting societal trends, this fact provided an important stick which enemies could use to beat the Order's leaders.

In January 1996, the SOD aborted plans for another Ulster Hall rally, which suggested that the movement had lost its initial momentum. But it did not vanish. Unlike its 1954 predecessor the O & P, whose back was broken within a year by swift disciplinary action from Grand Lodge, the SOD retained a hard core of 500–1,000 activists who could be mobilized to harass internal opponents.[81] Grand Lodge also began to try and contain the movement, albeit through a consensual approach. This began with an invitation to meet Central Committee in March. The members of the SOD stalled for several months before meeting the committee in May. In between, this internecine strife was played out in the media and in private correspondence. David Dowey, for example, demanded an apology from Smyth. Smyth responded that he did 'not consider that I have anything to apologise for...I am of the opinion that a number of [SOD] Brethren owe me an apology'.[82] The May meeting had been billed by the media as a 'showdown', with Joel Patton striking a combative pose. 'There's been talk of an inquisition or a clampdown, but the mood of our people is that we would not accept that,' the SOD leader proclaimed before the showdown.[83]

At the meeting, members of the SOD packed the proceedings with some twenty belligerent supporters and Dowey refused to sit before Smyth as per Orange custom. Smyth, though known as a stern chairman, failed to take Dowey to task for his insubordination, preferring to tread carefully.[84] He emphasized that the meeting was not 'disciplinary' but was designed to seek clarification. When the members of the SOD walked in, he asked them whether they would 'adhere to and uphold' their obligations as Orangemen. While Patton agreed, Dowey objected to the question, stating that he expected them to present their position. 'This is not a trial,' responded Smyth, and at this point an SOD member, William Bigger, presented his case. A prepared presentation by the SOD complained of ill treatment by Grand Lodge and zeroed in on membership decline, arguing that the Order needed to rediscover its *raison d'être*. For the SOD, the Order should remember why it was formed, '[for Protestants] to defend themselves...from murderous attack by the Roman Catholic Irish'. The members of the SOD also threatened legal action against Brian Kennaway for his report—adding that existing copies should be withdrawn and pulped—and demanded an apology from Warren Porter for his remarks.

Bigger presented grievances pertaining to Kennaway's account of the Ulster Hall meeting, printed in the Grand Lodge reports. Claiming it was inaccurate, he demanded an apology from Grand Lodge and a recalling of all report books. At this point, Smyth interjected, 'What is sauce for the goose is sauce for the gander', and reminded the SODs that they had broken Law 10 (against speaking to the media as an Orange representative without Grand Lodge assent). In addition, the members of the SOD had misrepresented Smyth's words in their organ, the *Orange Banner*, which accused Smyth of speaking to Sinn Fein. Moreover, Smyth challenged, Patton, the SOD leader, had appeared on a television programme with a 'convicted republican terrorist'. Dowey objected to this line of questioning and took his seat only after repeatedly being asked by the chairman, Thomas Reid, to do so. Patton evaded Smyth's questions, preferrring instead to address himself to the chairman.

Patton and his acolytes defended their actions as being in the best interests of the Order while Smyth repeatedly drew their attention to violations of Orange law, underlining the split between Smyth's traditionalist Orangeism and the rebellious SOD Orangeism, with its central focus on the broader principle of Orange and Protestant ethnic interest. Next, Denis Watson probed inaccuracies in Bigger's testimony regarding a telephone call between Patton and Watson. Bigger had alleged that 'senior Orangemen' had talked to Sinn Fein, namely Robert Saulters and Jeffrey Donaldson. Awestruck, Saulters replied that he had never met any Sinn Fein people, but only some Quaker representatives. Meanwhile, the Rev. Porter noted that a video of the Ulster Hall rally showed Kennaway's report to be largely accurate. The Education Committee traditionalist Kennaway then provocatively asked about leaks of the report on the members of the SOD to the media, and the Antrim SOD member John McGrath (who remains very active within Grand Lodge today) strenuously denied this. Kennaway asked again, and Dowey retorted that it was a 'ridiculous stupid question' and asked for the names of those besides Kennaway who were involved in compiling the report on the Ulster Hall rally. Clearly a sharp rift was opening up between militants and moderates, with Smyth and Central Committee largely backing the moderates. To this end, Smyth refused to release the names, no doubt partly for safety reasons.[85]

The SOD spokesman Harold Price changed tack to appeal for unity, whereupon William Foy of Cavan, incensed by the SOD's disparaging remarks about Eire Orangemen, intoned, 'what about the Brethren of the Republic?' Price distanced himself from Dowey's Ulster Hall rantings by saying he had said nothing about southern Orangemen. The SOD member Walter Millar, who had once chased Sean O'Callaghan from the field at Drumcree brandishing an umbrella, again took the offensive by calling on Kennaway to withdraw his charge of a Sinn Fein leak, and added, 'we will not accept lap dog status'.[86] Kennaway in turn interjected to clarify his charge, and Dowey again dismissed this as 'an absurd question'. Things became even pettier when Bigger accused Grand Lodge of withdrawing business from his travel company, which was denied by Smyth.

Grand Lodge representatives were determined to get answers to some of the outrageous statements made by the members of the SOD at Ulster Hall. Douglas Caldwell of County Londonderry enquired why the SOD had not dropped the name 'Drumcree' from its title as per the wishes of the Portadown

District master, Harold Gracey. Patton claimed to have sought clarification from Gracey, who had apparently advised him that 'he had never said that', whereupon Watson stated that twice in the Armagh County minutes, Gracey had requested this and had reiterated it 'only yesterday'. Smyth next addressed the group's remarks about Grand Lodge being run by 'old men with one and a half brain cells between them'. Dowey combatively owned up to the remarks, saying he made them through observation, whereupon Smyth snidely commented that Dowey 'must therefore have physiatric [sic] knowledge'.

Each side had extracted its pound of flesh, but the members of the SOD had come out looking amateurish and vindictive. Nonetheless, they continued to press their demands, asking what Grand Lodge had done about their suggested reforms. Bigger also repudiated the group's DUP connections, claiming that neither the DUP nor the Free Presbyterians were behind the movement (though undoubtedly many of its supporters were DUP men). The Grand Secretary appealed for unity, and members of Central Committee implored the group to cease its publicity and work for change within the system. However, Millar, while conceding some points, maintained that the 'system doesn't work'. In conclusion, Smyth took a moderately conciliatory line. He admitted his own fallibility as Grand Master, noted that some of the SOD reforms were real issues, and did not discipline the members.[87]

By June, Grand Lodge had still failed to take action, opting instead for a new addition to the rules and regulations:

The Grand Orange Lodge of Ireland affirms that membership of or involvement with any organisation or group, purporting to be of the Loyal Orange Institution of Ireland [i.e. SOD], working outside the structure of the Grand Orange Lodge of Ireland and/or operating without the authority of the Grand Orange Lodge of Ireland, for the purpose of changing the structure or effecting the policy of the Loyal Orange Institution, is incompatible with membership of that Institution.[88]

The Order did, however, urge unity and decry 'party squabbling' in its third Twelfth Resolution, noting that a house divided cannot stand.[89]

7

From Victory to Defeat: Drumcree, 1996–1998

As the second Drumcree marching season approached in 1996, a propaganda war broke out between Loyalists and Republicans, and the RUC Chief Constable, Hugh Annesley, kept both sides guessing as to his final decision. In a reprise of 1995, Orangemen, joined by many paramilitary elements, began massing in their thousands. In the crowd, different currents collided. Though united in their determination to get the march down the road, David Trimble, Ian Paisley, Joel Patton, Martin Smyth, and the paramilitary leaders possessed varying agendas and vied for leadership of the event. The tragic death of the Catholic taxi driver Michael McGoldrick showed that the paramilitary element had few qualms about venting its spleen through violence. On the other hand, Trimble tried to calm Unionists, uproot paramilitary influence, and negotiate a quid pro quo to allow Catholic residents to march into Portadown. Privately, he briefed Patrick Mayhew on the threat posed by the UVF leader Billy Wright and the digger that had appeared at the field, which could be used to batter police barricades and allow Loyalists through to attack Catholic residents.[1]

Smyth and the Orange Order's marshals, though they failed to claim responsibility for the actions of non-Orange supporters, did—to their credit—try to calm some of the wilder elements at Drumcree.[2] However, they could scarcely contain this throng of thousands. Just as important was the key influence wielded by Wright over Harold Gracey. Whether through intimidation or because of his overwhelming desire for his district to be allowed to march the Garvaghy Road, Gracey failed to repudiate Wright and kept in regular communication with him.[3] Last-minute negotiations involving the COI bishop Robin Eames, the Catholic cardinal Cahan Daly, and the leaders of the Presbyterian and Methodist churches were interrupted by the news that the Order would, as in 1995, be allowed to parade down the road (minus bands and supporters). The principal reason was that the RUC had underestimated the resolve of the Orangemen, the numbers which Loyalists could mobilize, and the havoc which the paramilitaries could wreak. The counter-option was to bring in a large army presence, but RUC leaders feared that a 'bloody Sunday for Protestants' might ensue, with several demonstrators being shot dead.

Unprepared and with police lines stretched, the RUC decided that allowing the march down the road would lead to less trouble than banning it. In the House of Commons, Mayhew tried to deflect criticism of the decision: 'to describe it as capitulation . . . is inappropriate language. It is a striking of a balance in the light of changing circumstances.'[4] However, some suggest that public order was not the only reason for the RUC's decision. The Tory Unionist Lord Cranborne, for instance, maintains that Trimble's reputation within the Unionist community had been hammered by his willingness to allow the half-Irish American Senator George Mitchell to chair peace talks. Allowing the march down the road restored Trimble's stock of political capital, thereby keeping negotiations on track.[5] As evidence, in the December Grand Lodge report, Smyth's address to the membership linked Orangemen's fate to Trimble, lamenting that 'we are blamed and David Trimble has been vilified for seeking to prevent tragedy in Portadown'.[6] Yet in the very moment of the Orangemen's victory there lay the seeds of its ultimate defeat as Britain, Ireland, and the world once again associated the Orangemen with sectarian violence and intimidation. One concerned Orangeman decried the lack of Grand Lodge media planning for Drumcree, remarking: 'the institution was slaughtered in the propaganda war . . . the fight for Ulster will be won by the side that makes best use of the media . . . it is no longer sufficient to have a just cause . . . it is time we realised we are at war and acted accordingly'.[7] The Grand Lodge paid heed to this internal criticism, and the Orange publicity machine would become a great deal more sophisticated in the decade to come. Nonetheless, the loss in the propaganda war was to have immediate negative consequences for Orangeism. The outcry from Northern Nationalists and the Irish government's Department of Foreign Affairs was expected. However, the Orangemen did not fully anticipate the fallout, which emerges in Mayhew's reply to his questioners at the height of the Drumcree crisis: 'The hon. Gentleman has spoken about a commission . . . and I agree with the Church leaders and those who speak of the need for an early review . . . We shall therefore be looking sympathetically and urgently at some means by which an independent and external eye can be cast upon the matter [of parades] with a view to making recommendations.'[8] The upshot of this was the North review of parades, which would later develop into the Parades Commission (PC), the bête noire of Orangeism. Needless to say, the Order later opposed the North report.[9]

Meanwhile, the SOD continued to wreak havoc inside and outside Orange halls, particularly in Antrim. Much of the storm concerned Grand Lodge's apparent 'softness' on Nationalists. One of the key taboos of Unionist and Orange life is political or religious contact with Catholics, especially if cordial or voluntary. Politically, working on split local councils with SDLP (though not Sinn Fein) councillors was decried by the SOD, but accepted by many Orangemen as an inevitability. On the other hand, discussions that the new Orange Grand Master, Bobby Saulters, allegedly had with John Hume of the SDLP drew opprobrium from the grassroots—even those who backed Saulters against the SOD.[10] On the religious side, attendance at Catholic funerals and baptisms was frowned upon but, as we saw earlier, was deemed acceptable where the individual was fulfilling an official duty. Smyth's sharing of a table with Catholics at a prayer breakfasts—a more voluntary act of 'fraternising with the opposition'—was, by contrast, viewed with great disfavour by many Orangemen. Likewise, when the Grand Lodge defended the rights of Catholics to worship without running the gauntlet of Loyalist intimidation at Harryville, County Antrim, in late 1996, it was denounced by hardliners such as the SOD. In the Orange report of proceedings, Smyth called for Orangemen 'not to impede Roman Catholics worshipping... [since]... we stand for Civil & Religious [liberty]', while Saulters and the Antrim Grand Master Robert McElroy openly supported the civil rights of Catholic worshippers at Harryville.[11]

Another Orangeman to face the wrath of many was David Trimble, who attended two Catholic funerals and met the Pope in early 1999. 'If any other Orangeman went to meet the Pope he would face expulsion,' charged Portadown District's David Jones, but despite a district-level resolution against him, Grand Lodge did no more than send a letter to Trimble and have Saulters remind him of his Orange obligations.[12] A much more serious taboo was marrying a Roman Catholic (Orange Law 4). In the mid 1990s, the Grand Lodge of Canada voted by a narrow margin to repeal Law 4 in a move which pitted the more liberal Newfoundland half of the Order against the more conservative Ontario wing. One reason for the move was that social changes had led to such a high degree of inter-faith marriage that the law was affecting potential recruitment.[13] In 2000, the US branch considered the same move. In both cases, Grand Lodge resigned itself to these developments, merely expressing its disapproval in written form to the jurisdictions.[14]

One of the more rigorously enforced taboos within Orangeism was a refusal to negotiate with Nationalists, especially if tainted by violent Republicanism. This was true even if negotiations were mediated by a third party. Hence the SODs homed in on the Grand Lodge's tentative attempts to negotiate indirectly with Catholic residents in the overwhelmingly Nationalist town of Dunloy through the independent Mediation Network.[15] In addition to a regular campaign of media sniping at Saulters's leadership and Grand Lodge from the right, the SOD mobilized for direct action. In March 1997, busloads of SOD men disrupted the County Antrim Grand Lodge sessions at Carnlea. An attempt to hold the sessions a month later was also physically disrupted. Though Antrim leaders spoke of the SOD's 'bully boy tactics' and

Saulters denounced it publicly for its 'thuggery', words were not matched by disciplinary action and no members were suspended.

Privately, the newly appointed Saulters was dismayed by events. In a speech to Grand Lodge, he bewailed the bad publicity which the Harryville pickets had brought on the Institution. He stressed that he had shown restraint by not taking any disciplinary action against Orange brethren wearing collarettes at Harryville. Remarking on the breaking of windows at the Catholic chapel by Loyalists and the assassination of a policeman, he mused, 'Are we taking over from the I.R.A. or the Ku Klux Klan? . . . by our silence we condone these acts of atrocity.' Saulters next paid tribute to the moderate Mayor of Antrim for condemning the Loyalist violence and threw up his hands at the membership for its criticism of his indirect dialogue with residents at Dunloy. 'Brethren,' he began, 'quite frankly I no longer know what this Membership wants . . . we have the case where one Lodge is given all they supposedly wanted [in terms of a right to parade] . . . and they refuse to accept it, another Lodge . . . gains what they want and a number of Brethren condemn their action, I can only assume that those who are complaining . . . have no idea of the difficulties involved . . . and have never been in the situation of having to organise a contentious parade.' Saulters ended by castigating those (undoubtedly SOD supporters) who had delivered an avalanche of abusive correspondence to him by letter and telephone. He claimed to have switched to answering calls only from his answering machine 'to protect my wife and family. The next step is ex-directory which I didn't want to do as other Orangemen might call, but some of the language is choice'.[16]

One of the encouraging signs for the leadership was the strong measure of support for Grand Lodge that came from an internal Orange Commission, which recommended that the structure of Grand Lodge be retained, despite SOD demands. This recommendation met with universal approval across all counties consulted. On the other hand, the Commission did attempt to endorse many SOD reforms, thereby indicating the SOD's surreptitious influence. Yet, interestingly, the more 'reformist' proposals which expressed some of the SOD's demands (such as reducing the number of deputy grand masters and chaplains at Grand Lodge) were opposed by counties and districts representing half or more of the membership. Likewise, five of eight county lodges and ten districts objected to the SOD-inspired demand that county representation at Grand Lodge should follow the numerical strength of each county.[17]

Correspondence from grassroots lodges also backed Grand Lodge and upbraided the SOD for sowing division within the ranks. This suggests that the members of the SOD were probably random individuals who failed to dominate their lodges and districts. 'Members have been alarmed at the amount of brethren who style themselves prominent Orangemen,' wrote the secretary of Sandy Row District 5 in Belfast. 'By their action some members are doing what our enemies have not succeeded in doing in over 200 years.' Sandy Row called on Grand Lodge to discipline the members of the SOD, as did Whiterock LOL 974 from the Shankill.[18] The same message came from LOL 550 in Saintfield, County Down, LOL 15 in Comber, County Down, City of Londonderry District 5, LOL 621 (Waterside, Londonderry), and LOL 60 (Scarva, Tandragee, Armagh). No letter expressed support for the SOD, though three (from Magherafelt District, County Londonderry, Bessbrook District, Armagh, and Markethill District, Armagh) were critical of Grand Lodge for indirectly negotiating with residents' groups or lacking a parades strategy. All lodges pleaded for unity and an end to the public bickering between the SOD and Grand Lodge.[19]

This was a vain hope. The struggle between the SOD and Grand Lodge raged throughout 1997 and would not reach its nadir until the following year. Battles were taking place locally and provincially. In Patton's home county of Tyrone, he had tried to mobilize a movement to oust the traditionalist leadership of a lodge in the 90 per cent Catholic town of Dromore, where lodge officers had sat down with church leaders (including Catholic clergy) to negotiate over marching. Despite a successful parade, SOD hardliners and Paisleyites viewed marching rights as non-negotiable and thus fingered the traditionalist Orange negotiators as traitors. Joel Patton and the deputy master of the Dromore Lodge, Gerald Marshall, were behind a no-confidence motion in the traditionalists under the Grand Secretary, Charlie Kenwell. The motion split the forty-three members and failed by only one vote.[20] Patton next tried to mobilize against Kenwell and others at the Tyrone county meeting, but failed spectacularly, with 69 opposed to the SOD, 9 for, and 3 abstentions, suggesting that Patton had little support in his own county. As the Tyrone secretary Reid announced to Grand Lodge in May, the vote was 'clear and decisive . . . [we] were not going to take much more'. Reid also promised to pursue charges against Tyrone brethren who were involved in the Antrim disruptions.[21] Notwithstanding its endorsement from the membership, the Grand Lodge hesitated to discipline Patton and other members of the SOD. At Central Committee in May, the leadership considered the aftermath of the SOD's Antrim obstructions. Several of those present called for action in line with the tighter rules on discipline outlined the previous year. However, Central Committee ultimately decided to co-opt (or as critics would say, appease) the SOD, prompted by a letter from Markethill District, Portadown, Armagh, urging Grand Lodge to 'work towards a reconciliation' with the SOD.[22]

For instance, by June, Patton, who had routinely failed to turn up for meetings, defied higher lodge authority, broke Orange laws against speaking to the media, and attacked his fellow Orangemen, appeared at the June Grand Lodge meeting as an active participant. At the meeting, Grand Lodge agreed 'in the spirit of brotherhood and in the interest of maintaining unity' to an amnesty for all previous misdemeanours. Though it resolved to enforce discipline in the future, it subsequently failed to match actions with words.[23] Patton's was by no means the dominant voice, though, and it was in fact the UUP's David McNarry who spearheaded the hardline stance against entering into negotiations with the Mediation Network. This motion was backed by Patton and Gracey of Portadown, but was opposed by traditionalists like Warren Porter and Leitrim's John Richardson. Patton was also able to obtain certain clarifications and amendments to Orange policy on media and parading. For example, he wanted to know if the Order would speak to residents' groups *without* an obvious affiliation to Sinn Fein/IRA. In the end, Grand Lodge, led by McNarry, approved a compromise measure on an 82–18 vote which opposed negotiation with residents or mediators unless they met a high standard of 'trustworthiness'.[24]

In addition to gaining a voice at Grand Lodge and shaping the Orange Commission report on Grand Lodge restructuring, SOD men came to dominate a new 'strategy committee' of Antrim County Lodge.[25] In contrast with the situations of 1953–4 or 1959–60, this militant protest movement was thus able quickly to penetrate the Orange power structure even as the Order's elite tried to contain the movement's subversive energies. As in 1995 but unlike the 1950s protest movements the SOD used violent intimidation, and they did so without the backing of any of the established counties. By contrast, in the 1950s, county elites in Antrim and Belfast extended sympathy and backing to the rebels. Already, the SOD was beginning to shape Orange policy. The proposal to set up a commission to examine the structure of the Order was initiated by a Belfast lodge and presented to Grand Lodge in December 1995, just after the SOD Ulster Hall rally. The Commission's remit included the need to 'study and address concerns' raised at the December meeting by the SOD and the Commission's report, which we will come to later, clearly reflected SOD concerns.[26]

The attempt to mollify Patton by bringing him inside the Grand Lodge ultimately failed. In the lead-up to the 1997 marching season, Patton was a regular commentator in the press, and banged away at his core demands of no negotiation with residents, a reform of Grand Lodge democracy, and the resignation of Saulters. Grand Lodge responded by attacking the divisiveness of the members of the SOD. Led by traditionalists like Saulters, Denis Watson, the Rev. Warren Porter, Smyth, the Rev. William Bingham, and the Rev. Brian Kennaway, the leadership braved the mutinous winds and continued with its pragmatic course, earning a degree of media praise in the process. Bingham, Watson, and Gracey wrote to Tony Blair, the newly elected British Prime Minister, assuring him that they would comport themselves well and pleading for the Drumcree Church parade to be permitted to return via the Garvaghy Road.[27] This Orange letter subsequently worked its way into a government 'game plan' for Drumcree.[28]

In the end, the Drumcree parade was allowed to take place in 1997. The reasons for this remain unclear, however.[29] Security calculations on the part of the police (i.e. which side was in a position to cause more trouble) probably played the leading role, and the Northern Ireland Office's 'game plan' revolves around conflict resolution, with the need to work through 'influencers' like Saulters and Trimble to achieve moderation. The game plan comes across as overly optimistic in its failure to appreciate the strength of the 'contact' taboo, and in its underestimate of how paramilitaries could intimidate Portadown Orangemen, who could in turn constrain traditionalist Orange leaders. What is interesting is that the 'least worst' outcome—as expressed by the British government, Northern Ireland Office, and RUC—is identified as a controlled march.[30] This no doubt reflected the balance of intimidation (i.e. 'public order considerations'), as the RUC and the Secretary of State Mo Mowlam unwisely revealed after the event. It is true that Blair wished to shore up Trimble's position in the Unionist community since Trimble seemed to be more open than his predecessor Molyneaux to making a deal—as evinced by his willingness to meet with the Catholic primate and to enter talks with Sinn Fein representatives for the first time.[31] Yet if this was a factor it was of limited importance since all documents suggest that public order considerations were paramount in police and Northern Ireland Office thinking.

A surge of Nationalist rioting and invective followed Drumcree III. In the chaotic few days between the Drumcree Church parade and the Twelfth, the RUC tried to regain control. The Orange Order helped in this task. One of its crucial decisions was to coordinate the re-routing of Orange Twelfth parades from four contested areas. Parades planned for Shambles (Armagh), Lower Ormeau (Belfast), Londonderry City, and Newry were put on hold for 'the greater good of the Province' and to avoid loss of life.[32] This action was not, however, a Grand Lodge-driven one. It appears instead to have been initiated by the county and district lodges themselves after being contacted by the RUC, who shared shocking intelligence with the county lodge officials—such as the presence of IRA snipers along some of the routes—which these Orange local elites found 'in the main matching up with what we were aware of . . . after long and heart searching deliberation we were more than satisfied that we could not go ahead . . . None were any sadder than ourselves that the decision had to be taken and we could understand why some were annoyed.'[33]

Could political calculation have played any role here? Dean Godson, drawing on David Trimble's remarks, contends that the British were concerned by Trimble's flagging support after he agreed to Senator George Mitchell's chairmanship of the peace talks. One way of shoring up Trimble was to ensure that the 1997 march could proceed at Drumcree.[34] While there is no evidence to suggest that the Order made any deals with the RUC, it is clear that the RUC, as one of its ancillary arguments, raised the issue of its decision to permit the march. But the local Orange leaders would not have sacrificed their own parades for the brethren at Drumcree—instead, the RUC had to demonstrate a strong security risk to its members. The only possibility for British influence was therefore through the RUC and its ability to (1) manipulate intelligence and thereby trick the Orangemen into backing down; and (2) mollify the Order by assuring a march at Drumcree. There was some evidence for this at the November meeting, where Londonderry City Orangemen told the RUC that:

> We feel to some degree that. . . even though the situation appeared to merit what we were told. . . in fact we were not being given the full truth of the situation and that we were conned. This would be a despicable policing decision and we require an honest answer. . . . [In addition] Last time the basis of the argument was on what would happen at Garvaghy Rd. This should have no bearing on policing at other venues on other dates and can we be assured that in future policing will be on merit?

Watson also later charged that 'Ronnie Flanagan may have overstated the situation in an attempt to force those lodges to re-route.'[35]

The county and district Orangemen who agreed to call off or re-route their parades never once mentioned Drumcree at the July discussions, and it is clear that the RUC decision to permit an Orange march there had little direct bearing on their decision. These local Orange leaders were under intense pressure—electoral, moral, and physical—from their grassroots not to 'surrender' their local routes, and thus the suggestion that the local parades were called off in exchange for the right to march at Drumcree cannot be sustained. Indeed, looking back on the event at a highly charged meeting with the RUC Chief Constable in November, the Londonderry City Orange leaders recounted how, after their decision to re-route,

> we had still to sell the idea to our grass roots members. . . we met with [district]. . . and all private lodge [masters] in Drumahoe later that evening. A further meeting was held on the following evening (11th July). . . the bulk of members agreed to abide by our decision, nevertheless some rebelled for a time on the 12th July morning and some for a longer period. After 12th July. . . we took loads of abuse. . . we have been having a tough passage. . . particularly our wives and families. The DGCM had to change phone numbers. We have managed to bring the membership along with us and have been re-elected for 1998, but, as we said at the time, our diversion was for once only.[36]

The intimidation of Orangemen by paramilitary elements is often underappreciated. In 1985, when Orangemen were prevented by police from parading the 'tunnel' in Portadown, they marched up to police lines in protest and then turned away. One onlooker recalls how the massed crowd of Loyalist stone-throwers heaped abuse on the departing Orangemen, taunting them as 'Lundies' (traitors).[37] In 1997, when the RUC Chief Constable Ronnie Flanagan was permitted by Smyth to try to sell an alternate Drumcree route to the Order, a senior Portadown Orangeman told him that even if this was acceptable, he could not agree to it because Loyalist thugs would burn the

Orangemen's houses down. 'The delegate did not mention [the UVF paramilitary leader] Billy Wright by name,' note Chris Ryder and Vincent Kearney, 'but that was who he meant.'[38]

The courageous stand on the part of the four county and district Orange leaders in July 1997 was designed to avert bloodshed and enhanced the Orange public image and its political capital, but was inevitably viewed as a betrayal by the SOD and its fellow travellers and pinned on conspirators at the highest levels of Grand Lodge. The *Orange Banner*, the official organ of the SOD, wrote:

A clique of senior Orangemen from within the Central and Education Committees, led by Revs [Warren] Porter and [Brian] Kennaway, began to meet in secret to devise a plan to overturn the clear mandate given by the grass roots of our Institution [i.e. no meetings with residents or surrendering of parade routes]. Part of the betrayal...included the undermining of Brethren in Dunloy...the first action taken by members of the Spirit of Drumcree was to halt this betrayal...in Cloughmills, County Antrim Orangemen backed up this action by causing County Officers to reverse their decision to meet Dunloy residents [a decision later declared void by Grand Lodge]...The sinister plot by the clique was revealed to everyone in the summer of 1997 when four significant traditional Twelfth Parades were surrendered in a clandestine and arbitrary manner...It was clear to us that unless decisive action was taken the situation would spiral out of control and our Institution would be destroyed.[39]

One of the 'cliques' mentioned was the Education Committee (EC), an institutional bastion of traditionalist Orangeism. Though vigorous in its desire to promote the Protestant collective memory through histories and lectures, and to protect the Protestant character of the state school curriculum, the EC realized it needed to improve the Order's public image. Evangelism was its watchword, not secrecy, and it sought to engage with the wider community in order to improve the perception of the Order in the wider society.

Led by clergymen, the EC pioneered a more media-friendly strategy for the Order as early as the 1970s when Canon S. E. Long, a long-time chair of the Press Committee and EC activist, spoke of the need for 'media training'.[40] By the mid 1980s, this cultural evangelism was kicking into high gear both within and without the Order. Inside the Institution, the EC under the Rev. Fred Baillie and Clifford Smyth had begun the process, speaking of the need to travel abroad to fight misrepresentation of the Order and for the Education Committee 'generally to become a "fighting" think-tank'. The goal was to be education of both the Protestant community and those outside it.[41] Outside the Order, David Trimble and his Ulster Society for the Promotion of Ulster–British Heritage and Culture had begun to work, sensing that government cultural funding would be more accessible to a non-Orange body.[42] In practice, the two bodies functioned separately but maintained important contacts, and most if not all Ulster Society personnel would have been Orangemen. Both contributed to a History Working Group report and noted the opportunities presented by the new government discourse of 'cultural heritage'.[43]

In 1990, the Rev. Brian Kennaway assumed leadership of the committee from Clifford Smyth (himself a modernizer), and began to take it in an even more pragmatic and evangelistic direction. We have seen how Kennaway, a Belfast Presbyterian cleric, raised his voice against troublemakers in Belfast parades from the mid 1980s. At Grand Lodge in the 1980s and 1990s, he emphasized a pragmatic approach which sought to propound a positive image of Orangeism even if it meant breaking taboos regarding contact with 'the enemy'. The debate over contact with Nationalists pits pragmatists, who see contact as a chance positively to put across the Order's rational case, against purists, who view contact with Catholics as a violation of the boundary between sacred and profane. In early 1996, Kennaway's EC showed its pragmatism by addressing various external gatherings, including the Irish Association in Dublin, the Ulster People's College, the Columbanus Community, and a conference on 'Varieties of Scottishness' at Queen's University. It legitimized its actions with reference to its mission statement, which committed itself to 'engage in the process of continuing to educate . . . the general public in the truths and principles of the Reformed Religion, and our historical and cultural heritage'.[44] A year later, letters were received from several Catholic colleges expressing appreciation for Kennaway's 'Protestant View of St. Patrick' pamphlet and seeking to invite EC members to address their pupils.[45] Kennaway also presided over the committee's exploration of the new Northern Ireland human rights agenda, which emerged out of the 1998 Good Friday Agreement and was connected with the European Convention on Human Rights.[46]

Kennaway's evangelism, which had the ear of Central Committee, was bound to collide eventually with the rebellious militancy of the SOD. The two sides met in dramatic fashion on the evening of 12 September 1997. Inside the House of Orange on Dublin Road in Belfast, Kennaway chaired a meeting of the EC. After a reading from Ephesians, he presented correspondence from Alistair Graham of the newly formed PC, which had been established as part of the Public Order (NI) 1998 bill following Irish government, Northern Nationalist, and world press response to the violence of Drumcree 1997. The PC had been opposed root and branch by Orangemen, who, with some justification, considered it anti-Orange by virtue of the fact that Protestants tended to express their culture through parading at about ten times the frequency of Catholics. As Trimble remarked, this meant that Nationalist transgressions of Protestant space like the high-speed car 'cavalcading' of the Gaelic Athletic Association did not fall under the PC's remit.[47] Despite its antagonism to the PC, the pragmatists of the EC reasoned that dialogue was preferable to the symbolic puritanism (but practical powerlessness) of boycotting the PC. In the letter, the PC's chairman, Alistair Graham, wrote:

Having noted the Education Committee's many publications and other recent initiatives aimed at enhancing understanding of the Orange Order and various facets of Orangeism, the Commission would be pleased to meet you and as many members of your Committee as possible, to explore your views on what steps we might take in pursuit of the educational dimension to our remit.[48]

In the meeting, the EC was split on the issue of whether to meet the PC. Two recent articles in *Sunday Life* had leaked news of the meeting, fed by leaks from disgruntled EC members. Among those opposing the meeting were Nelson McCausland, the current convenor, George Patton, the Order's Executive Officer, Grand Treasurer Mervyn Bishop, Grand Secretary John McCrea, and Roger Bradley. During the meeting, Graham Montgomery, a young grammar school teacher, spoke for the majority when he claimed that the committee could not wait for the twice-yearly meeting of Grand Lodge to review its decisions and still fulfil its educational outreach remit. Patton, however, demurred. McCrea agreed with Patton, noting that while correspondence had flowed between the PC and Grand Lodge, a meeting with the PC would 'undermine the Grand Master's position'. At this, Kennaway replied that Grand Lodge had not forbidden the EC to meet the PC. McCausland said that he was 'suspicious of the motives' of the commissioners and felt that more time was required to prepare, but did not have an objection in principle to the meeting.

Some at the meeting, including McCrea and Bishop, were worried that the PC would try to draw the Orangemen into negotiations over the 1998 parades. In the end, Kennaway asked for a vote on whether to meet the committee to discuss educational matters only. The vote was 8–4 in favour. At this stage, George Russell, who had left the meeting, returned to inform those inside that a 'protest' was going on outside the building.[49] Not only this, but the demonstrators were members of the SOD, mobilized by Joel Patton, and they barricaded the members of the EC in the House of Orange for an hour and a quarter. Only the conservative dissenters, Bishop, Patton, and McCrea, were able to leave unmolested. At this point, Montgomery told the others that he would consider resigning from the committee—a fact reprinted in *Sunday Life*, suggesting that leaks from anti-Kennaway committee members were a regular feature at this point.[50]

After they arrived late at the meeting with the PC, Graham tried to reassure the Orangemen that he wanted to educate the public about parades from the Orange point of view so as to increase mutual understanding and reduce 'mayhem on the streets'. Even these moderate Orangemen were very wary of being drawn into wider debates, so they insisted that the meeting be only about education. Graham soon left the meeting, to be replaced by David Hewitt and Berna McIvor. The discussion thus turned to the difficulties experienced by the Orangemen in getting their pamphlets into schools. Here the PC promised to try and get schools to hear the 'moderate and sensible Orange case' and added that it might be able to 'open doors' for the Order.[51]

The debriefing meeting took place on the 19th. Some committee members who had not attended the PC meeting, notably T. Ross, were keen to cover themselves, and insisted that the names of those who attended be included in the minutes. Nelson McCausland, who did not attend this meeting, protested that minutes of the meeting were not included, hence his absence. He wanted a copy of the letter of invitation from the PC, but this was refused since, as Warren Loane pointed out, he had heard the letter read aloud. These more conservative dissenters failed to dominate the meeting, however. As if to answer the naysayers, the Orange archivist Cecil Kilpatrick insisted on an addition to the minutes stating that the committee had been held against its will by the members of the SOD. He also added that the meeting with the PC had been useful, contained no traps, and raised no unnecessary fears. Finally, Kennaway was reconfirmed in office (and in his decision to meet the PC) by the remaining members of the committee.[52]

At subsequent meetings, existing rifts deepened between the traditionalist majority and the bloc of conservative dissenters, some of whom were probably involved in leaking committee business to their acolytes. A letter from McCrea to Saulters reported that the SOD demonstrators had behaved 'courteously' to McCrea, George Patton, and Bishop when they left, and McCrea made the highly implausible and disgraceful assertion that Kennaway was the source of the leaks to the press. In McCrea's words, 'my personal opinion is...that the Convenor [Kennaway]...leaked this information to basically turn the attention away from himself to the Grand Secretary and the Grand Treasurer. I have to the best of my knowledge adhered to the Policy of Grand Lodge'.[53] This accusation beggars belief, and represented an attempt by the more conservative faction to distance itself from the traditionalist (but unpopular) wing of the EC and to also minimize friction with the more numerous SOD splinter group which was intimidating the Grand Lodge elite.

Before rushing to condemn the conservatives, it is important to understand the difficult position that Patton, McCrea, and Bishop—as Grand Lodge members—were in as a result of SOD pressure. Kennaway's committee had simply moved too far ahead of mainstream Orange opinion.[54] This was initially revealed in a series of letters from grassroots lodges such as Muckamore 1422 (Antrim), 1934 (Belfast), Carrickfergus District 19 (Antrim), and Antrim District 13 (Antrim). Antrim Grand Lodge also supported the sentiments expressed. The text of the letters is generally temperate and draws attention to the EC's breach of Grand Lodge policy. LOL 1934 referred to the PC as a 'quango paid for and elected by the Northern Ireland Office' which could not be 'educated'. While accusing the EC of defying Grand Lodge, it was careful to express appreciation for the EC's past good work. Carrickfergus District declared that the EC had 'overstepped the mark and are no longer representative of grassroots opinion'. Most lodges wanted the EC to be reformed or restructured, to focus more narrowly on defending the Protestant curriculum and less on its outreach function.[55]

Meanwhile, the aggrieved traditionalists on the EC sought to bring internal charges (for violations of Orange law) against the members of the SOD for their blockade despite the discouragement of some among the conservative minority of the EC. The traditionalists received some support from Grand Lodge when a 'senior source' told the press that 'If they [the members of the SOD] are found guilty, the situation is that you cannot just do something like that and get away with it'.[56] However, the committee charged with looking into the preferment of charges was led by the more cautious members of the EC, notably McCrea and George Patton, who were keenly aware of the SOD's challenge to Grand Lodge on their right flank.[57] Patton's position paper on the SOD homed in on its violation of Laws 18 (wearing of regalia in inappropriate situation) and 23 ('Conduct Unbecoming an Orangeman'). The paper argued that for Grand Lodge to bring a charge, it would have to affect the entire Institution rather than a local lodge. The paper further recommended that charges initially be brought either by the individuals affected or at county level.[58] Later, the Central Committee agreed to proceed with the charges against the SOD, with action to be taken at county level.[59]

Joel Patton and the other SOD men vowed to resist any charges, and were true to their word. SOD supporters first disrupted a county meeting in Portadown on 3 December, when the Armagh Orangeman Alec Newell was to be tried for his part in the blockade. This episode ended in pushing and shoving outside the hall.[60] Two nights later, the Tyrone SOD leaders Joel Patton and Walter Millar—whom Ruth Dudley Edwards once described as a 'hatchet-faced man'—were tried and charged by County Tyrone Grand Lodge in a remote tin-roofed lodge in Newtownsville.[61] However, rulings would need to go through the slowly turning wheels of Grand Lodge before expulsion or suspension could take place. In the meantime, Patton and Millar publicly tore up the charges against them, and Patton taunted his accusers by claiming: 'Those who brought the charges do not have the courage to go through with what they started.'[62] This comment was an indirect reference to the fact that Kennaway and several other EC members did not attend the Tyrone meeting, for fear of their own personal safety. In the *Orange Banner*, the members of the SOD pitted the EC 'clique' (named as only Kennaway, Montgomery, Hatch, Richardson, Whitten, Loane, and Kilpatrick—and thus excluding the conservatives) against the martyr-like 'Drumcree Five' who were charged in Antrim, Tyrone, and Armagh. 'Unable to pick on individuals, Kennaway's mob ran scared and failed to even turn up,' boasted Patton.[63]

The SOD had a well-orchestrated campaign of 'civil disobedience' with tactics that ironically would have made left-wing civil rights demonstrators proud. Rather than occupy UC Berkeley, however, Patton and his henchmen chose the more modest two-storey surroundings of the House of Orange, the

Orange headquarters. Several times a target of IRA bombs, Orange HQ was on the second floor of a drab, white-fronted modern block with blackout windows, situated—for protection—above some fast-food establishments on Dublin Road, one of the city's main arteries.[64] At 4.30 p.m. on 9 December, six SOD men entered the House of Orange and asked the Executive Officer George Patton for the keys, saying they needed to photocopy documents and wanted to stay late to hold a meeting. Grand Secretary John McCrea also conversed with some of the men.[65] After obtaining the keys, the SOD men called Joel Patton, triumphally declaring to their leader: 'The building is taken. It's ours.' This plot had been hatched over several weeks and was now bearing fruit.[66]

The SOD's audacity knew no bounds. Joel Patton organized fifty SOD supporters to occupy the building. They covered it with posters calling for Saulters's resignation and an end to 'betrayal' and remained overnight. They faxed major news media to inform them of the occupation. When delegates to the Grand Lodge sessions arrived the next day, they were met by between thirty and 100 SOD supporters who crowded around the building and prevented delegates from meeting.[67] Never before had a splinter group been so confident in its challenge to the Orange hierarchy. The ginger group that became the IOO in 1903 never did more than interrupt a platform proceeding. The O & P rebels of 1953–4 were active in the press, held a rally, and did some heckling, but never disrupted meetings or Grand Lodge sessions.

An obvious question that the evidence begs is whether McCrea and George Patton were complicit in the occupation. This seems doubtful. The atmosphere at Orange HQ tends to be informal, functional, and convivial. McCrea and Patton, if they recognized the men, may have feared that they were up to no good. If so, they probably felt uncomfortable denying them access because of the need for Grand Lodge to be perceived by rank-and-file members to be open to all shades of the grassroots membership—and thereby to be debunking SOD accusations. In any case, the event provided the SOD with lots of publicity. The SOD men themselves justified the action as a spirited move which foiled the Grand Lodge 'clique's' sinister plans to bring in an RUC 'ring of steel' to keep the 'ordinary Orangeman' away as it elected 'the puppet Saulters'. In conclusion, they wrote, 'The secret clique are desperately clinging on to power, prepared to capitulate, surrender and destroy the Orange Order.'[68]

After being forced to hold its sessions in West Belfast, where Saulters was re-elected as Grand Master, Grand Lodge issued a strongly worded statement:

The Grand Orange Lodge of Ireland meeting in West Belfast Orange Hall on Wednesday, 10 December 1997 abhors the conduct exhibited in the 'House of Orange' today by persons who call themselves Brethren. Such conduct and act of defiance is reprehensible. Grand Lodge categorically states that the only course for those persons to take is to resign forthwith from the Institution. Persons not prepared to accept the Rules of the Institution are unwelcome and are unworthy to be called Members of the Loyal Orange Institution.[69]

Ill. 11   Grand Master Robert Saulters, Past Master Martin Smyth and Kenneth Watson, Past Antrim Grand Master, c. 1997 —Saulters took over from Smyth as Grand Master in 1996. Lacking Smyth's gravitas, Saulters was buffeted by both hardline and liberal pressures on Grand Lodge.

County Armagh had urged that Grand Lodge deal with the matter of the SOD once and for all. Orange leaders proceeded cautiously, first obtaining legal counsel on what charges could be laid against the SOD occupiers. Alan McAlister, whom the Order solicited for an opinion, believed that the occupation itself was not against the law, but that charges could be laid in the case of the disruption of the Portadown meeting. David Brewster, a barrister and Orangeman from County Londonderry, felt that while some 'smaller fry' might be charged, the ringleaders had not broken any law. Those at the meeting thus concurred that little could be done and that 'no offence meriting expulsion' under Orange rules was committed. One voice noted that Central Committee might need to pass a resolution specifically defining the SOD's actions as falling under the law against 'defiance of lodge authority' and that participation in these events should be considered under the rubric of the Orange law against 'conduct unbecoming an Orangeman'. Another suggested that one solution was to write to those involved asking whether they agreed to abide by Orange law. A negative response would constitute grounds for dismissal.[70]

A swift attempt to expel the SOD occupiers would have been morally upright and courageous under the circumstances. But in this case, Grand Lodge was to turn the other cheek. This began when someone at the meeting mentioned the unmentionable: 'There is of course the difficulty of implementation'.[71] As Kennaway notes, a strong vein of fear imbued this 'difficulty'. This was related to the paramilitary connections of some SOD supporters. For instance, Ivor Knox Young, master of LOL 9 in Portadown District, was one of those who stood near Joel Patton for a photo opportunity during the occupation of the House of Orange. Young later reappeared in a paramilitary display at a Drumcree stand-off with fifty other Loyalists, including the famed UDA gangster Johnny 'Mad Dog' Adair. Kennaway charges Grand Lodge with running scared of these men: 'The fact that his [Young's] photograph [later] appeared widely in the media, and that no disciplinary action was taken, indicated the unwillingness of the leadership to take on their own hard men.'[72] The bravery and moral correctness of Kennaway's stand does not detract from the fact that in the Northern Ireland setting, the threat from paramilitaries was, and remains, very real. Just as fear of the IRA kept some candidates from allowing their names to go forward to replace Martin Smyth as Grand Master, trepidation at the thought of a visit by UVF or UDA hard men led some to keep their heads below the parapet. Moreover, not only did Orange elites face a physical threat, but they also feared for their very legitimacy at a time when the members of the SOD were openly flouting Grand Lodge authority.

The first step in the Grand Lodge's conciliatory approach was what one Orange trustee called the 'need for a charm offensive'.[73] This began with an unofficial meeting in early January between Grand Lodge officers (including Saulters) and members of the SOD. The secretary of County Antrim, Drew Davison, first broached the idea and approached Grand Secretary John McCrea (also from Antrim), who—along with his sympathetic Antrim colleague William Leathem—helped organize the talks.[74] At the meeting, Joel Patton was positively effusive, stating that he 'appreciated the opportunity' to be at the meeting to 'break the ice' between the camps. Dowey, the hot-headed, self-proclaimed 'sectarian bigot', also struck a conciliatory note, declaring himself to be 'anxious to dispel the fallacy of a split'. Discussion began with the common ground of the need for unity in the face of a press and a Northern Ireland Office which sought a split. In a curious reversal of power, Saulters and McCrea found themselves explaining their apprently inadequate conduct to the SOD leaders during the 1997 Drumcree crisis. In relation to the SOD's tactics, David Dowey averred that while some 'boys have been boisterous', no weapons were carried. The mood was getting so chummy by this juncture that Davison sought to push for a joint statement of reconciliation. However, some of those present felt that the 'time was not yet right' and that the matter would need to be approved at Grand Lodge and Central Committee. The members of the SOD did not yield much. When queried by Mervyn Bishop about violence at Drumcree and whether Joel Patton could ensure no violence, Patton replied that he couldn't give that assurance.[75]

At Central Committee two days later, Saulters informed those present that the Grand Lodge officers had been treated with respect. This news was greeted with a palpable sense of relief by a Central Committee eager for unity and a number of those present congratulated Saulters on his initiative. Despite this, concern was expressed that Central Committee's strategy for disciplining the members of the SOD was being leaked to members.[76] At a follow-up meeting between the members of the SOD and the Orange leadership, it was noted that while most on Central Committee were positive about the talks, others reacted with 'stunned silence'. In terms of concrete policy, Patton commended Grand Lodge's decision to oppose the PC. In a further testament to SOD influence, this unofficial meeting agreed to revisit the reform paper previously submitted to Grand Lodge after the Ulster Hall rally on 14 November 1995. A discussion ensured over the SOD's principal demands. The demands of 1995 included:

1. The immediate resignation of Martin Smyth as Grand Master
2. Direct, popular elections for Grand Master and other top offices (rather than these being chosen by elected county leaders)
3. The election of an Annual Congress of Orange delegates, elected by private lodges—a policy-making body which would oversee the Order's future direction
4. No voluntary re-routing of parades
5. No talks with Sinn Fein/IRA or surrogate groups
6. Grand Lodge to disaffiliate immediately from the UUP.

Point 1 was moot and all could agree on point 5, though difficulties arose on some other points as well as on some of the addenda to the SOD's demands. For instance, the SOD, which saw the Order as a self-defence organization, disagreed with the idea of it as a religious organization and stated that there was a big gulf in perception between the leadership and the masses on this point. This underscores the long-standing difference between the 'respectable' leadership and 'rough' rank and file noted by Dominic Bryan.[77] Saulters agreed that the Order should act politically, but still felt that it was 'a religious organisation'. McCrea tried to conciliate by stressing that the Order merely had 'a strong religious base'. The nub of the issue for the SOD was whether the Order's 'religious base' would impede taking a strong stand on issues. The Orange leaders felt that the majority of Grand Lodge would be prepared to take a stand, and Joel Patton emphasized the need for Grand Lodge to take a lead. In a departure from the tone in his *Orange Banner*, Patton astutely commented that the Order had four constituent elements, cultural, political, religious, and social, and thus could legitimately take a political stand. Dowey did not shrink from showing his true colours and spoke of the Order's role as a 'physical defense' organization. 'Would Grand Lodge be prepared to take a stand in a hypothetical [military] situation', he probed. Patton added—no doubt with Kennaway, Porter, and Martin Smyth in mind—that there was a disproportionate influence of clerics in the association. This was not rebutted or challenged, and confirms some of Kennaway's observations that for some elements of the Order, 'there is a scarcely disguised distrust of "the clergy" and an unwillingness to listen to their advice'.[78]

All told, a surprising degree of agreement would emerge during the meeting between the SOD and the Orange leaders, whom the members of the SOD had recently referred to as 'traitors', a 'clique', and 'old men'. For example, when the discussion turned to the SOD's demands 4 and 5, the Grand Lodge men assured the SOD members that they would not give credibility to either the PC or the residents' groups and that these promises would be 'fed into' the Grand Lodge Strategy Committee. Interestingly, Grand Lodge members offered little resistance on point 6 (re disaffiliation from the UUP), saying that this was 'going to happen' and it was just a matter of timing, which 'was important in light of the forthcoming referendum [on the Belfast Agreement of 1998]'. Dowey also expressed his opinion that Grand Lodge officers should not be officers in any political party, though he recognized the difficulties this presented. He claimed that his basic position was that the Order should be free of political manipulation.[79]

These meetings indicate that the SOD was exercising substantial influence over the direction of Orange policy as Orange leaders attempted to keep it sweet. SOD influences, suitably 'fed into' Orange committees by Orange leaders, thereby encompassed both disaffiliation from the UUP and discouraging contact with the PC. A selection of Orange leaders (Saulters and the County Antrim contingent of McCrea, Leathem, and Davison) were holding meetings with the SOD without the prior approval of Grand Lodge. Furthermore, few of the details of these meetings were presented to either Central Committee or Grand Lodge. Yet it is crucial to note that the Order's solicitor had advised them not to proceed against the SOD men because their case might not withstand legal scrutiny. The Order was thus advised to engage the SOD men so as to avert the possibility of either letting them off the hook (a propaganda victory for them) or losing a case against them. There is no indication of any affinity between Watson, McCrea, and the SOD men at these meetings.[80]

At the following session of Central Committee, divisions emerged more clearly into the open when the issue of discipline arose. Enquiring into counsel's opinion on how to proceed against the SOD, the traditionalist Rev. Porter worried aloud that Grand Lodge meetings with the SOD would prejudice charges against them. Porter then asked McCrea for the names of the four brethren whom McCrea had met in the building on the fateful night of the occupation. McCrea at first equivocated, saying that he was concerned that the names would be leaked to the press, whereupon Porter asked what harm that could bring. Colin Shilliday then backed Porter, urging McCrea to yield the names, but Grand Treasurer Mervyn Bishop interjected that 'we must search our conscience as to what is going on in this Central Committee'. McCrea protected his SOD contacts and never did tell, but Kennaway informed the meeting that he was aware that Bros Dowey, Jordan, and Smyth (two of whom formed part of Patton's much vaunted 'Drumcree Five') were in the building on 9 December. After Grand Lodge heard a legal counsel's opinion, it agreed to issue a resolution pertaining to the SOD occupation.

But the cadre of McCrea & Co. was not finished yet. Davison weighed in on McCrea's side, cautioning those present that in pursuing the members of the SOD, the Order was 'losing sight of the real issues' while the way forward was not to continue down the route of punishment. The Rev. Porter was having none of this, and, after Saulters admitted to a second meeting with the members of the SOD, asked why they had not been challenged over their outrageous press statements. As a Christian, he agreed with reconciliation but only if there were signs of contrition, whereupon he asked Saulters if there were any. Saulters would only say that he was optimistic, but 'couldn't make promises', and that the talks were frank. Colin Shilliday backed Porter and added that while he was in favour of unity, his sources suggested that the members of the SOD still sought to target certain brethren (i.e. the 'clique'). Finally, a consideration of charges at county level found that all cases were still pending in Tyrone, Armagh, and Antrim.[81]

Saulters, McCrea, and others had in fact prepared a statement designed to reconcile Grand Lodge and the members of the SOD. In the various versions of the statement, the Order's leadership pretended that there was a moral equivalence between the members of the SOD and the elected Grand Lodge elite: 'Having witnessed the hurt on both sides we are genuinely sorry that this has happened and believe that the most positive response is to move forward together . . . in a spirit of "brotherly love and loyalty".'[82] Kennaway has labelled this 'appeasement', but in the face of physical threats and a possible SOD challenge to Grand Lodge legitimacy, was it the correct decision?[83] In the end, Kennaway proved prescient. The SOD had been temporarily pacified, but they had never disavowed violence as a tactic and their version of the 'armalite and ballot box' strategy was producing tangible results.

Thus at a further meeting with Grand Lodge officers, the members of the SOD claimed that after consulting with their supporters, it emerged that the SOD ranks generally backed talks with Grand Lodge, but were also 'cynical', and thus they withheld final approval from Grand Lodge. At this meeting, Saulters also queried Joel Patton about the SOD's incendiary *Orange Banner* and noted some 'nasty comment'. 'It is ours,' Patton admitted, but he justified it as largely for 'internal consumption'. McCrea hastily added that the *Banner* had come out before the reconciliation talks began. At no point did Saulters or McCrea—who had collectively been vilified by the *Banner*—ever demand an apology. The meeting ended with the SOD men voicing their concerns that the PC and residents were targeting vulnerable lodges and members (to entice them into discussions) and that Grand Lodge needed to send a firm signal down the Orange structure that there were to be no discussions with the PC or residents.[84]

Where did the membership stand on all of this? For the most part, the membership was disgusted by the SOD's repeated press appearances and their divisive, belligerent tone. Even a relatively 'macho' Orangeman like the Sandy Row District leader George Chittick, who sympathized with many SOD aims, was critical of its methods.[85] In policy terms, the SOD reforms were backed only in so far as they dovetailed with existing Grand Lodge thinking, and there are no grassroots resolutions calling upon Grand Lodge to introduce direct elections or an annual convention as per the SOD demands. In one respect, though, the membership indirectly supported the SOD against Grand Lodge. This concerns the link between the UUP and the Order. We can glean this from the results of the Order's Commission report of 1997, which drew on a survey that obtained a healthy 41 per cent response rate from the membership. Results show that as early as 1996–7, 65 per cent of the membership felt that the Order 'should not be affiliated with any political party'.[86]

In addition to its membership survey, the LOI Commission report debated proposed reforms to the Order. The relatively cerebral committee brought together the Rev. Warren Porter, the local Orange historian Trevor Geary (Armagh), the author and University of Ulster PhD David Hume, and a selection of others including Willie Ross, MP. The Commission received submissions from several quarters within the Order, but the most important came from the SOD. The SOD's policy reforms were much more positive than its public pronouncements and all pointed in the direction of populist, direct democracy, including:

1. The Grand Master to stand for annual, direct election with all members voting.
2. Grand Lodge representation by population (which would shift influence away from the traditionalist Republic of Ireland lodges).
3. A reduction in the number of *ex officio* and honorary seats for assistant and deputy grand masters and chaplains at Grand Lodge. Grand Lodge would instead more directly reflect the votes of members on a 'one man one vote' basis. The irony of this demand was not lost on Martin Smyth, who in December 1995 likened such demands to those of the Nationalist civil rights movement of 1968–9.[87]
4. Committees to be subservient to Grand Lodge and report regularly. This was no doubt a dig at the ideological autonomy of the EC.
5. Central Committee (i.e. the 'clique') to be abolished. Grand Lodge should take up the slack by meeting monthly instead of twice a year. In essence,

this reform would place policy power in the hands of a directly elected Orange 'parliament' and its backbenches rather than the 'cabinet' of elites in Central Committee.

6. An increase in frequency of elections to four to six per year for county and district officers.

7. Annual Convention to decide policy and direction for the Order.[88]

The LOI Commission took on board many SOD recommendations. Thus the Commission endorsed a slimming down in the membership of several committees and a reduction in the number of deputy grand masters and deputy grand chaplains permitted to sit in Grand Lodge. The Commission members felt that the office of Deputy Grand Master was 'almost honorary', and hence deputy grand masters could be excluded from Grand Lodge. Likewise, the rationale given for reducing clerical influence was that the average number of deputy grand chaplains attending Grand Lodge seldom exceeded twelve or fifteen, and that the status of Deputy Grand Chaplain would be enhanced by reducing the number eligible to attend Grand Lodge to just twenty-four. This was half of the SOD's demand, but still represented a major reduction. The latter might be seen as a relatively weak logical argument and thus a doff of the cap to SOD pressure.

In another nod to SOD demands, the LOI Commission endorsed the view that the representation of Grand Lodge should reflect the number of Orangemen in each jurisdiction. It also approved the idea of term limits to posts at all levels of the Order, with a break of at least two years before an individual resumes office. Finally, Grand Lodge was to sit four times per year rather than twice annually. Taken as a whole, these reforms addressed many SOD concerns, and—to be fair—improved the already high degree of democratic legitimacy within the Order. The report was a blow for traditionalists, in that it removed the right of many honorary or long-serving elites (like the deputies) to make policy. This made Grand Lodge less 'clubby' by chopping 140 bodies from its guest list, but it also reduced its scope to chart policy independently of the grassroots or to 'lead' them—all of which reinforced the growing populism of the organization.[89]

But the Commission's report was not a clean sweep for the SOD. One of the principal reasons for this must have been the forceful rejection of certain SOD-inspired reforms by both Martin Smyth and a majority of county lodges in 1996–7, when the interim report was floated.[90] In addition, the EC was singled out for a positive mention and many other specialist committees were praised. The report also stressed the need for better vetting of candidates through local inspection committees and improved discipline on parade, though this was to be exercised only through local lodge masters 'exert[ing] their authority'.[91] The report decisively rejected the notion of 'direct democracy' in favour of an improved representative democracy and rebuffed the SOD demand to abolish the Central Committee. The suggestions that the Grand Master stand for office each year and that a convention should decide policy never saw the light of day. Instead, the Commission proposed a set of annual regional conferences and subjected part of the Central Committee to five-year term limits (excluding the Grand Master and Grand Secretary from this requirement). Finally, it reaffirmed the historic UUP–Orange link, asserting that 'While we recognise that our membership includes those of other unionist groupings and many with no party affiliation, the Commission is strongly of the opinion that the unionist people's interest is best served by the Institution being associated with the party which we initially helped form.'[92] The latter recommendation received endorsement at a conference of private lodge masters which took place in late 1997. The motion to disaffiliate from the UUP fell by 484–369 with 71 abstentions.[93]

George Patton also evaluated the LOI Commission's recommendations. He agreed with the thrust of the Commission's views, but wanted things taken further by bringing district representation directly to Grand Lodge. He wanted the composition of Central Committee re-examined so as to decrease the voting power of small counties like those in the Republic. 'Currently Leitrim with two Lodges is entitled to equal representation with Antrim with its 247 lodges,' Patton noted. His proposal sought to exclude all counties with fewer than fifty lodges (thus wiping out the more liberal Republic of Ireland representation) and make further representation proportional to membership. Patton also endorsed a Political Affairs Committee, composed of Orangemen who did not hold political offices above the branch level. This committee could thus lobby and meet all parties without the taint of being associated with a particular party.[94]

At this time, Patton, the genial and relatively neutral Executive Officer, was involved in the political high-wire act of trying to satisfy various constituencies within the Order. He was embroiled in the SOD occupation controversy, involved in the reconciliation meetings with them and thus in close contact with McCrea and other Antrim Orangemen. Antrim's views may have shaped Patton's, but in any case, Antrim put forth its own set of proposals. These endorsed his views but went further and called for the adoption of the SOD aim of a directly elected Grand Master who should face annual election.[95] In the end, however, such proposals failed to make inroads at Grand Lodge. Let us not underestimate the impact of the SOD, however. This group had assailed the leadership of the Orange Order on Twelfth platforms, in its own publications, and in the media. It had intimidated the leadership of the Order and disrupted county and Grand Lodge sessions. Its reform agenda achieved half implementation, making a much bigger dent than the populist agitators of 1953–4 or 1959–60.

1998 would see the SOD break apart as its leaders were finally brought to book for their transgressions and the movement's popular energies were absorbed by a rightward shift in the Order. On the other side of the ideological spectrum, the EC was eventually pressured into a restructuring which culminated in the demise of its open, evangelical radicalism. The Order's democratic structure means that it tends to tack to the centre of its constituency's opinion in all jurisdictions where it operates.[96] In a strange irony, both the SOD and the EC were in a sense doomed and thus they had something in common! Their fates were also to remain intertwined, and throughout 1998 the two forces vied for influence within the Order and again came into open conflict.

This first surfaced at the Central Committee meeting of 21 March, when the delegates collectively decided to have only one further meeting with the SOD. Brian Kennaway asked whether the SOD had showed any signs of remorse and added that he was still receiving its literature. Saulters replied that Joel Patton had owned up to the *Orange Banner*. He also failed to report any expressions of remorse.[97] The action then moved to County Antrim, where two Antrim SOD men, Willy Smith and David Tweed (a former Ireland rugby international), were being charged by members of the EC, including Kennaway, Kilpatrick, Montgomery, Richardson, and Whitten. Not all EC members could confirm that Tweed and Richardson had *both* used foul language and physically abused members of the committee. But the evidence from some witnesses—notably Richard Whitten—was damning. County Antrim, home of McCrea and Drew Davison, which was relatively hostile territory for the EC, took the view that the charges were not sufficient to suspend the men. However, in view of the patchy case put by the EC witnesses, it is far from clear that Antrim's decision could have gone the other way.[98]

At Grand Lodge, the mood was finally beginning to sour on the SOD. A large number of those present, notably Billy Kennedy, the Rev. Tom Taylor, the Rev. Gerald Sproule, and Warren Porter called on Joel Patton to dissolve his group and express remorse. H. Mitchell Cummings spoke of 'mafia tactics' used by the SOD, and J. Allen (Down) urged Patton to dissolve the SOD. Martin Smyth wanted an understanding from the SOD that it would not continue intimidating families of Orange leaders and adding the addresses of county masters to its posters. David McNarry, while evincing some sympathy for some of Patton's reforms, also called for the SOD to disband. Only Davison would defend Patton, saying it was 'unfair' to ask him to dissolve. At the end, James Molyneaux called for better communication of the work of Grand Lodge to the membership to dispel notions of a 'fuddy duddy' leadership.[99]

Subsequent letters suggest that the membership felt the same way as the leadership about the SOD. LOL 1892, from Belfast, provides an example. In a January 1998 letter, it expressed its anger at the way in which the SOD 'flaunted' [sic] Orange laws. The SOD, claimed 1892, 'persistently inform the press that THEY speak for the rank and file. They do not speak for anyone within the membership of 1892 . . . Their most recent, rebellious debacle in early December [1997 occupation] cannot go unchallenged by this Institution.'[100] In July 1998, the same lodge excoriated Grand Lodge for its 'appeasement' of the SOD in accepting 'this group's bigoted and sectarian stand, in contravention to the qualifications of an Orangeman and the basis of what our forefathers fought and died for. . . civil and religious liberty. . . [The SOD's] pure and unadulterated sectarianism that has brought shame on the colours which we wear. . . must end now and we urge our District Officers to act with expediency.' This was from a no-nonsense lodge which actively opposed the PC.[101] Another lodge spoke of Patton bringing the Order's public image into 'serious disrepute'.[102]

The events at Drumcree 1998 were unkind to the Order. Once it had secured the Good Friday Agreement in April 1998, there was less of an incentive for the British to press for pro-Unionist concessions at Drumcree. The newly created PC delayed its ruling until after the Agreement was inked, and then delivered its verdict, which included a re-routing of the Drumcree event.[103] Loyalist mobilization was for nought as the RUC and Army mobilized 'one of the biggest security operations for years' replete with razor wire, closed-circuit cameras and a fourteen-foot-wide moat. At the field, traditionalists like Graham Montgomery faced invective and physical jostling from Joel Patton and others. Many Loyalists and Orangemen viewed Drumcree 1998 as a last stand and thought force of numbers would turn the tide as in previous years. The public disorder that followed saw over 500 attacks on the security forces, but the latter were too well dug in this time. Over 2,500 public order incidents occurred province-wide owing to sympathy actions, and Catholics were intimidated in Protestant areas. In Antrim, the entire Nationalist town of Dunloy was blockaded. Scenes of violent young Orangemen were broadcast throughout the UK and the world, tarnishing the Order's image once again.[104]

In the midst of the mayhem on 12 July, tragedy struck when Loyalist thugs petrol-bombed the home of Christine Quinn, a Catholic living in a mainly Protestant estate in Ballymoney, County Antrim, killing her three sons. Although the Order was not involved in the killings, the media and major public figures leapt to this conclusion and the killings became associated with the Order and Drumcree in a public relations fiasco. In a controversial move that later attracted the ire of many in the Orange Order, the RUC Chief Constable wrongly blamed the Order for the Quinn murders. The COI bishop Robin Eames asked those at Drumcree to call off their protest. More significantly, at a packed sermon in Pomeroy, the Armagh Grand Chaplain William Bingham, who had bargained hard for the Order's right to march the road and mistakenly believed the RUC Chief Constable's message, preached a message of sorrow which would later be interpreted as a message of 'surrender' by hardliners: 'After last night's atrocious act a fifteen-minute walk down the Garvaghy Road. . . would be a very hollow victory because it would be in the shadow of three coffins of little boys. . . I believe the Orange Order needs to

Ill. 12 Drumcree—Orange demonstration with Drumcree Church in the background. The involvement of loyalist paramilitaries and the televised scenes of violent clashes with police tarnished the image of Orangeism in the world media and split the Institution.

call off its protests because we can't control them. Drumcree is rapidly getting out of our hands, we have to back off'.[105]

As the dust settled on a major Orange defeat, Kennaway and other EC traditionalists appealed to Grand Lodge to re-hear the charges against the SOD. At the hearing in October, Grand Lodge concurred with Antrim's decision not to prosecute the SOD men because of the admittedly conflicting nature of the various EC members' testimonies, but it did accede to the EC members' appeal regarding the Tyrone meeting which was broken up by SOD bullying. However, events on the ground in Tyrone soon did Kennaway's and the traditionalists' work for them. Pomeroy District in Tyrone had a thirty-year tradition of holding a non-political, purely religious platform and denying the opportunity even for MPs to speak.[106] But on the platform at Pomeroy on 13 July 1998, Joel Patton and Walter Millar heckled the Tyrone Grand Secretary Perry Reid and the Rev. William Bingham. As Millar and Patton approached the stage, they were prevented by several others from ascending and fisticuffs broke out in front of the world's cameras. As Reid asked those present to observe a minute's silence to remember the Somme dead, the SOD men cursed, 'We'll remember you.' The episode reduced the affable Reid to tears and was the last straw for Pomeroy District.[107] Despite being warned off by some in Grand Lodge, the courageous district charged and expelled both Patton and Millar. This was then appealed up to the county.

Events moved swiftly thereafter. On 28 August, County Tyrone summoned Patton and Millar to hear the charges against them. The tense meeting was kicked off by the SOD sympathizer Paul Coote, who, while disavowing membership of the group, warned that the Order stood to lose 2,000 members if the two were expelled. He added that charges should also be brought against William Bingham, David Trimble, John Taylor, and Reg Empey for supporting the new Good Friday Agreement. The county Grand Master Thomas Reid was having none of this and ruled Coote out of order, retorting that he was not going to be threatened and that politics should not enter into the meeting.[108] In the end, the county suspended Patton and Millar until they agreed to appear to hear the charges. This motion was passed by 55–0 with 10 abstainers, all of whom were sympathetic to Patton. This suggests that only a minority in Tyrone backed the SOD. At the next meeting of Tyrone County Lodge, Patton and Millar finally turned up. Thomas Reid explained that Pomeroy District had suffered seven dead and economic boycotting in the Troubles, and that part of its traditional parade route had been banned by the PC. The SOD attack on a religious service was, in his opinion, an attack on the very basis of the Order and showed contempt for it.

In their defence, Patton and Millar cited the provocative presence of Ruth Dudley Edwards ('no friend of the Order') and the ex-IRA informer and Trimble advisor Sean O'Callaghan. Patton yelled 'IRA' at O'Callaghan while Millar chased him with an umbrella, and at the hearing the SOD pair complained that Orange marshals failed to remove these *provocateurs* despite Patton's request. They also expressed great disquiet at the presence of the traditionalist Bingham for his statements following the Quinn murders.[109] After hearing a number of witnesses, Patton offered his swansong:

I am 32 years in the Order and . . . [have given] all to the Order. My record is exemplary. It seems like so many wasted years. This county has been betrayed. I saw red when I saw O'Callaghan . . . It was unwise to invite the Rev. Bingham . . . We are conceding that it was a wrong act on our part but I ask the question, 'Who is the bigger offender?' . . . I concede that I challenged the platform out of conscience. My son [who was involved in a fight with the son of a Tyrone county official] is now being victimised because of it. I can't help the way I am and I will not change for any man.

This little ditty didn't help and the charged men lost on a 52–12 vote with 1 abstention.[110] In the end, Patton appealed to the only person he thought could save him, William McCrea.[111] But by this point, Grand Lodge was only too pleased to wash its hands of the troublesome creature, and the three-year saga of the SOD came to its end, having rocked the Institution from top to bottom.

Overall, the SOD altered the direction of the entire Orange policy ship. In 1996–7, the Order's leadership was up for grabs and its policies were drifting in an evangelical, moderate direction. Traditionalist 'liberals' like William Bingham and Brian Kennaway were encouraged to put their names forward for the post of Grand Master to replace Smyth in 1996 and might have got the job.[112] Saulters eventually won by default, but his immediate circle included many moderates, including Watson (who later tacked to the DUP), Kennaway, Bingham, and others.[113] By 1998, however, the liberal 'moment' had passed. The SOD's tactics of 1995–8 put the leadership on notice that they had attackers on their right flank. Central Committee and Grand Lodge responded by moving rightwards, clipping the wings of the EC, and suing for peace with the SOD. Where it once equivocated on the subject of meeting the likes of John Hume and the PC, the leadership now stood four-square against negotiation.

8

Breaking the Link: Orange–UUP Relations after the Good Friday Agreement

We saw that the rise in parade-related conflict from 1995 led to major convulsions within the Order as its cultural power was diminished by residents' groups and RUC-backed parading restrictions. In early 1998, the historic Good Friday Agreement (GFA), signed by David Trimble's UUP, the SDLP, and Sinn Fein, was to shatter Orangeism's political certainties. These opened new divisions within the Order which largely mapped onto the traditionalist–hardline fissures over Drumcree.

Many believe that in 1973 Faulkner's Unionists were pressured or outwitted into making compromises which the wider Unionist community could never accept.[1] Unionists rejected Sunningdale by voting against Faulkner's UPNI and joining the Orange-assisted 1974 UWC strike. In 1998, by contrast, the GFA was endorsed by around 53 per cent of the Unionist electorate and encountered little organized Unionist mass action.[2] Moreover, Trimble was consistently able to win the approval of the Ulster Unionist Council in the run up to the agreement, something Faulkner failed to do.[3] Why the difference between 1973 and 1998? Trimble would say that the GFA was a better deal for Unionists because it secured the removal of the irredentist Articles 2 and 3 from the Irish Constitution, ended the unpopular Anglo-Irish Agreement (AIA), and stripped down the remit of the north-south (strand II) bodies from their 1973 interpretation.[4]

Another piece of conventional wisdom holds that middle-class, non-voting, 'garden centre' Protestants turned out in 1998 for the GFA in a way they never had before (or have since). This has subsequently influenced UUP belief in the existence of a constituency of progressive, middle-class 'civic Unionists' who would jump aboard the UUP ship once the party proved its non-sectarianism by cutting its ties to Orangeism.[5] However, the *2001 Northern Ireland Election Study* shows this analysis to be a myth. The white-collar upper- and middle-class turnout improved marginally in 1998 over 1997, but the

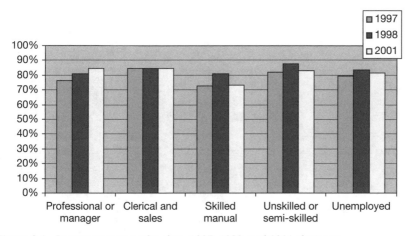

Figure 8.1 Protestant turnout by class: 1997, 1998, and 2001 elections

Source: H. Clarke et al., *General Election in Northern Ireland, 2001* [computer file], Colchester: (UK Data Archive, SN 4622 (March 2003).

greater increase was recorded for the skilled working class—the most solidly Orange constituency. Moreover, there was no major difference in turnout by class in any election. It seems that the 1998 referendum merely heightened interest across all classes. All told, there is no sign of the mythical middle-class 'garden centre Prod', saviour of liberal Unionism (see Figure 8.1).

The pundits' focus on high politics, voters' rational calculations about the benefits of the deal, and short-run events fails to address the question of mass response. Here we need to pay more attention to symbolic issues and their instinctive 'resonance' within the Unionist population. First of all, Trimble enjoyed a strong reputation owing to his repeated appearances at Drumcree and his ability to see the Orangemen down the Garvaghy Road between 1995 and 1997. In 1995, the *Orange Standard* referred to Trimble as a 'cult figure' among Portadown Orangemen and an excellent choice for UUP leader.[6] Secondly, the IRA ceasefire of 1994 almost certainly contributed to optimism among the Unionist masses, and the UUP warned during the campaign that a 'no' could lead to a return of more bloodshed.[7] This reinforced a trend toward Unionist liberalism. For instance, surveys show that, across all indicators, Protestants became more willing to sanction residential, school, and workplace mixing with Catholics between 1989 and the 1998 Agreement. Even the proportion opposed to inter-faith marriage steadily declined to little more than a third by 1998. Notice that during the period in which Protestant attitudes were softening, the number of Protestants and security force personnel killed by Republicans was in sharp decline (see Figure 8.2).

Yet Figure 8.2 also shows that the rosy picture imploded after 1998 as the decade-long trend towards more favourable attitudes to mixing with

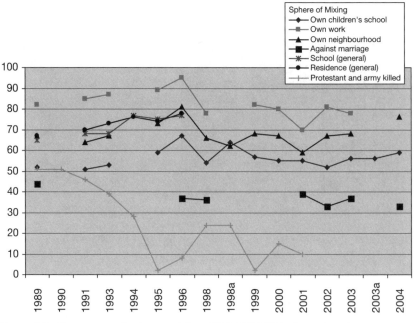

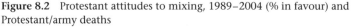

Figure 8.2 Protestant attitudes to mixing, 1989–2004 (% in favour) and Protestant/army deaths

Source: ARK Surveys On-Line time series data <http://www.ark.ac.uk/>, accessed 2005. (*Note*: Years labelled 'a' refer to the second of two surveys in the same year.)

Catholics peaked and then declined. Meanwhile, Protestant attitudes towards the GFA rapidly turned cold when they discovered some of the outriders of the Agreement. Principal opposition from Unionists centred on: (1) Sinn Fein taking its place in government without IRA decommissioning; (2) police reform, extending to 50:50 recruitment of Catholics and Protestants and the abolition of the sacred symbol of the RUC; and (3) the quick release of Republican prisoners, many of whom were implicated in the murder of Protestant civilians and policemen. None of these was predicted by the mass of the Unionist electorate, and even many UUP politicians did not fully understand how completely these measures would be implemented. The UUP pro-Agreement stalwart Reg Empey ridiculed suggestions of having Sinn Fein's Gerry Adams in government by likening this to having 'Hitler in a synagogue'.[8] Whether this belief was sincerely held or merely a ploy is uncertain, but it reveals the kind of assumptions then current. Though Protestant support for the GFA has ebbed and flowed, enthusiasm for it has plummeted since the April 1998 signing (see Figure 8.3). In November 2003, a Millward Brown poll in Ulster showed that just 16 per cent of Protestants wished to see the GFA implemented in its current form.[9]

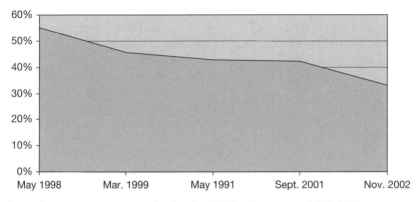

Figure 8.3 Protestant support for the Good Friday Agreement, 1998–2002

Sources: BBC <http://news.bbc.co.uk/1/hi/northern_ireland/1552632.stm>, accessed 2005; C. Irwin, *The People's Peace Process in Northern Ireland* (Basingstoke: Palgrave, 2002).

The Orange Order and the Good Friday Agreement

The Order was closely focused on parading issues and its own internal fissures with the SOD in 1997. The GFA was signed by Trimble on 10 April, and the referendum was held six weeks later on 23 May. Media speculation was that the Order would come out against the deal, adversely affecting an upcoming UUC vote. There was also speculation about Martin Smyth, who had not yet declared for the anti-Agreement side.[10] On 15 April, the Grand Lodge met. Two main issues dominated the meeting. First was an old issue: the Grand Lodge's opinion about whether to discipline the SOD and Joel Patton. Next came the new issue: Grand Lodge's position on the GFA. This generated heated discussion. Tom Taylor, Armagh's Deputy Grand Chaplain, struck first, declaring that his conscience would not allow him to support the GFA. The prospect of Gerry Adams in government was considered objectionable, and Taylor cited the fact that seven Republican murders had occurred in his district of Tynan and Middletown. This opener received applause and was followed by the weighty opinion of James Molyneaux. Molyneaux, like Jeffrey Donaldson, had in fact failed to appear publicly on anti-Agreement platforms despite being privately against the GFA—something which may have had something to do with Trimble's and Tony Blair's private pressure on the two to remain loyal to the party.[11] But at Grand Lodge, Molyneaux was far less equivocal. He stated that he had 'no axe to grind' (presumably against Trimble), but that he and Smyth were 'totally opposed to the Agreement'. Furthermore, Molyneaux wanted action to 'disarm the mechanism' of the GFA and sought Orange backing to put the government under pressure not to proceed. He pointed out that the Order could not wait five weeks but had to act in the first two weeks when Trimble was vulnerable.

The Orange outlaw Joel Patton was also present and warned that 'eyes' were 'on Grand Lodge today', and he urged a clear and concise decision against the GFA and the giving of a 'lead' to the masses on this issue. His hardline *gravitas* may have helped the anti-GFA cause within Grand Lodge, but was nowhere near as decisive as Molyneaux's intervention. George Watson said he was 'encouraged by the support of Lord Molyneaux' and that he was simply 'amazed that David Trimble could sign up despite having said he wouldn't'. The Rev. William Malcolmson expressed similar disbelief: 'was David Trimble out of his mind', he asked. Evidently many in the Order sincerely believed in Trimble because of his support for them at Drumcree and were blindsided by his acquiescing in the GFA. One by one, speaker after speaker came out against the Agreement—partly as a result of peer pressure, but also owing to deeply held belief. The Rev. McMeekin spoke of a 'seething feeling' within the Protestant community that was 'about to erupt'.

Yet there were several delegates prepared to defend the Agreement. Sam Foster from Fermanagh, a pro-Trimble UUP activist who was subsequently elected to the Assembly in 1998, acknowledged the pain of prisoner releases and decommissioning, which 'hurt deeply'. But he stressed that Protestants had to be realistic in the face of a 40 per cent Nationalist population. He pointed out that under the GFA, the Union was safe and had been acknowledged by Nationalists and the Irish government. He celebrated the fact that the Anglo-Irish Agreement and its Maryfield secretariat were going. 'Weighing one against the other', Foster said, he would be 'saying yes' to the GFA. Foster was followed by David McNarry, another pro-Trimble UUP who was later elected to the Assembly. McNarry tried to stress the hidden gains from the GFA: its emasculation of cross-border bodies and its stipulation that quangos would be centralized under Stormont control. He declared that he would go to war or prison for his country, and asked whether anyone had a 'great plan through simply saying "no"'. Finally, he put his faith in 'David Trimble's judgment', which he said he had backed for the past two years. This shows that Trimble's stock was still reasonably good and that he had not yet become the Orange hate figure he would later on. Next, the Rev. Gerald Sproule, Grand Chaplain, invoked Scripture to back the Agreement. 'Trust the Lord', he said, and added that he hadn't heard of a solid alternative to the GFA. The Rev. Warren Porter also backed the 'yes' camp, challenging Molyneaux to withdraw his comments about the Order getting involved against the GFA since Grand Lodge should only be responsible for its own membership.

This was all the yardage the pro-Agreement camp would get, and the UUP MP Willie Ross followed its salvo with a dissection of the deal's flaws, which was greeted with applause. Smyth dispelled any speculation as to his views by telling his audience that he was 'shellshocked' by the Agreement, and had been assured before he left (presumably referring to the Unionist party headquarters) that nothing would be decided. Citing Sunningdale, he cautioned that there would be 'no democracy' under the GFA, that the Unionist people were being 'led like a lamb to the slaughter', and that he would argue against the GFA at the next UUC meeting. He urged the Order to get its people out to the polls 'to vote as we want them to vote'. Grand Secretary John McCrea took a more measured approach, saying he disliked many aspects of the GFA but urging everyone to read it in detail and discouraging Grand Lodge from coming out clearly against.[12]

Fifteen had spoken against and just five for the GFA. Molyneaux now put a resolution in front of the 100-odd assembled delegates: 'The Grand Orange Lodge of Ireland takes note of the acceptance by the participants to the talks process of the document of 10th April 1998 but failing clarification of certain vital issues cannot recommend it to the people of Ulster.' This statement was endorsed by 76–10, with 1 abstention, showing just how powerful anti-Agreement feeling was at Grand Lodge even at this early stage. But there was hesitation: polls had shown significant Protestant support for the deal, and Grand Lodge's official remit was to respect the 'civil and religious liberty' of all and not directly tell its members how to vote. Therefore when Londonderry's legendary Billy Douglas submitted a tougher resolution than Molyneaux's simply worded as 'This Grand Lodge says NO to the Agreement', it went down to defeat by 70–22.[13]

Nevertheless, Molyneaux's resolution clearly signalled Grand Lodge's disapproval of the GFA. This should have come as no surprise. The Order has always sought a return to Stormont majoritarianism and has consistently rejected all post-1972 constitutional initiatives based on either executive power-sharing or North–South bodies. Only the DUP has a similar stance. Yet a return to Stormont majoritarianism was the preference of just 20–33 per cent of the Protestant population, less than the proportion favouring integration and certainly less than the majority of more than 70 per cent who were willing to accept power-sharing.[14] Why would the Order align itself with its opponent Paisley? First of all, it might not have opposed an agreement which excluded Sinn Fein, limited the Republic's influence to bilateral talking shops, and relegated Nationalist power-sharing to toothless Stormont committees. Even so, we cannot be sure that the Order's innate caution and its impulse to insist on the 'same as the rest of the UK' might not have scuppered even a 'Good Friday-lite'.

We also shouldn't overestimate the leadership's power. The Order is a bottom-up organization which had become increasingly populist. The ideological location of its rank and file is thus at least as important as the leadership's wishes, and is best described as conservative but not militant. This is clear from recent survey work on the Order. Just 34 per cent of roughly 300 Orangemen surveyed claim to have voted for the GFA in 1998, compared with the 53 per cent of the Protestant public who endorsed it that year. In 2004, just 12 per cent of Orangemen surveyed still backed the GFA, many fewer than the roughly 25–30 per cent of the Unionist electorate who continue to support it.[15] The Order today is a highly democratic organization which is responsive to its members' views. We saw that Grand Lodge had officially stood against its militants on issues of paramilitarism, violence against the RUC and Catholics, and support for Paisley. It is therefore difficult to ascribe the Order's 'no' Unionism to the influence of militants. Rather, the Order had, as usual, taken an accurate reading of its members' preferences and had avoided committing itself to modernizing political change in advance of a clear mandate from its grassroots. All of this pointed to an anti-Agreement UUP position as the natural comfort zone for Orange leaders.

The Order's resolution was greeted with dismay by the UUP leadership and Tony Blair. John Taylor (an Orangeman like most UUP MPs) told the Order that its anti-Agreement stance was a mistake given majority Protestant support. Fearing its ability to swing a tight vote, Blair desperately tried to persuade the Orangemen to back the Agreement. Accordingly, an Orange delegation consisting of Saulters, McCrea, Mervyn Bishop, Denis Watson, and George Patton was invited to meet Tony Blair, Mo Mowlam, and some civil servants at 10 Downing Street. The pre-game noises from the Order were not overly enthusiastic, but Saulters promised to keep an open mind.[16]

Mowlam began by discussing the prisoners issue. She tried to reassure the Orangemen that the bill did not provide for a 'general amnesty' but would only establish an independent body which would consider cases on an individual basis. Blair then arrived and Saulters thanked him for his time. Blair in turn said he was 'delighted' to meet the Order. Saulters then began by insisting that decommissioning not be voluntary and added that the GFA made no mention of guns having to be handed in. Blair responded that an independent commission would report on this within two years. He said that in the meantime, Sinn Fein was expected to abide by the rules of non-violence, though he acknowledged that 'there is a question of whether or not people are genuine or tactical when they speak of non violence'. Blair also reiterated that the 'principle of consent is pretty strong'.

McCrea then asked for assurances that Sinn Fein would be excluded if it returned to violence. Blair claimed that he had assurances from the other parties but that this decision ultimately lay in the parties' hands. However, he was at pains to underline the fact that, unlike the Framework Documents, Unionist Assembly members could bring the Assembly down and the British and Irish governments would be unable to impose policy from above. He added that sensitive issues would require cross-community consent and that decisions made by north–south bodies would require unanimity. When questioned by Bishop about whether this was the last chance for the Agreement, Blair insisted that this was so. McCrea, who showed an incisive sense for the important questions, probed Blair on the North–South Council, stating that the SDLP had claimed it had executive powers. Blair referred to the SDLP statement as 'words and phrases' and assured his guests that Trimble's bottom line stipulated no executive powers without the assent of the Assembly.

Discussion then returned to the matter of prisoners. Bishop disagreed with Mowlam's press statements about Loyalist prisoners like Johnny Adair and Michael Stone being the 'unsung heroes' of the peace process. In a query that must have made Mowlam squirm, he spoke of their 'heinous crimes' and the fact that prisoners were getting political recognition. Blair replied that 'this is the most difficult part' and that the prisoners were out on licence rather than receiving a general amnesty. The condition was that their organization must have given up violence for good. Blair added that this was not the situation 'we . . . want to be in, but it is part of the resolution'. Watson then came to the point by asking the Prime Minister, 'Where is the morality of this?' Blair tried to defuse the emotion by conceding that these were 'perfectly reasonable points', but pragmatically stated that if prisoners were 'nowhere in this package you wouldn't have a package'.

'[This is a] sad reflection,' replied Watson provocatively. 'The Agreement is Prisoner driven.' Watson then spoke of the events at Tullyvallen Orange Hall in South Armagh where Republican hitmen killed four Orangemen and would have wiped out the entire lodge but for the return fire provided by an off-duty RUC man attending the lodge meeting.[17] Few of the perpetrators of the massacre had been apprehended, and the thought that even if arrested they would simply be set free was unacceptable to Watson. The Agreement, said Watson, was unacceptable from a 'moral/christian viewpoint'. Blair took a different view, however, and argued that '[we have to] accept that but judgements have to be made. It [the GFA] will do more to preserve life and bring justice to people.' Blair tried to express sympathy for the Orangemen's feelings by offering that 'emotionally most people find this [forgiving violent offenders] most difficult. Attacks on halls must also be a problem for you.'

McCrea then asked what provision there was to deal with further Republican violence. The Prime Minister assured him that offenders would be 'brought back in', if they committed new acts of violence, but conceded that 'there is clarification needed on this'. McCrea worried aloud that those getting out would train the next generation of terrorists, but Blair stuck to his message that prisoner releases were part of the deal and that it was the 'whole package or nothing'. Blair then tried—much as Terence O'Neill once did—to locate the Orangemen within the broader picture of world opinion. He spoke of how the British government's freedom of movement (presumably in favour of the Unionist interest) was constrained by Sinn Fein's political credibility in the 'Outside World [of] America and the Republic of Ireland'. There would be no more respectability for Sinn Fein if they took up violence, Blair added, and said that the British government would act if Sinn Fein again took up arms. He implored his Orange guests to 'give those Sinn Fein who want [it] the opportunity to cross the bridge to democracy' and spoke of an unprecedented opportunity.

It was nearing the end of a meeting in which Blair and the Orangemen had done almost all of the talking, with Mowlam and the civil servants virtually silent. Sounding a practical note, McCrea asked whether there was a possibility or mechanisms for changing the Agreement. Blair said that while '[we] don't want to change . . . clarification will have to be made—clarification not alteration'. As a sweetener, Blair raised the subject of money for victims, which he said he had discussed with Jeffrey Donaldson, and said that he had met the Chancellor of the Exchequer, Gordon Brown, and 'hoped to be able' to provide this. McCrea ended by evincing concern about the security situation, and then the Orangemen thanked the Prime Minister for his time.

It had been a cordial meeting, but with limited meeting of minds. The Order had tried to impress its moral case on the Prime Minister, with all the grievances born of thirty years of terror. The Prime Minister in turn had tried to convince his interlocutors of the 'big' picture: that this was a historic chance to wean Sinn Fein away from violence and thus reduce the possibility of more of the pain and suffering that the Orangemen were describing. The Order's moral philosophy was based on inviolable Kantian first principles (deontology), while that of Blair was based on utilitarian results (consequentialism). If leading philosophers cannot agree on which approach is better, we can hardly expect Blair and the Orangemen to concur. On the practical side, the Order felt that keeping as many prisoners behind bars as possible was the best way towards a more peaceful society as this would prevent the training of a new generation and reinforce the principle that crime doesn't pay. On the other hand, Blair argued that compromises were necessary to wean terrorists off their old habits and inculcate the habits of democracy and peace. In the short run, the IRA has stopped its aggression, but paramilitaries who do not respect the law still run amok on many estates, legitimating their criminal activities by their 'political' status. Only in the long run will it become apparent whether imprisonment or release made the most sense, but, once again, expecting the two parties to agree on such intractable issues is too optimistic.

Soon after the meeting, the Grand Lodge released a statement that, having heard the Prime Minister's response to its concerns, it found that its objections were 'unalterable'. As a result, though the Grand Lodge, as an organization committed to civil and religious liberty, could not instruct its members how to vote, it remained 'unable to recommend the Agreement to the people of Ulster'. Its main complaints were:

1. Dublin interference in the internal affairs of Northern Ireland
2. The prospect of an undemocratically accountable Assembly
3. The prospect of unrepentant terrorists in the Executive of the proposed Assembly
4. The Maryfield Secretariat and the Anglo Irish Agreement in another guise

Decommissioning was also noted as a concern.[18]

While debate was taking place at the highest levels, grassroots members were wrestling with the issue. The attitude of the more defensive section of Orange opinion was firmly against an agreement well before the ink was dry. As early as September 1997, for instance, York Lodge in Belfast submitted a resolution calling 'upon the Orange Institution...to immediately set up Action Committees to prepare for Practical Resistance in the event of Ulster's Constitution [*sic*] Position being... affected by the success of Pan Nationalist's Plans in the so called Peace Talks'.[19]

Yet in other parts of the province, things were different. Tyrone, which as we will see is the strongest pro-Agreement county within the Order, hosted a particularly acrimonious debate. The SOD was in the forefront of pushing an anti-Agreement agenda, and Walter Millar and Joel Patton claimed at a county meeting on 6 May that twelve of the nineteen lodges in their district (Killyman 1) were anti-GFA. Mitchell Cummings felt that politics should not be discussed until after Grand Lodge had given a lead on the issue, but the Rev. Culbertson urged a strong 'no'. Richard Reid asked that both sides of the issue be considered and that the decision be left up to individuals to decide for themselves. Another speaker, Paul Bell, in turn expressed his opposition to the GFA. Cummings then re-entered the picture reading a letter from David Trimble and mentioning that Trimble had offered to address a county meeting 'on any part of the Agreement'. Patton brusquely intervened and, ironically, enquired about the legality of reading such a letter in a lodge meeting. Another delegate spoke against the GFA, but was again countered by a member, James Emery, who said there were many points 'for' and 'against' and that the county should not take a position. Andrew Scott argued that voting on this issue would merely divide the lodge and, regardless of the decision, 'what will we achieve?' It is interesting that even at this early date, pro-Agreement sympathizers had to couch their arguments in the language of neutrality while opponents were quite openly campaigning for a 'no'.

It was now time to take the pulse of County Tyrone Grand Lodge. Ivan Cooper proposed that 'this county Grand Lodge reject this Agreement', seconded by the notorious Millar. Cummings then proposed an amendment that 'we take no decisions and leave it to the individual's conscience', which was seconded by Richard Reid from Pomeroy District (the district which was soon to expel Millar and Patton). Reid was pro-Agreement, a delegate to the UUC who represented the Mid-Ulster constituency association rather than the Order.[20] The county Grand Master decided to put the amendment to the floor, and it was passed by 35–30 with 6 abstentions. This then became a motion and only those entitled to vote at county level (i.e. excluding visitors like Patton and Millar) cast a ballot. The vote now split by 35–27 with 6 abstentions. Most of those supporting the amendment would have been pro-Agreement, so this vote indicates a county pretty evenly split in its sympathies. The minutes record that: 'Some members including many of the visitors present [many of whom were part of the SOD] felt very disturbed at the decision taken by the County Grand Lodge and there was evidence of dissent against various Officers and members of the County. . . . The County Grand Master ruled that the Lodge adjourn for supper which was served by the ladies.'[21]

The debate in Tyrone shows that a good deal of diversity of opinion on the GFA existed within the Order in 1998 and that more liberal border Unionists in Tyrone (and to a lesser extent Fermanagh) could plough a different furrow from Grand Lodge. Nevertheless, the fact that the 'no' camp could almost prevail in the most liberal Orange county as early as 6 May 1998 also suggests that the GFA would have to swim against the current of Orange opinion from the outset. As Unionist opinion soured on the Agreement after May 1998, Orange campaigning against it became more overt. As in the post-Sunningdale period, the Order became the nexus around which 'no' Unionism coalesced. In an echo of its leading role in forming the UUUC in the mid 1970s and coordinating anti-AIA protests in the mid 1980s, the Order put its weight behind a 'Declaration and Pledge of the United Unionists' which brought together DUP, UK Unionist Party, and anti-Agreement UUP elements. The document was read out by Saulters, who was flanked by the UUP MPs Roy Beggs, Clifford Forsythe, Willie Ross, William Thompson, and Martin Smyth as well as the DUP leader, Ian Paisley, his deputy, Peter Robinson, and the UK Unionist MP Robert McCartney. 'We solemnly pledge ourselves and urge our fellow citizens to ensure, by every lawful means, the rejection of an Agreement designed to destroy the Union,' read Saulters. Saulters and the eight politicians then signed copies of the document.[22]

This offended some in the Order like the Trimble loyalist Sam Foster. 'We are in a very sad and very bad time,' he lamented. People like him (i.e. traditionalists) 'were disillusioned because of the direction we appeared to be going'. Foster forcefully complained that 'Grand Lodge had been wrong to get involved in the . . . Referendum Campaign and . . . the "House of Orange" should not have been used for a "No" Photo Call'.[23] William Bingham told the press that 'there are many Orangemen who are open to be persuaded to vote Yes. . . . The Order should not seek to persuade members to vote Yes or No, but should seek clarification on matters of concern and then let people make up their own minds.' Indeed, a small group of Orangemen calling themselves 'Spirit of the Union' formed to support the GFA.[24]

Other pro-Agreement Orangemen expressed their disappointment in Orange meetings. The Rev. Gerald Sproule, in a subsequent Central Committee meeting, lamented the appearance of Paisley and McCartney at Grand Lodge. After William Leathem criticized Trimble's lieutenant David McNarry for his media attack on Saulters, Sproule said it was a tragedy when the Order began to 'name names'. Sproule derided what he called the Order's 'persecution complex' and optimistically called upon Grand Lodge to recognize that 'we have lots of friends, the general public support this Institution . . . we should encourage that support. Let's not always be looking suspiciously on [them]'. This did not please McCrea, who sardonically replied that while 'we talk with our friends', the Order should ensure that 'our friends [i.e. Trimble and the UUP] are not betraying us. . . [It is] sometimes difficult to tell who your friends actually are.'[25] The assembled delegates then voted on whether Unionist candidates should take their place in the new Northern Ireland Assembly which would be formed under the GFA. Here the Order was prepared to be pragmatic, with eighty-seven supporting participation and just Joel Patton and two others opposed.

The previous exchange showed that the pro-Agreement forces, though not afraid to articulate their views, were in a decided minority among Orangemen and on the defensive even during the early stages of the GFA when the Agreement still commanded a slim majority of the votes of Protestant Ulster. As support for the GFA slipped within the Unionist community in late 1998 and early 1999, pressure was increasingly brought to bear on the most liberal elements within the Order.

The Demise of the Education Committee

Given the modernizing thrust of the Education Committee (EC), it is unsurprising that its traditionalist members formed a solidly pro-Agreement bloc. Meanwhile, the SOD was in the forefront of pushing the anti-Agreement case. But these two lines of cleavage did not neatly overlap. Most Orangemen opposed the SOD for its methods and its flagrant disrespect for Orange laws, and this was reflected in the expulsion of Patton and Millar in late 1998. On the other hand, most Orangemen also opposed the GFA. This means they backed the EC's disciplinary case against the SOD, but were critical of the way the EC 'pushed the envelope' of modernization within the Institution over issues like meeting the PC and supporting the Agreement.[26] The EC's chief adversary at Grand Lodge was Grand Secretary John McCrea. McCrea was an early opponent of the EC's evangelism, and went out of his way in mid 1997 to criticize some of its publications, once raising the astounding observation that King Billy was facing the wrong way in an EC leaflet!

In December 1997, a Paisley-leaning Belfast Orangeman named James Heyburn nominated Councillor Nelson McCausland for the post of convenor of the EC, charging that 'some of us do not like the direction the Education Committee is taking'. McCausland had a history of running on both the Independent and United Unionist tickets, switching from the UUP to the DUP as early as 2001.[27] Heyburn's proposal failed, winning just seven backers, but the wheels of change were set in train.[28] 1998 began with conflict within the EC between McCausland and Kennaway and their rival factions.[29] McCausland complained that Kennaway had obstructed the accession of the more conservative Rev. Mervyn Gibson and Alvin Mullan onto the committee. Sure enough, when McCausland put Gibson's nomination to a vote in the EC, it was defeated.[30] McCausland also complained that Kennaway's EC had failed to adequately repudiate the contents of a Republican book which mentioned McCausland and which David Trimble and others had denounced as a hoax.[31]

As noted, letters from various lodges had attacked the EC's decision to meet the PC in December 1997. One from LOL 1422 in Belfast followed this up by a suggestion that the entire remit of the committee be investigated.[32] This submission (possibly prearranged) was taken up with gusto by elements in Grand Lodge, notably McCrea and, later, Denis Watson. Brian Kennaway alleges that a 'whispering campaign' had begun against the EC after December 1997, and it soon found itself under investigation by Grand Lodge. It also appears that EC members were kept in the dark about the process, with Grand Lodge failing to provide Kennaway and other EC members with copies of the investigating committee minutes and other documents. At best, insensitivity was shown to the traditionalists on the EC. At worst, protocol was breached.[33] In February 1999, Grand Lodge appointed a committee to consider the remit of the EC. The investigating committee included Kennaway's old foes McCrea and Davison, though some traditionalists like Colin Shilliday were also on it.[34]

Meanwhile, Kennaway was questioned regarding the budget for the EC's dinner at Stormont 1798 commemorative, with the charge being that the finances were not in order. This line of questioning came from nowhere and drew an angry response from Kennaway.[35] Journalists, academics, and the lord mayors of Belfast and Dublin had been invited to the dinner, another example of the EC's evangelical, outreach approach to Orangeism. The presence of the Catholic Mayor of Dublin drew objections from some within the Order (notably Joel Patton, who was still active at the time), and Saulters told Kennaway he could not attend the dinner as this would split the Order and weaken his position vis-à-vis the hardline faction:

I believe for me to attend the Dinner on 12th June will again bring the wrath of many members down on me and Grand Lodge Officers, I therefore thank you and the Education Committee for the invitation but must decline for the sake of harmony within Grand Lodge.... I dare not cause further controversy... Brethren whom I had thought would fully support me as they have done in the past now threaten me with their resignation.[36]

Throughout 1999, the investigating committee probed the EC, asking for minutes, querying the finances for the 1798 dinner, and generally making life difficult for EC traditionalists. Meetings were fraught with tension, with the EC men responding defensively to accusations that they had exceeded their remit in meeting the PC and had failed to consult adequately with Grand Lodge with regard to the dinner. Kennaway's long tenure as chairman opened him up to accusations of domination—and it was suggested that he rotate the position. Antrim's Drew Davison complained about the lack of 'breadth' in the EC and the rejection of conservative candidates like Mervyn Gibson, Alvin Mullan, and others. Although the lone traditionalist on the investigating committee, Colin Shilliday, defended the EC's decisions, the weight of opinion was stacked against it.[37]

The investigating committee tabled its report at the June 1999 Grand Lodge meeting, and called for a radical restructuring of the EC into three discrete subcommittees dealing with publications, education, and public relations. All were to be placed under tight Grand Lodge oversight and their remits were to be highly circumscribed. Kennaway was told to give up the chair by 2001, offered the relatively pedestrian publications post, and excluded from the more high-profile areas. EC traditionalists were then publicly humiliated in front of Grand Lodge by the report, which criticized the EC for failing to rotate the chairmanship (held by Kennaway for some ten years), failing to consult Grand Lodge adequately on its activities, and generally not being 'open' in its approach. EC members were now obliged to present Grand Secretary Denis Watson with the names of anyone attending external conferences. Two Grand Lodge men, Kelly and McKeown, felt that the EC should be allowed to respond to the report. However, David McNarry (perhaps seeking to shore up his hardline credentials so as to offset his pro-Trimble image), seconded by the SOD sympathizer John McGrath, proposed the immediate adoption of the report of the investigating committee. This was approved by 77–22 with 9 abstentions.[38]

In legal terms, the EC *had* probably exceeded its remit, and failed to rotate the chair, or to consult Grand Lodge adequately in some of its initiatives. Under a more modernizing leadership, such initiatives would be excused as innovative, but with the leadership under pressure from the SOD-inspired right, the EC's actions exposed the leadership to criticism and thus the EC was a luxury that Grand Lodge could no longer afford. As Clifford Smyth later observed, Kennaway never really commanded a large, vocal following comparable to the SOD and could thus be more easily brushed aside.[39] In June 2000, after refusing to meet with Grand Lodge officers to discuss the new EC remit, Kennaway and the EC traditionalists resigned en masse and publicly denounced the leadership.[40]

Party vs Order

The Orange Order's public opposition to the GFA set it firmly against the UUP, the party which the Order was instrumental in helping to form in 1905. The Order had a long history of tangling with Stormont Unionist leaders over particular policies, and hence the launch of Stormont Mark II in 1998 reopened a familiar story. One clear difference of course was that the Order was no longer an 'insider' pillar within a corporatist system, as in the period from 1922 until the late 1960s. Few elite networks bound Grand Lodge to the UUP executive. Most active Orangemen who were in the UUP (i.e. Martin Smyth, Denis Watson, Drew Nelson, David Brewster, Lord Molyneaux) were anti-Agreement. David McNarry was one of the few to balance a pro-Trimble stance with Orange activism but he constantly had to manage a high-wire act which involved playing the hardliner where he could while muting his open defence of Trimble at Grand Lodge. The Order's relationship to Trimble thus more closely resembled the adversarial relationship of the O'Neill–Faulkner years than the corporatist one of the Craig–Andrews–Brookeborough era.

The Order's favoured tactic for bringing down unpopular UUP leaders like O'Neill and Faulkner was to sponsor and swing a no-confidence vote by the UUC.[41] The roughly 900-member UUC is the governing body of the party. The UUP's constitution mandates a special meeting of the UUC at the request of just sixty party members. Many of these rules are the legacy of the UUC's fissiparous umbrella structure, in which a number of affiliated bodies like the Orange Order and Young Unionists, as well as constituency associations, came together to form the party in 1905. The party's diffuse structure resembles that of the Order, and is unique among the parties of Northern Ireland. It is noticeably different from that of the DUP, which is far more disciplined, centralized, and hierarchical.[42] After late 1999, anti-Agreement UUP members—notably Jeffrey Donaldson—repeatedly used the UUP's party rules to engineer repeated UUC 'crisis' meetings. These helped to interrupt the smooth working of the GFA-based Peace Process and forced Trimble to placate the grassroots constantly before signing up to new GFA initiatives.[43]

Within the UUC, the Orange Order occupies a position not unlike that of the trade unions within the British Labour Party. Each Orange County Lodge has a number of delegates which it is permitted to send to the UUC. In all, the Order has 15 per cent of the total UUC delegates. However, this accounts only for the Order's direct influence. If we include the UUC delegates who happen to be in the Orange Order but are not official Orange delegates, the total Orange component of the UUC rises to over 50 per cent.[44] Does this mean that the Orange Order can control the UUC? In the post-GFA period, as in the past, loyalty to the party often overrode loyalty to the Order. This was clear when reformist leaders like O'Neill and Faulkner often gained UUC majorities despite having few supporters within Grand Lodge. They fortified themselves against the popular Unionism of the Order by cultivating personal and party loyalty and establishing a support base within the 100-odd UUP party executive. Within the executive, an inner circle of confidants surrounded the leader. In Trimble's case, this largely consisted of young, well-educated 'baby barristers': modernizers with few connections to rural, Orange Ulster.[45]

Trimble's leadership was strongly tested by the signing of the GFA, but this was only the beginning of the struggle. The IRA's failure to decommission, increasing restrictions on Orange parading from July 1998, and the Patten commission's proposals on police reform (particularly the threatened removal of the cherished name 'Royal Ulster Constabulary') contributed to weakened support for the GFA within the UUC. This was partly staved off by Trimble's refusal—for nineteen months—to allow the Assembly and executive to launch without prior IRA decommissioning. The US mediator George Mitchell managed to cajole Sinn Fein into making a strongly pro-decommissioning statement, and after Mitchell coordinated a modus vivendi on actual decommissioning between Sinn Fein and the UUP, the matter was put to the UUC. On 27 November 1999, the UUC voted by 59–41 per cent to take its place in an executive which included Sinn Fein.[46]

Though Trimble's margin had dropped to under 60 per cent from the 71 per cent support received in May 1998, both were a far cry from the level of support for the pro-Agreement camp at Grand Lodge in May 1998, which was less than 25 per cent. This begs the question of (1) what the 117 Orange delegates to the UUC were up to; and (2) how the rest of the UUC Orange members reconciled their Orange and party loyalties. Recent research allows us to be relatively precise about this. The first point is that the Orange factor is important. In March 2000, the former Orange Grand Master Martin Smyth challenged Trimble for the UUP leadership, campaigning against an Agreement which Smyth viewed as deficient on issues like policing, decommissioning, and parading. Though perceived as less charismatic than the other main anti-GFA figure, Jeffrey Donaldson, Smyth did much better than expected, losing the UUC vote to Trimble by a margin of just 57–43 per cent.

In a statistical analysis of the vote, the strongest predictors were age and occupation. Those under 34 (especially if under 24) were hostile to Trimble, while older delegates (especially those over 55) were strongly in support. In terms of occupation, an odd mix of professionals, civil servants, and those in clerical employment and trades backed Smyth, while senior managers and teachers opposed him. Wealthier delegates tended to back Trimble over the less well off. Even with all these factors constant, Orange membership was a significant ($p < .01$) predictor of an anti-Agreement vote—a stronger influence on the vote than income. This analysis showed that Orangeism was an anti-Agreement influence, but it also demonstrated that the Orange vote was split. In the survey, Smyth had the edge over Trimble among Orange voters by only 51–49 per cent.[47]

This finding would corroborate much of what we know from the other main Orange jurisdictions in Canada and Scotland, where the Orange vote proved immensely difficult to mobilize en bloc.[48] Does this mean that one's Orangeism says little more about one's beliefs than one's income? Before we accept this implication of the Tonge–Evans study, we need to look more

Table 8.1 The Social Profile of the UUC and Orange Order in Comparative Perspective (99% sample)

	Top 12 MOSAIC postcode classes	Rural 8 MOSAIC postcode classes	Bottom 7 MOSAIC postcode classes	Cases in study (N)
Orange bloc UUC delegates	45.7%	36.2%	12.4%	105
UUC delegates total	44.3%	35.9%	8.4%	879
Grand Orange Lodge office-bearers	34.7%	44.4%	9.7%	144
Northern Ireland population average	32.5%	18.1%	22.9%	1.6m

Sources: Kaufmann and Patterson, 'The Dynamics of Intra-Party Support'; NI MOSAIC 2002.

closely at the UUC and its Orangemen in Table 8.1. 45 per cent of UUC delegates live in the top twelve postcode areas, and there is no difference in this respect between Orange delegates and other UUC delegates. In other words, UUC Orangemen are a fairly select social bunch within the Order: older, more urban and better-heeled than the Orange masses. This may account for their modestly pro-Trimble stance.[49]

We also need to consider the difference between Orange delegates and those whose membership in the Order was more nominal. We obtained data on 113 of 117 Orange delegates from UUP party strategists and found that just a quarter of Orange delegates to the UUC backed the GFA. On the other hand, two-thirds of the other 749 delegates for whom we had information backed the accord. We were also able to identify twenty-two Orange office-bearers (masters or secretaries at any level) who were *not* part of the 117-strong Orange delegation. These individuals took a much more favourable view of Trimble and the GFA (52.6 per cent) than the Orange official delegates (25 per cent). This also helps explain why the proportion of Orangemen backing the GFA in the Tonge–Evans study (49 per cent)—whose Orange respondents are probably mostly nominal members—vastly exceeds the proportion (25 per cent) in our study of the 113 official Orange delegates. Table 8.2 also shows how Orange delegate support for the Agreement and Trimble drops substantially among those who hold office. We may surmise from this that Orange *activism*—in the form of being a lodge master or secretary—and Orange *representation* (i.e. being part of the Order's 117-strong delegation) make one more likely to privilege one's Orange loyalty over that of the party. As Table 8.2 shows, those like Smyth and Molyneaux who *both* were active in the Order and were Orange-appointed delegates were extremely unlikely to back the Agreement (12.8 per cent). As Smyth insisted, he was 'first... an Orangeman, then a politician'.[50]

Table 8.2 Orange Delegates' Stance towards the GFA: The Role of Party Section and Orange Activism

Characteristic	Pro-Agreement	N	Sample
Non-Orange delegates	66.3%	704	91%
Orange office-bearers outside Orange bloc	52.6%	22	86%
Non-office-bearers in Orange bloc	32.9%	73	94%
Orange office-bearers in Orange bloc	12.8%	40	98%

Source: Kaufmann and Patterson, 'The Dynamics of Intra-Party Support'.

Orange activism and representation is not the whole story, however. As the case of Tyrone vs Grand Lodge showed, even within official Orange delegates we find a great deal of diversity. This in turn permeates the opinions of the delegates whom each county sends to the UUC. County UUC delegates know each other and meet frequently. Since all must be party men, they tend to be appointed more discreetly than other Orange office-holders and do not have to be proposed on the floor of the County Lodge. Instead, candidates are 'approached' by existing UUC delegates, thereby perpetuating an elite network. Grand Lodge tries to get the UUC delegates to do its bidding by calling UUC delegate meetings, but these are often poorly attended.[51] For instance, in March 2002, Grand Lodge called a meeting of delegates to discuss UUP policy and insisted that the county and grand lodges rather than the UUC delegates would 'decide the way forward'.[52] However, at the meeting, just forty-three of the 113 delegates turned up. At a crucial meeting in June 1999, just thirty-five attended.[53] The self-contained, independent nature of the county delegate networks contributes to a great deal of diversity when it comes to UUC voting. Figure 8.4 shows that Tyrone County Grand Lodge was over 70 per cent pro-Agreement in 2002, by far the highest level of support in the Order. On the other hand, in Antrim and Belfast, delegates opposed the GFA to a man, confirming a long-standing historical tendency in both counties towards rebel Orangeism.[54]

The stance of the respective county lodges was partly related to local Unionist voting patterns, since Fermanagh is a bastion of UUP support, and North Antrim and parts of Belfast are strongly DUP. Yet this does not provide the strongest explanation. In statistical tests based on the eighteen Northern Ireland constituencies, we found that Orange delegates residing in 'border' councils (often with a high Catholic population and high Orange participation rate) differed very little from non-Orange delegates in their views. However, in north-east Ulster, being Orange was an important political statement that signalled a much stronger anti-GFA stance. The map in Figure 8.5 shows the difference in support for the GFA between Orange and non-Orange UUC delegates by constituency of residence. Note the darker shading in the north-east, which indicates that Antrim and Belfast County delegates formed

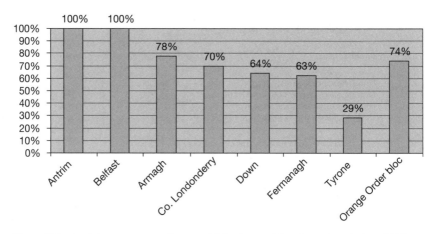

Figure 8.4 Anti-Agreement sentiment within Orange bloc, by county lodge, 2003

Source: Kaufmann and Patterson, 'The Dynamics of Intra-Party Support'. (*Note*: There were no Orange delegates in Derry City.)

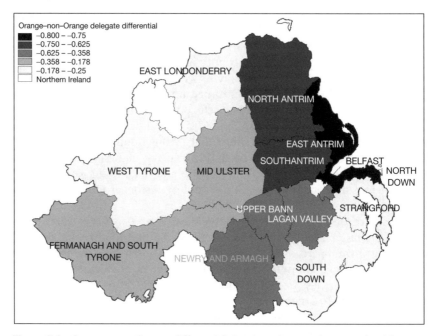

Figure 8.5 Orange–non-Orange differentials in stance by constituency of residence

Source: Kaufmann and Patterson, 'The Dynamics of Intra-Party Support'. (*Note*: There were no Orange members in Foyle or West Belfast: these areas are unshaded and unlabelled.)

networks that were highly insulated from the UUP constituency associations in these two counties.[55]

UUC–Orange relations

The Order's public antipathy to the Agreement and Trimble's deepening unpopularity after Drumcree 1998 led to a severe schism between the UUP and the Orange Order. Within the Order, calls to break the official link with the UUP were increasingly heard. Within the UUP, modernizers like Trimble yearned for the day when the party could cut its Orange ties, reach out to moderate Catholics, and embrace a more rational, 'civic' Unionism.[56]

As soon as he had taken the reins from Molyneaux in 1995, Trimble began thinking of ways to modernize the structure of the UUP to change it from a federation to a more centralized body. In March 1995, these modernizing plans were adopted by the UUC. In meetings with the Order, Trimble, the party president Josias Cunningham and Jeffrey Donaldson sought to assure the Orangemen that they were not trying in any way to remove a 'sectarian millstone' from around their necks, as portrayed in the media. It didn't hurt that both were Orangemen in good standing.[57] By March 1998, Trimble raised plans for a UUC–Orange Commission to consider reforming the link between the two entities as part of a wider scheme to modernize the structure of the UUP.[58] He also gave private assurances to John Gorman, a Catholic UUP candidate in North Down, that the formal links would be broken. For Gorman, the Order was 'a positively anti-Roman Catholic body with a degree of sectarianism in its organisation', and he chastised it for being out of step with the UUP on the GFA issue.[59]

Correspondence between the Order and the UUC reveals that the UUP was careful to stress that the reorganization was not intended as a way of breaking the link but rather as an end in itself designed to modernize archaic party structures. In truth it was both, since the UUP leadership wanted to reach the liberal wing of Unionist and Catholic opinion, and the conservative organizations and constituency associations—like the Orangemen or Donaldson's Lagan Valley association—were the main barrier standing in the way of this. Josias Cunningham told Denis Watson that the Order could no longer maintain bloc representation under the new structure. Rather, the new arrangement would result in 'tighter disciplinary processes and efficient communication'. He added that 'although such a change may attract [new] members (including Roman Catholics) . . . this is purely coincidental'. Having said this, Cunningham did broach the more sensitive issues. He contended that Orangemen who were also members of constituency branches could vote in both forums and thus achieve 'double representation' for themselves. He then asked the Order to produce its own proposal for change.[60] Following a meeting with the Order, Cunningham proposed an interim measure whereby Orangemen currently on the UUC who were paid-up members in good standing in their party branches could remain UUC members for a further two years after the reforms. Beyond this point, they would lose their places.[61]

Within the Order, the strongest supporters of retaining the link between the Order and the UUP were anti-Agreement members of the UUP.[62] Tonge and Evans's analysis shows that support for Smyth over Trimble was as good a predictor of support for retaining the Orange link as Orange membership itself.[63] This meant that Orange UUP MLAs who opposed the Agreement were among the first to sound the alarm over the threat of a UUP–Orange divorce. Peter Weir, for example, a clever and articulate MLA from North Antrim, circularized his colleagues at Stormont as follows:

As you are aware the Party Leader [Trimble] has now set out on a rapid attempt to radically alter the structure of the Ulster Unionist Party. There is a clear attempt to remove the Orange Order and the Young Unionists from having representation, in part because these organisations are seen as an embarrassment to the Leader, but more importantly a political obstacle to the direction he wishes to take the Party in. It might even be part of a wider agenda connected with the political process. However colleagues should be aware that we are in a stronger position to prevent this witch hunt than we appear.

Citing the need for a two-thirds vote to amend the party constitution, Weir urged his anti-Agreement colleagues to 'stick together' to defeat the proposals so as to ensure that reform occurred 'for the right motives, in the right manner, and with the key prerequisite of consensus . . . we can only lose if we allow ourselves to be outmanouvred [sic]'.[64]

Did Weir represent the main body of Orange opinion? The question has a long history. We saw that anti-UUP feeling was often expressed by the DUP, Independent and Labour-minded sections of the grassroots, and a minority at Grand Lodge in the 1950s and 1960s. In 1981, a correspondent to Grand Lodge complained of too much coverage of the UUP in the *Orange Standard*.[65] In late 1994, Smyth raised the question of the link and asked county lodges to report back. The issue was then raised at a conference of all lodge masters in Northern Ireland in 1995. Recall that despite SOD campaigning, the vote for disaffiliation went down to defeat. The final tally among lodge masters was just 369 for a divorce, 484 against, and 71 abstentions. The feeling among the rank and file was different: in 1996-7, the LOI Commission found 65 per cent of members endorsing disaffiliation. Despite this, Commission sided with lodge masters rather than the mass membership and endorsed a retention of the link as in the best interests of the Order.[66]

Discontent remained within the SOD fringe between 1995 and 1998, but even the rebellious County Antrim Grand Lodge endorsed the link in 1996.[67] Later, an Orange working party endorsed the 1997 LOI Commission recommendations to retain the link.[68] Trimble's signing of the GFA rocked this complacency. In March 1999, County Antrim passed a resolution to break the link and endorsed a vote of no confidence in Trimble.[69] The disaffiliation vote in Antrim was 51–12 in favour with 16 abstentions, but nobody in Antrim spoke up for Trimble and the no-confidence resolution was passed by 78–0.[70] The vehemence of Orange denunciations of Trimble stemmed from their belief that he had 'faked it' at Drumcree and used the Order purely to advance his career.[71] Dunmurry (Antrim) LOL 1046 expressed similar views:

Despite assurances from [Trimble] of 'No guns—No government' the Northern Ireland Assembly is now up and running and terrorists from both sides of the community now sit in Stormont, all pals together and content to vote through a 30% increase on the pieces of silver being handed out. Grand Lodge urged its delegates to the special meeting held by the UUP in the Waterfront Hall to vote against the recommendations put to the meeting. In view of this, the question must be asked why so many members . . . are sitting on various committees at Stormont but cannot find time to sit in their lodge rooms? Despite the oath taken by all members when joining the Orange Order, that it is for no private or personal gain, we feel that certain members have used our colours to push themselves forward in their political careers. We . . . recommend that the Orange Institution takes the initiative by breaking all links with the Ulster Unionist Party as soon as possible.[72]

In response to pressures like these, an Orange committee began to consider the link, but deliberated at a snail's pace. This brought criticism from the traditionalist Orange Grand Chaplain, the Rev. Warren Porter, who accused his own Order of foot-dragging and inconsistency. For Porter, the Order's membership opposed the UUP, yet the Order continued to send delegates to a party 'which they really want to destroy'. Porter then resigned from the Orange–UUP liaison committee in disgust.[73] In June 2000, the Orange committee, despite its deliberations, stated that Grand Lodge was 'not in favour' of breaking the link.[74] In view of the appetite for change within both Order and party, the obvious question was why the resistance? George Patton, writing to his fellow Orangeman and UUP MP Jeffrey Donaldson, who also opposed the GFA, put the matter succinctly. 'Many Lodges (my own for example) felt [in 1995] that it would be better if there was an amicably agreed change [to break the link]. The mood is now different in light of what has been perceived as a hostile move to "get rid of" the Institution.'[75] While the Order resisted moves to break the link, it privately sought legal advice on how best to secure its assets within the UUP in the event of a forced split.[76] Clearly, the new rift was a split unlike any before.

Undaunted, the UUP continued to push its reform agenda. UUP officials realized that they would have great difficulty achieving the two-thirds UUC vote required to break the link, so they took a path of less resistance, the legal route. They argued that under new Westminster legislation, the Orange Order could not be part of the UUC owing to the nature of its funding. The Order rejected this legal approach after taking advice from its solicitors, prompting an open battle with UUP modernizers.[77] Stymied, the UUP executive sought to implement reform of affiliation fees which would hit the anti-Agreement Orange Order and Young Unionists and thus curtail the frequent UUC 'crisis' meetings which the 'Antis' were using to undermine Trimble's leadership. The crux of the matter was that constituency associations paid fees while the Orange Order and other affiliated bodies did not. As a quid pro quo, affiliated bodies like the Orange Order could only attend UUC meetings (as opposed to more frequent committee meetings) and the UUP frequently used Orange facilities gratis.

In early 2002, the UUC's Trimbleite Executive Committee sought to force the Order and other affiliated bodies to assume the responsibilities of constituency associations and pay a new fee of £100 per delegate.[78] David Brewster, a lawyer and Orangeman as well as an anti-Agreement UUC delegate, felt that while the UUC had a case, the Order was in a good position to ask what new services it would get for the higher fee and to demand some compensation for UUP use of Orange halls. He also pointed to the fact that Order delegates who were also members of a branch would in effect be paying twice.[79] Brewster later added that the Order would need to insist on assuming its full voting rights in the Executive Council. He recommended that the Order drag out the appeal procedure as long as possible and if necessary call a special Council meeting if any of its members were suspended for non-payment of fees. He also raised the point that Orange members of the UUP executive should be 'mandated' by Grand Lodge to vote against enforcement of the new rules and be held accountable by Grand Lodge if they failed to do so.[80] Brewster did suggest meeting the UUC, but it took months of moving to and fro between the Order and the UUP before a mutually acceptable date was arranged. It seems that the Order proved the more difficult partner in this awkward dance.[81]

By mid 2002, the UUP appeared to be making peace with the Order. Drew Nelson, a prominent Orangeman who is now Grand Secretary, drafted the UUC Rules Review Committee's position paper on the link. Several meetings also took place between the Order and the committee. Nelson's paper endorsed a consensus that the relationship between the Order and party should not be broken, but would instead be altered in a way that would not affect the long-standing association between the two.[82] The new proposal sought to introduce a £60 fee per delegate in 2003, with a £10 increase for four years until the £100 fee was attained.[83] Patton described the new proposals as more 'realistic' and offered to put these to the County lodges.[84]

County Orange delegates next considered the fee increase and the nature of the link. In all counties, there was a near-unanimous desire to retain the link. Belfast probably represented the views of many, declaring that they should 'stay within the Party and fight [our] corner'. Only County Londonderry was split, with some favouring retention and others a breaking of the link. In terms of fees, virtually all—including the traditional Unionists of Fermanagh and Tyrone—complained that a fee of £100 was high. County Down vowed to fight it.[85] None of this impressed modernizers within the UUP. In Cooper's address to the party faithful in Londonderry, he extolled the virtues of pro-Agreement Unionism and savaged the Order's delaying tactics:

> I deeply regret that for the last two years, since Joe Cunningham's death, we have been bogged down in a continually frustrating set of discussions with the Orange Order. We have gone round in circles and eventually ended up back at square one, the Order not being prepared to accept the need for change. Your Rules Committee will now decide . . . whether to allow this roadblock to stymie many of the other changes we want to implement. I am convinced that this party should not allow one particular interest group to prevent progress. But I have to face the reality that the Order's opposition would make it unlikely that we can obtain the necessary two-thirds majority . . . do we go for the radical and complete set of new rules favoured by Joe Cunningham? Or do we go for a hot patch of compromise changes, which leaves the need to modernise the linkage with affiliated bodies to another day?[86]

In the meantime, the lack of progress on decommissioning led to a continual weakening of Trimble's position. Republicans were also implicated in an audacious break-in at Castlereagh Intelligence Centre and were linked to FARC guerillas in Colombia. Revelations that an IRA spy ring was operating at Stormont—the so-called 'Stormontgate affair' which the Sinn Fein and British intelligence operative Denis Donaldson later claimed was a British Special Branch hoax—led to the raiding of Sinn Fein party offices and the fourth suspension of the devolved institutions.[87] The GFA was in tatters and anti-Agreement forces were on the march, something reflected in the selection and deselection of UUP candidates ahead of the Assembly elections planned for May 2003.[88] Overall, just 42 per cent of the UUC backed breaking the link, forcing UUP modernizers to abandon the Trimble–Cunningham dream of cutting Orange ties.[89] They now merely sought to reform the relationship so that Orange representation would be at the behest of constituency associations rather than the county Orange lodges.[90]

The UUP had proposed a compromise whereby each constituency association would reserve a number of UUC places for paid-up local branch members who were Orangemen (or members of other affiliated bodies). However, since this would create a body of Orange delegates speaking for the Order yet outside the jurisdiction of the county or grand lodges, this was deemed to violate Orange law.[91] A meeting of Orange UUC delegates in early 2003 showed that the mood among Orangemen was defiant. John McCrea opened the proceedings with a sketch of the past months' news stories, one of which spoke of buying out the Orange Order. 'Who really is trying to get us out?, he asked. 'Does Mr. Blair want us out? Is the IRA involved? Mr. Blair has a lot to answer for. [The Order] must remain within the UUC . . . New rules need $\frac{2}{3}$

majority [of the UUC].' He spoke of meddling with rules put in place by 'our forefathers'.

For the anti-Agreement MP Willie Ross, the '[Orange] Institution has a part to play in politics that is why our enemies want to get rid of [us]'. Ross opposed the reforms from both an Orange and a party viewpoint, stating that the new rules would move power away from the UUC to the executive. To counter this, his proposed amendments would 'ensure [that the] "status quo" will exist...8 of 14 officers on the current [UUP] officer team were full time politicians [which is] not healthy'. After criticizing the party for spending 'money like it is going out of fashion' on the referendum, Ross related that he had been denied access to other associations' documents by the party and noted that his constituency, East Londonderry, was the only one to oppose a reform of the Orange–UUC link.

Within the Order, the question of Orange control over its delegates was paramount. At a meeting of Orange UUC delegates, a speaker named Gilpin mentioned that two Order delegates had been 'given clear/concise guidance tonight' on how to vote at the next UUC meeting. Maynard Hanna then asked about the '400 Orange members and friends' who attended the UUC. 'Can they be pressurised?' he asked. This question was not answered, but the reality was almost certainly a 'no', given the diffuse authority structures of the Order. Fees were another bone of contention, and Jackie McCallister spoke of being told by County Down that if they didn't pay they would not be allowed to vote. This led to delegates paying out of pocket, which McCallister considered 'morally corrupt'. McCrea urged that no one rush to pay but that the matter be discussed with the Grand Secretary and George Patton. Dawson Baillie concurred with McCrea that no payments should be made until 'red letters' were received. Views differed somewhat by county. In Down, the general consensus was in favour of paying the £60 affiliation fee. A delegate named Randall from Belfast felt this was too high, however, and favoured a £10 fee. In the end, Baillie and Harold Doherty called for a press release and a record of the meeting to be sent to all Orange delegates and for those present to try to influence their fellow delegates. They reiterated the need for Orange delegates to attend the next meeting as a 'matter of utmost urgency'.[92]

Towards the end of the meeting, McCrea recounted an accusation from Fred Crowe, a UUP officer not in the Order, that DUP men were being sent by the Order to UUC meetings. McCrea denied this, and claimed he had told Crowe to substantiate it. Thus it appears that within the Orange anti-Agreement camp, there was still loyalty to the UUP. This was not the case for others, however. Peter Weir, Nelson McCausland, William Leathem, and Denis Watson were among the many Orangemen to make the leap to the DUP during 2001-3. Finally, on 29 November 2003, the UUP, the only party to govern Northern Ireland since Partition in 1921, lost its primary position as the leading Protestant party to the DUP of the Rev. Ian Paisley. Salt was

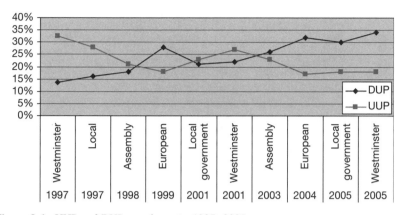

Figure 8.6 UUP and DUP popular vote, 1997–2005
Source: ARK NI Election Study, 1998.

later rubbed in the wounds when Jeffrey Donaldson, Arlene Foster, and Norah Beare defected to the victorious DUP.[93]

This was the denouement of a story of steady UUP decline. Between 1997 and 2005, the DUP's share of the Unionist vote rose steadily at the expense of the UUP. Figure 8.6 gives the chronological trend, which suggests some volatility. In reality, this is an artefact of the different rules and conditions for each type of election and conceals the fact that in each separate variety of contest (i.e. Westminster, local, Assembly, European), the UUP lost support to the DUP in straight-line fashion over this period.

Part of the explanation lies in the growing unpopularity of Trimble and the GFA. Yet we also need to be cognizant of the generational factor, which is not as amenable to policy change. A statistical analysis of a major 2001 election survey reveals that even in a year when the UUP edged ahead of the DUP in the popular vote by 27–23 per cent, by far the strongest positive (+) predictor of a UUP vote was age, as shown in Figure 8.7. Younger generations who had grown up with the Troubles—irrespective of class—were already turned off by the UUP in 2001. The better-educated opted for the UUP, but many who voted against the party were disaffected by the personalities and institutions of the 'establishment', from Trimble and the UUP to Blair, the Assembly, and Westminster.

Patterns in Orange voting were similar to those in the province as a whole. A 2004 survey returned by some 300 Orangemen shows that a bare majority of Orangemen were already in the DUP camp by 2001. Results also indicate that the Order supported the DUP to a greater extent than the Unionist population, despite the history of acrimony between the Order and the DUP leader, Ian Paisley (see Table 8.3). Statistical analysis of the results shows that—as in the Unionist population as a whole—age was the most significant background

227

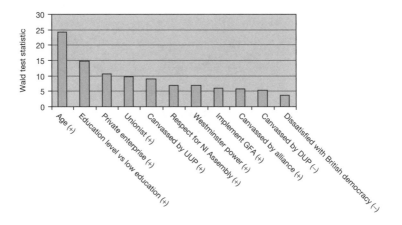

Figure 8.7 Predictors of support for the UUP in the 2001 election (Protestants only), by Wald test statistic

Source: H. Clarke et al., *General Election in Northern Ireland 2001*.

Table 8.3 Unionist and Orange Voting, 2001–2004

Election	Voter type	Party voted for		
		DUP	UUP	Other
2001 Westminster	Orange Order members	48.9	45.3	1.9
2001 Westminster	All Unionist voters	45.0	53.6	1.4
2003 Assembly	All Unionist voters	51.2	45.2	3.6
2004 European election	All Unionist voters	63.8	33.2	3.0
If election tomorrow	Orange Order members	64.9	29.2	3.5

Source: Tonge and Evans, 'Eating the Oranges', 11.

variable. Orangemen aged under 35 were far more likely to vote DUP than those over 55. The authors also found that Orangemen who supported retaining the UUP–Orange link were much less likely than others to support the DUP. This finding questions the Rev. Warren Porter's contention that DUP-leaning Orangemen pushed to retain the link so as to destroy the UUP.

Yet if the Order leaned towards the DUP, how can we explain the anomaly that the strongest Orange areas (in the border counties) are not the strongest DUP areas? Indeed, quite the contrary is the case. The map in Figure 8.8 shows UUP strength by district electoral area in 1993 in the 101 district electoral areas. If we look at voting in the three district council elections of 1993, 1997, and 2001, we find that the strongest predictor of UUP support, that is, a high ratio of UUP to DUP votes, is COI population ($z = 5.5$). Orange strength among Protestants is also mildly significant ($z = 2.4$) and predicts a UUP advantage if we leave County Antrim out of the analysis. The only other significant variables are the Protestant unemployment rate ($z = 3.3$)

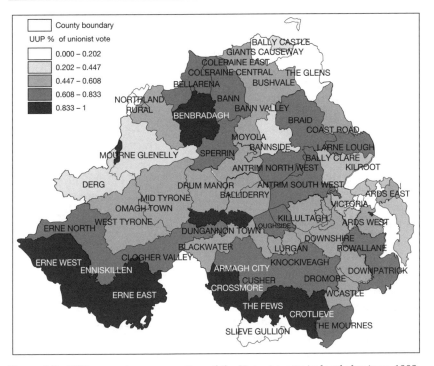

Figure 8.8 UUP support as a proportion of the Unionist vote in local elections, 1993

Source: ARK NI Elections Study, 1998; Northern Ireland Census 1991; based upon Ordnance Survey of Northern Ireland (OSNI) DEA digital boundaries 1993. © Crown copyright

and the local Catholic proportion of the population ($z = 2.5$). The higher the proportion of Catholics, the stronger the UUP advantage, whereas the higher the unemployment rate, the greater the DUP edge over the UUP (see Figure 8.8).[94]

How does this square with the DUP leanings of Orangemen discovered by Tonge and Evans? Once again, we need to bear in mind the nuances of intra-Orange voting behaviour. First of all, Orangemen in north-east Ulster, especially Antrim, lean to the DUP more than those in border counties.[95] To some degree, Tonge and Evans picked this up when they discovered that urban Orangemen from Belfast and Derry were much more likely than others to vote DUP.[96] Henry Patterson and I also found in our postcode analysis of the UUC that Orangemen from border areas like Tyrone and Fermanagh were much more likely to back the GFA than those in Antrim, North Down, and Belfast.

Finally, Christopher Farrington's qualitative research on local government shows that the UUP has an inbuilt advantage over the DUP in all counties bar Antrim, owing to its 'social capital' of connections with the Orange Order. To be blunt, the UUP has established itself first, and its network of halls and connections with UUP local branches are more robust. The DUP is simply 'out of the loop'. As Farrington remarks, 'at a basic level, most UUP branch meetings take place at Orange halls, whereas, with one exception, DUP meetings do not'. Moreover, endorsement from the Orange Order provides a powerful advantage to a candidate which non-Orangemen like the Craigavon councillor Fred Crowe readily acknowledge.[97]

Reference to this local connection was made at an Orange delegates' meeting, where a Tyrone member accused the UUP leadership of 'running scared' and suggested that 'the Orange Order really are the financiers of the Party as so many Orange members are the backbone of the Branches . . . [I am] glad to note that the general consensus is we keep the link and fight from within.'[98] This does not mean that the DUP could not take ground from the UUP, but it had a harder row to hoe—especially at local level. In explaining DUP gains, Farrington notes how Troubles-driven population movements from Derry and West Belfast into Waterside and Castlereagh Borough Council enabled the DUP to put roots down in these areas, which became core zones of strength for Paisley. In addition, the DUP's strength in North Antrim and especially Ballymena Borough Council owes little to the DUP's Free Presbyterian connections, which are often an electoral liability. More important is the way the DUP has appropriated the role of the UUP in North Antrim, with DUP politicians speaking at local Orange Twelfth platforms, Orange Arch erections, and banner unfurlings. This is slowly starting to spread outside the DUP's heartlands to constituencies like South Down. As the South Down MLA Jim Wells of the DUP told Farrington, because of his Orange credentials, 'I get invited to lots of functions and banner unfurlings and hall openings and it keeps me in contact with grass roots Unionism.'[99]

Rapprochement with Dr Paisley

Ian Paisley's career, as we saw in the first few chapters, has been defined by his desire to carve out a niche for himself to the right of the traditional institutions of Unionism: the mainline churches (especially the COI), the Orange Order, and the UUP. Beginning with his defection from the Order and Presbyterian Church in the early 1950s, he proved a thorn in the side of the mainstream Unionist institutions. Although the Order tried at various points to co-opt Paisley, his cantankerous response to its unity overtures ensured that a freeze in relations between the two bodies set in. At times of crisis, as in the 1970s and 1980s, the DUP acceded to Unionist unity overtures and even electoral pacts, but as we have seen these relationships were often fraught with tension. Instead, Paisley forged links with the outcasts of Unionism: namely his own church and the Independent Orange Order.

The hostile attitude of Paisley's Free Presbyterian Church towards the Order and the mainstream churches was reciprocated in 1951 by the Order's decision to close its halls to Free Presbyterians and to bar Free Presbyterian clergymen from serving as Orange chaplains. Yet there were those within the Order—often DUP-inclined—who sought to heal the wounds. In December 1975, Robert Overend from Londonderry County Lodge raised the issue of a Free Presbyterian minister who was rejected as a chaplain owing to the rules, but Martin Smyth would not acquiesce on this point. The forging of a united political party was floated during the tense days of 1975, but as Central Committee soon realized, 'Dr Paisley's party would not forgo their independent action or identity' and therefore a retrenchment into the 'old UUP' was favoured.[100]

A year later, John Brown from Antrim and William Douglas suggested talks with the IOO, though little came of this.[101] The matter of Free Presbyterian clergy becoming chaplains also reared its head again, in 1977. At the instigation of Thomas Passmore and George Watson of Belfast, a motion was proposed to amend Orange laws to allow members of any denomination (including Free Presbyterians) to become clergymen. Belfast's lodges contained a small number of Free Presbyterian members, which may have accounted for this motion (some 2.5 per cent of Belfast initiates in 1971, but under 0.5 per cent of 1965 initiates and just 1.7 per cent in 1986).[102] Of interest is that during discussions it became apparent that a number of chaplains in the Order in fact were Free Presbyterian clergymen, but this does not appear to have led to any moves to evict them.[103]

The motion to formally allow Free Presbyterian chaplains into the Order brought sustained opposition from many chaplains at Grand Lodge. The Rev. Tom Taylor asked why the matter had been raised again since it had already been dealt with a year earlier. The Rev. Lockhart warned that he would have to reconsider his position in the Order if Free Presbyterians were allowed to become chaplains. This stance was justified by what was claimed to be the Free Presbyterian Church's antagonism to other churches. One member of Grand Lodge, Esmond Harvey, stood up to defend his Free Presbyterian Church, saying that it was the only church in Northern Ireland 'which cared for the saving of souls'. At this remark, Smyth pointed to a mission in his church in which eight young people had pledged themselves to Christ. Smyth also related a story of how, at an IOO rally, the Moderator of the Free Presbyterian Church had stated that you could not be a Christian and a member of the Orange Order. This led the Free Presbyterian apologist to withdraw his remarks. One opponent of the Free Presbyterians, the Rev. McDonald, asked the case-closing question of whether the Free Presbyterians would 'join in prayers for the Province and other matters with Chaplains from other Protestant denominations', answering that from his own experience, 'they would not'. On a ballot, the motion to allow Free Presbyterian clergy to be chaplains was defeated 'by a substantial majority' of 65–35.[104]

Sections of the membership frequently pushed the Orange leadership to seek political unity. Orange cooperation with their arch-enemy Paisley was not easy, though, and relations continued to be sporadic and fraught with tension. Paisley was involved in organizing a number of mass rallies protesting the poor security situation in November and December 1981. He did so under the banner of the 'Third Force', which he claimed was an umbrella group for Unionist unity.[105] The UUP had sent William Douglas to attend Third Force meetings, and Douglas urged Orangemen to send a representative. At this, Lord Brookeborough pleaded for caution, saying that 'we are losing friends' over the formation of the Third Force movement and 'should not be contaminated by the DUP'. Others disagreed. George Watson referred to a recent unity resolution passed by Grand Lodge. Another delegate named Kennedy claimed that in South Armagh, the DUP and UUP were working together. In the end, the vote hung on a knife-edge, with 31 against, 30 in favour, and 4 abstentions.[106] In the past—with the exception of the UUUC period from 1974 to 1976—Paisley had found excuses not to attend Orange unity initiatives. The Orange Order had usually been more accommodating except where it sensed that Paisley was in the driver's seat. This was true of the UUAC strike of 1977 and was true with the Third Force rallies of 1981, hence Orange non-participation.

Such reticence was less evident among some DUP-inclined members from Antrim. One individual named John Henry called an 'Orange meeting' which, in the words of the county leaders, 'went overboard' in its search for unity.[107] Resolutions calling for admittance of the Free Presbyterians continued to flow in sporadically. In 1983, a lodge in Down put forth a resolution to this effect, even as the IOO was again banned from taking part in any Orange parade.[108] At the next Grand Lodge sessions, County Antrim reported improved relations with the IOO and spoke of cooperation 'over the past twenty years'.[109] The Rev. John Lockington called for discussions, and Smyth cautioned that the Order stood to lose members and influence to the IOO. In 1989, Grand Lodge was even bold enough to openly endorse the UUP candidate Jim Nicholson against his DUP opponent.[110]

There matters rested until 1992, when the Clifton Street Orange District invited a Free Presbyterian minister, the Rev. Ronald Johnston, to conduct a pre-Twelfth Orange service. Only pressure from the Free Presbyterians forced Johnston to decline.[111] A year later, Tom Haire of Belfast opened an old debate by proposing that Free Presbyterian clergy be admitted as chaplains. The motion was opposed by the Rev. Warren Porter and the Rev. Brian Kennaway, whose amendment (to exclude the Free Presbyterians) won easily by 54-19, and crushed its opponents by 54-3 on a second reading.[112] All told, except in Antrim, there was no evidence of growing DUP ties within the

Order. This was to change rapidly after the SOD's campaign and Trimble's signing of the GFA.

In late 1998, James Heyburn, a DUP-supporting, Free Presbyterian Orangeman from Belfast, proposed to rescind the Grand Lodge motion of 1951 which excluded clergy from 'unrecognized' denominations like the Free Presbyterians from becoming chaplains. This was seconded by Tom Haire. Most who spoke to the amendment were clergy calling for an inclusive spirit of brotherhood, though the Rev. J. Noble opposed the resolution because Free Presbyterians would not invite Presbyterian ministers to preach in their churches. Finally, David McNarry proposed an amendment which effectively endorsed the rule change but delayed implementation until a report was tabled. This motion won handily by 56–38 with 1 abstention, demonstrating a major shift in opinion over the space of just five years. The vote tapped an epochal shift in attitudes, but also reminded Heyburn that the old division between 'rebel' and 'traditionalist' remained.[113] A year later, the committee tabled its report accepting Free Presbyterians and urging a welcoming spirit to Protestant ministers of all denominations. The only obligation for new chaplains was to 'discourage controversy among Orangemen on any point of difference among or within the denominations'.[114]

Another unprecedented step took place the same year when anti-Agreement politicians dominated almost all Orange Twelfth platforms. Not all were UUP men. Nigel Dodds, a DUP MLA and recently initiated Orangeman, addressed the resolution on 'State'. On the same platform, the Free Presbyterian minister Ronald Johnston was the first of his sect to speak at this venue, addressing both the religious service and the standard resolution on 'Faith'.[115] We have seen how several prominent Orangemen like the new Grand Secretary, Denis Watson, moved to the DUP between 2001 and 2003. During this period, Grand Master Robert Saulters also left the UUP, making it clear at Grand Lodge in 2002 that he was 'not now a member of any political party'.[116] The DUP sensed a thaw in its fifty-year cold war with the Order, and the Order also sensed the rising power and ideological compatibility of the DUP. Now, when the Order had a problem, it no longer rushed to see the UUP.

For instance, a long-standing issue for the Order was the taxable status of Orange halls, which were charged higher rates than strictly 'community' halls. The campaign to reduce rates on Orange halls involved a meeting with *both* DUP and UUP representatives.[117] At the joint meeting, the DUP appeared the more cooperative and effective party. Saulters and George Patton met Paisley, and described the 'meeting [as] . . . very positive'. 'Dr. Paisley advised that he would immediately, in his capacity as an M.E.P. for Northern Ireland, demand that the Minister responsible together with the appropriate officials receive a Deputation from the Institution,' they related. On the other hand, the UUP's David McNarry had to apologize that since Trimble had launched a review of rates as First Minister, it was a conflict of interest for him to meet the

Order, and so McNarry would have to serve as Trimble's representative.[118] Over the next two years, the DUP played a leading role in helping the Order wring concessions from the government on rates and pressed insurers to offer cheaper hall insurance.[119] It appears that a relatively weak UUP, whose concerns had drifted away from those of the Order, was increasingly an irrelevant actor for Grand Lodge.

Rifts between 'traditional' and 'rebel' Unionism were being healed in other areas as well. The 1,000-member IOO, whose lodges had been expelled in 1903 and whose members had been prevented from walking in Orange parades in the past, began to be accepted by the Order. In December 2003, Ballymoney District LOL 16 in Antrim was given permission to develop a 'closer and better' relationship with the IOO. Grand Lodge was very much on board, and it was agreed that in the future, IOO lodges could apply to take part in Orange parades. Concerns were expressed about the compatibility of IOO and Orange doctrine and regalia, as well as the issue of expelled or suspended Orangemen walking with IOO lodges, but this was not deemed an impediment. In the end, a cordial mood prevailed and members of Grand Lodge agreed to meet their counterparts in the IOO to discuss links.[120]

Increasingly, the Order began to see itself as a bridge between the UUP and DUP, with a definite predisposition towards the policies of the latter. One member of the current EC enthused about a new, 'progressive' post-Paisley DUP.[121] Grand Lodge was a changed place, and for the first time lacked the instinctive ties to the old party. In March 2004, it passed a motion of no confidence in David Trimble by a wide margin, citing 'concession after concession . . . to republicanism, including the disbandment of the RUC, prisoner releases and so on'.[122] A year later, the Order finally decided the time was right to break the link. Symbolically it was Edward Stevenson, a UUP man and county master of Tyrone, the most pro-Agreement county, who tabled the resolution calling for the 'severing of all links' between the Grand Lodge of Ireland and the UUC.

John McCrea proposed an amendment that merely sought to avoid 'any formal association' in the future with any political party. The Rev. Culbertson seconded McCrea's proposal; he reminisced that 'it had been a glorious partnership in its time' and recalled the campaign against the Home Rule bill at the time of formation of the UUC in 1905. 'It was essential that any decision that day did not signal a retreat from politics.' So bitter was anti-UUP feeling by this time that McCrea and Culbertson's amendment fell by 33–68 with 8 abstentions while Stevenson's original resolution to 'sever' the ties was backed by 82–16 with 11 abstentions. As the report read, 'The vote brought to an end the historic link which had been formed a century before, when, in March 1905, the Ulster Unionist Council was formed by the Institution, constituency groups, and other bodies.'[123]

We must be careful not to see this as a DUP putsch within the Order. As events in 2004–5 showed, the DUP MLA Denis Watson was voted out as Grand Secretary in favour of Drew Nelson, a UUP activist. Meanwhile, Saulters supported David Burnside (UUP) in one constituency against a DUP Orangeman, and elsewhere supported a DUP candidate against a UUP Orangeman.[124] These photo opportunities tended to lead to condemnation from county Orangemen opposed to particular candidates. In County Down, the county master Eddie Keown, a pro-Agreement UUP MLA, was criticized for supporting Dermot Nesbitt (a non-Orange UUP candidate) against a DUP Orangeman. In Fermanagh, Grand Lodge formally expressed its disapproval of Saulters's appearance with Arlene Foster of the DUP, who was contesting the seat against the Orangeman Tom Elliott.[125] Meanwhile, leading anti-GFA members of the UUP like Willie Ross and Martin Smyth remained among the most identifiably 'Orange' of politicians.

The activity of 1998–2005 had seen a tectonic shift towards a closing of the great rifts which had torn apart Unionism for a century. The rebel tradition of Antrim and working-class Belfast, once a minority voice, has infused Unionists throughout the province. The rebel institutions—the DUP, Free Presbyterian Church, and IOO—are no longer shunned and are becoming part of the mainstream. Now, it is traditionalists who are on the back foot, especially in urban areas and among younger Protestants. The traditionalists' party, the UUP, has been smashed in recent elections, and the main traditional association, the Orange Order, is in decline and losing influence to independent marching bands and a culture of 'hip' paramilitarism. The Order increasingly feels pressure to adapt. Kennaway contends that the Order has begun to downgrade the influence of chaplains by limiting their representation at Grand Lodge and diluting the moral code of 'respectable' Orangeism.[126] Even the paramilitaries, as we shall see, are becoming a more prominent feature of urban Orange life than ever before. All told, it amounts to a social and political earthquake of defiant modernization. Unionism's rebel alter ego has moved into the driver's seat and the traditionalism of a century is shrinking back into the shadows.

9

The War against the Parades Commission

Parading has always been the top priority for the Orange Institution, and its significance for the Order cannot be reduced to the wider Unionist desire to assert communal dominance. Power over space plays a role, as Jarman and Bryan point out, but marching also has a meaning apart from the political and constitutional contest between Unionists and Nationalists. We see this in politically quiescent places like Rossnowlagh (Eire), Southport (England), and Orono (Ontario, Canada) or in the numerous parades in Northern Ireland that take place in heavily Protestant locales. Parading is about power, but we need not swallow the entire Loyalist story to see that it is also about culture, 'show', and conviviality. Consider the fact that a third of Orangemen never attend a meeting and only ever turn up on the Twelfth, while for many of the other two-thirds, the Twelfth is the pinnacle of their engagement.[1] Take the parade away, and you take away their 'day in the sun', the main reason for joining. This explains the ferocious Orange reaction to parade bans, particularly bans on main parades taking place around the Twelfth of July.

In the run-up to Drumcree 1998, the Order's new Parades Strategy Committee and its new full-time Executive Officer George Patton developed a series of tactics designed to win the propaganda war which they acknowledged they had been losing. The previous parades strategy was simply based on resisting any voluntary re-routing of parades, and Grand Lodge knew this was now insufficient. The new strategy would encompass communications, public relations, and protests. In the period before the 1998 Twelfth, the Parades Strategy Committee met fifteen times, twelve of them in July. The main topic discussed was the Lower Ormeau and Portadown and in particular the publicity campaign. The focus was to be on (1) 'Civil Rights . . . being denied to Orangemen'; (2) proving that '"contentious" routes were shared arterial routes'; and (3) fighting for 'parity for Orange culture'. The Order wanted to portray the residents' groups as self-segregationists, hence the slogans 'Accommodation not Segregation' and 'End Apartheid in Ulster' which graced Orange posters.[2]

Ill. 13 Silver Band, Rossnowlagh Parade, Donegal, Republic of Ireland —The artistry of silver bands in this depoliticised setting demonstrates that Orange marches are about culture as well as power.

Protestant vigils were organized and a rota created whereby all district lodges could visit Drumcree to mount non-violent protests.

Public relations played a much bigger role in 1998 than ever before. Though public relations and media training had been mooted sporadically in the past, there was a marked increase in the attention paid to public image after 1997. Among the innovations agreed following Drumcree 1997 were: (1) a wallet-size 'cheque card' printed with core Orange values and vision to be carried by all Orangemen for easy reference; (2) a full-time public relations officer at the House of Orange; (3) the introduction of county public relations and press officers backed by a committee in each county; (4) the 'need for discipline on parade and [when] dispersing'; (5) lodge masters guarding against bad image in the press; and (6) the strengthening of band contracts to ensure better discipline. As usual, action on these points was not as strong as the intent, but the Parades Strategy Committee did claim some success in 1998 saying that aspects of the strategy 'worked well'. The Order had 40,000 leaflets produced for the public, and an advertisement was taken out in *Sunday Life*. Grand Lodge attempted to coordinate its media efforts and impose some discipline on those speaking for the Order so as to be 'on message'. David McNarry stressed that the Order's 'charm offensive' and openness to the media allowed it to hold its own in the international publicity game until violence broke out on 8 July.[3]

The fiasco of Drumcree IV in 1998 led to an important new round of soul-searching within the organization which brought together ideas about parades strategy and public and media relations. The new thinking was also urgently required because many senior Orangemen recognized that they lacked an 'exit strategy' on Drumcree, caught between their demand to parade and their refusal to meet residents and the PC. In the aftermath, Smyth, whose voice as past Grand Master carried great authority, expressed 'grave concern at the spectacle of Brother contending against Brother in public'. Decrying 'an intolerant spirit', he warned that 'a sense of anarchy had crept into the Order over recent years . . . There could be no excuse for attacks on the Royal Ulster Constabulary who were simply doing their duty.' The Rev. Warren Porter, from a liberal angle, spoke of the need to 'strike a note of penitence . . . we cannot do a whitewash job or bury our head in the sand'. He spoke of how the Order had vowed that events would not evolve as in 1996 yet this had happened again. 'We must take control,' Porter urged, and he was backed by the Rev. Denis Bannerman, who worried openly about the Order's image abroad. There were many at Grand Lodge who resented this sermon from these clerical Orangemen, however, and Porter's resolution referring to Grand Lodge being in a 'spirit of deep penitence before Almighty God' and calling for 'every effort to [be made to] uphold the Christian principles of our order' failed to be adopted by a 57–37 vote, with 17 abstentions. For many, 'penitence' came too close to an admission of guilt, which they felt was unfair under the circumstances.[4]

Even so, the sense of despair and disappointment remained. In its post-Drumcree reassessment, the Order—in consultation with Portadown District—developed two discussion papers which were circulated to all counties and districts. Acknowledging that the 'intensive' strategy of 5–13 July could not be sustained year-round, the paper sought instead to 'regain' public sympathy for Portadown's right to march at Drumcree by lower-key, year-round actions. Non-violence and adherence to the law formed the central tenets of the strategy. Confrontation with the security forces was to be avoided, and county and district lodges were to 'take control of all legitimate protests'. A petition was to be circulated and sent to 10 Downing Street, and protest actions based on 'traffic slowing, peaceful vigil, occupation and/or picketing of buildings' would be organized. Local protests were also proposed, but 'effective marshalling must be a priority to keep troublemakers away. Clear guidelines must be issued to those who wish to take part. Alcohol should be banned from the vicinity.'

Besides peaceful protest, the strategy sought to reach out to the media by being 'people friendly'. A series of events was organized around President Bill Clinton's visit on 4 September, including presenting him with a gift, holding a parade, emphasizing the Ulster-Scots connection to the USA and demonstrating aspects of Orange culture. The Order was to solicit MPs, MLAs, and local councillors and produce a regular press update on the Drumcree protest. Ironically, this was a major civil rights protest, with outrage to be replaced by a softer approach. A quiet but continual presence was to be arranged for Drumcree, and the Order hoped to be able to 'regain the neutrality if not the support of many church figures' by meeting church leaders and encouraging better church attendance among the membership. 'Protests must be properly organised and controlled or else we will face the same difficulties which occurred in Phase 1 [July 1998],' warned the paper's authors. 'The Institution must not allow a situation to arise where it is again required to go into crisis management.'

For the civil rights campaign, the Order resolved to work on its image. Possibly taking a leaf from the notebook of Ruth Dudley Edwards, the authors declared that 'publicity and PR will be vital to Phase 2. We must begin to repair relations and regain any good will and support which was lost. Members should be discouraged from being hostile towards the press.' Finally, they stressed a unified message and clear channels of communication flowing through appointed spokespersons.

In the second paper, the authors spoke of the broader parades strategy beyond Drumcree. The central planks of the Order's approach to the parades problem revolved around a boycott of both the PC and residents' groups, since the former discriminated against the Order and the latter were connected to Sinn Fein/IRA, 'who have not ended their terrorist campaign'. That said, the paper impressed upon its readers the

need to take advantage of the opportunities our strategy allows . . . to engage with all others, even those not sympathetic to our cause. As an Institution we should become proactive in making contacts with as many groups in civic society with whom it would be beneficial to talk . . . parties, all religious leaders, businessmen, pressure groups . . . our cause is just. It must be stressed however, we will not negotiate on the issue of parades, as no one should be required to barter or grovel for their civil rights.

The angle of discussions with outsiders was to proceed from a very modern, secular, 'equal rights' framework shaped by the multiculturalist ethos of the times which had suffused the Good Friday Agreement (GFA). Some of the issues to be foregrounded included: (1) discrimination against Orangemen 'by those in business and power', not least with regard to employment and promotion—especially in the RUC; (2) freeing Orange Halls from rates, with monies to be put into cultural or charitable activities; (3) a demand to be treated equally when applying for cultural funding from Northern Irish, UK, or European sources; and (4) parity of 'recognition' between Orange and Nationalist culture in official publications. This multiculturalist language could have been lifted from Will Kymlicka's political theory, and the Order clearly understood the need to 'broaden the issue of parades into an equality debate, which can only assist us'. The authors, perhaps anticipating internal criticism from SOD hardliners who oppose anything evangelical as 'ecumenical' or a concession, added that 'nothing in our regulations . . . prevents such activity'.

In the final part of the paper, the Committee urged its members to take an active part in their local communities and boards. In addition, the idea of a civic forum was seen as a way of bypassing the PC. 'The Order should begin lobbying for a place on the new civic forum,' the authors began, and they spoke of 'local civic forums or similar bodies being used as a possible conduit to resolve the parading issue'. The committee wanted a forum with a broad remit so as not to single out the largely Unionist activity of parading. Forums would be for deliberation rather than enforcement, and would help achieve 'mutual understanding'. These would include Nationalists (and, though the report doesn't mention it, Republicans), and where there was objection to speaking directly to others, remarks 'can be directed at the chair. The model being the new assembly.' Forums would be constituted in all areas rather than merely in parade hot spots, and the Order would attempt to play its part in civil society. 'Resistance to our involvement will expose the bigotry and sectarianism . . . which has been practiced against this Institution for years.'

The document proposed several actions to bring this to life, including a new subcommittee to be formed from Orangemen knowledgeable in community politics and civic involvement, to suggest how the Order could become involved in local bodies. Second, an attempt would be made to train Orangemen with the potential to represent the Order on these bodies. Finally, direct talks were to begin with relevant external groups, organizations, parties, and individuals. Much of this agenda was shaped by the subclauses of the GFA, with their nebulous provisions for developing and funding civil society initiatives. At the same time, developments within Orangeism, best expressed by the Education Committee, played a role. Though the Education Committee was in the process of being sidelined, its evangelical spirit continued to influence Orange thinking at the highest levels.[5]

The response to the document was generally positive, but varied among counties and districts. Fermanagh's traditional Orangeism was evident in its response. It had already submitted a strongly worded resolution stressing the need to respect the law, and its reply to Grand Lodge was critical.[6] While Fermanagh supported the rights of Portadown District to walk the Garvaghy Road, it did 'not agree with the [confrontational] methods being used to achieve this' and added that 'now is not the right time to insist on exercising these rights. An attempt should be made to regain the "moral high ground" following the damage that has been done . . . through adverse Press.' Fermanagh wanted a return to religious principles and was worried that many in the wider Unionist community who ordinarily supported Orangeism were becoming alienated by the events at Drumcree. It also claimed that a number of its members felt Grand Lodge to have 'lost control of the situation' and that control needed to be re-established and 'law breakers. . . dealt with'. Finally Fermanagh did not support any of the proposals for protests outlined in the Parades Strategy documents. All of Fermanagh's sentiments were passed by an overwhelming majority, sending a very strong signal from this traditionalist border county in favour of moderation.[7]

It was much the same story in County Tyrone, another close-knit border county. Although it did not go as far as County Cavan, which called for the 'protest at Drumcree [to] cease' because of the 'enormous damage' inflicted on the Order's reputation, many in Tyrone were alienated by the images beamed to them on television.[8] While *most* districts backed Portadown's right to march the Garvaghy Road, some also felt that the events of 1998 'brought the order into disrepect'. Most districts were willing to send members on a rota basis for a quiet protest at Drumcree 'provided Portadown District could promise that there would be no paramilitary involvement and all gatherings were strictly marshalled'. The submission was also critical of Portadown District, decrying the 'lack of any positive strategy. . . as to how they intended getting down the Garvaghy Road. In reality it was their problem and they should be making more positive and definitive steps to solve it in a peaceful and dignified way.' Tyrone also contested the point that a peaceful strategy had worked in 1998 since scenes of confrontation were broadcast on 9 July.[9] Not surprisingly, some in Tyrone reported that when they went to Portadown in 1998 in support of Drumcree, they were told they were not wanted or required.[10]

Annahoe District Lodge 6 in Tyrone, on a 12–5 vote, submitted a resolution that 'some elements of the [Drumcree] protest have been divisive and not in the best interests of our illustrious institution. We therefore recommend that the Drumcree protest be suspended'.[11] Castlecaulfield District Lodge 4 in the same county emphasized that the '"hanger on" element' needed to be better controlled and kept away. Moreover, 'an effective way must be found to deal with [SOD] dissidents within our Order. The brethren present were disgusted with the outrageous scenes which took place at the platform in Pomeroy.'[12] Strabane District 14 in north-west Tyrone worried about the dangers of 'exposing ourselves to another humiliation'.[13] Stewartstown District Lodge 2, in the eastern part of Tyrone on the Lough Neagh shore, worried that 'because of our minority situation', any local protest would merely give Nationalists 'another opportunity to add another town to the list of contentious parades'.

That said, Stewartstown, and the county as a whole, generally gave a thumbs up to the cultural funding and public relations strategy espoused by the committee. Stewartstown wrote that, as in many districts, the local town was predominantly Roman Catholic, and hence the membership was drawn from the hinterlands. It felt it had to 'encourage some of our young people back into the towns' and that some of the recent cultural festivals in the town helped to promote a positive version of Protestant culture. Its handwritten but eloquent submission concluded by reminding Grand Lodge that in 'rural areas in particular the Protestant community look[s] to the Institution for leadership' and thus the district backed the call for local civil society involvement.

In concrete terms, the response from Tyrone was somewhat piecemeal and apathetic. Those who bothered to reply to Grand Lodge's Parades Strategy gave hesitant support to some of the milder protest actions like a petition, but none backed more active local protests, traffic slowing, and demonstrations. Many of the comments were fatalistic: some regarded petitions as a 'futile exercise' while most felt that local demonstrations had been tried before without success.

Many of the [Tyrone] towns and villages now had Protestant minorities and it was felt that we would only be adding to our own local future problems if we were to protest in many of the Districts . . . the recent atrocity in Omagh [bombing of centre] has caused so much grief within all sections of the community that any immediate action over these next weeks and months would be seen as very insensitive.

The Omagh bombing also shaped Tyrone's response to President Clinton: Alan Rainey, as vice-chairman of Omagh District Council, replied that he would have to be involved in Clinton's visit to Omagh and 'in such a case it would be very difficult to snub him'.[14] Evidence from Orangemen in Fermanagh, Tyrone, and the Republic shows that border Unionism seems to lead to a more conciliatory approach vis-à-vis Nationalists. Likewise, Londonderry City Lodge, reflecting on its minority status, spoke of its hopes to have a Twelfth in the city next year, hence the need for a 'softly softly' approach to any protests.[15]

County Down, by contrast, on a resolution put forth by its Grand Treasurer and David McNarry, gave strong support to the Grand Lodge proposals. However, there was considerable opposition from quiescent districts who did not support the call for protests, and the resolution only squeaked through by 27–21 with 9 abstentions.[16] County Antrim's response was markedly less critical of Grand Lodge, and generally approved all proposals. It also urged Orange clergymen to exert their influence on their colleagues to support Harold Gracey at Drumcree and desist from criticizing the Order. Despite its tough stance, Antrim was pragmatic and felt that 'because of our stand not to get involved with the Parades Commission etc. we had lost ground . . . it was now time to carefully study the proposals for a Civic Forum'. Although some districts (likely for hardline reasons) criticized some of the proposals, '[most who] criticise don't have much of an alternative'.[17]

Belfast gave a strong endorsement to the committee's strategy paper, albeit with caveats. It did not support active local demonstrations as it was 'fearful of [these] . . . leading to trouble on the streets once again'. Belfast backed protests against the PC but wanted nothing to do with President Clinton, 'a discredited individual' (owing to the Lewinsky scandal). Belfast also revealed that it was split over whether to get involved in 'direct contact' with the PC. It acknowledged that 'politically things are moving and perhaps this aspect will have to be reviewed later on, either 1998 or 1999'. Belfast further agreed that the Order needed to become more 'outward looking' and involved in community institutions.[18] Whitewell Temperance LOL 533 spoke for a significant section of the county when it challenged Grand Lodge that

maybe it is time to have some communication with the 'Republican' Parades Commission. This may seem a U-turn but how can we defend our corner if we do not put it across to this group. Maybe we should also look at setting up a line of communication with residence [sic] groups. We are loosing [sic] the battle could this be a way of reversing the slide.'[19]

County Londonderry expressed some similar sentiments: 'a few members thought that it might be possible to negotiate in a limited way with the Parades Commission'. This county also called for more financial contributions to local churches and church missions in order to mend fences with the clergy, and criticized traffic slowing as something which would hinder the Orange cause.[20] Armagh endorsed the strategy *tout court*, with the proviso that meeting Clinton might not be wise since 'it would take only a few Brethren to shout abuse at him for the world's media to portray the Institution in an even worse light than it already does'.[21] Taken as a whole, the response from the grassroots shows exasperation with the Drumcree situation and a desire for a return to respectability. The Order was firmly against confrontation and abhorred any idea of forcing its way down the Garvaghy Road. A new strategy needed to be found, and most gave direct or tacit agreement to the new approach based on improved public relations and engagement in civil society. There was provision in the GFA for a civic forum, and the Order resolved to play a key role in its agenda. This was backed by all counties, though some expressed hesitation or caution as they were unsure of the new forum's composition or agenda.[22]

Replies from the counties to the Order's Parades Strategy document suggest that some were tentatively willing to explore negotiations with the PC and Nationalist residents' groups. This was taken up by a special meeting of Central Committee, where Eddie Keown (Grand Master of County Down and a pro-Agreement UUC delegate representing the South Down constituency association) asked those present to consider meeting the PC. 'We cannot win by force of numbers,' added Martin Smyth, adding that therefore the Grand Lodge 'must take them to court'. On a vote, the committee decided by 17–7 to ask Grand Lodge to approve a delegation to meet the PC, a daring move guaranteed to upset hardliners. Colin Shilliday urged those present to 'bring those with you who are broadly sympathetic [to meeting the PC]', but when William McKeown (another pro-Agreement UUP branch delegate) put a resolution to Grand Lodge to meet the PC, many of the proponents—perhaps sensing the mood of the majority at Grand Lodge—fell silent. David McNarry then scuttled the ship by proposing an amendment rejecting McKeown's initiative, which was passed by 52–4 with just 4 abstentions.[23]

The continued boycott of the PC reinforced the Order's policy of locking horns with the British government and its approach to the Peace Process. In an earlier report to members, the Order described the new public processions bill as 'racist in that it only applies to one part of the United Kingdom'. The PC was seen as 'a new quango which will promote disorder'. The bill was seemingly aimed, argued the Orangemen, 'at curtailing our parades' and attacking '[our] faith and culture. Government have either misunderstood or taken the easy option of dealing with the law abiding population to placate republicans.' The non-recognition of 'traditional' parades (part of the government's desire to promote equality) was viewed as disregarding the importance of parading for Protestant culture. At a meeting with the Secretary of State for Northern Ireland, Mo Mowlam, and the Minister of State at the Northern Ireland Office, Adam Ingram, the Order complained of Mowlam's attitude and her limited attendance of only ten minutes.[24]

The quiet following the marching season was broken in September when a Loyalist mob in Portadown claimed the life of Constable Frankie O'Reilly in Portadown. William Bingham and Denis Watson made a point of attending the Catholic-born O'Reilly's funeral but sensed anger from other mourners, who blamed the Order for his death.[25] The Orange glasnost continued into the autumn as Grand Lodge officers met with a succession of officials. At a meeting with the American Consul General, the Order pressed her as to why they were not included in the list of those to be met by the President. Otherwise, the meeting was cordial, with the Orangemen presenting their case for their parading culture and the Consul General appearing keen to accommodate the Orangemen. George Patton noted that the meeting helped to present the Order's credentials and had 'opened doors' for a future presentation of its case.[26] Yet there was a limit to how far such changes could go. A proposal emanating from the Parades Strategy Committee to participate in a conference with speakers from the Nationalist–Republican community and residents' groups got the thumbs down by a 14–6 margin at Central Committee.[27]

In the autumn, the Order published a document marked 'secret—eyes only' entitled the 'Drumcree Winter Initiative'. The document was a blueprint for achieving success at Drumcree and appears to have been the brain-child of the Parades Strategy Committee, with a key role played by David McNarry. It contained a step-by-step set of proposals which effectively sought to win concessions on the Drumcree issue by offering to meet with church leaders (including the Catholic archbishop Sean Brady), suspend Drumcree protests, engage in indirect dialogue with Nationalist residents, and participate in civic bodies dedicated to reconciliation. This was arguably the most advanced piece of diplomatic strategy ever devised by the Institution and showed the emergence of a new political maturity. The document exhibited cautious movement from previous Orange positions in that the Order was willing to have Portadown District enter into an independent body to resolve the issue of Drumcree. The position paper further stated that 'the manner in which Garvaghy Road Residents Group are involved in this process. . . cannot be vetoed by the Institution, providing, there is equity in approach'.

In return, the Order wanted to parade the Garvaghy Road on 29 November and demanded a suspension of the PC until a review of the legislation was complete. In addition, Grand Lodge sought funding to help promote Orange traditions and culture, though it was simultaneously open to accommodating and understanding the 'traditions and culture of others'. Finally, the 'Winter Initiative' document stipulated that any agreement must not be used as a 'political bargaining chip' (i.e. a trade of Drumcree for Orange backing of the GFA before decommissioning) and that the Order would not engage in direct talks with either Sinn Fein/IRA (i.e. residents' groups) or the PC.[28] This was not revolutionary stuff, and Ryder and Kearney are correct to state that the document was 'stillborn' since the previous year's proximity talks had foundered on the residents' bottom line that a parade could not be a precondition.[29] This said, the Initiative did arise out of a genuine Orange desire to avoid violence and open itself up to dialogue.

The Winter Initiative began with a meeting with supportive local press figures, notably David Montgomery (Mirror Group) and Geoff Martin, editor of the *News Letter*. Neither was designated 'Bro', suggesting that they were not Orangemen as their predecessors were thirty years ago. Montgomery began by telling the assembled Orangemen that the Prime Minister realized he needed the Orange Order on board to ensure a peaceful society in Northern Ireland. The Orange Order, Republicans, and Prime Minister were the focus of these transactions, noted Montgomery. 'If the initiative works we will have the high moral ground enabling us to move forward, and we will see the transformation of the Institution into a modern, outward looking, constructive organisation,' he enthused. He commented that the Peace Process would be in danger if the Orange Order was not recognized or permitted to return home along its traditional route. McNarry also announced that Portadown District was on board and that if all went well with the visit to the Prime Minister, then Harold Gracey would call a halt to all protests.[30]

The willingness on Portadown's part to engage in dialogue as part of an Orange 'sub-peace process' indicated a genuinely new-found degree of flexibility, even if it was short of what was required. Meanwhile, the Winter Initiative continued to unfold. Montgomery's shuttle diplomacy helped to set up a meeting with the COI archbishop Robin Eames, who in turn contacted

Archbishop Brady.[31] While Montgomery and Martin were busy meeting Mowlam, McNarry contacted George Patton with the upbeat message 'I can see it all just coming together.' A more sober call the following day from Montgomery adopted a cloak-and-dagger tone:

things are pretty difficult at the level above. There has been contact on your issue with the other side. He [Trimble] had spoken to a contact last night. They are taking this very seriously. There is a meeting this morning but this will be very secret. There is an awareness that there must be a reciprocal gesture from them [Nationalists]. He [Trimble] is having Dinner with the Prime Minister on Thursday Night . . . and then on Saturday Evening at Chequers . . . he[Trimble] doesn't believe we (the Orange) can move until we see something from the other side. He [Trimble] stated that we . . . are offering something very valuable in this process. The republicans must reciprocate and they are receptive. Mr. Blair will get behind and act as referee.[32]

A week later, McNarry called George Patton and told him he had spoken to Montgomery, who had been with Blair on Saturday. Montgomery described Blair as 'up for the whole thing', keen on the Civic Forum, and impressed with Orange initiative. 'This is testing the other side,' McNarry glowed. Montgomery was of the opinion that 'this is the Prime Minister—we need to get our choreography right'. McNarry further related that George Quigley had set up the meeting with the Catholic and COI Archbishops.[33] Patton was positive if more cautious: he wanted to know what the 'other side' (i.e. Republicans) were told and whether the meeting with church leaders would 'allow us to remain within our policy regarding residents groups'.[34] This was important given the trouble which the SOD could cause and the potential in a highly populist organization for hardliners to accuse Grand Lodge of 'selling out' the Orange cause.

The twelve-point briefing paper for the meeting with church leaders, also marked 'secret—eyes only', put the accent on moderate Orangeism's track record: the leaders' support for Catholic worshippers at Harryville, the faith and family aspects of the Order, the Order's criticism of violence, its desire to work with the Assembly, and the fact that it included both pro- and anti-GFA members in its ranks. Orange good faith was demonstrated by its willingness to engage in dialogue with others, like the archbishops.[35] Quigley chaired the meeting, and Archbishop Eames began by preaching the need for dialogue, which could take place without any surrender of Orange principle. Eames added that he accepted the importance of the symbolism of the parade for the Order. On the other hand, Archbishop Brady, while willing to do what he could, put a strong Nationalist case to the Order which did not mince words. He said he shared the views of his [Nationalist] community and added that Portadown Catholics wanted to talk about a range of issues including poverty and their future in the town. For Brady, the PC had determined that 'never again will they [the Nationalist residents] be bullied into submission. They [the Nationalist residents] believe they have the support of the British and Irish governments, Europe and the Assembly.' Brady lambasted the Order's 'constant parades' as unhelpful and worried that some would use a parade to create mayhem. He stressed to his Orange audience that there must be dialogue without preconditions and that 'it is a real put down to say we won't talk to you'.

At this point, Quigley tried to conciliate by urging those present to try to put themselves in each other's shoes in order to get at some shared interest. Quigley remarked that the Unionists and Orangemen felt they were losing out and all communities felt threatened. He emphasized that there had to be something that everyone could live with even if it was not their preferred option. Eames then asked whether the Order had a new approach and any practical suggestions to put on the table. Denis Watson replied that the Order was willing to go into proximity talks with Nationalist residents. Quigley then optimistically sized up the situation as 'a jigsaw shaping up'. But Gracey, who had been holding back, chose this moment to let loose. Pouring cold water on Quigley's summary, he injected the dour note that he was listening to a lot of politics but didn't really trust politicians. He spoke of proximity talks as a 'pressure cooker' in which one couldn't leave the talks until one had signed up to something. Gracey recounted how his district was the first to be formed in the Order and said he had 'eventually' managed to persuade it in 1985–6 to accept re-routing away from the 'tunnel'. He then underscored his bottom line: 'Our traditional route must be maintained.' Gracey ended by declaring that he would not be happy in proximity talks but would allow McNarry to go in as his deputy.

The Portadown Orange officer David Burrows suggested that the socioeconomic concerns could be addressed by the Civic Forum. 'We [are] willing to participate,' Burrows told the clergymen, though 'the Forum could also be a hard sell to our people. Parade—then we can build bridges.' The Rev. Mervyn Gibson then sounded a harder note, reminding the clergymen that the Order received no thanks for the steps [towards non-violence] they had taken in 1998 and that 'no one should have to negotiate for parades'. Gibson called for a stop to the demonization of the Order, as this would 'give us a space'. Archbishop Eames agreed with Gibson's last point, but then asked his Orange audience whether there were any conditions under which they could get closer to meeting the residents. Brady seconded Eames, stating that the residents would be able to understand Gracey and his Orangemen's concerns (if the two met). Gracey remained unimpressed, though, angrily declaring that 'Portadown will not be participating in a civic forum or anything else until the parade [Drumcree] is completed'. Flummoxed by this, Eames asked Gracey, 'can Garvaghy Road [Nationalist residents] really understand if they don't hear it [from Gracey]?' In summary, Quigley said it was a useful and honest meeting and urged all sides to talk about solutions—even if in separate rooms.[36]

Little ground had shifted between Gracey and the residents, but it is clear that Grand Lodge and McNarry were genuinely trying to drag Gracey towards dialogue—even if the Order's starting position was a guaranteed parade and the suspension of the PC. The Winter Initiative continued to roll on three days later when members of Grand Lodge met Blair, his chief of staff Jonathan Powell, Bill Jeffries of the Northern Ireland Office (NIO), and Alistair Campbell to discuss matters relating to parading and Protestant culture. Gracey implored the Prime Minister to see things from Portadown District's perspective. He spoke of its tradition, its compromise over the Obins Street route in 1986, and the good behaviour of its members on parade. He stated that the Order 'did our best to control violence'. He then pointed out that his district had called off its street protests when asked to do so by David Trimble, but had received no reciprocation from the NIO or Trimble. 'People find there is no other choice but to sit there [Drumcree] until we have our civil rights restored,' he claimed. Gracey also spoke of the 'black propaganda' of the Quinn murders being associated with the Order and contended that the Orange marching routes were arterial roads rather than roads on a housing estate.

Denis Watson then took a more consensual role, stating the Order wanted to participate in a negotiation process and was willing to engage in civil society as well as proximity talks with local Nationalist residents. He asked the Prime Minister whether mechanisms were available to promote and fund Protestant culture. Robert Overend then presented the Order's printed submission against the PC, and Patton expressed the position that the Order's views were not being taken on board when major decisions were made, as with the North review of parades. Patton then stated the Orange position that the PC impinged on Orange 'civil liberties'. After digesting the initial presentation, Blair cautioned that 'there is no question of tying decommissioning into the Parade getting approval'. However, he said he wanted to reach a position where all parades could proceed. 'I want to see parades,' Blair continued, and said that he had 'never been under any illusion that [the] Parades Commission represents only the least best option'.

'My personal view is [that] the Orange Order is a respectable body that contributes to the life of society in Northern Ireland,' the Prime Minister said. He supported the need to 'educate people as to what the Orange Order is all about', spoke of the Order's long traditions and deeply held principles, and insisted that he would 'help by being positive'. John McCrea complained of the adverse publicity that the Order was getting, and Blair seemed to empathize. 'We have got to find a way of resolving Drumcree,' Blair said. 'I will play my part by saying what the Order is about. I am desperate to get Drumcree sorted out,' he added. At this, Gracey, who had adopted an uncompromising tone throughout, said that Drumcree was not the problem but rather the Garvaghy Road, and that he couldn't understand the lack of toleration displayed by the local residents. 'I want the road open for my children and grandchildren,' he demanded. 'If Portadown is beaten [the] Orange Order is beaten [and] Unionism is beaten.' Gracey, who described himself as 'not a violent person', vowed to 'attempt to keep violence down' but also stressed the depth of feeling among alienated young people in Portadown.

McNarry then adopted a tough line, asserting that the Order was 'not in the business of negotiation—we believe we have unfinished business on Garvaghy Road . . . For Harold Gracey to still be there at Christmas is inhumane'. He then told the Prime Minister that 'When we leave here we will be asked did we sell out? What did we get?' McNarry therefore appealed to Blair to use his good offices to ensure a breakthrough (via Sinn Fein to the residents' groups or directly through the PC). In conclusion, McCrea laid out the Order's principal demands, which included a parade down Garvaghy Road by the end of 1998 and a disbanding of the PC. He also asked the Prime Minister to inaugurate an initiative which would help promote Orange culture. The Prime Minister probably knew he could not accede to McCrea's parading demands, but seized the opportunity to move on the less explosive cultural promotion issue by saying he would study it very carefully.[37]

Attention next moved to the less contentious ground of the review into the future of the Orange Order offered by the Prime Minister. This was chaired by George Quigley and accepted by McNarry on behalf of the Order.[38] A letter to the Prime Minister spoke of the Orange sense of having been marginalized and welcomed a new body which might promote and protect 'all aspects of heritage, culture and tradition' with new funding.[39] The Prime Minister's reply was favourable, and he said he had charged his Secretary of State to speak with cultural organizations and that this work would be 'completed very soon'. The letter promised draft terms of reference for the new initiative by Christmas and concluded by encouraging the Order to consider the part it might play within the cultural-diversity facet of the millennium celebrations.[40] As the end of 1998 approached and it appeared that Portadown would not parade in 1998, a new letter from the new Grand Secretary Denis Watson called off the cultural initiative since 'I am sure you will appreciate that it would be impossible for this Institution to become fully involved whilst Portadown District still await the restoration of their right to walk their traditional route'. Nevertheless, Watson did not close off dialogue but ended by suggesting terms of reference for the new cultural initiative.[41]

Months went by with little willingness on the part of either Orangemen or Nationalist residents to compromise on their respective preconditions demanding or opposing the Drumcree parade. Both invested their hopes in the wider political choreography of the Peace Process. David Trimble was central because he had yet to give his final stamp of approval to Unionist involvement in the new Assembly. This gave him some leverage within the Peace Process which he hoped to be able to exploit for the benefit of the Order. Trimble wanted to resolve the Drumcree issue and, according to Dean

Godson, sincerely believed that most of the members of Portadown District (in his constituency) were decent people. His intermediary with the Order and No. 10, David Montgomery, felt that Trimble 'had an ace to play'. If he could get the Orangemen through, he could stretch the UUC far enough to launch the devolved institutions and go into a government with Sinn Fein. Trimble believed that he could get the Order to negotiate with Nationalist residents, and that this would show the world that the Portadown Orangemen were less intransigent than the residents. He also hoped it might discredit the PC, which he felt was a top-down relic of the Direct Rule years and should instead be accountable to the new Northen Ireland Assembly.

Trimble hoped that a programme of economic development in Portadown coupled with Sinn Fein pressure on Brendan McKenna, leader of the Garvaghy Road Residents Coalition, might be enough to win the day. His plan was to have Portadown District Lodge finally meet the residents and call off its regular protests. A local civic forum would be established to discuss parading issues in which both parties would take part. The forum would have its format facilitated by the First Minister and deputy Minister in the Assembly and would be signed by the parties and Blair. In exchange, the Drumcree parade would be permitted to proceed. Godson claims from private sources that Portadown District Lodge backed this proposal by a 70–5 margin.[42] However, it agreed only to act through Trimble, thereby preserving the Orange–Nationalist contact taboo.[43] At Grand Lodge, there was more resistance to Trimble's plan. One delegate, citing McNarry's alleged proposal to meet the residents, called this a 'backward step'. 'Portadown will not be speaking to Residents Groups,' added David Burrows. McNarry quickly denied that he supported the idea of directly meeting Nationalist residents, though such a step would certainly have made McNarry's Trimble–Orange high-wire act easier.[44] Around the same time, Grand Master Robert Saulters, already under fire from hardliners for meeting the Irish president Mary McAleese and the Taoiseach Bertie Ahern, was similarly forced by the Parades Strategy Committee to backtrack on his previously stated view that the Order would have to meet Nationalist residents.[45] There seems to have been little further debate on the matter.

Trimble braved the harsh winds of criticism from within the Unionist fold to meet Brendan McKenna in May. However, neither McKenna nor local residents were in a mood to compromise. McKenna knew that the PC would rule in June and felt no need to make a move. A British proposal (authored by Frank Blair) did gain his approval, but involved trading Portadown's right to march for a funding package for Orange culture and hall rates relief. When presented to local Orangemen, they saw red. 'It was exactly what the residents had been asking for,' recalls David Burrows. 'We were being asked to agree to have one more parade and then no more in return for money . . . It seemed like [Frank] Blair had completely ignored everything we said.' At a subsequent meeting with Tony Blair and Jonathan Powell, the Portadown District legal advisor, Richard Monteith, was so outraged by the terms of the deal that he threw the proposal in front of the Prime Minister and shouted at him and Powell. Blair then sternly raised his voice and told Monteith he would not be intimidated, whereupon the solicitor sat down.[46]

Frantic efforts by Blair to get the two sides to talk came to nought. The Prime Minister assured Orangemen that he couldn't see why a march could not take place and would try to find a way for this to occur. However, Sinn Fein pressure failed to materialize, there was no movement by residents, and the march was banned by the PC. As Godson notes, the PC had worked in the British and Irish governments' strategic interest. 'In the new dispensation, Orangemen could no longer set the pace of events . . . as in 1995, 1996 and 1997. With Trimble at their side on the barricades, outside of the framework of the institutions of state, the Orangemen could win.' With Trimble signed up to the GFA and absent from the barricades, the Orangemen lost their leverage. For Godson, this demonstrates a weakness in the Trimbleite philosophy that greater influence could be had within government than outside it. Critically, Trimble was not willing to abandon the Peace Process for the sake of Drumcree, 'and the Government knew it'. Despite the fact that a win at Drumcree would help Trimble take his seat in the executive with Sinn Fein, the British reckoned they could get Trimble on their side without conceding this point.[47]

March or no march, the COI primate Robin Eames was keen to avoid further scenes of violence outside Drumcree COI Church. Owing to the COI's decentralized structure, Eames had little control over the Rev. John Pickering, the Drumcree rector, and his local select vestry. Pickering thus refused a Church of Ireland petition not to allow Portadown Orangemen to participate in his morning service. Although he had received gifts and correspondence from the Order, there can be little doubt that his decision was motivated by the sympathies of his local congregation.[48] Though powerless to prevent the Orangemen from attending Drumcree Church, Eames called on the Order to honour three pledges before being allowed to congregate there in July. These involved the Order obeying the law and protesting away from church property.[49] Eames implored the Order to consider its moral responsibility to bring people onto the streets only if they could be controlled. He urged the Orangemen to tackle the PC in the courts rather than through protest. He also stressed his concern that 'the worship of Almighty God is sullied by violence' and wanted protests disassociated from the church. A legal advisor named Mr Plunkett suggested that the Order could use the Northern Ireland Assembly, Parliament, and the European Court of Justice to press its claims. A media protest (away from Drumcree) could be part of the strategy. In conclusion, Eames reiterated his belief that he did not believe a protest at Drumcree could be peaceful under the circumstances.[50]

Despite being banned from marching the Drumcree route by the PC, the Order generally stuck to Eames's three pledges and helped to defuse tension by not providing catering to the gathered throng. The marchers approached police lines, handed in a letter of protest, and then returned home. Most protesters dispersed and the event passed off much more peacefully than the RUC dared hope. Here we see that a concerted Orange effort to change things at Drumcree had a positive effect. Yet this good behaviour did not buy the Order any new concessions. In the week between Drumcree Sunday and the Twelfth, Grand Lodge officers and Harold Gracey met the Prime Minister and were disheartened to learn that there was no guarantee of a parade in Portadown that year. Accusing the Prime Minister of betraying his earlier promises, they stormed out of No. 10. Government officials claim that the Orangemen had confused Blair's *belief* that a march would take place with a *promise* that he could engineer this outcome.[51]

The Death of Drumcree?

No parades have taken place at Drumcree since 1997. After the devolved institutions were launched in November 1999, the Order definitively lost any bargaining power (via Trimble) that it may have had. The intensity of Drumcree protests remained high, though, and violence on the scale of 1996–9 took place at Drumcree in 2000, when the Loyalist paramiltary leader Johnny 'Mad Dog' Adair was the star of the show. But these events proved increasingly contentious and futile. For instance, Portadown District's frantic calls in July 2000 to continue street protests led the Orange politicians James Molyneaux and Jeffrey Donaldson to condemn the violence, though Grand Lodge failed to do so.[52] Grand Lodge's and Portadown's actions sparked division within the Order and outright condemnation from some quarters. One of several letters came from Omagh District in Tyrone, which reprimanded 'some Grand Lodge Officers [who] are completely out of touch with grass roots opinion and if the present disorder and lawlessness, in the name of Orangeism, is allowed to continue it will lead to ultimate destruction'. These sentiments were 'unanimously' endorsed by Tyrone County Lodge.[53] At Grand Lodge, concern about paramilitary involvement and the lack of discipline was widely expressed. Even some Antrim lodges assailed Portadown's actions.[54] In 2001, violence declined significantly in comparison with 2000, and since 2002, the protest has passed off peacefully. Increasingly, the Drumcree protest has become ritualized, with some fifty parade applications deluging the PC each year and regular quiet marches to a lightly manned police line.[55]

Gradually, the realization began to dawn that the only way to break the Drumcree logjam was through a court challenge against the PC at the European level. The basic outlines of the Order's court challenge had been in the works for several months. In May 1999, a set of principles was laid out authorizing Orange solicitors to prepare a brief on the matter.[56] In early 2000, the Orange solicitor Richard Monteith pleaded with Armagh County Lodge to meet the PC, claiming that such a meeting was vital to show that the Order had exhausted all avenues of action and could thereby mount a convincing legal case against the PC. Amazingly, the motion was adopted by Armagh and backed by Portadown District and its deputy master David Burrows. Lodges in Armagh, including Portadown District, voted by a 3–1 margin to alter their policy and enter into talks with the PC.[57] Armagh's initiative drew strength from the desire of districts affected by parade restrictions to change the policy of Grand Lodge. Thus at the March 2000 sessions of Grand Lodge, seven of fourteen affected districts favoured limited contact in order to make the Orange case, two favoured full contact (i.e. negotiation), and only four backed the current Grand Lodge policy of no contact. In terms of residents' groups, all but one district backed the current policy of no contact.[58]

Nonetheless, in order to become policy, the Armagh resolution to meet the PC had to be ratified at Grand Lodge by representatives from Protestant-majority areas (largely in Antrim and Down) where parades were uncontentious. Those in favour argued that the present boycott was not working and that Portadown, being in the 'front line' at Drumcree, should have its wish to meet the PC respected. Those against claimed that nothing had changed since Grand Lodge took a 'principled decision' not to speak to the 'anti-Orange' PC.[59] Despite the legendary Harold Gracey speaking in favour of the resolution, it went down to defeat by a 2–1 margin. Denis Watson declined to speak up for Armagh's bill, and privately opposed it. This upset Richard Monteith, who attacked Watson's stance the next time the two met, claiming that Watson had betrayed Armagh's brethren.[60] The next five years would be defined by the tension between districts who wanted to meet the PC and the majority in the Order who favoured a continued embargo.

A number of efforts were made by third parties to resolve the dispute. The South African mediator Brian Currin initially gained the trust of Order, but the deal he brokered with McKenna—offering a perpetual guarantee of non-interference in a Drumcree parade if a new route was taken—was rejected by the Order. Currin, to no avail, reiterated the message that European, British, and Northern Ireland human rights law could not override a decision based on a threat to public order. The Order also continued to rebuff the concerns of Monteith and another Orange-friendly lawyer, Austen Morgan, that failure to meet with the PC was counter-productive for any Orange legal challenge.[61] The British were becoming increasingly exasperated at Grand Lodge's refusal to engage. These frustrations burst forth at a meeting with the Secretary of State, Peter Mandelson.

Orange records describe Mandelson as being 'aggressive' towards George Patton and Watson over Drumcree, as Mandelson insisted that they meet residents or the PC or engage with Brian Currin. Watson reminded Mandelson that Portadown had taken steps to meet the PC, but Mandelson shot back:

'you are expected to do a fair bit more'. When Grand Treasurer Mervyn Bishop queried Mandelson about the double standard of not speaking to terrorists in Sierra Leone despite engaging with the terrorist IRA, Mandelson, according to the report, 'became very uncomfortable'.[62] Some months later, the Rev. Pickering of Drumcree Church also did his best to seek a solution. When Pickering asked Saulters why he wouldn't meet the PC, Saulters replied that the PC requires the Order to meet with residents, which they refused on principle to do. 'Why talk to the middle man [the PC]', observed Saulters, instead of going straight to Brendan McKenna? Pickering could do little but agree with his logic.[63]

The flurry of local contacts between the PC and local Orangemen in Portadown and other flashpoint areas distressed Grand Lodge but emboldened the PC. 'Did you only mean the Grand Lodge Officers do not talk to these people [the PC]?', Saulters asked Grand Lodge delegates. 'It would appear so, as I am getting an inferiority complex...Nearly every time you open a newspaper there are Brethren talking or debating with these people.'[64] Two secret documents later discovered by the PSNI during the 'Stormontgate' raid on the home of the Sinn Fein executive (and alleged British agent) Denis Donaldson showed the extent of Orange–PC contacts. These documents—excerpts of PC meeting minutes in June–July 2001—underscore that the PC was aware of serious divisions within the Order over whether to negotiate with it. This undoubtedly strengthened its resolve. In Bellaghy, Parades Commissioners reported that while the Order wouldn't negotiate, the 'Grand Master and [Grand] Secretary [are] happy to talk'. Bellaghy officers seem to have indicated that they would have been happy to engage with the PC were it not for Grand Lodge restrictions. In July, PC internal minutes revealed that the Order 'have been asking their leadership to enter talks' and that the Grand Lodge's refusal to countenance talks with the PC had led three Orangemen to resign. 'Now [is] the time to squeeze the Orange Order,' the minutes noted. On 3–5 July, the minutes again spoke of splits within the Order and the fact that Keady District (Armagh) and Derry City Orangemen were working to reduce tension rather than protesting against their inability to march.

PC strategy was affected by these Orange 'leaks'. For example, it appears that elements within the PC were wary of the Order's use of 'high positions' (through its UUP connections with the British) to get Nationalist residents to submit. It also worried about its Drumcree decision withstanding an Orange legal challenge.[65] Aware of divisions within the Order, the PC seems to have identified the leadership as the main stumbling block. Thus it tried to offer an olive branch to Grand Lodge. The new PC chairman Tony Holland positively glowed about a new mood within Orangeism: 'The great achievement...is that the Grand Lodge has entered into some form of engagement with the commission. That, I think, is a seismic shift and one that deserves to be recognised.'[66] Holland's remarks proved premature, and failed to recognize the difference between the willingness of affected interface districts to negotiate and the unaffected majority within the Order which resolutely opposed the PC—especially the latter's insistence that the Order negotiate with residents. Even affected districts were generally willing to meet the PC only to plead their case, and were not seeking engagement with residents along the lines of the Apprentice Boys or Royal Black Preceptory, who had both made deals with Derry residents which permitted them to march.[67] Central Committee recommended meeting Holland 'to challenge him', and Holland's letter was seriously discussed at Grand Lodge. Yet the moral stance against meeting the PC held. Within Grand Lodge it was felt that no one should meet the PC until after the proposed Quigley review of the PC.[68]

Though shunning the PC, Grand Lodge tried to act where it could. It strenuously tried to attain official representation on the new Civic Forum to plead its case. This sixty-member cross-community body emerged out of the GFA and was launched on 9 October 2000 by Seamus Mallon of the SDLP and David Trimble as a way of enhancing participatory democracy.[69] On 24 October, the DUP tabled a motion urging the First Minister's department to appoint a representative of Grand Lodge to the Civic Forum. This motion failed, with many UUP MLAs voting against it. In an early test of Orange influence in the new Stormont, nine letters were sent from Grand Lodge to Trimble and eight other UUP MLAs who were members of the Orange Order, claiming that these legislators had violated their Orange obligations. They were asked to account for their legislative behaviour on the issues of both the Civic Forum and Sunday betting (i.e. permitting them).[70]

Trimble coordinated the reply on behalf of the MLAs, which he said would obviate the need for MLAs to reply individually. He began by claiming that the Orange request was unprecedented. 'They [letters] seem to be directed specifically at Ulster Unionist members and some of the letters I have seen are couched in explicitly hostile language which is less than we expect from a sister organisation.' Trimble went on to introduce a partisan tone into the letter, arguing that

at no point during the debate to approve these arrangements, did the DUP, nor any other member (including the Grand Secretary [Denis Watson] . . . who sits as a [DUP] Member for Upper Bann) raise the issue of direct Orange representation . . . It is odd, therefore, that they raise the issue now, when nothing can be done about it. No doubt you will wish to take this issue up with those members!

Trimble's defensive dig at anti-Agreement Unionism shows how estranged he was from the Grand Lodge. Yet he also took care to point out that he had personally spoken to applicants for the culture category within the Forum who were both members of Grand Lodge. He stressed that Gordon Lucy, an Orangeman, had been appointed for this post. Also, Trimble wrote that he had decided that there had to be someone in the Civic Forum who could give an effective defence of the right to march. Consequently I appointed Brother Richard Monteith...I have first hand evidence as to his effectiveness in dealing with the legal and political representatives of the Garvaghy Road Residents' Coalition...he would be an effective counter to [Nationalist Donncha] MacNiallis...One of my other nominees is also an Orangeman.

While defending his Orange credentials, Trimble ended on a combative note, declaring that he did not accept that Orangemen were accountable to their lodge for their voting record and that Orange 'legislators...are accountable only to their electorate, their Party and their individual conscience'.[71]

All the MLAs bar Reg Empey (who took six months to reply) responded within a matter of months, and many expressed displeasure at being called to account. Despite Trimble's talk of the Order as the UUP's 'sister organisation', the MLAs' replies indicate that they saw the relationship between the Order and the party as essentially one of lobbyist and lobbied. For Trimble, 'all Ulster Unionist Members, whether Orangemen or not, [should]...be open to sincere representations about issues which touch on religious and cultural matters of concern to the Order'.[72] For Jim Wilson, while he was

very willing to listen to any representations...[these] would be on the clear understanding that [they]...would be taken into consideration and would be weighed against my conscience. I trust you will convey to Grand Lodge that I will not be providing any explanation to that body for any subsequent vote of mine cast in the Assembly that I would not give to the public as a whole.[73]

Ivan Davis, a Lagan Valley MLA, adopted a cordial tone, but made reference to 'the varying attitudes of my Orange colleagues in relation to the Belfast Agreement' as well as Saulters's statement to Ballymena Orangemen in 1998 calling for meetings with local residents' groups. Incisively drawing attention to Saulters's about-turn, Davis insisted: 'I believe the Grand Master will eventually be proved right.'[74]

Grand Lodge wrote back to the MLAs denying any pro-DUP bias and adding—somewhat questionably in light of the historical evidence—that letters to MLAs were not unprecedented.[75] Around the same time, Grand Lodge had few qualms about pressing *both* Trimble and Paisley to act on the parading issue by seeking to abolish the PC. Increasingly, the Order was lobbying both parties to get action—a new departure in its political strategy.[76] The Order was preaching to the converted, but the British government was in no mood to change course as the comments of the successive secretaries of state Mandelson and Reid indicated.

During 2000–1, Grand Lodge began its war of attrition with the PC. Noting the 'administrative problems' created by a series of written challenges to the PC's parade restrictions, it urged lodges to send more. It also asked lodges to affix appendices to their '11/1' parade request forms.[77] Meanwhile, the Order peppered the press with criticisms of PC decisions and statements.[78] This cut little ice with John Reid, who was unwilling to play ball with the Order. In a bruising meeting, Reid and two NIO officials insisted that the Order 'must' enter into discussions with residents, the PC, or the Currin Initiative. When Grand Lodge Officers pointed out that (against official Grand Lodge policy) Portadown District had met both residents and the PC, Reid questioned whether these meetings were 'meaningful'. When queried by the Orangemen as to what would be considered 'meaningful', David Watkins of the NIO challenged the Order to 'take a judicial review if we [Order] did not consider their [the NIO's] interpretation correct'. Reid also reiterated his support for the PC.[79]

Meanwhile, Grand Lodge continued to invest its hopes in a legal challenge to the PC. David Brewster, a UUP activist and Orange lawyer from Limavady, felt that recent legal developments, like the judgment in the Dunloy parade case, provided some grounds for optimism. The 'no right to be offended' stance of residents had not been upheld, which could undermine the PC. Moreover, Brewster advocated a proactive policy of pressing the Secretary of State to replace the PC with another body to deal with parades that would have much more limited powers. This proposal was widely applauded and unanimously endorsed by 112 delegates, with only 2 abstentions. On the other hand, a proposal to speak to the PC was defeated by 80-16, with 8 abstentions. Even Gracey equivocated, saying he 'personally would not' speak to the PC, though he thought that if others wanted to do so that was 'up to them'.[80]

Privately, Brewster was less optimistic. 'This [parading issue] is not one which commends itself to the liberal Human Rights Establishment here,' he wrote to George Patton. In contrast to the USA, where the American Civil Liberties Union had even defended extremist groups like the Nazis, no such agenda existed in Northern Ireland. Nonetheless, Brewster felt that it was important to use the human rights machinery in Northern Ireland, however inadequate it was, and to 'confront' existing human rights groups to 'expose their own agendae'. Confronting the human rights establishment would mean they would be faced with 'the invidious choice of snubbing the Orange as it tries to go down the road of Human Rights, or being seen to support our campaign in the context of human rights'. Proposed tactics included educating the membership about their options, seeking Orange group representation on statutory bodies, and coordinating legal action. In a more humorous vein, Brewster acknowledged that a petition and a conference were 'a complete waste of time', but felt these could also help build community awareness and educate the membership. Finally, he proposed a human rights handbook for lodges and the need for familiarity with the vocabulary and techniques of the human rights lobby. 'Such apparent steps towards a culture [of] Human Rights would also play well with the liberal establishment and might make it more difficult for the government to demonise the order.'[81]

The Orange shift from public protests to legal and political challenges meant that Grand Lodge set great store by the Quigley review of the PC, pressing British officials like John Reid for a timetable.[82] After a month of hearing nothing from him, Watson criticized the Secretary of State: 'In a recent speech you referred to the fact that Northern Ireland must not become a "cold place for Protestants". Such concern does not equate with the "off-hand" approach adopted to the largest Protestant organisation in Northern Ireland'. Obviously alarmed, Reid responded courteously to Watson the same day.[83] Meanwhile, an extensive brief, 'The Case Against the Parades Commission', was compiled by George Patton, and Grand Lodge Officers met Sir George Quigley to discuss their concerns.[84] This did not go unnoticed by the PC. PC minutes released to the Order under the 'Stormontgate' affair show that it worried about its Drumcree decision 'withstand[ing] any judicial review by LOL No. 1 [Portadown District]'.[85]

Unfortunately for the Order, the Quigley review suggested that the European Convention on Human Rights (ECHR), which influenced similar British and Northern Ireland legislation, would not protect the Order's right to march in the face of threats to public order or countervailing rights including freedom from noise.[86] The main Quigley recommendations involved little more than calling for a new body to facilitate dispute resolution between local parties and transferring the right to decide on parades from the PC back to the police. There was no hint of abolishing the PC or putting it under Stormont control, though the report did hint that the name 'Parades Commission' was not sacrosanct.[87] The Quigley report also approvingly cited statistics from the North report on parading which showed 44 per cent of Protestants and 80 per cent of Catholics backing the principle that paraders should obtain consent from the other community before parading. 46 per cent of Protestants felt that marchers should meet residents before marching, and 77 per cent of Protestants agreed that in the absence of local agreement a settlement should be imposed (by the RUC, government, or an independent commission).[88]

The Order responded with dismay to Quigley's report. Though claiming that Quigley stated that the PC 'had not worked' (a questionable interpretation of the report), the Order felt that the report took insufficient account of the strength of the ECHR's protections of freedom of assembly.[89] Grand Lodge thus began a steady appeal process, turning to the liberal Ulster Human Rights Watch (UHRW) as a potential ally.[90] In February 2003, the Order held a meeting at its new headquarters in East Belfast, bringing together representatives of the Loyal Orders and UHRW as well as DUP and UUP officials to discuss Quigley. While the Loyal Order representatives were downcast about the report, the UUP officials said that they were more positive than the others. The DUP, on the other hand, backed the Loyal Orders in their critical view. Ian Paisley Jun. urged the kind of resolve against the PC that allowed the Protestant community to see off the Anglo-Irish Agreement. Richard Monteith was more interested in promoting a legal challenge which he felt the Order could win.[91]

At a subsequent meeting between Grand Lodge officers and the new Secretary of State, Paul Murphy, Murphy noted that there was 'a lot of sense' in the Orange criticisms and promised further consultation after sounding out the Nationalist community. Murphy's tone was much more courteous than that of his predecessors Mandelson and John Reid, perhaps because of the reduced level of violence at Drumcree and the government's own decision to review the PC's workings. Thus he noted that the majority of parades were peaceful and spoke of improvement since the 1990s.[92] Earlier, PSNI raids on Sinn Fein offices at Stormont revealed considerable leaks of sensitive information from the PC to Republicans, adding to Orange suspicion of the PC. Whether 'Stormontgate' was a hoax cooked up by British intelligence or the result of real IRA spying remains contested, but the damage it did to Unionist confidence in the Peace Process was considerable.[93] This may have stiffened resistance to the raft of mediators, government officials, the media and church leaders who called for the Order to meet the PC. Even a letter from the secretary of the vestry of Drumcree Church urging Grand Lodge to grant permission to Portadown District to go to the PC failed to sway enough Grand Lodge delegates to change its policy.[94]

Within the Order, certain spirits flagged. Some members from the Republic, who complained that Drumcree had tarnished their image, suggested that Portadown District should abandon its aim of marching the Garvaghy Road and return via its outbound route. Another member from the Republic felt 'there was more to the Orange Order than marching' and implied that the Order had maintained a better class of (non-political) member in the Republic. Apathy was also a problem on the Order's Human Rights Committee, which met representatives of UHRW to discuss police handling of the Dunloy parade ban at Easter 2003. 'Lack of attendance and different persons attending at subsequent meetings results in the [Human Rights] committee having to revisit' various issues, reported the disgruntled committee chairman.[95] Apathy was similarly identified as the cause of a poor response rate to questionnaires sent by the Order to its younger members.[96] When a motion was tabled at Grand Lodge to levy £5 per district to fund legal action for a test case against the PC, this was defeated by 59–49 with 8 abstaining.[97]

Though stymied by apathy and caution from directly approaching districts for cash, the Order's leaders continued to pursue their human rights strategy, one of the few policy avenues still open to them. In April 2004, Antrim Grand Lodge attempted to show engagement with Nationalist residents in the town of Dunloy ahead of a scheduled parade. Despite a 'charm offensive' in which

120 Nationalist residents of Dunloy were sent letters inviting them to an Orange 'Faith and Heritage' exhibition in Ballymoney, the march was banned by the PC. The PC claimed that despite its overtures, the Order's refusal to negotiate with residents or meet the PC showed that it had not meaningfully engaged with residents.[98] Antrim Lodge sought and obtained a judicial review of the PC's decision at Dunloy, and was greatly encouraged by this. At the next Grand Lodge meeting, delegates voted unanimously to broaden the remit of the Orange legal fund to include general challenges to legislation 'which denies us our fundamental Human Rights'.[99]

Politically, the Order hoped to put pressure on the British and Irish governments. This was already going on indirectly in the form of lobbying through DUP and, to a lesser degree, UUP representatives. In 2004, the Order sent a delegation to Westminster, including the UUP MP Willie Ross and Grand Secretary Denis Watson, to present evidence pertaining to the PC and the Public Procession (NI) Act of 1998.[100] At Westminster, the Northern Ireland Affairs Committee, chaired by Michael Mates, considered testimony it had received from all quarters. Things began badly when Mates enquired after correspondence from the PC which Watson denied receiving. Ross then testified against the Quigley review, claiming that its complexity would make things worse. He reminded Mates of his earlier testimony regarding the PC in which he claimed the legislation could allow Sinn Fein to create '100 Drumcrees' if it wanted to. Ross later testified that he lived in a mostly Nationalist area where the IRA could at any point decide to 'switch on' its objection to local Orange marches.[101]

Martin Smyth had managed to get on the Parliamentary Questioning Committee, and under his questioning, Robert Saulters said that the Belfast County treasurer (Mervyn Bishop) had directly met Sinn Fein in 1995 when the first disputes arose (over Lower Ormeau). After two years of mediation with Sinn Fein and the RUC, an agreement had been reached. But 'everything was thrown out because the Sinn Fein community centre and the heavy squad came in with baseball bats and it was all off'.[102] This therefore proved that contacts with Republican residents' groups were futile. Later, debate focused on the transparency of the PC, with Watson and Ross urging the PC to reveal who was making allegations against the Order. The chair claimed that this would compromise witnesses' security, while the Orangemen argued that without seeing the submissions, they had no way of challenging malicious allegations.[103]

The Order's consultation with UHRW was paying off and shaping its overall strategy. This organization had previously focused its criticism on police brutality towards Nationalist protesters during the marching season, but had now come to be persuaded of the Order's case.[104] It submitted one of the most telling memorandums to the committee, which excoriated the Quigley report and the PC. UHRW's main criticisms of the report were as follows:

1. Its failure to outline and discuss restrictions on (Nationalist) protests against Orange parades;

2. Its restriction on the rights of Orangemen to assemble peacefully and a failure to guarantee Orangemen's freedoms (through police protection against protesters);

3. Its omission of Article 9 of the ECHR regarding the 'right to manifest one's religion publicly and to try to convince one's neighbour through appropriate means';

4. The problem of terrorist-influenced residents' groups. 'If the new recommendations become legislation, terrorist-influenced residents groups will be given even more efficient means of undermining others' rights to freedom of peaceful assembly and freedom of religion through the threat of violence.'

In conclusion, UHRW's brief came down strongly in favour of the Orangemen, and claimed that nothing in the ECHR supported the rights of those (i.e. residents) who seek to destroy another's (i.e. Orangemen's) freedoms. 'The duty of the State is to forbid practices which aim at the destruction of human rights and fundamental freedoms,' charged the report. 'It must not encourage through legislation those [i.e. IRA-inspired residents' groups] who through their activity and actions aim at annihilating the rights of others.'[105] The UHRW's stance contrasts greatly with the PC's view that it was balancing the rights of marchers with the rights of residents to protest and be free of intimidation. The Orangemen's testimony reflected what they believed was their legal ace card. Ross, for example, warned Mates and the Northern Ireland Committee that 'any legislation which arises from Quigley will have to comply with the European Convention of Human Rights'.

Ross acknowledged that the police could always stop a parade on public order grounds, but added that the ECHR makes determinations on the basis of civil rights, not public order, and it 'does set down a number of very definite absolutes [i.e. freedom of religious expression and assembly], despite what some folk [i.e. the PC] are trying to say'.[106] Given the ECHR's previous decisions, outlined in the Quigley report, it was unlikely that the Order would win the right to march.[107] However, it is possible that the ECHR could rule against the PC and tilt the normative case against the residents' groups. Quite clearly, the Order's goal is to first win the moral rather than practical high ground. Thus there was—and is—no point in the Order making a deal with the PC that would prejudice its case against the PC. UHRW had greatly bolstered Orange hopes, and in December 2004, Grand Lodge voted to make a payment towards the group's costs.[108] This policy marked a 360-degree shift from the 1980s, when the Order preferred to base its case for parading on 'tradition' and rejected Northern Ireland's human rights infrastructure as morally deficient.

Yet Grand Lodge's legal progress was deemed insufficient by many of those lodges whose parades had been restricted. As noted, a third of most lodges' members turn up only on the Twelfth and it is the highlight for most Orangemen. Thus bans greatly hurt membership numbers. Portadown, for example, lost a third of its membership during 1999–2004 when the Drumcree parade failed to take place.[109] It simply couldn't afford to wait for Grand Lodge's legal proceedings. After the debates of 2001, when Armagh's wishes were overruled by Grand Lodge, Portadown continued to pursue an independent policy with the PC. In April 2004, Portadown District leaders took part in a PC field trip to South Africa, accompanied by PSNI officers and Parade Commissioners (Nationalist residents boycotted the trip).[110]

This action led Saulters to raise the possibility of expulsion or suspension for the Portadown men who went to South Africa. But Richard Reid claimed the rule against contacting the PC was not practical, and David Burrows of Portadown District contended that the policy of shunning the PC should be changed. The decisions of the PC and PSNI needed to be challenged, said Burrows. Grand Lodge policy might have been right in the past, 'but not now', he continued. Saulters did not issue any suspensions, but he refused to put any motion to the meeting to rescind the policy prohibiting contact with the PC on the grounds that 'we already know where we stand. It [is] time for a bit of discipline'.[111] At a special meeting a few weeks later, Saulters railed against the news that members of Portadown District had met the PC and Irish government officials on the evening of the recent Grand Lodge meeting.

Since Wednesday I have learned that Portadown District has met representatives from the Department of Foreign Affairs from Dublin . . . [they] also met the Garvaghy Road Residents . . . was a deal done with these people? There was also a meeting in Belfast with Brian Curr[in], the South African whom the Officers of Portadown [following their South African trip] assured myself was no longer in the picture . . . was a deal also done there?

Saulters then asked the membership what would be done to ensure that no further breaches of Grand Lodge policy (against meeting the PC) took place. He warned that the Quigley review would have major ramifications for all and called for a united front. The Rev. Dickinson, he noted, was concerned that 'Portadown District was talking to everyone apart from Grand Lodge. He [Dickinson] felt that the District should be suspended until their conduct was considered.' This was backed by George Watson and seconded by Dickinson. Others, on the other hand, wanted to give Portadown a chance to respond. Reid claimed that the twenty-two districts facing parade restrictions were in a different situation from the rest of the Order.[112] Much of the pressure to relent came from members on the front line who wanted their Twelfth back. They felt that just as the Order had got over its advice in the 1980s not to make submissions to the Fair Employment Agency (for fear of recognizing it), it should do the same with the PC. One annoyed Londonderry City member who resigned in 2002 wrote:

Let me make it clear that it is not over the arrangements of the parade this year, but with the non-arrangements that the City Grand Lodge did not make over the last number of years. It is about time that the City Grand Lodge took on board that we live in a Nationalist/Republican city and the leadership must negotiate with the powers that be so that our culture is not lost forever. If and when the leadership take on board what Number 4 District [City of Derry] did this year, then I will reconsider rejoining at some date.[113]

Another in Belfast opined:

I feel that the virtual loss of the Ormeau Road due to the fact that Grand Lodge has tied the hands of my good friend the District Master Noel Liggett, as to who we talk to and who we don't has caused untold damage . . . it is the Order who [need to] move themselves into the here and now, not to be hindered by unworkable principles that cost us influence, friends, roads and membership, including my own.[114]

Derry City Lodge had recently had its election annulled and its minute books confiscated because of its willingness to negotiate with the PC, but Robert Overend from County Londonderry challenged this kind of reasoning, arguing against Richard Reid that in Bellaghy they were re-routed but—unlike the Royal Black brethren who negotiated—did not go to the PC. Others warned that the NIO was trying to divide the Order over the issue. It was then decided that Armagh County Lodge should investigate Portadown's actions and report back within ten days. Watson agreed to withdraw his motion of suspension of Portadown. The vote was then passed overwhelmingly, by 75–3 with 12 abstentions.[115]

We have seen that Armagh had backed Portadown District since early 2000, supporting Richard Monteith's argument that the Order needed to speak to the PC to make its case. Though overruled by Grand Lodge, Portadown and Armagh proved unwilling to comply. At the following sessions in September, it emerged that Portadown was continuing to defy Grand Lodge. In correspondence, it was revealed that Portadown had attended a PC clinic at which four commissioners were present. 'That is more members of the Commission . . . than there has been present when they have been issuing their stupid determinations signed by Peter Quinn during the summer months,' quipped Saulters. Letters from both County Armagh and Portadown District lodges were deemed unsatisfactory by Saulters and others, and most felt that further investigation was needed. Some spoke up for Portadown District, speaking of their 'unenviable position' and the fact that other jurisdictions had also met the PC. The speaker was correct, but this served only to underline the inability of Saulters and Grand Lodge to enforce Orange policy on recalcitrant counties and districts. Saulters then issued a circular to all lodges based on a summary of his address, which reiterated the Grand Lodge policy of no contact with the PC. This was followed by a round of applause from the assembled Orangemen and a vote of confidence from senior members of the Institution.[116]

All the while, noises of support for Portadown came from local quarters like the *Portadown Times* and the hardline *Loyalist News*, both of which castigated Grand Lodge for its opposition to Portadown. An anonymous member in *Sunday Life* accused Saulters of waiting until the (recent) death of Harold Gracey before tackling Portadown District over its actions. Saulters retorted that Gracey had always said he would not meet the PC. Saulters also said he had always supported Portadown and had been lambasted by clerics (both within and outside the Order) for this and that 'people [who forget this previous support for Portadown] had short memories'.[117]

In December, correspondence from Armagh was received by Grand Lodge contesting the view that Portadown had broken the rules. David Burrows had also pleaded his case with Saulters. The issue, claimed Portadown and Armagh, was merely a misunderstanding over the specifics of Grand Lodge policy, something which could be cleared up when new guidelines were drawn up. Many knew this to be fudge, and the fractures could not be so easily papered over. In the new Orange elections, the serving Grand Secretary, Denis Watson, a DUP MLA from Armagh who had held the post for six turbulent years, was defeated. On a 78–41 count, the post passed to the Lisburn solicitor and UUP member Drew Nelson.[118] In spite of Armagh's disobedience, the basics of Orange policy remained intact, and were given a boost from the results of a pilot survey of some 300 Orangemen carried out by the University of Salford.[119] This revealed that 87 per cent wished to see the PC abolished. On the more pragmatic question of whether to negotiate with the PC, 56 per cent of those surveyed endorsed Grand Lodge policy of no contact, as against 31 per cent who wanted contact.[120] This suggests that there is backing, albeit fragile, for Grand Lodge policy, but that Grand Lodge needs to be vigilant in order to maintain a majority in favour of its policy course.

Politically, the parading issue remains one of the great ancillary issues of the GFA, along with decommissioning and police reform. Parading decisions played a role in shoring up Trimble ahead of the GFA in 1998, and despite the ostensible independence of the PC (or, under Quigley, the PSNI), parading remains a political issue that will not go away. The British government has the capacity to abolish the PC and put pressure on the police, and as long as this is the case, all parties have something to play for. The DUP in particular continues to press the British on the urgent need to address this issue in seeking an overall settlement.[121] However, the British government has stood by the PC. In January 2005, after the Northern Ireland Affairs Committee's deliberations, Westminster decided to back the PC against Quigley's limited recommendations that the PC lose its power to determine parading decisions and shelved Quigley's report. Despite UUP and DUP criticism, the NIO minister Ian Pearson announced in February 2005: 'I have decided that a case has not been made to make fundamental changes to parading arrangements in Northern Ireland.' Worse still, Pearson introduced a measure that would require supporters of Orange parades to register with the authorities. This seems to have been pushed through over the objections of an Orange deputation which expressed concern about PC control over spectators and the 'impracticable and unacceptable' notion that Orange parade organizers should be held accountable for the actions of spectators.[122] At the same meeting, the Grand Master's Advisory Group under the leadership of the Education Committee activist the Rev. Mervyn Gibson reported its findings. Gibson recommended that the existing Grand Lodge policy of no contact be retained, but said that the Order would be prepared to consider a replacement body with a wider remit that included all aspects of cultural expression. Members were warned that the PC was keen to have engagement from the Order to get Orangemen to 'meet with republicans, who in any case ha[ve] no desire to see parades proceed'. This reaffirmation of existing policy received a substantial endorsement of 84–24 from the assembled Grand Lodge delegates.[123]

British policy, however, remains unchanged. In September 2005, the latest in a succession of secretaries of state for Northern Ireland, Peter Hain, defied DUP and Orange pressure and again spoke in favour of retaining the PC.[124] Hain's previous political activity within the Labour government showed considerable evidence of Nationalist sympathies, and he even counselled a phased British withdrawal from Northern Ireland in the seventies and eighties against official Labour policy. Even in the 1990s, his statements marked him out as a Republican sympathizer.[125] Further bad news came in November when Hain announced the results of Stormont's Review of Public Administration. This legislation promises to slash the number of district councils from twenty-six to seven and disqualify local councillors from simultaneously serving as MLAs. Though ostensibly predating the GFA, this review also has severe implications for sectarian politics and will lead to the creation of three Nationalist-controlled super-councils in the west, three Unionist-dominated ones in the east, and a ferociously contested Belfast super-council.[126] The devolution of certain powers to the councils—many of them Nationalist—could be interpreted as strengthening the degree of Nationalist political power at the expense of British control. This may have been designed to put pressure on the DUP and other anti-Agreement Unionists to accede to a relaunch of the Assembly.

Meanwhile rifts continue within the Order between the centre and districts where parading is restricted, especially Portadown. The extent of policy divergence between Grand Lodge and Portadown was revealed in December 2005, when two leading Portadown Orangemen, Burrows and Don MacKay, joined the PC. Both expressed a willingness to listen to residents' concerns, and will play a part on a PC determined to see mediation between Orange marchers and Nationalist residents. Despite the objections of Brendan McKenna that this would lead to an 'unbalanced' PC that would alter its previous rulings, the PC's new chairman, Roger Poole, said he was 'delighted' that the two had joined. Though Poole hoped this would lead to fresh talks with the Order, Grand Lodge, despite expressing 'interest' in the new developments, continued to reject the PC as 'fundamentally flawed'. The rift between Portadown and Grand Lodge was obvious when Burrows and MacKay acknowledged that they had not cleared their appointments with Grand Lodge. Referring to his decision to join the PC, Burrows brazenly declared to reporters, 'I never asked anyone.' [127] He simultaneously resigned as deputy master of Portadown District.[128]

Evidently, Orange political pressure has failed to dislodge the British government from its pro-PC position. There is an inherent contradiction between a policy of trying to abolish the PC and trying to work within it for change. A boycott of the PC is intended to make a moral statement that the Order will not recognize the legitimacy of an institution that it believes to be unfairly targeting Orange culture while neglecting the wider issue of cultural parity. It is also intended to put pressure on the British and Irish governments to change their strategy and abolish the PC. Portadown's engagement with the PC through legal and political channels undermines this strategy. Or does it? We have already witnessed Grand Lodge using Portadown's involvement with residents and the PC as a sign of good faith in negotiations with the Secretary of State and other government officials. If little comes of Portadown's overtures to the PC, this may well support Richard Monteith's argument that evidence of engagement will allow Grand Lodge to make a stronger human rights case for its abolition. With the PC unlikely to alter its established policy course, this leaves the legal approach as the most promising avenue for future Orange action on the issue which most concerns it: parading.

10

Segmenting the Orange: The Future of Orangeism in the Twenty-First Century

Parading is the issue which most concerns Orangemen today, but membership loss is the most pressing long-term concern, a lightning rod used by both hardliners and moderates to agitate for change. 'For many years, the Orange Institution has been in decline. Our membership has decreased alarmingly,' thundered the *Orange Banner*, official organ of the SOD. 'Managing our decline is no longer acceptable . . . If the Orange institution is not to die a slow and undignified death we must rekindle the spirit of the [Battle of the] Diamond.' To 'stop the rot', the SOD wanted Grand Lodge to mount a militant defence of the Orange cause and rally Unionists to Orangeism as the main defender of the Protestant interest.[1]

On the other hand, the traditionalist moderates of the old (pre-2000) Education Committee believe that the very militancy of the SOD has suffused the Order, driving away members, especially middle-class members. For Austen Morgan, a London-based barrister close to David Trimble and sympathetic to Unionism, the Order needs to abandon its insistence on the 'principle' of no contact with the PC and residents or face 'increasing pro-nationalist stances by the United Kingdom government under pressure from Dublin, more Drumcrees, and a continuing loss of members, leading to a rump organisation at once impotent and despised'. Morgan believes that engagement and openness will pay a public relations and political dividend for the Order, 'preventing the decline in numbers, and consequent loss of status in the majority community'.[2] Chris Ryder and Vincent Kearney suggest that the small number of militants attracted into the Order since 1995 has been greatly offset by the loss of more liberal, middle-class members.[3]

Where does the truth lie with respect to membership? Many Orangemen who leave the organization simply cease paying their dues and are suspended. A great many others pay their final debts but resign their membership. In combining these categories, we can get some idea of how many leave. During the three years 2000–2, roughly 1,200 Orangemen officially left the organization, amounting to a loss of just over 1 per cent of the total membership per year. Before we ask whether this is a large or small amount, let us consider the question of why these individuals pass out of the Orange Institution. Those who resign their membership are asked to explain their reasons on a special form. Most write 'personal' and so leave us guessing at their motives. However, a minority give a written response, and these provide an interesting insight into the motives of those who leave. One clerical member and a past master of his lodge passionately wrote:

My reasons for non attendance are simple....My rector who is a personal friend suffered humiliation at the hands of thugs in July 1998, all because he said during his sermon that the Brethren at Drumcree should stand back and let the forces of law and order deal with the thugs who had infiltrated the Protest...I personally will not abide with the thugs who started shooting at the police and the army. These points which I have made tended to wean me off Orangeism. Make no mistake you are aware and I am aware that quite a lot of the Brethren attending the rally would have known a lot of the thugs who were there to cause nothing but trouble and bring discredit on the Orange Order. Yes Brian I feel I cannot continue being a member until the house is in order.[4]

Another criticized the stance of both his district and Grand Lodge:

To suggest that 'social crime' is justified and inevitable and that some members of the security forces should now be regarded as 'enemies of the Protestant people' is self destructive and dangerous in the extreme. I would expect it from the likes of Adams and McGuinness but not an Orangeman. The rules of the Order make it plain—I refer to the qualification of candidates...'That he (the candidate) will to the utmost of his power, support and maintain the laws and constitution of the realm'...To go to the extreme of inventing ludicrous stories with no basis in fact in an attempt to excuse the actions of those who attacked the security forces at Drumcree with deadly force is unconscionable. Their actions did the Orange Order more damage than Sinn Fein/IRA ever could and our refusal to condemn their actions damages the Order even more. I realise, however that at the September meeting I was alone in arguing against the more extreme viewpoint. It seems that I am out of step with the brethren of [local district] and probably the majority of the Order as a whole.[5]

For another member, the death of the RUC constable Frankie O'Reilly at Drumcree in 1998 touched a little too close to home:

The brutal and unwarranted murder of Constable Frank O'Reilly has really convinced me that it is regrettably time to consider my future as a member of the Order I have loved to be part of for the past twenty-eight years. Frankie leaves behind a shattered and heartbroken family—his wife Janice, Steven (10), Gary ($3\frac{1}{2}$) and little Sarah (14 weeks). Although in a mixed marriage situation Frankie often attended our church with his wife and young family. Janice, who is in membership of our Church...took the vows, with Frankie at her side, at the baptism of Gary...I must say that this is another tragic opportunity for Portadown District to call off their Drumcree protest which is providing a conduit for violent, evil, and irreligious people to vent their heinous deeds on the forces of law and order, who have had to face the IRA and their kindred organisations in defence of freedom over the past twenty-nine years.[6]

Others, however, saw things differently.

As a young man I joined the Orange Order some years ago . . . I believed when I joined . . . that I was joining an organisation that was there to defend my Protestant culture, instead now I see a group of old men who are content to sit and just let our culture be eroded and taken away from us. As defenders of the faith, Portadown District have done little or nothing . . . Harold Gracey and his Officers have no guts not like in 1995 and 1996 when we had men who were not Orangemen [who] took up the challenge. Ay they done what had to be done and we got down the Garvaghy Road. Sadly some of these men are not with us today. I feel now the Orange Order no longer has anything to offer me . . . So as a young Protestant I am disgusted with the Order and wish to resign immediately.[7]

For other hardliners, the problem was Trimble and the Agreement. In the words of one who handed in his collarette: '[The] UUP has too much influence on the Orange Order . . . I do not wish to walk behind "YES" men who are "Orange" while parading, yet prepared to hand Ulster over.'[8]

The question that immediately arises is where the balance of opinion lies. There is some evidence that during the height of the Drumcree conflict in 1998, anti-Drumcree sentiment led to significant resignations from the Order. In that year, 21 of the 302 Orangemen who resigned cited Drumcree or gave a liberal' reason for their departure while only 6 gave 'hardline' reasons.[9] In 1999 once again, 'liberal' leavers outnumbered hardliners: 13 of the 325 who resigned gave a 'liberal' reason (almost all over Drumcree) and just 5 a hardline one. An important minority of the 'liberal' conscientious objectors were churchmen and long-serving members. In addition, a handful of others resigned because of peer pressure within organizations like the RUC.[10] By 2000, the number of resignations dropped to 132, with an even balance between 8 'liberal' and 8 hardline written responses. Some hardliners were anti-Agreement, others wanted tougher action at Drumcree, and some criticized the lack of 'leadership'.[11]

Yet we need to keep the political responses in perspective since we have solid evidence of political motivation for only a small proportion of those leaving. 2001 was a more typical year, with just two hardline responses and one 'liberal' one out of 151. In 2002, such issues were effectively absent. This foregrounds some of the more mundane reasons that dominate the resignation list. In 2002, for example, just 50 of the 152 resigners gave a reason for leaving. Work, other obligations, illness, or loss of interest accounted for over 80 per cent of the *stated* reasons, with local or national politics comprising less than 10 per cent.[12] Of course there may have been a groundswell of those leaving for reasons of conscience who simply cited 'personal' as their explanation. But this is far from apparent. One way of trying to tease out an answer is to look at the postcodes of those who resigned during 1998–2003. Liberal commentators suggest that Ulster's professional and business classes have left the Order over its confrontational and increasingly sectarian image post-Drumcree.[13] Chris McGimpsey, a former UUP MLA and councillor, speaks of the folding of middle-class Belfast lodges like the Press Lodge and membership declines in the elite Eldon 7 Lodge and Cross of St Patrick 688. 'The middle classes are not joining', he says, because they don't want to be associated with anything even remotely connected with the Troubles. McGimpsey believes that the Order is becoming almost exclusively working-class and that in a generation, politicians like himself will not be in membership.[14]

This said, there are good reasons to doubt that recent events have had any great impact on the class composition of the Order. If we look at those who resigned during 1998–2003, 767 individuals of the roughly 1,200 could be assigned a postcode. Table 10.1 compares the MOSAIC postcode classification of those who left with a sample of 3,368 'stayers': Orange private lodge masters and secretaries in 2001. Curiously, those who resign live in slightly lower-class postcodes than those who remain. Fewer are from the top twelve postcode classes and slightly more from the bottom seven. Where there is a significant difference is between rural and urban postcodes: urbanites in the Order are over twice as likely as rural dwellers to leave.

Perhaps it is the case that many who leave opt to let their membership lapse with dues unpaid. Once again, though, an analysis of 296 suspensions in the 2000–2 period shows that those who are suspended are twice as likely to live in urban postcodes as those who leave. In class terms, there is an important difference between those who resign and those who are suspended. Whereas resigners have close to the same social profile as 'stayers', those who are suspended are twice as likely as those who stay to be from the poorest postcode sectors (see Table 10.2). This is unsurprising as poorer Orangemen would be expected to have a hard time paying their dues off. All told, the people leaving the Order today through resignation and suspension are urbanites and generally poorer than the average Orangeman.

Table 10.1 The Class and Rural/Urban Score of Stayers vs Resigners, 1998–2003

	Rural MOSAIC 2004* postcode classes	Bottom 7 (non-rural) MOSAIC* postcode classes	Top 12 (non-rural) MOSAIC* postcode classes	Cases
Stayers: Local lodge masters and secretaries, 2001	35.3%	12.4%	58.7%	3,368
Resigners, 1998–2003	15.8%	18.3%	53%	767

Sources: NI MOSAIC 2004; GOLI resignation forms, 1998–2003; GOLI membership returns, 2001.

Table 10.2 The Class and Rural/Urban Score of Stayers vs Suspended Members, 2000–2002

	Rural *MOSAIC 2004 postcode classes	Bottom 7 (non-rural) *MOSAIC postcode classes	Top 12 (non-rural) *MOSAIC postcode classes	Cases
Stayers: local lodge masters and secretaries, 2001	44%	22%	58%	1,429
Suspended, 2000–2	21%	35%	41%	296

Sources: NI MOSAIC 2002; GOLI suspension forms, 2000–2; GOLI membership returns, 2001.

Loss of members through resignation or suspension should not be overemphazised, however. Associations are dynamic entities that are constantly shedding and replenishing members, especially in cities—where intake and outflow are both high. For instance, over a fifteen-year period from 1905 to 1919, the Orange Order in Canada initiated 138,000 men and suspended 99,000. This resulted in one ex-Orangeman in the country for every active member.[15] In Belfast, total membership peaked in the mid 1950s and began to decline seriously by the early 1960s. The reason has little to do with an increase in the rate at which existing members left. In the 1950s and early 1960s (I sampled 1953, 1956, and 1960), during a period of buoyant membership, roughly 200–300 men, between 1.4 and 2 per cent of the total membership, *officially* left the Order in Belfast each year. This rose to 4–7 per cent during 1968-73, a period of largely *rising* membership, but declined to 2 per cent by 1975, during a period of sharp membership decline![16] In 2000–2, by contrast, the rate of official exit in Belfast was just 0.5 to 1 per cent of total membership per year.[17]

In Derry City, the records of District 1 show that 10–15 per cent of members left *annually* in the 1950s and 1960s. Grand Lodge records show that between 5 and 8 per cent of membership left annually in the city as a whole, but this is almost certainly an underestimate of actual departures. Yet even as large numbers flowed out, many joined or returned to the fold, so membership held steady until 1963, when a slow decline set in. Derry's ability to attract or reinstate large numbers of new members was key to its success, and when recruiting flagged, membership began to fall. The occupations of the Londonderry City District 1 officers in 1961 and 1971 seem to be among the most middle-class of any I have seen in the Order, with a majority in the professions, business, or services.[18] So it seems likely that the Troubles and the reform of the local government franchise caused many in the city's middle-class to spurn the offer to join or to let their membership lapse.

Let us examine the figures for Belfast (the only place for which we have separate initiation and outflow figures) more closely. By looking at Belfast, we

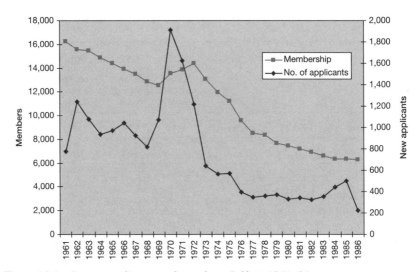

Figure 10.1 Orange applicants and members, Belfast, 1961–86
Source: Belfast County initiation forms, 1961–86; GOLI membership returns.

can see that initiation decline, rather than outflows of older members, largely tells the story. Note how the initiation line ('New applicants') in Figure 10.1 tends to predict membership with a one-year lag effect. Despite peaks of interest during the Troubles and around the signing of the AIA, the Order's level of recruiting has declined to the point where just 38 per cent of all lodges attracted *any* new members during 1989–97.[19] Clearly the Order in Belfast has dwindled because it has been unable to attract new members in their late teens and twenties at the same level as it once did. This casts doubt on the thesis that a growing exodus of any kind—never mind a middle-class one—is to blame for the Order's decline in the city. The same was true in Toronto. In 1921, the 11,000 Orangemen of greater Toronto (population 650,000) formed about the same proportion of the city's Protestant population as is true in Belfast today. Initiations in Toronto were around 1,000 per year until the early 1920s—about the same as in Belfast in the early 1960s. As in Belfast, though, initiations in Toronto declined sharply, to under 650 by 1930 and under 250 by 1935. Outflows were highest in 1920 and shrank thereafter. Nonetheless, by 1961, membership was barely a third of its 1931 level.[20]

Figure 10.2 shows the relationships between the initiation rate, the outflow rate (membership loss taking into account new initiates), and total membership in Belfast during 1961–87. Statistical analysis using two time-series regression methods shows that the previous year's initiations are a better predictor of membership levels during this twenty-five-year period than the number who leave the Order in a given year. In fact, around half of the variation in membership can be predicted by the number of

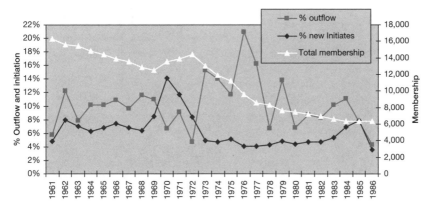

Figure 10.2 Orange inflows, outflows, and membership, Belfast, 1961–87
Sources: Belfast County initiation forms, 1961–86; GOLI membership returns.

initiates in the previous year. While initiation is consistently significant sta-
tistically, the number flowing out is on the borderline or insignificant. In
other words, declining initiation largely tells the story about membership
decline.[21]

Could it be that young middle-class potential recruits are being repelled
by the Order? This is very unlikely. First of all, middle-class members have
always been thin on the ground in Belfast. To determine the trends, I have
sampled the complete applicant pool for Belfast for five years: 1961, 1965,
1971, 1981, and 1986. Results are shown in Figure 10.3. In 1961, less than
2 per cent of initiates held professional or managerial occupations. Even if we
include students and clerks, we arrive at a figure of only about 8 per cent. At
the peak of the Troubles in 1971, this figure rose slightly, but then returned
to about the 8 per cent level (including students).[22] The truly impressive shift
actually has less to do with the middle class than with the decline of Belfast's
skilled industrial base. This hit the Order hard as the proportion of apprentices
shrank from 20 per cent in 1961 to almost nothing by 1986, while the ranks of
unemployed initiates swelled from zero in 1971 to 12 per cent by 1986. Chris
McGimpsey remarks that in some lodges in Belfast, nearly half the members
are unemployed.[23] Many others are unskilled workers.

Apart from the fact that these members will have trouble paying their dues,
they also reduce the status and cultural capital ('connections') associated with
Orange membership, and this may also be affecting recruitment. Overall,
though, a class analysis only provides part of the story. At £60 per year
plus £40 on the Twelfth, Orange membership is not expensive, but the cost
may be enough to deter a pool of potential members.[24] Yet this fails to fully
explain why the Order recruits so few unemployed and unskilled Belfast youth
while other forms of activity like independent band parading and, on a more

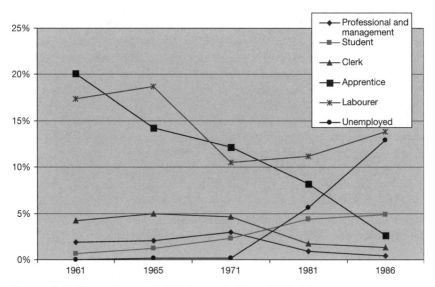

Figure 10.3 Occupations of Belfast Orange initiates, 1961–86
Sources: Belfast County initiation forms, 1961–86.

mundane level, live sports and pubs, are popular with the same category of people.

In addition, there is no relationship between unemployment rates and Orange initiation rates over time, and thus the higher proportion of unemployed Belfast recruits does not indicate that unemployment was affecting membership. For instance, unemployment in the province as a whole began to rise from 5 per cent in 1975 to its peak in 1986–7 at 17 per cent.[25] Seen this way, the Order's initiates in 1986 merely reflected the occupational make-up of working-class Protestant Belfast. In tests with some thirty variables, Belfast initiations were significantly related only to Northern Ireland marriage rates, with more marriages (implying traditional values) linked to higher recruiting. Most economic factors, key events, and Troubles-related fatalities had no impact. Only the number of television licences—which jumped in the 1960s and then levelled off—was of borderline significance. Here, perhaps, is evidence that cultural change has had a more pronounced effect than deindustrialization or the Troubles when it comes to initiations in Belfast.[26]

Orange Decline in Comparative Perspective

In 1920, more than 100,000 Orangemen—twice the Northern Ireland membership—lived in what is now Canada. In the colony of Newfoundland,

274

which joined Canada in 1949, 35 per cent of Protestant adult males were Orangemen, a figure nearly twice as high as in Northern Ireland. The city of Toronto was largely controlled by Orange mayors until 1960, and the Order influenced employment in the police force, Toronto Transit Commission, and other public bodies. Numerous provincial premiers and four Canadian prime ministers were Orangemen in the period 1830–1970, but today, Canadian Orangeism is a small, largely aged cultural fraternity with little more than 5,000 members.[27] The former Education Committee chairman Brian Kennaway, drawing on the Canadian research of Cecil Houston and William Smyth, adds that Canadian Orange membership plummeted because Orangemen failed to adapt and abandon their 'garrison mentality'.[28] This may be so, but Canadian membership decline is very mysterious. Culturally, Unionism in Canada began to slowly wane after World War I while the sense of Canadian national identity was strengthened. This was very noticeable between 1940 and 1960, when the balance of Canadians switched their preferences from British to Canadian symbols for the flag, anthem, police, and military.[29] Secularization and liberalism can be safely excluded as factors since they took place later, in the 1960s.

Less glamorous explanations based on socio-economic change are important as well. Major declines hit all branches of the Canadian Order in the 1920s and 1930s. The same pattern afflicted the Oddfellows, a life insurance fraternity, but had no impact on the Masons. Some surmise that working-class and rural fraternities like the Order and Oddfellows suffered because of the rise of alternative forms of social security, while the more middle-class Masons were unaffected.[30] Less contentious is what happened in the post-1960 period. This time, all Canadian fraternities including the Masons suffered, as did unions and churches. The political scientist Robert Putnam has charted a similar path for some 100 major American chapter-based associations. The cumulative membership curve suggests a general pattern of post-war growth and post-1960 decline, which Putnam attributes to a decline in 'social capital' or connectedness between strangers. Using individual survey data, he finds that all forms of organized, face-to-face social contact from bowling leagues to fraternities have declined. Half of this effect is attributable to the replacement of a 'joining' generation born between 1910 and 1940 with the non-joining baby boom and generation 'X' cohorts born thereafter. A further quarter comes from increased television consumption, and the rest from diverse effects like the changing role of women and longer working and commuting times.[31]

Peter Hall famously argued that Britain had not suffered the same social capital decline as the United States, and hence Putnam's work did not apply.[32] However, more recent analyses have questioned Hall's methodology and findings, especially for the British majority that identify themselves as working-class. 'The social institutions that were the mainstay of working-class participation—mutual aid societies, clubs, labour unions—have disappeared or changed,' write Grenier and Wright. 'We would conclude, contrary to Hall's analysis, that Britain indeed may have experienced a decline in "social capital" strikingly similar to that of the United States.'[33] Another interesting study, conducted by two Freemasons with scientific backgrounds from the trend-setting Internet Lodge, take the argument still further. These authors looked at the number of years for which individual candidates remained in the Masons from initiation to resignation in eight lodges across Britain, Canada, Australia, and the United States. The authors' wealth of individual-level data on the five-year 'initiating class' of 1945–9 up to 1990–4 allowed them to track individuals' membership careers cross-nationally. They found that by the year 2000 the average length of membership had declined from between fifteen and twenty-five years for the 'class' of 1950–4 to between five and seven years for the 'class' of 1985–9. The declines occurred roughly in proportion across all countries, leading the authors to conclude that 'each succeeding cohort remained within the Craft [Masons] for a shorter period of time and all lodges show a very marked fall in membership duration from the second half of the 1970s onwards'.[34] With this trend in mind, we can better appreciate the exasperation that the Orange Grand Secretary Denis Watson felt at the Orange conference at Templepatrick in 2003 when he derided certain lodges for acting as a 'conveyor belt' for members from initiation through suspension.[35]

A cursory glance at post-1945 membership trends within worldwide Orangeism shows a picture of recent decline, with the Order in Northern Ireland faring better than its Canadian cousin but worse than that in Scotland. If we bear in mind that the Scottish ladies' organization (which was bigger than the men's one until the 1960s) began to decline by 1960, and the Scottish juniors by 1970, it seems that the general trend largely follows a Putnamite path as young people simply opted for other ways to occupy their spare time. Some suggest that drinking clubs and pubs in urban working-class areas may fulfil a function as social centres not dissimilar to that of the Order.[36] There are further reasons for suspecting that this may be the case. A comparison with the Freemasons is interesting. The Masons are a Protestant fraternity with a similar ritual and symbol structure to the Orange Order, though unlike the Order they are avowedly apolitical and do not discuss religion in the lodge room. They are also a far more urban and upper-income fraternity than the Order, as we saw in Table 6.3. We have good data for County Down Masons which shows that there are roughly the same number of Masons and Orangemen in the county. Both organizations have experienced post-1960 decline: decline set in ten years later among the County Down Masons, but has proceeded more sharply than the decline among the more rural County Down Orangemen in the past twenty-five years. (see Figure 10.4) This is a different picture from that in Canada during 1920–60, when the Masons grew while the Orange Order declined rapidly.[37]

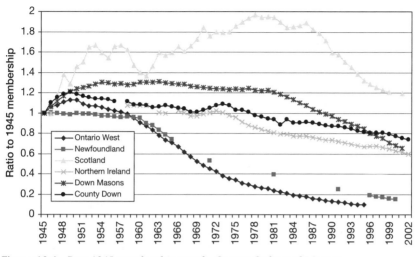

Figure 10.4   Post-1945 membership trends, Orange Order and Masons

Source: Kaufmann, 'The Orange Order in Ontario, Newfoundland, Scotland and Northern Ireland'.

Geographic Patterns

The most reliable statistics tend to be from the census, but censuses have been taken only every ten to fifteen years in Northern Ireland. To add to the complexity, census boundaries changed in the early 1970s. Looking at the 1891–1971 period at county level with statistical tools, we find that Orange participation rates among Protestant men are highest in counties and county boroughs with high Roman Catholic and COI populations. Orange participation is especially strong in Nationalist areas like South Down, South Armagh, Derry, and West Belfast. This reflects a community mobilization response in the face of adversity. The historical pattern of stronger traditional Unionism in COI border counties like Fermanagh also holds. But things are changing as rebel Unionism takes hold in the urban parts of border counties. If we look at smaller geographies like the 101 district electoral areas (DEAs) in the 1991–2001 period we find that the proportion of people who are Catholic or COI is no longer significant. Instead, close-knit, rural DEAs with few migrants from other DEAs are the strongholds of Orangeism. Urban centres like Derry that have experienced Protestant population movement exemplify the kind of area that is now inhospitable to Orangeism.[38] The same trend appears to have occurred in Glasgow and Liverpool when Orange lodges failed to make the transition from inner-city wards to suburban estates.[39] It seems that Orangeism and geographic mobility do not mix except in the case of frontier settlement, as in rural Canada. By contrast, the suburban frontiersmen of the

277

twentieth century in both Britain and Canada failed to form or join lodges in their new surroundings.[40]

Rural areas with small numbers of migrants from outside the locale tend to have stronger Orange memberships and have experienced fewer membership losses in the post-1960 period. Figures 10.5 and 10.6 map the fact that Belfast, Londonderry City, and smaller urban centres are weak Orange areas, as indicated by light colours. Even in the western Orange heartland, larger towns like Dungannon, Lurgan, and Cookstown form light patches of weak Orangeism within the fiercely Orange rural hinterland. This is not because there are fewer Protestants in the towns, but because young people in the towns are not joining the Order. The same pattern obtains in Canada, especially in Newfoundland, where St John's (urban) Protestants have long stood out as less Orange than their rural 'outport' co-religionists.[41] In 1961 and 1971, this pattern was much less evident in Northern Ireland. Belfast had a similar proportion of adult male Protestants in membership (15–20 per cent) to Antrim and Down, while Londonderry City was a tower of Orange strength that rivalled Fermanagh or Tyrone in the Orangeism of its Protestant population (27–30 per cent).[42] The same was true of Portadown and other major towns. Much has changed in the last thirty to forty years.

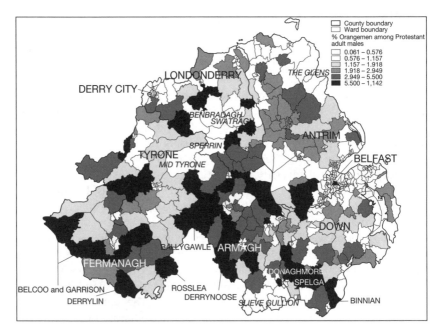

Figure 10.5 Orange density by ward, Northern Ireland, 1991

Sources: GOLI membership returns; Northern Ireland Census 1991; based upon Ordnance Survey of Northern Ireland (OSNI) digital boundaries 1984 © Crown copyright.

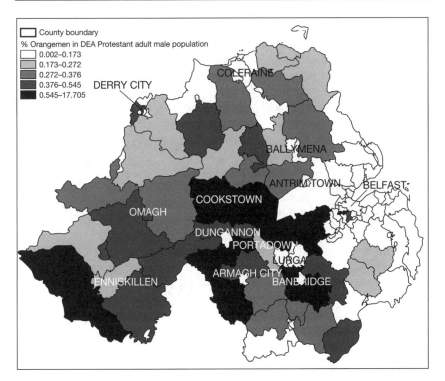

Figure 10.6 Orange density by District Electoral Area, Northern Ireland, 1991
Sources: GOLI membership returns; OSNI DEA boundaries 1984; Northern Ireland Census 1991.

Figure 10.7 shows that even in the short period 1991–2001, the hardest-hit (lighter-coloured) districts of membership are often in geographically small—hence populous—districts like Armagh city, Antrim, or sections of metropolitan Belfast and Derry city. Further losses are noticeable in North Down and parts of North Antrim. If we factor in the wider Protestant population shift to the suburbs of Belfast in North Down and South Antrim, the urban decline appears even more glaring. All told, these patterns represent a continuation of the collapse of urban Orangeism which resembles patterns found in Canada.

Trends in the Masons are not vastly different, though we have data only at county or multi-county level so cannot prise apart rural and urban areas. Broadly speaking, the biggest recorded declines in membership during 1975–90 in both organizations were east of the Bann, while more rural Tyrone, Fermanagh, and Armagh suffered less (see Figure 10.8). The main divergence in Londonderry and Donegal has to do with an exceptionally good Masonic performance in the city of Londonderry, where the Masons have maintained membership extremely well while the Order has declined sharply.[43] What this means for the Order is that rural areas where a large proportion of Protestants

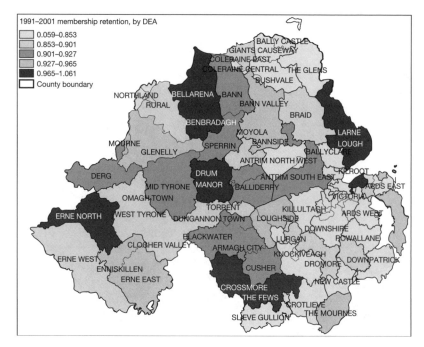

Figure 10.7 Orange membership retention, 1991–2001, by District Electoral Area
Sources: GOLI membership returns; OSNI DEA boundaries 1993.

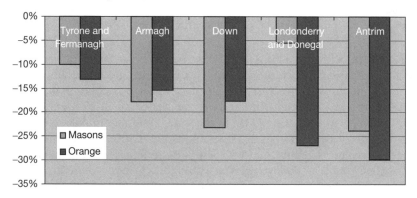

Figure 10.8 Orange and Masonic membership decline, 1975–90, by county
Sources: Grand Lodge of Ireland (Freemasons) membership returns; GOLI membership returns.

are already in membership remain much as they were, while in urban areas the Order is becoming like its dwindling Canadian cousin. Urbanity is linked with lower social capital, higher mobility, and more competing attractions, all of which may be contributing to the decline of Orangeism in Ulster's cities and towns. However, the 'Putnam effects' of generational turnover and television consumption are not strictly urban phenomena. Clearly there is more to the decline than social capital loss in the Unionist community.

This brings us to secularization. The results of major social surveys in Northern Ireland since 1978 show an important decline in the proportion of Protestants attending church (see Figure 10.9). In 1998, those aged over 65 were more than twice as likely to darken a church door as those under 34.[44] Census figures show a jump in those declaring themselves non-religious or refusing to state a religion, from 7 to 14 per cent.[45] Recent figures seem to show a levelling off or slight reversal of secularizing trends, though one cannot be precise about this because of slight variation in the survey question. It is nonetheless evident that secularization seems to have run in parallel with Orange and Masonic decline. This may be because of the religious basis of both institutions or because both church and association membership are forms of social capital which are suffering decline among more recent generations.

On the other hand, Orangeism has always been a bridge between church-goers and non-attenders.[46] Considerable evidence suggests that many Orange-men are unchurched, hence secularization would have relatively little impact. For instance, just 42 per cent of almost 20,000 Orangemen who responded told an Orange internal survey that they attend Orange church services.[47] When Denis Watson addressed an Orange conference in 2003, he bemoaned the falling quality and irreligiousness of new recruits. 'Church attendance should be taken . . . [over] a regular period rather than just a few Sundays before the proposed initiation,' he complained. 'In some lodges, "alleged" church attendance is glossed over . . . [and] even if the answer [is] negative, it's ignored anyway.'[48]

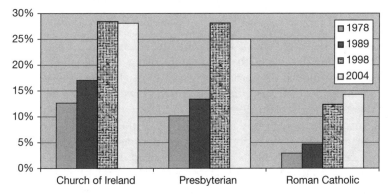

Figure 10.9 Proportion 'never attending' church, by denomination, 1978–2004

Sources: E. Moxon-Browne, *Northern Ireland Social Attitudes Survey, 1978* [computer file], Colchester: UK Data Archive, SN 1347 (1980); Social and Community Planning Research, *Northern Ireland Social Attitutes Survey, 1989–91*; Devine and Dowds, *Northern Ireland Life and Times Survey, 1998*; Devine and Dowds, *Northern Ireland Life and Times Survey, 2004*.

We also need to be aware of sharp changes in working-class youth culture. Independent marching band parades have been rising steadily in the past few decades as Orange membership has declined. The attractions of a more instantly gratifying urban Loyalist culture of sport, drink, and pseudo-paramilitarist machismo have been noted by both the Order's supporters and its detractors. Impatient to 'kick the Pope' in their music and parade more frequently, younger working-class or unemployed men are 'translating' Orange tradition away from the lodge room. Faced with the new Loyalist culture, time-honoured Orange traditions of ritual, religious symbolism, and lodge business have a hard time competing.[49]

Diagnosing the Decline

Though our best data come from the census, there is a body of annual data for the recent period that can help us to unravel the puzzle of membership loss. To begin with, there is no significant relationship between unemployment and Orange membership over time. Unemployment in Ulster rose by 12 percentage points from 1975 to 1987, then fell by 12 points from 1987 to 2002. All the while, Orange membership continued to slip. Instead, in statistical tests, the most important correlate of Orange decline appears to be the expansion of communications. Road network expansion is a proxy for a certain kind of modernization and the decline of close-knit social contacts, and has proceeded fairly steadily in the second half of the twentieth century. Armed with the annual figure for Troubles-related killings and the annual spread of the Northern Ireland road network, we can predict almost 99 per cent of the variation in Orange membership during 1959–2002. Road expansion explains the trend, and Troubles violence predicts the bumps (see Figure 10.10).

One might be suspicious of this result since Orangeism's steady fall may link it with anything else that is steadily rising or falling. For instance, generational turnover, the kernel of Putnam's 'social capital' thesis, may also be producing this kind of a trend. Importantly, a lowest common denominator of 'modernization' explains 99 per cent of the variation in the expansion of roads, cars, flights and family allowances in Northern Ireland over the past thirty years. This 'modernization' factor has the same power as road expansion when it comes to predicting Orange membership decline. Yet if we look at many of the modernizing trends across thirty independent annual statistics encompassing education, communications, demography and economics, their growth trend doesn't fit the rate of Orange membership decline nearly as well as road expansion. Figure 10.11 summarizes the results of tests using this data across three different models. Put simply, more mobility depresses Orange membership while more violent ethnic conflict increases it. This dovetails

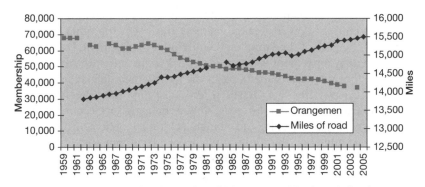

Figure 10.10 Orange membership and road expansion in Northern Ireland, 1959–2005

Sources: GOLI membership returns; *Ulster Yearbook*; *Northern Ireland Annual Abstract of Statistics*; Northern Ireland Statistical Research Agency <http://www.nisra.gov.uk/>

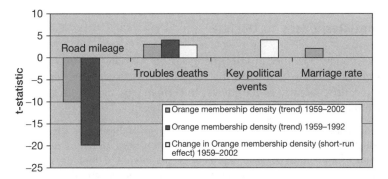

Figure 10.11 Predictors of Orange membership strength among Protestants, 1959–2002 and 1959–1992

with results from our geographic analysis in Figure 10.7 which found that Orangeism was strongest in DEAs with fewer migrants from other areas, that is, less mobility. Besides mobility, few other factors count. Moreover, the 'positive' effects of the Troubles for the Order's growth are outweighed by more than three to one (t = 9.94 vs 3.09 in Figure 10.11) by the negative effects of road expansion. The close relationship between variables makes it impossible to distinguish perfectly between economic factors like mobility or wealth and cultural ones like secularization. What evidence we have suggests that mobility is a more important economic determinant of membership loss than rising wealth or deindustrialization. Cultural factors (television, marriage rates) seem to impact most heavily on recruitment, but overall, mobility trends appear more important than cultural ones in explaining Orange decline. We can say with considerable certainty that Troubles-related deaths, though a

283

medium-strength predictor, are the only factor related to *both* long-run trends and short-term changes in Orange membership.[50] On the other hand, key events like the peak of the Troubles, the Anglo-Irish Agreement, Drumcree, or the Good Friday Agreement (GFA) tend to catalyse membership growth in the short term, but these gains are 'blips' in the trend which quickly fade away.

In whatever way the data are sliced, the most important determinants of membership are anchored in less sexy, slowly changing socioeconomic trends related to geographic mobility and changing cultural practices. In a perceptive display of its ailments, the Order invited Robert Putnam to address Grand Lodge on these questions in late 2005. The evidence is that television has a modest effect on recruitment, providing mild support for Putnam's analysis. Putnam's theory also appears to be borne out in the Orange membership trend, but since we have no way of parsing out the steady effects of generational replacement from those of road expansion, we cannot definitively confirm his theory.

Orange Responses to Decline

Concern about membership decline has been episodic within the Order, but Orange leaders have tended to shy away from discussing this vexed question until recently. As early as World War II, Fermanagh—which certainly did not have a recruiting problem—wrote to Grand Lodge to take steps to:

Make our grand old Order more attractive to young men throughout Ulster. [With] the introduction of cinemas, wireless, dances, badminton, bus facilities for reaching towns, etc, some measure must be taken to provide greater interest in our lodge meetings if we are to attract the younger generation to our ranks and having enrolled them, to retain their interest in the Institution . . . . [There is] no inducement to young men in country districts to travel perhaps a couple of miles on a winter's night in order to attend their lodge.[51]

When Grand Lodge responded that this was a county matter, Fermanagh's leaders wrote back immediately to 'express our surprise and disappointment at the reply sent by the Grand Lodge of Ireland'.[52] Little was said about membership until the early 1980s. Even then, where attention was paid to trends, this tended to focus on strengthening the relatively small junior movement through new activities.[53] As late as 1997, the LOI Commission put membership losses down to local population movements in places like Belfast and the city of Londonderry.[54] A committee appointed to look at 16–25-year-olds in the Order favoured stronger connections to youth groups, churches, and school boards and the creation of more of a 'family atmosphere' around Orange halls.[55] But as losses mounted, cries for action became more urgent. In the Republic, counties recently urged Grand Lodge to allow them to admit members aged as young as 15.[56] In Antrim, the ex-SOD hardliner

John McGrath called for mixed junior lodges to prevent them from folding altogether.[57]

In 2001, Castlewellan District in County Down wrote to the county expressing concern over the 'decline of membership of our Institution'.[58] Denis Watson spoke directly to this question at an Orange conference. Noting the poor quality of new recruits, he proceeded to berate the assembled delegates for failing to actively pursue new members actively and lead by example.[59] The extent to which such moral exhortations can affect membership must nevertheless be questioned in view of the economic, social, and cultural trends which are putting the squeeze on new initiations.

The Orange Order and the Protestant Clergy

Younger Ulster Protestants tend to vote DUP and show few signs of adopting more 'liberal' attitudes towards ethnic relations.[60] Their lack of interest in the Orange Order cannot therefore be linked to a 'post-sectarian' ideology such as perhaps appeared in Liverpool in the 1960s. Meanwhile, the middle classes left the Order long ago, and thus their opinion simply cannot affect the Order's membership. Yet it is possible that the Order's political activities have impacted upon a significant category of middle-class member: clergymen. The exact number of clergy in the Order is a matter of some dispute, being hidden by the steady number of chaplains at Grand Lodge level. In 1988, a survey of close to 500 Northern Ireland clergy found that 12 per cent were Orange members, with higher proportions among the COI and Presbyterians than among Methodists. In addition, many supported the Order by participating in Orange events: 29 per cent of COI clergy, 19 per cent of Presbyterian ministers, and 11 per cent of Methodist clerics were willing to do this.[61]

In the late twentieth century there was a steady decline in clerical participation. This trend was certainly absent in 1951, when a County Down request to appoint a lay chaplain was turned down and the lodge was told by Central Committee that lay chaplains were not allowed above the district level.[62] But by 1969, Cliftonville District, with 1,500 members, complained that it had just three clergy and none was suitable for office owing to their poor attendance.[63] In mid 1975, the Rules Committee finally recognized the reality of the changes that had already taken place and approved new Orange laws that would allow laymen to serve as private and district lodge chaplains.[64] By 1996, the Order began to consider creating the office of Lay County Grand Chaplain.[65] Under 0.5 per cent of respondents to the LOI Commission report were ministers, suggesting that total clerical membership in the Order is under 200.[66]

An important contingent—arguably the majority—of Orange chaplains are moderates like Warren Porter, William Bingham, Brian Kennaway, S. E. Long, and John Lockington. Their Orangeism sits uneasily alongside their membership in parent churches in which a majority favour an ecumenical approach towards the Roman Catholic Church. On the other hand, an important minority are also conservatives, such as the Rev. Mervyn Gibson, Stephen Dickinson, Ron Johnston, and the late John Brown. The majority sentiment among Orange chaplains is nevertheless moderate, and this was made clear at a 'chaplains' meeting' of twenty of them in 1997. On the parades question, the chaplains called for 'rational and realistic' decisions rather than simply 'sentimental' or 'emotional' ones. 'The Institution is vastly more than its public processions,' they wrote, in pointed reference to the Drumcree conflict.[67] Drumcree seems to have had an important effect on Orange clergy. Kennaway identifies three prominent ministers who resigned during 1997–2003, and the records show a number of others who left for this reason. In addition, several high-profile ministers who stayed in membership resigned from positions of leadership during this period. Kennaway also charges sections of the Order with being overtly anti-clerical, and suggests that this may have motivated the decision to reduce the representation of deputy grand chaplains on Central Committee in 1998.[68] All told, Drumcree did affect the position of clergymen within the Order, but clerical participation was already on the wane.

Discipline

One of the bugbears of clerical Orangemen is poor discipline. Kennaway's recent book exhaustively cites numerous instances of criminal and paramilitary activity among Orangemen which has gone unpunished by Grand Lodge. The case of the unruly 'Old Boyne Heroes' LOL 633 in Belfast, known as the 'UVF Lodge', is perhaps the most egregious example of paramilitary influence in the Order going unchecked. The lodge has many paramilitary members, and its bannerette honours five UVF men killed in the Troubles.[69] The important question that needs to be posed is whether matters have ever been different. Bryan argues that there has always been a tension between the 'rough' rank and file and 'respectable' elite traditions within Orangeism.[70] Orange laws which stipulate that members must first be expelled by their private lodge before being expelled by Grand Lodge helped to insulate deviants from expulsion for years. This suggests that Grand Lodge's willingness to discipline its members has never been strong. Indeed, only in 2001 was the Grand Master given the direct power to expel or suspend members who commit an offence. This power has rarely been exercised.[71]

The cases of Gusty Spence and Robert Williamson are instructive. Spence and Williamson were founder members of the reformed UVF paramilitary group in the mid 1960s, and were convicted of the murder of a Catholic barman on the Shankill Road in 1966. Spence's lodge, Prince Albert Temperance LOL 1892 in Belfast's Cliftonville District, contained many relatives and supporters who resisted his expulsion. Some traditionalists on Central Committee asked why these 'murderers' had not been expelled immediately, but the majority were more cautious and equivocal, seeking not to ruffle local sympathies. Rather than expel Spence, Central Committee, on a resolution from the Rev. John Brown, deferred the matter pending the outcome of a petition signed by hundreds of Shankill Road residents.[72] Spence and Williamson were only expelled a year later, after the Belfast County Master Martin Smyth (no doubt with Grand Lodge backing) put pressure on Cliftonville District and LOL 1892 to move against the two killers.[73] The Order employed a similarly cautious approach after the protests against the Anglo-Irish Agreement in 1986, when a resolution was received urging action against a Belfast Orangeman who attended a UVF paramilitary funeral. As in the Spence–Williamson case, Central Committee moved glacially, claiming that it was hard to 'prove' the individual's UVF connection, and citing the member's 'good standing' with his lodge. In the end, Grand Lodge agreed not to contest Belfast County's decision and did not proceed with expulsion.[74]

At Drumcree 2002, fifteen men known as the 'Drumcree Fifteen' were charged with 'riotous behaviour'; they were convicted at Belfast Crown Court and received suspended sentences. Many were Orangemen, and this caused tense debate within Grand Lodge.[75] After Portadown's David Burrows called for lodges to support the Drumcree protest by providing marshals, the traditionalist Richard Reid asked how many of those charged by police at the 2002 protest had been disciplined. Grand Secretary Denis Watson advised that some had already been dealt with and that other lodges were awaiting evidence. At this, Jackie McCallister told Grand Lodge that one of those charged had been acquitted at court of any wrongdoing and that the court had been critical of the police in bringing the case when 'there was clearly no case to answer'. He then attacked Brethren like Reid who condemned the events at Drumcree 'without being aware of the situation on the ground'.[76] Despite McCallister's defence, several of those charged by police confessed to their crimes. Even in the face of this evidence, Grand Lodge backed them up, with Saulters going so far as to accuse the courts and police of setting up the men. Kennaway suggests that Grand Lodge's defence of the convicted men's actions is an 'unprecedented' departure from the Order's 200-year-old tradition of respecting the law.[77]

The events of 2002–3 led the Rev. Denis Bannerman, a moderate Orange Grand Chaplain, to resign in protest. Still, Saulters was unrepentant. Referring to the resignation of the Rev. Denis Bannerman from the Grand Chaplaincy, and the latter's comments about obeying the lawful authority, the Grand Master said that 'not recognising the Parades Commission could also be defined as not recognising the lawful authority'. In other words, Saulters was reading a degree of latitude into Orange law rather than following it to the letter. This flexibility could thereby allow Grand Lodge to override its own statute in pursuit of a broader policy goal—or give moral support to those like the rioters who were seen to be working to advance the Orange cause. Thus Saulters in his December 2003 address to members informed them that 'Portadown brethren had asked for the large barrier . . . police had decided on the smaller barrier instead . . . an attempt to ensure that the PSNI were able to get at the brethren. People could lose their tempers in such situations.' Yet while three Orangemen were 'charged with riotous assembly for throwing stones, it was clear that certain people [i.e. Bannerman and other clergymen] in the province were quick to forgive IRA murderers. The Orange Institution had been formed to protect Protestants and the day that the Grand Master did not stand up for his members was a time when something was going wrong,' concluded Saulters.[78]

The Order has never been successful in quashing political dissent within its ranks and it has a similarly poor record in establishing central control over discipline. These trends did not originate under Saulters but actually remain unchanged from the pre-Troubles era. For example, detailed expulsion forms reaching back to 1964 show a very low level of ejection from the Order. Roughly a third of those expelled from the Institution during 1964–2002 committed the offence of marrying or cohabiting with a Catholic, and a further 11 per cent were ejected for participating in Catholic religious events like baptisms, services, or funerals. The proportion of Catholic-related offences has fluctuated from year to year over the period, but has hovered at around 45 per cent of all expulsions with no sign of recent change. Expulsions for crimes, fraud, and poor discipline (disciplinary expulsions) comprise around half of the total. Though they have never exceeded twenty cases per year, Figure 10.12 shows a good deal of variation in rates of disciplinary expulsions. The evidence is not clear-cut, but there does appear to be a slight decrease in the rate since the late 1980s, providing some ammunition for those who charge the Order with lowering its standards. However, given the annual variation in expulsions and the small numbers involved, we should exercise caution in interpreting these figures. Certainly there is no basis for arguing that Grand Lodge has greatly shifted its practices in recent years, since the power to expel has been sparingly exercised since before the Troubles began in 1968–9.

Recall that urbanites were disproportionately represented among suspended and resigning members. The expulsion data show a similar pattern and sketch the 'rebelliousness' of the Orange tradition in Belfast, Antrim, and parts of County Londonderry. Dividing total expulsions over 1964–2002 by 1991 membership figures, we find that the more law-abiding jurisdictions are in the border counties, while 'rebel' Antrim and Belfast head the list of offending counties (see Figure 10.13).

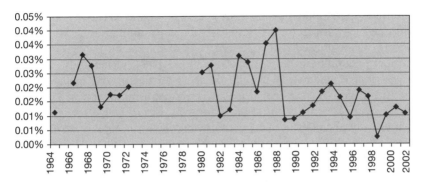

Figure 10.12 Expulsions for criminality and poor discipline as a percentage of total membership, 1964–2002

Sources: GOLI expulsion forms, 1964–2002; GOLI membership returns.

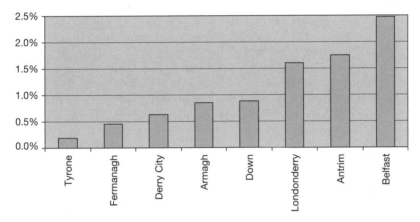

Figure 10.13 Expulsion rate per member (1991 base), by county, 1964–2002

Sources: GOLI expulsion forms, 1964–2002; GOLI membership returns.

The Order's caution in expelling deviants must be balanced with an appreciation for the very real stand taken by the Institution against paramilitary violence. This is partly related to the Order's founding obligations, and partly linked to its long-standing connections to the established forces of law and order, including the UDR and RUC. The Order thus prided itself on being law-abiding and respectable in contrast to what it saw as the indulgent attitude towards paramilitarism of many within the Nationalist community. As noted earlier, the Orange opposition to paramilitarism is real. Concerns about UVF and other Loyalist paramilitary activity first surfaced in Orange circles in 1966.[79] In 1972, some on Central Committee were reticent about giving wholehearted support to William Craig's Vanguard movement owing to its UDA connections. The leadership also rejected calls to support the 'Orange

289

Volunteers' paramilitary group.[80] In late 1974, Grand Master Martin Smyth continued to warn Central Committee about paramilitaries.[81] A year later, concern was expressed that representatives of the Grand Lodge of Scotland had met paramilitaries in Northern Ireland.[82] The leadership also implored lodges to give guidance to young members on staying out of paramilitary activity. In late 1976, a lodge in Ballymena (Antrim) sought to change its title to Ulster Defence Association Volunteers. Grand Lodge sent the matter back to Ballymena District Lodge, indicating the unacceptable nature of this title.[83] The lodge subsequently agreed to change the title to Ulster Defence Volunteers, despite being defended by the hardline Central Committee men George Morrison (Antrim) and William Douglas (Londonderry).[84]

Throughout his long tenure as Grand Master from 1973 to 1996, Smyth encouraged young Protestants to serve in the RUC reserve and UDR rather than join paramilitaries. In 1978, a Grand Lodge statement responded to the 'frequent' comment that members needed alternative channels to 'burn up' their 'energies'. Grand Lodge responded that the 'obvious answer' to this conundrum was to encourage the members to serve in the RUC, its reserve, and the UDR, where there was plenty to be done.[85] In 1981, in the wake of violence following the hunger strike and Unionist rallies protesting at the security situation, Coleraine District Lodge proposed to 'form an army' and asked private lodges to consider the matter and report back to the district lodge. Grand Lodge quietly let this proposal die.[86] In subsequent years, it regularly criticized paramilitaries and Loyalist terrorism.[87] Smyth also urged the Order to be more selective in screening against paramilitary recruits.[88] More recently, Portadown's Harold Gracey co-sponsored a resolution condemning the 'murderous' Orange Volunteers for usurping the 'Orange' label.[89] In 2001, Central Committee continued to express concern about the Orange Volunteers and called upon Twelfth platform speakers to condemn anti-social behaviour and paramilitarism.[90] Grand Lodge's 2004 resolution on 'State' again made its stance clear: 'We utterly condemn the paramilitaries, loyalist and republican, for crimes by which they dominate and destroy the lives of people and their communities. We condemn, too, the arsonists, vandals, burglars and petty thieves. The present level of lawlessness with its victims of all ages must be ended by the forces of law and order.'[91]

The Order leadership's stand against paramilitarism is beyond dispute and shows that there is no question of the Order ever having been in league with the paramilitaries. On the other hand, Orange leaders have also tended to see Protestant prisoners as symbols of the community whose interests need to be safeguarded. Thus in 1973, concern was expressed within Central Committee about Loyalist prisoners in the Maze prison, 'not all of them Orangemen', who it was felt were being held 'unduly'.[92] During 1981–2, the Order helped plead the cases of Gusty Spence and Robert Williamson with the Secretary of State and expressed unhappiness about the state of Spence's health.[93] A year later, Grand Lodge issued a statement demanding the segregation of Loyalist political prisoners to ensure their safety and resolved to take the matter up with the Secretary of State.[94] More recently, in 1999, Grand Lodge supported a lodge's call for an enquiry into the death of the UVF and LVF paramilitary leader 'Mad' Billy Wright in the Maze prison.[95]

In addition, the Order's strong RUC and UDR connections, as well as its 'traditionalist' respect for law and order, rubs up against its 'rebel' sympathy for defenders of the Protestant ethnic interest. Thus it has been willing to engage with pan-Loyalist bodies which include paramilitary representation. For instance, while wary of its UDA links, the Order (along with the UUP) backed Bill Craig's Vanguard movement in the early 1970s. Grand Lodge's equivocation over the activities of the shadowy Paisleyite USC in 1977 provides another example.[96] More recently, the Order has become involved in the Protestant–Unionist–Loyalist (PUL) network, which brings together representatives from across the spectrum of Loyalism.[97] The Rev. Mervyn Gibson, a key Belfast clergyman who also serves on the Order's Education Committee and the PUL, has developed a particularly important liaison role with paramilitaries through his chairmanship of the Loyalist Commission. Part of this activity is directed at pacifying the paramilitaries, but it also demonstrates the Order's shared identity with its wayward Loyalist cousins.

The Loyalist Commission first arose out of parading disputes in the Ardoyne, a contested Protestant–Catholic interface area of North Belfast, in 2001. As at the Whiterock parade in West Belfast, there had been violence here since the start of the Troubles.[98] The response from Loyalist paramilitaries and their supporters (which included rank-and-file Orangemen) was to picket a local Catholic institution. In the case of the Dunloy re-routing, Harryville Church was targeted. The Ardoyne re-routing led to the harassment of Catholic primary schoolchildren and their parents at Holy Cross School. Televised pictures of Loyalists shouting abuse at schoolchildren wrought considerable damage to the Protestant cause. In an attempt to defuse the dispute, a new Loyalist Commission was formed which included representatives of the main paramilitary organizations, the UDA and UVF, as well as trusted clergymen like Gibson and the Rev. William Murphy, a former Maze prison chaplain.[99] The Loyalist Commission has also helped to pacify Loyalist paramilitary wars like that between the UVF and Johnny 'Mad Dog' Adair's UFF (Ulster Freedom Fighters) or the UVF feud with the LVF in 2004–5. In 2003, the Loyalist Commission came under fire for continuing to include the UDA despite the latter's role in the murder of a 21-year-old Shankill man, Alan McCullough. It emerged that the leading Orangeman and Trimble advisor David McNarry played a role in the Commission. McNarry defended his position, claiming he was 'spiritually moved' by clergymen (like Gibson) on the Commission and felt it was important to engage with paramilitaries to work for peace.[100]

The complexity of the Orange stance is also evident in its approach to the marching bands that it hires for parades and the spectators who line the streets to watch parades. Together, the youthful bands and spectators often relegate the Orange marchers and platform speakers to a sideshow. Many of the spectators and some bandsmen may be identified by the blue plastic bags of cheap corner-shop alcohol that they carry with them. This 'blue bag brigade' tends to dominate the ranks of troublemakers. The Order's attitude to these supporters is ambivalent and reflects conflicting impulses. On the one hand, serious action has been taken against unruly bands. Band contracts dating from the 1980s banned paramilitary insignia, and this rule has generally been adhered to, though infringements led the topic to be seriously discussed at the meeting of Scottish, English, and Ulster Orange leaders at Liverpool in 2002.[101] Violent behaviour by bands on parade and on ferries across the Irish Sea are another pressing concern, and many Ulster and Scottish bands have been banned from taking part in Orange parades. A particularly nasty incident concerned members of four Scottish bands returning from Northern Ireland.

Ill. 14 Platform at the Field, Belfast Twelfth, 2005 —The speeches at the field in Belfast are a peripheral part of the Twelfth, and highlight the limited political consciousness of many Orange and Unionist spectators.

Ill. 15 Crude UDA paramilitary band banner —Though a majority of Orangemen disapprove of paramilitarism, the paramilitaries' rebel Unionism is so popular among urban youth that it has made significant inroads in some city lodges.

Stena Line wrote to the Orange Executive Officer George Patton as follows: 'Members [of the band(s)] were involved in serious hooligan activity and loutish behaviour . . . violent and intimidating behaviour . . . included bottle throwing, fighting (with bottles), lewd and sectarian chants and even the manhandling of children travelling on board.'[102]

A re-run took place a year later, when Stena described the involvement of a band from Cloughfern (Antrim) 'in serious hooligan activity and loutish behaviour . . . violent and intimidating behaviour . . . included smashing bottles, damage to tables, lewd and sectarian chants and even defacing uniforms'.[103] In both cases, the Order cooperated quickly with Stena Line and banned the bands from taking part in future Orange parades.[104] Other evidence indicates that the leadership is trying to exert control over band behaviour but faces practical limitations on its power. In a faxed letter to Grand Lodge, the Orange solicitor David Brewster suggested an addition to the band contract compelling bands to make a deposit which would be retained if they failed to obey the law. Brewster discussed the possibility of requiring bands to indemnify themselves, though he acknowledged that most bands would not have insurance and would probably refuse to accept this condition.[105]

Faced with unruly bands and spectators and a minority of 'rough' lodges and members, the Order's leadership finds itself with limited powers to assert its authority. Its inability to control its supporters at Ardoyne, Drumcree, and elsewhere is consistently used by opponents of Orangeism to call for further restrictions on Orange parades. In response, Orange leaders just as vocally defend their right to parade and disavow responsibility for the actions of spectators. But the Order does not look upon its spectators as a necessary evil in need of reform. Instead, its leadership tends to balance its desire for respectability (typified by calls for supporters to be disciplined) with a sensitivity to locals' 'rougher' standards and a shared sympathy with the Loyalist motivations of 'blue bag' supporters. An Orange report to the PC on the violence-ridden

Ill. 16 Bandsmen Drinking at the Field, Belfast Twelfth, 2005 —The lack of respectability of many bandsmen highlights the clash between traditional Orangeism and the new loyalist youth culture.

Twelfth parade at Ardoyne in North Belfast reveals that the Order is willing to defend the rights of its supporters despite their 'immoral' behaviour.

On 12 July 2002, two North Belfast lodge feeder parades passed between Protestant territory and the Catholic Ardoyne flashpoint area. Supporters were banned from accompanying the parades on their outbound route past the Ardoyne but were permitted to return home along the route. The PC chairman Tony Holland charged that supporters of the parade were under the influence of alcohol and behaved poorly. The Orange report defended the supporters' behaviour. As for the issue of alcohol among supporters: 'We would have strong moral views on the abuse of alcohol but are amazed at the moral judgement imposed by the Parades Commission. It is not for the Parades Commission to set themselves up as some type of religious police. This is Belfast not some Fundamentalist State.' The report also absolved the Order of responsibility for isolating troublemakers. 'Despite excellent work by the stewards and marshals they should not really be held responsible for this . . . how on earth . . . with the parade under attack could they remove some of the supporters and leave them to face potentially serious assault from the so-called protestors?'[106]

At times, the Order has allowed the shared ethnic interest between itself and its supporters to verge on support for violence. For instance, PC documents leaked during the 'Stormontgate' affair showed certain West Belfast Orangemen appearing to admit that Orange actions fuelled the disorder at the Whiterock parade of 2000, though this may have been a tactical argument designed to get the next parade through. If the parade was not permitted up the Ainsworth Link, warned West Belfast Orangemen, there would be 'violence for days' from local Loyalists.[107] A reprise of these events took place in September 2005 when the Whiterock parade (previously re-routed in July) was again re-routed from Springfield Road to the Mackies factory site. This decision followed in the wake of a number of perceived concessions to Nationalists, including the release of the Shankill bomber Sean Kelly, the announcement of the disbandment of the Royal Irish Regiment home battalions, and the return of the Colombia Three. The result was some of the worst rioting since the end of the Troubles. Over 100 bullets were fired at police, many of which found the metal of police vans but luckily failed to hit any officers. More than 150 blast bombs and 1,000 petrol bombs were thrown at the riot and over 100 vehicles hijacked. The response was linked to both paramilitary orchestration and popular anger over concessions to Nationalists.[108]

In the aftermath, the British government withdrew its recognition of the ceasefires of the UVF and the Red Hand Commando, a small Loyalist paramilitary group often associated with the UVF. Northern Ireland's chief constable, Sir Hugh Orde, claimed that the Order was 'largely responsible' for the rioting because it had called for support on the streets for a march along a banned route. Despite scenes of Orangemen clearly involved in the riot, the response from Orange leaders was remarkably equivocal. The Belfast County Grand Master, Dawson Baillie, was unrepentant. 'As far as I am concerned the violence was started by the police,' he charged. In addition, Baillie initially refused to condemn the violence. Only later, when pressed, did he allow that he did not condone it. Asked if he would do things differently if he had the weekend over again he retorted: 'Not one thing.'[109]

Saulters walked a path closer to the traditional Orange line than Baillie, beginning by condemning the violence and expressing sadness at it. However, even Saulters accused the police of instigating the riot and declared that while 'this does not excuse the violence . . . it does go some way to explaining it'. He added: 'For years we have seen nationalists achieve what they want by violence and the threat of violence. In these circumstances, when frustrated and with no other option, we should not be surprised that some individuals resort to violence.' Saulters told the press that 'decent and responsible men have been goaded into behaving out of character by the authorities and their insistence on appeasing and rewarding nationalists at the expense of loyalists'.[110] Though always careful to defend the Unionist community, previous Orange leaders would have tried to isolate paramilitary elements as the source of trouble and urge respectability. Drumcree provides only a partial exception since Orange leaders pinned the blame on extra-Orange elements. Thus the Whiterock statements show an unprecedented equivocation on the violence issue reaching up to the highest layers of the Institution.

In the aftermath of the riot, a report produced by the Grand Lodge (clearly written from Belfast's point of view) for its members focused on criticizing the heavy-handedness of the police and blasting the media for biased coverage. Peter Hain, 'with his United Ireland agenda' was fingered as public enemy number one. Hain's left-wing support for Irish Nationalism came back to haunt him as Orange writers resurrected a quote from 1986 in which he remarked: 'I think it's helpful, from the point of view of people who wish to seek a united Ireland, to have the loyalist community in open revolt.' The US envoy Mitchell Reiss was derided as 'hardly a good friend of unionism', and liberal Protestant clerics and business people were dismissed as the 'usual suspects'. While not denying that Orangemen were involved in violence, the report flagged several instances of verbal and physical abuse of bandsmen and spectators by the police. The report suggested a 'caucus' of anti-Orange, anti-Loyalist forces with Hain at its apex. The aim of the police and the PC decision, it claimed, was to defeat the Order and demoralize Shankill Loyalists in order to convince Republicans of the neutrality of the police. 'The rioting was bad', the report admitted. 'But what of the lonely graves in country cemeteries . . . the children who should have had their fathers watch them grow up . . . the maimed, the injured in body and mind?'

At several points, the report repeated the point that violence paid off for Sinn Fein/IRA. 'The perception of the Loyalist community . . . is that violence does pay,' it argued. Citing the presence of Sinn Fein in government and the release of the convicted IRA killer Sean Kelly, the report's Belfast author declared: 'I challenge the Secretary of State . . . is it any wonder that the perception is that violence pays?' The report went on to issue an unprecedented degree of approval of rioting as a political act:

The news highlighted the hijacking and burning of a bus at Bangor, during which passengers were robbed. . . .The truth was very different. The bus was stopped and boarded by two young men, one of whom had a gun or imitation firearm. A person on the bus . . . started to ring the police on a mobile phone and the phone was taken off them. That constituted what was being portrayed as the robbery of passengers. The phone was later, we understand, returned through a politician and a clergyman.

Though not denying that the bus was burned, the Grand Lodge report complained that the press portrayed the event as a 'criminally inspired act', denying 'the rather obvious truth that there was a strong political element to what had occurred'.

'People were terrorised', admitted the report, but the 'government propaganda machine' was dividing Unionism by 'portraying the rioting as the work of mindless thugs. The reality is that the violence was a clear warning that the pressure pot within working-class communities was about to explode.' In describing the riot, the report alleges that police water cannon drenched onlookers, prompting an armed response from the paramilitaries.[111] At Grand

Lodge, the whole episode magnified splits between border traditionalists and the largely north-eastern-based rebels. A letter from a Tyrone district lodge spoke of the riot as a 'public relations disaster' which had damaged the Order. The letter's author spoke of policemen from his church who had been injured and parishioners who had lost their cars to rioters. The Rev. Culbertson agreed with the sentiments of the letter, as did the County Down Grand Master, Eddie Keown. Keown contended that there should have been an 'immediate condemnation of the violence' and that the Order could not afford to be 'associated with lawbreakers or paramilitaries'. He called for an 'urgent re-establishment of relationships with opinion formers'. Others expressed worry about the public relations impact of the riot.

Others took a more rebellious line, however. Several speakers from the affected Shankill District in Belfast were at pains to stress the factors (PSNI provocation, release of Kelly, repeated parade bans) that led to the rioting. One Shankill speaker named Mawhinney said that while he did not 'condone' violence, 'to condemn it was equally difficult' given PSNI brutality. Gibson agreed, saying that his information was that the PSNI was instructed to 'have a go' at the Orangemen. Both Gibson and Dawson Baillie underscored the anger produced by an underreported police brutality. They received some support from a Free Presbyterian, the Rev. Ron Johnston of Belfast, who reminded Grand Lodge that 'William Johnston of Ballykilbeg had broken the law' while 'there were deeper issues involved in the rioting'. The issue led to a cleft in views at the highest levels between rebels and traditionalists. Martin Smyth made a particularly poignant defence of the traditionalist case. The Order had to stand by its traditional principles, he argued. 'The Institution did not want the Grand Master to give leadership [i.e. condemn violence], and no PR effort could save the Order from its own folly.'[112]

Toleration of violence is not a perspective shared by most Orangemen. Orange survey research indicates that just 20 per cent of Orangemen feel that Loyalist violence is sometimes 'justifiable'.[113] This raises the question of why Orange leaders like Saulters and Baillie would equivocate on violence. In many ways, the question mirrors debates which emerged during the height of the Drumcree conflict during 1995–2001. In both cases, the Orange leadership found that extra-Orange support from youth and paramilitaries was helping to advance an Orange cause. Hence we may surmise that a shared Loyalism overrode differences between Orangemen and non-Orangemen on the violence issue and helped to bend the Order's unequivocal traditional commitment to law and order. But this is only part of the story.

A further factor is the growing estrangement between the Order and the police. During Martin Smyth's leadership, many in the Order identified with the mission of the police since they had served—or knew those who had served—in the RUC or UDR. However, police reform altered this relationship. The GFA included a police reform rider designed to answer to Nationalist grievances about the 90 per cent Protestant domination of the RUC. In truth, IRA targeting of 'disloyal' Catholic policemen was more of a cause of Catholic under-recruitment than Protestant discrimination, but the GFA needed to get the policing issue right in order to resolve the security problem. The government's Patten report on police reform which emerged in the wake of the GFA led eventually to the RUC being renamed the PSNI and introduced compulsory 50–50 recruiting along religious lines in order to bolster the Catholic presence in the police force.

Police reform, along with parading, north–south bodies, and decommissioning, is a staple of Orange opposition to the GFA.[114] Orange concerns that quotas rather than merit would determine recruitment and promotion were voiced regularly to the police. In 1997, Fermanagh Orangemen complained about discrimination against known Orangemen in their local RUC detachment. Subsequent reforms introduced the practice of mandatory 'notification' of fraternal memberships, which initially included the Orange Order but not the Nationalist Gaelic Athletic Association. This 'outing' of Orange officers was bitterly resented by the Order, and the Orange charge that notification violates Orange officers' freedom of expression formed part of its Parades Strategy of 1998–9. As of 2005, the notification issue was at the heart of conflict between the Order and the police. These issues are having real effects. Evidence from 1998–2003 shows that a number of Orange policemen who resigned cited a conflict of interest between their professional and Orange commitments. The frosty reception that some RUC men serving at Drumcree received in their lodges and on police lines (including being taunted by fellow Orangemen who knew them by name) prompted some to resign. The Patten Commission revealed that fewer than 1 per cent (300 officers) of the police force declared themselves to be Orangemen, a fact corroborated by the Order's internal survey of 1997.[115]

The fraying of Orange ties to the police—symbolic, political, and personal—combined with growing conflict over marching after 1995 to alienate the Order from the police. Tense meetings with local detachments, media sparring with the Chief Constable over parades, and conflict on the ground were the main forms of interaction with the Crown's forces of law and order. As with Orange ties to the Unionist political establishment and even the British government, the decline of links to the police marks a further step in the drift of the Order from its 'insider' position in Northern Irish society to an 'outsider' lobby alienated from the political structure whose interests it used to view as its own. Bryan and Jarman note that parades tend to follow the power that provides protection for marchers.[116] Where once it was the police who got the Order through hostile Catholic territory, now the only possible guarantors of Orange marching rights are the paramilitaries. The Troubles had already begun to undercut the reliability of the RUC's protective role, and it was the UDA that helped the Order march down Obins Street in Portadown in 1972. Still, such events were comparatively rare since most parades went uncontested and unrestricted. By the late 1990s, things had changed: the RUC was frequently mobilized to restrict Orange marches, and only threats from 'Mad' Billy Wright's UVF and non-Orange supporters could help sway the authorities over the Garvaghy Road route during 1995–7.

The willingness of Grand Lodge and the Belfast County and Portadown District lodges during 1995–2005 to empathize with the violent or unruly behaviour of supporters and certain 'rough' Orangemen seems to suggest the emergence of a new dispensation. Growing alienation from the police and the political system is partly behind this. But two further ingredients need to be considered: the change in urban Loyalist youth culture and paramilitary intimidation. We have already seen how the urban loyalist teenagers and 'twenty-somethings' that the Order desperately needs to recruit have become increasingly bored with their inherited fraternal and political traditions. This is especially true among the working-class and unemployed base of Belfast Orangeism. Young urban Loyalists, whether Orange or not, are often critical of the Order for not 'standing up' (i.e. taking action) for Loyalism. Belfast Orange leaders like Dawson Baillie are acutely aware of the need to win the backing of this key demographic if the Orange Order is to survive.[117]

Just as important is the pressure which young supporters and paramilitary men can exert on the Order. Belfast County officers often operate in territory where paramilitary membership exceeds that of the Order. The balance of power certainly favours the paramilitaries. Paramilitary control in inner-city Loyalist areas means that the Order comes into contact with paramilitary protection rackets that operate along parade routes. According to Mervyn Gibson, local paramilitaries play an important role in policing the 'blue bag brigade' of young urban supporters at Orange parades in Belfast like the recent September 2005 Whiterock march. Indeed, Belfast County officers have publicly thanked local paramilitary men for their protection services and are uniquely vulnerable to paramilitary demands.[118] These demands can come in various forms, like the requirement that the Order desist from barring paramilitary members from its lodges or expelling known paramilitary men—some of whom have committed criminal acts or behaved in an undisciplined manner while on parade. In the end, the sword is mightier than the pen, and the Orangemen must do the paramilitaries' bidding.[119]

Paramilitaries can also form part of the 'Loyalist community' of non-Orangemen that can harass Orangemen for acceding too meekly to PC re-routing decisions. We noted the abuse hurled at Orangemen at the 'tunnel' in Portadown during a protest march to police lines in 1986 and the threats to the families of district and county leaders who agreed to re-routings ahead of the 1997 marching season. Some of this sentiment was transmitted by West Belfast Orange spokesmen (likely the district officers) to the PC in 2000. Orange representatives—speaking against the policy of Grand Lodge—told of the 'extreme pressure' which the local community could exert over local Orangemen to defend their traditional routes. They said that local Orangemen were being abused in the streets by the local Loyalist community and accused of cowardice. They reported a fear of violence and paramilitaries taking over and threatened that further violence would occur if the parade was re-routed again.[120] According to Gibson, spectators levelled similar opprobrium upon West Belfast Orangemen for acceding to the PC decision to re-route the initial (June) 2005 Whiterock parade.[121] A further issue concerns relations between 'angry' rank-and-file Orangemen and the Orange leaders responsible for the safety of their men. The former leader of Sandy Row District (Belfast) George Chittick relates how he worked behind the scenes with police to ensure that significant police presence removed the possibility of conflict between his district's men and Nationalist rioters. A similar police presence at Drumcree and other hot spots allows marchers to avoid the risk of being attacked while saving face within their own community.[122]

Much of the problem in parade conflict situations is caused by the perception that public order decisions and politics can influence the PC's determinations. Although the PC is legally independent of political interference, its com-missioners represent divergent political agendas and have political antennae sensitive to how their decisions will be perceived. Thus politics implicitly affects decisions. Each parade application is reviewed afresh and previously re-routed parades may de facto be opened up in exchange for concessions elsewhere in the Peace Process. This creates a combustible climate and moral hazard which encourages Orange marchers and residents alike to strike fear into the hearts of police and politicians. The balance of threat to public order between Unionists and Nationalists is seen as a key determinant of a favourable decision. Secondly, the fact that each decision is in play encour-ages residents and marchers to exaggerate their grievances to win the political battle. Parading, it seems, has become a political football. 'We need a deal on parading once and for all,' argues Gibson.[123] Gibson is correct, though his prescription of replacing the PC is beside the point since moral hazard will be created no matter which body adjudicates. Instead, the situation calls for stable routes which should be impervious to demographic change. This means that certain routes should be declared permanently open and others permanently closed, thereby reducing the stakes which each side can play for. Prospective buyers in the housing market would simply have to take into consideration the unalterable fact of the routes' existence.[124]

The Order's Public Image Revisited

In the wake of the 1998 Drumcree parade ban, Orange leaders acknowl-edged that parade violence had done serious harm to the Order's cause through projecting a bad public image. The Order's Parades Strategy and Drumcree Winter Initiative of 1998–9 therefore decisively embraced the 'soft' logic of secular human rights and public relations. Though traditionalists in Kennaway's Education Committee resigned en bloc in 2000, their spirit of evangelizing to outsiders continued in the attempts by the Order to sharpen up its image at home and abroad. To this end, the Order developed a public relations working party in 2000.[125] In the lead-up to the 2002 marching season, the Order invested a good deal in media consultants to train its spokesmen and hold media seminars.[126] It was so impressed by the work of the public relations firm 'Reputation Matters' that its services were retained in subsequent years. An Orange Communications Committee was also established with a view to developing an efficient twenty-four-hour press response facility, and there was talk of building the Orange 'brand'. Wary of its lack of profile in donating to non-sectarian charities, the Order contributed £1,000 to Cancer Research UK and urged more from its members so as to 'develop a reputation as a respected and responsible organisation'.[127]

The Order also seeks friends abroad. As noted previously, it has been concerned about adverse media propaganda in the UK and USA since the 1920s. Curiously—in contrast to its pessimistic realism in other matters—it has consistently displayed a starry-eyed optimism that if only it could present its case to the world properly, it can win over the public. We see this optimism in the occasional trips to the USA by leading Orangemen between 1969 and the present to counter what was perceived as the propaganda advantage of Republicans there. The Order even considered setting up an information office near the UN headquarters in New York with the cooperation of the Grand Orange Lodge of America. Though meetings with government and private officials were often described as fruitful, few points seemed to come from this.[128] Few trips took place in the 1980s and 1990s, but in 1998, the Education Committee chairman Brian Kennaway visited the USA under the auspices of the Presbyterian Church, and lectured to American audiences on Orangeism.[129]

Yet the Order will have difficulty awakening the Ulster-Scots connection abroad. No one can deny the interest of the small number of genealogically conscious afficionados who recently established several lodges in Missouri and Alabama. While over half of the 40 million Americans with Irish ancestry are Protestant, most are simply 'old stock' Americans like Bill Clinton or George Bush who identify themselves as White Anglo-Saxon Protestants (WASPs) or Southerners. In addition, there is a serious antipathy towards white Anglo-Saxon Protestantism within the cultural elite that dominates the most prestigious universities and media outlets in North America and Britain. In the USA, this can be traced to the struggles between defenders of WASP nationalism and temperance, with their small-town 'dry' base, and 'wet' WASP cosmopolitans in the cities and their Catholic and Jewish immigrant allies. The conflict over the prohibition of alcohol during 1920–33 marked the first phase of this struggle. The wider battle ended only with the election of the first Catholic president (Kennedy) in 1960 and the civil rights movement of the late 1960s.

Today's version of this 'culture war' pits evangelical Christians and 'red-state' whites against an urban 'rainbow coalition' of white liberals and non-whites. For white liberals, the only version of whiteness that is marginally respectable is the ethnic whiteness of St Patrick's Day and Little Italy. White Protestantism is viewed as provincial or patrician, the opposite of multiculturalism, a ghost in the closet they wish to overcome through cosmopolitanism. In Canada and north-west England, the Orange Order was directly involved in WASP hegemony, and these nations' cultural elites also view WASPness as the 'other' against which multiculturalism defines itself.[130] This view of white Protestantism as illiberal, provincial, and non-cultural is a prejudice which any Orangemen or Ulster-Protestant has to grapple with in order to win the hearts and minds of metropolitan Britain and North America. The best hope for Orangemen is a revival of interest in the Ulster past among the conservative section of the electorate in North America. One pointer is the upsurge in interest in Scotch-Irish 'Jacksonian nationalism' by writers like Walter Russell Mead, Anatol Lieven, and Michael Lind. One study found a strong correlation between the proportion of Scotch-Irish in a state's population and its vote for George Bush's Republicans in 2004.[131]

The quest for international friends also extended to Israel when William Parkes of Lisburn District in Antrim requested that Grand Lodge look into the possibility of setting up an information office for the Order in Jerusalem. Parkes 'offered evidence' that the Jewish population would show 'much interest' in the Order, and the Grand Lodge reciprocated by forming a committee to study the feasibility of the project.[132] A year later, the committee reported that the Order should fund a house for displaced persons in Jerusalem. The report, authored by Parkes and Clifford Smyth, suggested that the home bear 'a Plaque which would explain the common bond between the Israeli people and the people of Ulster in their desire to maintain their own identity and resist terrorism and international lawlessness'. While some like the former Grand Master John Bryans spoke of 'the clear vision in the Bible of today's situation in the Middle East' with the 'Jews . . . reaping what they had sown', the proposal was passed by a majority at Grand Lodge.[133] Perhaps the notion of a tie to the Holy Land also had an appeal for the Ulster-Protestants as an Old Testament people, something which Don Akenson has pointed out.[134] As Grand Lodge remarked, 'The loyal people of Ulster will so act as not to lose for like Israel they know they can only lose once.'[135] The appearance of Star of David flags in Unionist areas in recent years bears testimony to the shared identity of these two covenantal peoples.

International efforts have been complemented by a changed attitude towards government funding. In the 1980s, David Trimble developed his Ulster Society partly to bid for public cultural funds denied to the Order by government funding bodies. In the 1990s this began to change, and today, the Order engages in strenuous attempts to capitalize on the community development and civil society funds of the GFA. Kennaway's Education Committee began the process of applying for cultural funding from bodies like the Community Relations Council (CRC), though its bid for funding for the 1798 bicentenary was rejected.[136] The Education Committee appealed against the decision, and then submitted applications to the CRC for three new posts of community development worker, economic development worker (rural areas), and women's development worker.[137] A year later, the GFA's funding was part of the Order's world-view, and it participated in exhibits of Protestant culture like that at the flashy new Waterfront Hall in Belfast.[138] The Order also sought funding for a Protestant cultural and heritage centre from Stormont's new Department of Culture, Arts and Leisure, whose minister was the Orangeman Chris McGimpsey of the UUP.[139]

Ill. 17   Orange Band, Waterfront Festival, 29–30 March 1999 —In the 1990s, the Order realised it was a cultural organisation which could fit in well with the new liberal discourse of multiculturalism, cultural funding and group rights.

The post-Kennaway Education Committee also began seeking funds for a full-time educational officer within the Order.[140] The result was an initial one-year funded post.[141] By this time, grant funding had developed from an optional extra into something expected as part of the equality and cultural diversity provisions of the GFA. When funding was not forthcoming—as in the case of an Orange-linked Somme Association project—government decisions were appealed against.[142] Funds were in no sense minimal: the government's 'Diversity 21' conference channelled £20,000 to one lodge and £5,000 to the Education Committee.[143] In 2005, the Order met the European Commissioner in Northern Ireland to protest at the under-representation of Unionist areas in grant applications.[144] Concerned to project its image outwards, the Institution sought to participate in the Republic in the celebration of Cork's status as European Capital of Culture 2005. Several lodges applied to participate and were embraced by Cork organizers, only to be turned away at the last minute owing to Sinn Fein objections.[145] Other proposed projects included a 'Twelfth Survey' cultural-educational event and an 'Orangefest' at which participants would carry Exposition-like passports, finishing up with a showcase night at the Spectrum Centre. The new House of Orange was also increasingly used for exhibits of Orange and Unionist culture.[146]

Orangeism also seeks to market its marches and culture as a tourist attraction. In 2005, members of the Order's Education Committee held their first

Ill. 18 LOL 145 Ulster-Scots Emigrant Ship Float, Belfast Twelfth, 2005 —This local initiative affirms the Order's revived Ulster-Scots identity and promotes the Twelfth as a tourist attraction

talks with the Northern Ireland Tourist Board (NITB) in an attempt to insert Orange culture into the tourist brand promoted by the NITB. This would include promotion of the Twelfth as a civic attraction.[147] The Unionist peer Lord Laird of Artigarvan, a member of York LOL 145 in Belfast, was behind his lodge's path-breaking decision to ride a float in the 2004 Belfast Twelfth parade. He describes the move as an attempt to promote the pageantry of the parade as a tourist attraction and adds that this is an example of what the Order needs to do to secure its future.[148] The float represented an eighteenth-century emigrant ship, underlining the Ulster-Scots connection to America.

As noted, the Order has shown a disproportionate level of enthusiasm for its small, non-parading American branch.[149] Billy Kelly, editor of the *Orange Standard*, has helped to author a series of colourful pamphlets which detail the 'Scotch-Irish' (Ulster-Scots) connection in various American states and feature prominently in the House of Orange. The Ulster-Scots revival, which has also informed cultural societies like the Ulster Scots Agency, amounts to an important reorientation of Ulster-Protestant identity away from its Anglo-Irish side. This may reflect the continuing retrenchment of Protestants from Ireland into the six counties and now into the Presbyterian north-east of Ulster. Some privately lament this new development, which they view as sidelining the traditional Anglo-Irish aspect of Ulster-Protestants' heritage.[150]

It may also respond to the greater admiration for the rebel stand taken by many Presbyterian forefathers who overwhelmingly supported the Patriot side against the one-third of Americans who remained loyal to the Crown in the American Revolution.[151] Perhaps John McGrath, a one-time SOD activist from Antrim, put it best when he told me that 'Loyalty to the Crown is starting to fade...we see that the Queen is not the Protestant person and England not the Protestant country it once was.' McGrath takes pride in the United Irishmen and his Presbyterian forebears, claiming that they fought the prejudices of the COI elite and also battled the Irish Yeomanry. Their campaigns, he argues, were battles for liberty rather than a campaign to be part of a United Ireland. He claims that many Ulster-Protestants are beginning to appraise the legacy of the United Irishmen positively, noting with pride that his Antrim lodge sits at the foot of Donegal hill, where the 1798 rebellion started. A firm DUP man, McGrath noted (even in 2003) that well over 100 of the 116 members of his lodge were DUP supporters.[152] These are intimations of a shift to rebel Orangeism, away from a traditional 'Loyal' Orangeism based on the Anglo-Irish heritage, the UUP, the forces of the Crown, and the COI.

11

Conclusion

The history of the Orange Order since 1963 is one of modernization. The secularizing, individualist, egalitarian ethos which swept through all Western societies in the sixties was refracted by the particular environment of Northern Ireland into a unique trajectory of change. Instead of ushering in an age of liberal individualism, ethnic decline, and lifestyle subcultures, modernity led to a rise in ethnic fundamentalism among the generations which came of age during the Troubles. Like young Muslims in Pakistan or Egypt, Ulster's youth have rejected tradition in favour of the fundamentals (albeit of ethnicity rather than faith). This has refashioned Unionism and the Orange Order much as it is reshaping Hamas and Palestinian nationalism—all of which should lead us to question Francis Fukuyama's easy notion that all advanced societies are heading towards a liberal 'End of History' while ethnic nationalism is a growing pain of developing societies.

The Orange Order is an organization dedicated to advancing the cause of the Ulster-Protestant ethnic group in Northern Ireland. It is nationalist rather than integrationist in so far as most Orangemen endorse the vision of an Ulster 'nation' within a multinational UK. Though they describe themselves as 'British' and eschew independence, most call their homeland 'Ulster'. They favour devolution rather than Direct Rule and dream of a territorially defined six-county Ulster nation within Britain in which the Protestant majority is secure and the Catholic minority is loyal and content.

In its two centuries of existence, Orangeism has imbibed certain patterned responses. 'No' Unionism—a resistance to changes in the political status of Northern Ireland—is one of the strongest Orange impulses. This stems from the fact that Protestants long had a dominant position, and hence it was rational for them to resist changes which effectively meant greater equality for Catholics and a loss of Protestant power. This dogged resistance occasionally remains rational: a British government which knows it will encounter stiff opposition from Unionists will think twice before proposing measures which will redistribute Unionist power to Nationalists. But the danger in this strategy is twofold: the British may become exasperated and impose direct control, as in 1972, or they may enact policy by fiat, as in 1985. In this case, only Nationalists and the Irish government retain a hand in influencing policy. A further cost is the bad public relations that a strategy of resistance produces in the UK and elsewhere, which can ramp up pressure on Unionist negotiators. The same decision confronts the Order at the micro-level: if it boycotts quangos that deal with fair employment, lottery funds, or parading, it cannot influence the decisions of these bodies or procure grants from them. There is a danger that the romance of defiance may overwhelm the need for strategic engagement with these bodies. Conversely, the hardliners may sometimes be right: a well-timed, defiant stand, if charismatically voiced, can sometimes inspire the membership and force the government to back down, as in 1974, 1986, and, arguably, 1996.

In the late 1990s, Ruth Dudley Edwards described Ulster Orangemen as 'ordinary men in extraordinary circumstances'.[1] She was commenting on the way in which regular Ulster-Protestants, most of whom lacked a university education or professional background, found themselves in the spotlight of the world's media and in the drawing rooms of its politicians. It was not always so. In the 1950s, most of those at the helm of Orangeism were well-bred patrician or mercantile leaders of Ulster-Protestant society. The backgrounds, training, and connections of men like John Andrews, Lord Brookeborough and George Clark equipped them for the task of dealing with the more manageable challenge of Stormont, the local press and an arms-length British government. They were facilitated by a more deferential rank-and-file membership, which looked to the Grand Lodge elite as a source of collective status and even patronage. Orangeism remained a vibrant tradition in both urban and rural areas, and the Grand Lodge openly backed the Official Unionist Party. Any rebels against the system were effectively held in check.

Since the mid twentieth century, the balance of power has steadily shifted away from the old Ulster elite into the hands of a new generation. The catalyst for this were the reforms of the O'Neill years. The growth of the British welfare state in the 1960s flowed through to Northern Ireland and raised the issue of which group would benefit most. O'Neill came under increasing pressure from his British paymasters to redress discrimination against Catholics in housing allocation, public employment, and the electoral system. But steps in this direction were seen by the Unionist grassroots as unacceptable concessions, and the Grand Orange Lodge of Ireland, as defender of the Protestant ethnic interest, felt duty bound to oppose them. As Unionist Party and Orange aims diverged, a wedge was driven between the two entities, placing intermediaries like the Orange Grand Master George Clark under intolerable pressure. Within the Order, the old guard wrestled with a defiant new breed of Orange populists who cut their teeth in the campaign against the reforms of O'Neill.

John Bryans was a compromise candidate for Grand Master who bridged two worlds. The first was the clubby atmosphere of the Ulster 'squirearchy' with their pseudo-English accents and private school education, who banded together in elite lodges, held high positions in the government, and moved in the top circles of Ulster society. The second was the earthier mould of the Orange populists, who rose through the ranks at a time when the old elite was beginning to turn its back on Orange membership. Yoked to this was a social revolution among the Orange rank and file: within a generation, the top and bottom of the Order were drawn from the same social strata and Grand Lodge resembled the Unionist social average—a far cry from 1900 or even the 1950s. Many in the new generation were increasingly unwilling to worship at the altar of their social elites. Out of the political earthquake of O'Neillism and the social revolution within the ranks emerged new leaders like Martin Smyth, James Molyneaux, and William Douglas. They owed nothing to the traditional Ulster elite. As Orangemen first and UUP men second, they were at home in the informal atmosphere of the rural lodge hall or Twelfth parade. Andrew Jackson, a man of Ulster-Protestant descent who founded populism as an American presidential style, would have been proud of them.

Smyth was a Belfast man, and Molyneaux from Antrim, which is important. There had always been a rebel tradition in Ulster, with particular strength in Antrim, which is heavily Presbyterian, and working-class Belfast. This tradition generally remained recessive, and even when it reared its head, as in 1903 with the breakaway IOO, it was never able to effect a radical transformation. Even the great Antrim outlaw, Ian Paisley, proved unable to push rebel Unionism to the fore. When he emerged onto the Orange radar screen around 1950, he was viewed by mainstream clergy and the Grand Lodge as a crank who would go the way of previous firebrand preachers. But his unerring eye for political opportunity and the tumult of the sixties proved the Order wrong. Paisley's core of sympathizers grew to include some Orangemen, who tried without success for forty years to persuade the Grand Lodge to normalize relations with the rebellious Reverend.

By the 1950s, rebel Unionism had its own fraternity, the IOO, and its own church—Paisley's Free Presbyterians. The preferred party of Independent Unionism changed over the years, but found a permanent home in Paisley's DUP in 1971. Finally, the rebels' alternatives to the police force were paramilitary organizations like the UVF, reborn in 1966, and the UDA, formed in 1971. True, the 'secular bigots' in the paramilitaries countenanced violence while the Antrim evangelicals in Paisley's camp generally did not.[2] But Paisley organized groups like the UPV or Third Force and criticized the Order for excluding paramilitaries from United Unionism. Moreover, he was always quicker to resort to paramilitary threats and civil disobedience than his Orange cousins. Paisley's groups may have been toothless, but they underline his willingness to embrace the politics of paramilitarism.

Grand Lodge either proscribed or frowned upon membership in all rebel organizations. Members of most of these rebel entities were in the Order in small numbers, but the ethos of Orangeism was resolutely loyal and traditionalist. The pillars of traditional Unionism were the Official (Ulster) Unionist Party, mainstream churches—especially the COI—the Orange Order, and the forces of the Crown like the RUC and UDR. Each traditional organization had its own rebel adversary which it constantly tried to control. Even so, interaction between traditional and Independent Unionism often took place through sympathetic intermediaries. In the Orange Order, County Antrim Lodge and occasionally Belfast County Lodge served this function, reaching out to the IOO, Free Presbyterians and DUP to build bridges.

During the testing times of the Troubles, the Order steeled itself against any attempt by the Northern Ireland Prime Minister, Chichester-Clark, to make constitutional compromises, reform local government or restrict Orange marches. As with O'Neill, Orange pressure—conducted through the medium of the Ulster Unionist Council (UUC)—was a vital factor in Chichester-Clark's downfall. Brian Faulkner succeeded O'Neill and succumbed to the same fate as his predecessors, squeezed in the pincer of British-driven reform and Orange-led counter-reformation. Though Protestants, many Orangemen among them, were being killed at an alarming rate during these years, the Order did not flinch. It resisted political compromises and showed absolutely no willingness to make concessions to safety. Martin Smyth began playing an increasingly prominent role in these years, becoming Grand Master in 1973. Under his leadership, young Orangemen were encouraged to join the RUC reserve and UDR, two police organizations targeted by the IRA. Though Grand Lodge advised its members to hoard weapons in the event of a British withdrawal and a unilateral declaration of a United Ireland, it deserves credit for taking a stand against paramilitarism and encouraging its members to respect the law.

The negotiations which culminated in the Sunningdale Agreement of 1974 were rejected by the Order from the start. Nothing less than a return of a majoritarian Stormont would satisfy the bulk of Orangemen, though there were always members who dissented from this view. No longer comfortable with Faulkner's Unionist Party elite, the Orange Order had become a political outsider and served as the glue which bound together a United Unionist opposition front. United Unionism even brought Ian Paisley into its big tent, despite his obstructionism and political petulance towards the Order. Together, the United Unionists defeated Sunningdale and kept Faulkner's reformed Unionism at bay through the mid seventies. Though the Unionist front collapsed in 1977, the reconstituted UUP had successfully recast its image from liberal modernizer to anti-power-sharing bulwark. Smyth maintained a close relationship with the Deputy Grand Master James Molyneaux, who became UUP leader in 1979 after leading the 'no' Unionist MPs at Westminster. Throughout the 1970s, 1980s, and early 1990s, a succession of British initiatives designed to reconstitute the relationship between Protestant and

Catholic and to carve out a role for the Irish government crashed against the rock of Orange–UUP rejectionism.

'No' Unionism won elections for the UUP and kept Paisley at bay. Orangemen were naturally comfortable with a philosophy which resisted changes to the constitutional status of Northern Ireland, but did so within the confines of its traditional party. The important minority of Ulster-Protestant voters who endorsed power-sharing were probably not in the Order in significant numbers. Concentrated among the well-educated in greater Belfast, these 'civic' Unionists seem utterly absent from local, county, or Grand Lodge discussions. The Grand Lodge's political success in deflecting power-sharing proposals nonetheless distracted it from the tectonic plates shifting beneath its feet. The most worrying trend was membership. Though Orangeism commands power through the media and its supporters on the streets, its clout is inseparable from its vast membership. With one in five Protestant men in a lodge, the wider Orange network of ex-Orangemen, Orange families, and supporters encompassed a majority of the Unionist community at mid century. The steady slide in membership after 1972, especially in urban areas, was caused by slow-moving social trends related to geographic mobility and a decline in the social connectedness among the new generation of urban, working-class Protestant youth. Simply put, television, independent marching bands, Rangers' clubs, and Loyalist pubs were more attractive for leisure time than the formality of the lodge hall.

This was not the way it seemed to dissatisfied factions within the Orange Institution, each of which pinned membership decline on Orange policy. From the right, militants felt that the Order had failed to take 'action' on behalf of Protestant Ulster which might inspire young Unionists to join. This was despite the fact that previous inflows of hot-headed recruits into the Order who joined for political reasons after violent events tended to leave almost as soon as they arrived. From the left, traditionalists like many Orange chaplains and members of the Education Committee believed the Order had become too political and had failed to enforce band discipline, control unruly spectators, and present a positive public image. Traditionalists favoured a return to religious principles and an adherence to Orange law, which they felt would entice respectable middle-class and well-educated Unionists back into the Orange fold. In reality, much of the small middle-class membership had left the Order decades earlier, and those who leave the Order today tend to be poorer than the average Orangeman and concentrated in urban areas.

Drumcree served as a lightning rod for volatile grievances of both left and right. The return portion of Portadown District's centuries-old parade route to Drumcree Church had been re-routed in 1987, and local Orangemen felt that any further changes to the existing Garvaghy Road route were unacceptable. Many festering issues were brought to the surface by Drumcree. Catholic demographic incursion into Protestant areas, increased regulation of parades, and a decline in Protestant power all played a role. Perceived restrictions on Orangemen's rights to freedom of expression and assembly were undoubtedly important. But what rankled most was that Orangemen saw the hand of Sinn Fein behind the rise of so-called residents' groups in Derry, the Lower Ormeau Road in Belfast, and Portadown. Following close on the heels of a Republican cease fire, the rise of the residents' groups was seen as part of a deliberate Sinn Fein strategy to win hardline IRA approval and blacken the Order. There is much to be said for this analysis, though it is equally true that ordinary Nationalist residents were genuinely receptive to the idea that Orange parades should be re-routed away from their areas.

In 1995, 1996, and 1997, the Orange Order successfully paraded the Garvaghy Road route. Orange success owed much to the mass mobilization of Orange and extra-Orange Unionists at Drumcree. Police calculated that the threat from Loyalist paramilitaries, undisciplined Orangemen, and their youthful supporters was too great to ignore. This persuaded them to permit a token march through and suffer the consequences of inevitable Nationalist rioting. Many could see that success came at a price. The Order's reputation in the UK and the world—which had never been stellar—took a pounding. Some traditionalist Orangemen resigned their membership or gave up positions of leadership. In 1998, the RUC was determined not to be outgunned and raised an implacable barrier to Orangemen and their supporters. Since then, the Portadown Orange Order has never marched home via the Garvaghy Road. In the same year, an independent Parades Commission (PC) was established, and soon came to be loathed by Orangemen, who associated it with a rise in parade restrictions. The Order resolved to boycott the PC because it felt that the very *raison d'être* of the PC's existence, parade regulation, targeted Protestants since marching is a more central feature of Loyalist culture and Unionists parade at ten times the rate of Nationalists. All of this was viewed against a background of continuing 'concessions' to Nationalists as a result of the GFA on wider issues like decommissioning and police reform.

In 1995, traditionalist forces had the ear of Grand Lodge. The Grand Lodge's Education Committee, with its emphasis on outreach to the media, clergy, schools, universities and even the Republic of Ireland, was endorsed by the leadership. The new Grand Master, Bobby Saulters, defended the rights of Catholic worshippers against Loyalist picketers (some wearing Orange collarettes) at Harryville Chapel in Antrim. Drumcree, however, split the Order, and led to an open challenge to Grand Lodge by the militant 'Spirit of Drumcree' (SOD) faction. SOD militants broke up meetings, heckled Orange platform speakers, and even occupied Orange headquarters. Their demands were almost identical to those of the splinter Orange & Protestant (O & P) movement of 1954. These included a tougher stance in defence of a particular parade route, the reform of Central Committee and Grand Lodge to make them more accountable, and an end to the link with the UUP. Both movements held mass rallies, but while the O & P was crushed, Grand Lodge took on board many of the SOD's demands. While the O & P took care to couch its claims in temperate and religious language and eschewed bully tactics, the SOD was bolder: downplaying religion, sanctioning violence, and openly advocating liquor clubs as a means to boost membership. The SOD also targeted the Education Committee, barricading the members in Grand Lodge for having the temerity to meet the PC in 1997.

By 1998, the SOD was losing force because two of its leaders, Joel Patton and Walter Millar, had been expelled by their own private lodges and backed up by County Tyrone Grand Lodge. Nevertheless, several SOD demands worked their way into concrete reforms to the structure of Grand Lodge. More importantly, between 1997 and 1999, SOD activism combined with anti-Trimble sentiment to shift Grand Lodge policy to the right. Grand Lodge began to distance itself from the Education Committee and its outspoken chairman, the Rev. Brian Kennaway. In 2000, the traditionalist majority on the Education Committee resigned en masse, forced out by a behind-the-scenes campaign. The new Education Committee was reconstituted by a conservative minority centred on the DUP councillor Nelson McCausland which was more in tune with the sentiments of Grand Lodge and the grassroots.

Ill. 19 Rev. Brian Kennaway —This Presbyterian minister became Belfast County Grand Chaplain and later headed the reform-minded Education Committee which clashed with SOD militants after 1995. Thereafter, Kennaway rose to prominence through regular press appearances and a hard-hitting book which excoriates the Order's leaders for bending to the militants' agenda.

Grand Lodge in turn was sensitive to the new mood within the Unionist electorate. As the Orange Order is a bottom-up organization, the leadership tends to stay close to the centre of gravity of rural and working-class Protestant opinion, and the trajectory of this period is no different. The GFA's popularity within the Unionist electorate plummeted when it was learned that Sinn Fein would be in government without prior decommissioning. Reform of the RUC didn't help matters, and Trimble's stock began to sink. Although the UUP backed Trimble by a slim majority of 50–60 per cent between 1999 and 2003, three-quarters of Orange UUC delegates were anti-Agreement in 2003, and Martin Smyth's 2000 leadership campaign against Trimble fell by only a 57–43 margin. In the years to come, Orange delegates and their allies repeatedly blocked the desires of UUP modernizers like Trimble and James Cooper to break the Orange link and reconstitute the party along more centralized lines.

In late 2003, Ian Paisley's DUP defeated the UUP in the Assembly elections, for the first time in Northern Ireland history. Paisley won 51 per cent of Unionist votes, as against just 45 per cent cast for Trimble. In truth, if we account for variations in type of contest, the UUP had been losing ground to the DUP in every election since 1997. The GFA accounted for much of its unpopularity, but, as with Orangeism, slow-moving social changes were eroding support for traditional Unionism. In 1978 and 1992, younger Unionists significantly favoured the DUP over the UUP, but other factors were more important. In 2001, the latter was no longer true: age was by far the strongest predictor of a DUP vote as against a UUP one. Evidently, it was only a matter of time before the younger generation tossed out the UUP. These changes buffeted the Order as DUP influence began to increase. Saulters ceased his support for the UUP, and new DUP men like Grand Secretary Denis Watson held high positions in the Order. Today, many staunch UUP supporters remain within Grand Lodge, but—despite a few exceptions such as David McNarry—they do not support the Agreement. The Orange rank and file now leans slightly closer to the DUP than the median Unionist voter, with fewer than a third backing the UUP. In 2005, Grand Lodge recognized the inevitable and cut the 100-year cord binding party and Order. This is truly the beginning of a new era for Orange politics.

In the meantime, parading remains the core concern for the Order. Marching restrictions have always caused the Order to express outrage, and parade bans have generally been the number one issue for Orangemen. This is partly because parades express power over territory, but is equally due to the fact that for most Orangemen, the pageantry of the parade is the reason why they join. For this reason, local Orangemen are often much more willing than Grand Lodge to negotiate—via proxies—with Nationalists if they think this will get their parade back. A precedent for this was established by the Apprentice Boys of Derry, who negotiated with local mediators and residents' groups for the right to parade, and have held violence-free marches since 2001.[3] Since 2000, Portadown District, Derry City, Bellaghy, and other areas that have experienced parading restrictions have spoken to the PC in defiance of Grand Lodge policy. In 2005, two leading Portadown Orangemen joined the PC, again without the approval of Grand Lodge. Although a majority of Orangemen (two to one) endorse the current Grand Lodge policy of no contact with the Commission, the issue is proving extremely divisive, pitting

Orangemen from Nationalist-majority areas against those from zones with comfortable Protestant majorities.

Discipline is another bone of contention, with rebels arrayed against traditionalists. While political traditionalism is now on the defensive within the Order, most Orangemen remain critical of paramilitarism and violence at Orange parades. Though unruly Orangemen are seldom expelled for poor discipline or even criminal acts, this is nothing new. Through the years, the decentralized structure of the Order and its disciplinary mechanisms have protected many miscreants from expulsion. On the other hand, the collapse of Orange recruiting in the main cities and larger towns has created a vacuum which paramilitaries have been keen to fill. The remaining Orangemen in Belfast and other urban centres must make peace with paramilitary protection rackets and respond to an impatient, pseudo-paramilitary youth culture in order to parade and recruit younger members. The riot over the re-routed Whiterock parade in September 2005 took place within precisely this kind of urban Loyalist matrix.

The war of attrition against the Parades Commission convinced leading Orangemen that they should rethink their strategy and embrace many of the initiatives first championed by Kennaway's open-minded Education Committee. Media training, public relations, cultural exhibitions, and tourist promotion are increasingly part of the Orange lexicon. The language of multiculturalism and collective rights has also made an impact. Hence the cultural funding which has flowed from the civil society provisions of the Good Friday Agreement has led to a new culture of grant writing within Orangeism. Kennaway's emphasis on exploring the ECHR has been taken up with gusto by some of the more innovative Orange strategists like David Brewster, Richard Monteith, and Drew Nelson. Whereas the Order once spurned the logic of secular human rights, it now pins its hopes on a legal challenge to the PC.

The story of Orangeism in the second half of the twentieth century is one of continuity and adaptation. Poor media coverage, an indifferent British government, and reforms dictated from on high are problems that the Order has complained about throughout this period. Its response was also unwavering: to reject reform, and back traditional Unionist institutions, but to try to use mass public demonstrations, media releases, and private lobbying to win support. Its efforts have resulted in a public image of a conservative, stubborn organization. This image is essentially correct. The Order does not make voluntary concessions, but it will accept changes if these are seen as inevitable.

As an English-speaking Canadian, I first became interested in the Order's Canadian branch, which exceeded the Northern Irish organization in numbers until mid century. Several Canadian examples serve to illustrate how the Order changes. The Grand Lodge of Canada has a long history of resisting initiatives like bilingualism, funding for Catholic schools, or the reduction in monarchist symbols. True to form, it mobilized against the new Canadian flag proposed by the Liberal government of Lester Pearson in 1965, favouring the retention of the Union Jack. Yet within two decades, the Order was using the new flag on its own publications. Liberalism had nothing to do with the decision of these largely rural Tory voters. Shifts in the public mood and declining membership helped convince the Canadian leadership that it should adapt. Today, Canadian Orangemen regret the fact they were slow to respond to the new Canadian nationalism.[4]

The same can be said for the Grand Lodge of Canada's decision to abolish the law forbidding members to marry Roman Catholics in the mid 1990s. The reality of mixed marriage and a desire not to be out of touch with potential recruits in a period of falling membership helped to effect policy change. Likewise with joint Orange–Knights of Columbus functions: the two organizations share a common experience of trying to survive in a difficult social environment. In Northern Ireland, we saw how laws affecting attendance at Catholic funerals were overlooked in recognition of the reality of secular political life. The perceived permanence of the Equal Opportunities Commission and ECHR has also led to a relaxation of the previous Orange approach to these bodies. The same may yet transpire with the PC if it is seen to be a permanent body with which Orangemen can effectively work.

Most UUP MPs and MLAs have been Orangemen. During the Stormont period, just eleven of 149 MPs were not in the Order, and even in 1998, three-quarters of UUP MLAs were Orange.[5] Although opinions varied a great deal within the Order's UUC membership—particularly between official delegates and others, and between border and north-eastern delegates—Orangemen always constituted the backbone of 'no' Unionism within the party. The decentralized party structure of the UUP made it a relentlessly populist organization in which elite modernizers could be repeatedly challenged by the Orange grassroots. Second, the electoral and party system in Northern Ireland effectively consists of two sectarian blocs. Ethnicity, rather than class, region, or ideology, is the dominant electoral divide. In ethnic party systems, few votes can be won from the 'other side', so parties win by portraying themselves as the best defender of their ethnic group's particular interests and have no incentive to tack to the centre.[6] Whenever the UUP acted against the Ulster-Protestant ethnic interest, the Order could successfully mobilize Protestants against the party, often in collusion with Independent parties like the DUP.

The contrast with Canada and mainland Britain is stark. In these places, there is a Westminster system with pragmatic 'catch-all' parties like Liberal, Conservative, or Labour, based on class ideology. These systems encourage parties to reach to the centre for votes beyond their ethno-religious base. Lines of class and region cross-cut the ethno-religious cleavage, making it much harder to mobilize voters along ethnic lines. Residential segregation, which underpins ethnic appeals at ward and constituency level, is also much less pervasive (except in pre-war Liverpool). The Canadian Orange Order was relatively successful in getting Orangemen elected to office: four Canadian prime ministers, at least ten provincial leaders, and no fewer than thirty Toronto mayors were Orangemen. The Newfoundland House of Assembly was half Orange in 1885, and the Ontario Assembly a third Orange in 1920.

In policy terms, however, the Order scored few successes because the Tories generally sought to appeal to both conservative Catholics and Orangemen, leading to curious formations like the 'Orange–Green–Bleu' coalition of 1856–7, which united Orangemen with Irish and French Catholics. Party almost always trumped Order. To take several glaring examples: the Orange Prime Minister Mackenzie Bowell, seeking Catholic support, tried to force the Protestant-dominated province of Manitoba to reintroduce funding for Catholic schools in 1896; in 1960, the Ontario Orangeman Leslie Frost, premier of Ontario, introduced public funding for Catholic schools; in the 1920s, the Orangeman Sir John Gilmour, Secretary of State for Scotland, obeyed his party and rejected the Church of Scotland's gift-wrapped request to limit Irish immigration to Scotland in order to reduce this 'menace to the Scottish race'. All told, the Orange vote in both Canada and Scotland was extremely difficult to mobilize because it was cross-cut by class, regional, and ideological allegiances. This reduced its power and enabled leading politicians—even if Orangemen—to ride roughshod over it.[7]

There is no indication that the political culture of Northern Ireland is changing. On the contrary, newer generations are if anything more ethnically aware than previous ones. This means that the Order will continue to be a powerful political force in the province even if its membership continues to slide. The end of the UUP-Orange link will reduce the ability of Orangemen to engineer crises in the UUC. But the Order's independence from the UUP will give it greater power as a 'swing' force whose endorsement both parties compete for. The UUP will almost certainly be unable to win the Protestant vote if it tries to rely on the small 'civic Unionist' constituency and the equally minuscule pool of Catholic Unionists. Victory will require an appeal to traditionalist Orange voters in Nationalist-majority and rural areas where parading is an important issue. Should the political culture of the province change in such a way that the ethnic cleavage weakens, then the Order, as an Ulster-Protestant ethnic association, will, *ipso facto*, lose power.

Such a change is unlikely in Ulster because ethnicity is entwined with divergent political visions. In Canada and Scotland, Protestants and Catholics may have skirmished, but no one argued over who constituted the sovereign and legal authority in the land. In Newfoundland in 1948, the Catholic third of the population largely favoured independence and a majority of Protestants wanted to join Canada, but many Protestants also opted for independence. The same was true, in reverse, for Catholics, muting the explosiveness of the conflict. As secularization proceeded in the 1960s, Newfoundland Catholics and Protestants began to realize that their commonality as Newfoundlanders against the rest of Canada outweighed their ethno-religious differences, giving birth to Newfoundland nationalism. Scottish nationalism, though more strongly supported by Protestants, also benefits from the fact that both Catholic and Protestant Scots can identify themselves against England. In Canada, Catholic English-speakers soon found they had more in common with Protestants than with French Catholics. Meanwhile Canadian nationalism, as a new product, was able to attract Catholic and Protestant in equal measure. The current cultural ferment in Northern Ireland, by contrast, is towards a deepening, not a bridging, of the two traditions. Ulster-Protestant cultural nationalists, many Orangemen among them, speak of an Ulster-Scots revival, and some have tried to carve out a pre-Plantation myth of ancestry tied to figures like Cuchulainn and even Patrick.[8]

The Order itself, as the leading ethnic association among Protestants, is an important ingredient in the province's social fabric. Yet despite being an ethnic association, it has an inbuilt code of ethics based on Christianity and civil liberty. The chaplains built into its power structure have been in the forefront of its traditional suspicion of militancy and violence. The Order's constitution, 'The Qualifications of an Orangeman', and its laws oblige members to uphold the law and the right of all citizens to worship freely. Have the Order's actions measured up to its ethical standards? The report card is mixed. Orangeism's principal failing is its history of resisting measures designed to equalize the economic and political status of Catholics and Protestants. It has also reacted suspiciously to policies designed to increase inter-communal goodwill and has been far too equivocal about the violence caused by its Loyalist supporters and some unruly members. On the plus side, the Order took a difficult stand against paramilitarism at a time when many Protestants were being killed and intimidated by the IRA. It stood by the forces of law and order and discouraged violence against Catholics and the police even as Independent Unionists called for military action. This undoubtedly reduced the numbers of Catholics killed in retaliation for IRA attacks. Full-blown tit-for-tat vigilantism backed by major political actors on both sides would have produced a far bloodier situation that might have degenerated into the kind of civil war which gripped Lebanon in the 1970s.

Times are changing. Catholics and Protestants are now relatively equal in Northern Ireland in economic, demographic, and cultural terms. Politically, police reform and the GFA are also geared towards equalizing Catholic and Protestant. But there is a difference. Protestants have suffered downward mobility while Catholics have risen. This may have been necessary but it doesn't change the fact that these two trajectories produce different outlooks. None of this is helped by demographic trends which favour Catholics over Protestants for some time to come. The violence also leaves a bitter legacy. For many years, a minority of Catholics, including one Nationalist party, killed to advance their political ends. The non-violent Nationalist counterpart to the Orange Order, the Ancient Order of Hibernians, never gained the same influence over Nationalism as the Order did within Unionism. Clergy, a moderating force, are central to Orangeism but never played a role in the IRA. On the other side, Loyalists murdered and maimed many Catholics, but they did so without the support of the UUP, the Order, the churches, and most Protestants.

With Nationalist political success, violent nationalism has effectively ceased. Might the reversal of this process among Loyalists lead to violence? Most Protestants were once loyal to the Unionist Party and the police. This helped them identify with respectability and law and order. But police reform, parading conflicts, and the GFA have alienated many working-class Unionists from the police, the law, and the government. It is worth considering for a moment whether political Unionism, which has hitherto been law-abiding, could turn to violence as a political tool. Imagine if the Orange Order and a radical Unionist Party were to establish a similar relationship to Protestant paramilitaries as Sinn Fein long maintained with the provisional IRA. The new Unionist Party and Grand Lodge would pay lip service to non-violence, referring to paramilitary murders and mayhem as 'regrettable but understandable'. They would urge the governments of London, Dublin, and possibly Stormont to make concessions or face continued violence. This strategy of putting a gun to the politicians' heads unfortunately worked for Sinn Fein.

Some feel that paramilitary violence gave Unionists important political leverage in 1974, in 1986, and at Drumcree in 1996. As Paul Dixon writes, 'Without the physical resistance of unionists and the threat of violence . . . the British may well have eased Northern Ireland out of the Union. When the power of unionism has been demonstrated . . . political calculations have been reassessed.'[9] If British policy is fear-driven, the threat of violence will prove attractive to Orangemen lacking ties to traditional Unionism and its respectable ethos. Is such a scenario so far-fetched? Already, we see signs of this logic in Orange statements made at the height of the Drumcree and Whiterock parade conflicts. Traditionalist Orange objections to this 'unchristian' violence are countered by a highly modern narrative of victimhood, identity politics, and alienation which urban Loyalists have cleverly imbibed from their opponents. Protestant emigration and Catholic growth may lead to spiralling Unionist insecurity which could tip the scales in favour of violence.

The worst outcome would see an increasingly embattled Protestant minority bombing Dublin and killing Northern Nationalists to protest their inclusion (or imminent inclusion) in a United Ireland. The greatest hope—and fortunately a more likely one—is that the demographic ratio settles at 50:50 and all sides realize they can never achieve dominance. Some seek a 'civic Unionism' to appeal to Catholic voters. This makes a fine theory, but ignores the reality of Catholics' attachment to the Irish nation state. It is also unattractive in that it seeks to replace the rich cultural traditions of Nationalists and Unionists with a set of politico-legal abstractions. Perhaps it would be better to make a virtue out of necessity and recognize that sovereignty in Northern Ireland will always be shared between Britain and the Republic of Ireland. Each ethnic group would continue to develop and express its traditions without seeking to dominate the other and would, it is to be hoped, move towards what I have elsewhere described as 'liberal ethnicity'.[10] Nationalists should be able to feel that they live in a United Ireland, and Unionists to see themselves as members of a well-defined Ulster-Protestant nation within the UK. Dual flags, passports, histories, and cultural activities can help. Hopefully, growing communal confidence will breed trust and ensure that identities become more relaxed, leading to interaction and intermarriage between the two groups. The history of places as divergent as the Netherlands and Newfoundland suggests that ethnic power-sharing arrangements will fall away when they are no longer needed. Assimilation of outsiders on both sides can maintain ethnic distinctiveness without the need for enforced endogamy. Finally, those who want nothing to do with either tradition should also be able to find a space in Northern Ireland to call their own.

The Orange Order will continue to have a cultural role as custodian of the Ulster-Protestant collective memory even if Northern Ireland's political situation normalizes. However, the social trend towards mobility and non-joining will make it very difficult for the Order to tread water, never mind regain its former strength. That said, even if the Order declines in Ulster as it has done in Canada, it will retain greater influence in Northern Ireland because it shares the same ethnic aims as the wider Unionist population. In this situation, one could imagine the Order developing as a cultural association and ethnic lobby. Part Ulster-Scots Agency, part Ulster-Protestant political caucus, the new entity would have to sustain itself through cheque-writing 'associate members', corporate donors, and government grants. Lodges have not yet begun to close in significant numbers as they have in Canada, where lodge halls often serve as restaurants or heritage village attractions or simply lie in ruins. Indeed, the Orange lodge may one day disappear from many urban parts of Northern Ireland. But in the southern and western countryside, traditional Orangeism will remain vibrant, nourished by dynamics different in degree but not in kind from those expressed at the Diamond in 1795.

Notes

Chapter 1

1. GOLI membership returns, 2004; 'What does Orangeism Stand for Today?' <http://www.grandorange.org.uk/parades/orangeism_stand.html>, accessed 3 Feb. 2004.

2. The latter point was highlighted during partition when brethren from the three Ulster counties left behind in the Irish Republic stated that their obligations 'forbade disloyalty' to their new state despite their affections for Britain. Similar sentiments later animated Donegal brethren in the mid 1960s (over the use of 'God Save the Queen' on official county correspondence) and mid 1970s (over the singing of 'God Save the Queen') (GL, 1923; CC, 3 Dec. 1965, 6 June 1975). In Canada, the ambiguous and symbolic link between the Crown and the Canadian state allowed monarchist sentiments to remain well into the 1980s. Though the Grand Lodge acted in the 1980s to accept the new (1965) Canadian flag and 'Grand Lodge of Canada' designation, this new conception is very much contested and coexists uneasily with strong reservoirs of Loyalist sentiment within the Canadian Institution (Interview with Canadian Grand Secretary Norman Ritchie, Toronto, 14 Dec. 1999, Grand Lodge of Canada, Toronto; interview with Newfoundland past Grand Master Ralph Roberts, Cupids, Newfoundland, 19 Aug. 2003, Grand Lodge of Newfoundland, St John's).

3. Francis Fukuyama, *The End of History and the Last Man* (London: Hamish Hamilton, 1992).

4. Anthony Giddens, *Modernity and Self-Identity* (Cambridge: Polity Press, 1991).

5. GL, Dec. 1997, 15.

6. Eric Kaufmann, *The Rise and Fall of Anglo-America: The Decline of Dominant Ethnicity in the United States* (Cambridge, MA: Harvard University Press, 2004).

7. Interview with Newfoundland Grand Secretary Garland Baker and Andy Johnson, Conception Bay South, Newfoundland, Jan. 2002.

8. GOLI resignation forms, 1998–2003; see Ch. 8 for more on the prayer breakfast.

9. E. P. Kaufmann, 'Dominant Ethnicity: From Background to Foreground', in Eric Kaufmann, ed., *Rethinking Ethnicity: Majority Groups and Dominant Minorities* (London: Routledge, 2004), 1–14.

10. On Britannic nationalism, see Douglas Cole, 'Canada's "Nationalistic" Imperialists', *Journal of Canadian Studies*, 5/3 (1970), 45–6; John Darwin, 'A Third British

Empire? The Dominion Idea in Imperial Politics', in Judith Brown and Wm. Roger Louis, eds., *The Oxford History of the British Empire*, iv: *The Twentieth Century* (Oxford: Oxford University Press, 2005), 64–87.

11. On West Africa, see private correspondence with James Gibbs re the Ewe playwright and Orange founder Fiawoo, 17 Mar. 2003. See also David Brown, *Contemporary Nationalism* (London: Routledge, 2000), 116–18 on persecution of the Ewe by the Akan majority in Ghana. On Eire, see *Protestants in Community Life: Findings from a Donegal Survey* (Derry: Derry and Raphoe Action, June 2001), 3–7. On Scotland, see Eric Kaufmann, 'The Dynamics of Orangeism in Scotland: Social Sources of Political Influence in a Mass-Member Organization', *Social Science History*, 30/2 (2006), 263–92.

12. *The Orange Order: Forward within the Community* (Belfast: GOLI, Jan. 2003).

13. Anthony D. Smith, *National Identity* (London: Penguin, 1991).

14. B. O'Leary and J. McGarry, *Explaining Northern Ireland: Broken Images* (Oxford: Basil Blackwell, 1995), 212, 306; Steve Bruce, *The Edge of the Union: The Ulster Loyalist Political Vision* (Oxford: Oxford University Press, 1994).

15. Adrian Hastings, *The Construction of Nationhood: Ethnicity, Religion and Nationalism* (Cambridge and New York: Cambridge University Press, 1997); Connor Cruise O'Brien, *God-Land: Reflections on Religion and Nationalism* (Cambridge, MA: Harvard University Press, 1988); Donald Harman Akenson, *God's Peoples: Covenant and Land in South Africa, Israel, and Ulster* (Ithaca: Cornell University Press, 1992).

16. John Armstrong, *Nations before Nationalism* (Chapel Hill: University of North Carolina Press, 1982).

17. LOI Commission Report, 1997 (GOLI).

18. This shift in sensibility, used to describe recent shifts in Canadian political culture, also characterizes the Ulster Unionist community. See Peter C. Newman, *The Canadian Revolution: From Deference to Defiance* (Toronto: Viking, 1995).

19. Based on forty-five county-year samples at census years compiled from surviving county reports; hence there is a good deal of missing data—especially for Derry City, Fermanagh, and Armagh in the pre-1961 period. For detailed statistical ouput, see <http://www.sneps.net/OO/bk1stats.htm>.

20. Cecil Houston and William J. Smyth, *The Sash Canada Wore: A Historical Geography of the Orange Order in Canada* (Toronto and Buffalo: University of Toronto Press, 1980).

21. Mancur Olson, *The Rise and Decline of Nations: Economic Growth, Stagflation and Social Rigidities* (New Haven and London: Yale University Press, 1982); John McCarthy and Meyer Zald, 'Resource Mobilization and Social Movements: A Partial Theory', *American Journal of Sociology*, 82/6 (1977), 1212–41.

22. Interview with the Tyrone Orangeman and former EC member Henry Reid, near Omagh, 14 Mar. 2000.

23. R. Hague and M. Harrop, *Comparative Government and Politics: An Introduction* (5th edn, Basingstoke: Palgrave, 2001), ch. 10.

24. Dominic Bryan, *Orange Parades: The Politics of Ritual, Tradition and Control* (London: Pluto, 2000), 77, 180.

25. D. Horowitz, *Ethnic Groups in Conflict* (Berkeley: University of California Press, 1985), 347.

26. More discussion of the way in which organizations evolve structures in response to a particular environment can be found in Arthur L. Stinchcombe, *Constructing Social Theories* (Harcourt, Brace & World, 1968).

27. GL, June 1949, 16–17.

28. GL, June 1922, 14.

29. GL, 1926; SOD press release, 1997.

30. Bryan, *Orange Parades*, 102.

31. John Higham, *Strangers in the Land: Patterns of American Nativism, 1860–1925* (2nd edn, New Brunswick: Rutgers University Press, 1988).

32. County Tyrone Grand Lodge minutes, 28 Oct. 1967, courtesy of Tyrone Grand Lodge (held by the current secretary).

33. Bryan, *Orange Parades*, 102.

34. GL, Dec. 1935, 24.

35. CC, 5 Dec. 1968.

36. CC, 8 Dec. 1971.

37. CC, 7–8 Apr. 1972. 'The Twelfth' refers to the Order's annual 12 July parades, in which all local Orangemen are obliged to take part, and which are watched by thousands of mainly Unionist spectators. These take place all over Northern Ireland, but the largest event occurs in Belfast and finishes at a park or 'field' in Finaghy, North Belfast, where leading Orangemen and Unionist politicians make speeches from a platform.

38. Steve Bruce, *Comparative Protestant Politics* (Oxford: Oxford University Press, 1998), 6.

39. Fearghal Cochrane, *Unionist Politics* (Cork: Cork University Press, 2001), 83.

40. J. Todd, 'Two Traditions in Unionist Political Culture', *Irish Political Studies*, 2 (1987), 1–26. The Order was, for example, suspicious of the militancy of John Cormack and Alexander Ratcliffe in Scotland in the interwar period. In Canada, it distanced itself from the Protestant Protective Association, and in Northern Ireland it has kept Independent Unionism and the paramilitaries at arm's length.

41. Donald Harman Akenson, *The Irish in Ontario: A Study in Rural History* (Kingston and Montreal: McGill-Queen's University Press, 1984); Madeline A. Richard, *Ethnic Groups and Marital Choices: Ethnic History and Marital Assimilation in Canada, 1871 and 1971* (Vancouver: UBC Press, 1991).

42. Eric Kaufmann, 'The Orange Order in Ontario, Newfoundland, Scotland and Northern Ireland: A Macro-Social Analysis', in David A. Wilson, ed., *The Orange Order in Canada* (Dublin: Four Courts, forthcoming); Hereward Senior, *Orangeism, the Canadian Phase* (Toronto and New York: McGraw-Hill Ryerson, 1972); Houston and Smyth, *The Sash Canada Wore*.

43. Bryan, *Orange Parades*, 39, 45–7.

44. Ibid., 52–3.

45. Though he graces IOO Twelfth platforms, Paisley is not a member.

46. Interview with John McGrath, 6 Mar. 2003; CC, 27 Sept. 1963, 4 Dec. 1964, Apr. 1965; GL, June 1967, 14.

47. The Official Unionist Party, often simply called the 'Unionist Party', became known as the Ulster Unionist Party (UUP) in the early 1970s.

Chapter 2

1. Billy Kennedy, *News Letter* (Belfast, 3 Mar. 2005), 8.

2. Dominic Bryan, *Orange Parades: The Politics of Ritual, Tradition and Control* (London, Pluto, 2000).

3. GL, Dec. 1946, 48–55.

4. Henry Patterson and Eric Kaufmann, *Unionism and Orangeism in Northern Ireland since 1945* (Manchester: Manchester University Press, forthcoming).

5. Ibid.

6. CC, Oct. 1951; GL, Dec. 1951.

7. CC, Oct. 1952.

8. Patterson and Kaufmann, *Unionism and Orangeism*.

9. Bryan, *Orange Parades*, 76

10. CC, 29 July 1959; Patterson and Kaufmann, *Unionism and Orangeism*.

11. Patterson and Kaufmann, *Unionism and Orangeism*.

12. CC, 2 Oct. 1964, 4 Dec. 1964; Andrew Boyd, *Holy War in Belfast* (Tralee, Ireland: Anvil Books, 1969), ch. 11.

13. Martin Smyth—whose social origins did not lie with the elite—formed part of Central Committee's growing populist minority at this point, though his accession to the Grand Mastership in little more than five years led him to moderate these tendencies.

14. GL, June 1956, 12; Tyrone County Lodge minutes, 1959, courtesy of Tyrone Grand Lodge (held by the current secretary).

15. CC, 2 Oct. 1964.

16. CC, June 1952.

17. GL, Dec. 1965, 32.

18. Ibid.

19. G.W. Dunn, leader of the rebellious O & P, was a member of Ballymacarett LOL 1310 in 1954.

20. CC, Apr. 1965.

21. GL, June 1965, 8.

22. Letter from Lord Brookeborough, Richard Thornton, and George Elliott to Grand Secretary Walter Williams, 26 Mar. 1966.

23. Tyrone County minutes, 1966.

24. Letter from George Clark to Terence O'Neill, 1 Apr. 1966.

25. Letter from O'Neill to George Clark, 5 Apr. 1966.

26. Circular to lodges from Clark, 5 Apr. 1966.

27. CC, 3 June 1966; Bryan, *Orange Parades*.

28. CC, 3 June 1966.

29. CC, 3 Dec. 1966.

30. GL, June 1966, 15–30.

31. GL, June 1966, 14.

32. GL, June 1966, 13.

33. CC, 3 June 1966.

34. CC, 7 Oct. 1966.

35. CC, 10 May 1967.

36. Letter from Killyman District Lodge 1 secretary to County Tyrone Grand Lodge, 12 Oct. 1966; letter from David Martin, secretary of Tullyhogue LOL 111 (south of Cookstown, County Tyrone), undated, *c*. Oct. 1966.

37. CC, 7 Oct. 1966; GL, Dec. 1966, 9.

38. CC, 3 Dec. 1966.

39. GL, June 1967, 11–12.

40. CC, 3 Dec. 1966, 2 Feb. 1967.

41. CC, 10 Feb. 1967.

42. Ibid.

43. Ibid.

44. Minutes of meeting between Orange and government representatives, 14 Mar. 1967.

45. CC, 10 May 1967.

46. GL, June 1967, 18, 27–8.

47. Bryan, *Orange Parades*, 81–2; GL, Dec. 1968, 8.

48. CC, 10 Feb. 1967.

49. CC, 9 June 1967, 6 Oct. 1967; GL, June 1967.

50. CC, 5 Jan. 1968.

51. GL, Feb. 1968, 13.

52. CC, Jan. 1968.

53. GL, Feb. 1968; CC, 26 Apr. 1968.

54. GL, Feb. 1968, 16–17.

55. CC, 26 Apr. 1968.

56. Ibid.

57. GL, June 1968, p. 16; CC, 27 Sept. 1968.

58. CC, 5 Dec. 1968; GL, Dec. 1968.

59. *BT* (11 June 1968).

60. *News Letter* (Belfast, 12 June 1968).

61. GL, June 1968, 14.

62. *News Letter* (Belfast, 13 June 1968).

63. *BT* (13 June 1968).

64. GL, Feb. 1968, 18.

65. This will be discussed in more detail in Ch. 6.

66. CC, 26 Apr. 1968; GL, June 1968, 15.

67. Minutes of meeting between Orange and Unionist Party representatives, 28 Oct. 1968.

68. CC, 8 Nov. 1968.

69. *The Re-Shaping of Local Government* (Belfast: Government of Northern Ireland, 1967).

70. GL, Feb. 1968, 14.

71. GOLI special committee meeting minutes, 28 Feb. 1968.

72. CC, 26 Apr. 1968.

73. CC, 27 Sept. 1968.

74. Ibid.

75. CAIN events 1968, accessed Nov. 2005.

76. Graham Walker, *A History of the Ulster Unionist Party: Protest, Pragmatism and Pessimism* (Manchester: Manchester University Press, 2004), 166.

77. GL, Feb. 1968; CC, 8 Nov. 1968.

78. CC, 8 Nov. 1968. In the previous Central Committee meeting, Clark had asked Brown to forcefully make his case in the upcoming meeting with the government.

79. Minutes of meeting of Orange deputation, Prime Minister, and Minister of Home Affairs at Stormont Castle, 14 Nov. 1968.

80. Tyrone County Lodge minutes, 27 Nov. 1968; GL, Dec. 1968, 38.

81. GL, Dec. 1968, 34.

82. CC, 10 Jan. 1969.

83. Ruth Dudley Edwards, *The Faithful Tribe: An Intimate Portrait of the Loyal Institutions* (London: Harper Collins, 1999), 64.

84. For more on Henderson's activities as a leading UUP reformer, see Patterson and Kaufmann, *Unionism and Orangeism*.

85. Cliftonville District Lodge 3 (Belfast) minutes, 11 Feb. 1969.

86. Belfast County minutes, 11 Mar. 1969.

87. Ibid.

88. Walker, *History of the Ulster Unionist Party*, 171.

89. Cliftonville District Lodge 3 minutes, 25 Mar. 1969, 24 June 1969.

90. Cliftonville District Lodge 3 minutes; Belfast County report of proceedings, 1967–8.

91. Cliftonville District Lodge 3 minutes, 11 Feb. 1969, 25 Feb. 1969.

92. Cliftonville District Lodge 3 minutes; 1969–81; Brian Kennaway, *The Orange Order: A Tradition Betrayed* (London: Methuen, 2006).

93. Cliftonville District Lodge 3 minutes, Apr. 1969.

94. Tyrone County Lodge minutes, 26 Nov. 1969; GL, June 1969.

95. CAIN events 1968, accessed Nov. 2005.

96. Walker, *History of the Ulster Unionist Party*, 168–9, 172–3.

97. GL, June 1969, 17.

98. CAIN events 1969, accessed Nov. 2005.

Chapter 3

1. GL, June 1969, 9; CAIN events 1969, accessed Dec. 2005.

2. GL, Dec. 1969, 32–5.

3. Graham Walker, *A History of the Ulster Unionist Party: Protest, Pragmatism and Pessimism* (Manchester: Manchester University Press, 2004), 166–7, 175.

4. *The Reshaping of Local Government: Further Proposals Following Discussions and Consultations* (Belfast: Northern Ireland Government, July 1969).

5. Letter from Harold Cushnie to Grand Secretary Walter Williams, 23 July 1969.

6. Minutes of special meeting between Orange and Black local government reshaping committees, 23 Aug. 1969.

7. Minutes of local government reshaping meeting between Orange Order and the Northern Ireland government, 16 Sept. 1969.

8. Letter from W. R. Lewis of LOL 178 to Killyman District Lodge, County Tyrone, 24 Aug. 1969.

9. Letter from James Megaw, secretary of Richhill District 1 Lodge, to W. C. Moody, secretary of County Armagh Grand Lodge, 11 Sept. 1969; letter from Moody to Megaw, 17 Sept. 1969.

10. Minutes of meeting between James Chichester-Clark and Orange deputation, 21 Oct. 1969.

11. GL, Dec. 1969, 35–6.

12. GL, Dec. 1969, 37–9.

13. Dominic Bryan, *Orange Parades: The Politics of Ritual, Tradition and Control* (London: Pluto, 2000), 86–7.

14. For more on the culturalist hypothesis that ethnic groups whose ethno-history is linked to the Old Testament tend to perceive the world in a similar manner, see Don Akenson, *God's Peoples: Covenant and Land in South Africa, Israel, and Ulster* (Ithaca: Cornell University Press, 1992).

15. Letter from Grand Master John Bryars to Chichester-Clark, 11 Dec. 1969.

16. Letter from Chichester-Clark to Bryars, 20 Dec. 1969.

17. Letter from Bessbrook District 11 Lodge to Armagh County secretary William Moody, 14 Nov. 1969; letter from Armagh County Lodge to Williams, 17 Dec. 1969.

18. Letter from Williams to Chichester-Clark, 2 Jan. 1970; letter from Prime Minister's secretary to Williams, 9 Jan. 1970; GL, June 1970, 17.

19. Letter from Belfast County secretary to Grand Lodge, 18 Feb. 1970; letter from Williams to Chichester-Clark, 1 May 1970; letter from Chichester-Clark to Williams, 6 May 1970.

20. Bryan, *Orange Parades*, 88.
21. Minutes of meeting between Prime Minister and Orange deputation, 14 May 1970; letter from Sir Harold Black to Williams, 15 May 1970.
22. Minutes of meeting between Orange delegation, British government ministers, and Prime Minister, 7 July 1970.
23. GL, June 1970, 21.
24. Bryan, *Orange Parades*.
25. Letter from Tandragee District 4 to W. C. Moody, County Armagh Grand Secretary, 28 Oct. 1969.
26. GL, June 1970, 23.
27. Bryan, *Orange Parades*, 88.
28. Walker, *History of the Ulster Unionist Party*, 180.
29. CC, Mar. 1970.
30. Letter from Williams to Chichester-Clark, 16 Mar. 1970.
31. Letter from Chichester-Clark to Williams, 20 Mar. 1970.
32. CC, 6 May 1970, 5 June 1970.
33. Or Ulsterman-by-assimilation in the case of Carson, a Dubliner who later moved to the North.
34. Walker, *History of the Ulster Unionist Party*, 18–85.
35. Bryan, *Orange Parades*, 88–9.
36. GL, June 1970, 22–3.
37. CAIN events 1970, accessed Dec. 2005.
38. GL, June 1970, 17–21.
39. GL, June 1970, 20.
40. CC, 10 June 1970.
41. CC, 10 June 1970, 11–15.
42. CC, May 1970.
43. GL, June 1970, 22.
44. Walker, *History of the Ulster Unionist Party*, 206.
45. Ibid. 187.
46. Letter from Chichester-Clark to Bryans, 23 July 1970.
47. CC, 4 Aug. 1970.
48. Ibid.
49. Ibid.; Bryan, *Orange Parades*, 67.
50. CC, 4 Aug. 1970; County Tyrone minutes, 27 Oct. 1969, courtesy of Tyrone Grand Lodge (held by the current secretary).
51. CC, 4 Aug. 1970.
52. Letter from Bryans to Chichester-Clark, 14 Aug. 1970.
53. GL, Dec. 1970, 35.
54. Letter from Chichester-Clark to Williams, 13 Oct. 1970.

55. CC, 26 Oct. 1970; letter from Chichester-Clark's secretary to Williams, 12 Nov. 1970.

56. Letter from Rev. John Brown to Williams, 17 Nov. 1970.

57. CC, 26 Oct. 1970, 17 Nov. 1970.

58. GL, Dec. 1970, 34–42; letter from Williams to Chichester-Clark, 16 Sept. 1970; letter from Chichester-Clark to Williams, 26 Nov. 1970.

59. CC, 11 Sept. 1970.

60. Walker, *History of the Ulster Unionist Party*, 188.

61. GL, Dec. 1970, 40.

62. GL, Dec. 1970, 47.

63. CC, 9 Dec. 1970.

64. Minutes of a meeting between amalgamated committee and Chichester-Clark, 21 Dec. 1970.

65. Walker, *History of the Ulster Unionist Party*, 188–9.

66. Belfast County report of proceedings, 1968–9.

67. Belfast County minutes, 10 June 1969.

68. GL, Dec. 1970, 46.

69. GL, handwritten minutes, 9 June 1971.

70. GL, June 1971, 10.

71. CC, June 1977.

72. CC, 8 Mar. 1971.

73. CC, 4 June 1971.

74. CC, 8 Mar. 1971; CAIN events 1971, accessed Dec. 2005.

75. Walker, *History of the Ulster Unionist Party*, 188–90.

76. CC, 8 Mar. 1971. Clark held a leading role in both the Order and the UUP, and leading Orangemen like Brown and Smyth were cognizant of the need to back him, with Brown asking what the Order could do to bolster Clark's position at the next meeting of the UUP Standing Committee.

77. CC, 8 Mar. 1971; GL, June 1971, 11.

78. CC, 4 June 1971; GL, handwritten minutes, 9 June 1971.

79. GL, handwritten minutes, 9 June 1971; GL, June 1971, 12.

80. GL, June 1971, 13.

81. GL, Dec. 1971, 13–15.

82. Neil Jarman, and D. Bryan, *From Riots to Rights: Nationalist Parades in the North of Ireland* (Coleraine: Centre for the Study of Conflict,University of Ulster, 1998), 64.

83. CC, 17 June 1971, emphasis added.

84. CC, 17 June 1971.

85. Bryan, *Orange Parades*.

86. GL, June 1971, 27–8, emphasis added.

87. Jarman and Bryan, *From Riots to Rights*, 64, 92.

88. GL, Dec. 1971, 12.

89. Jarman and Bryan, *From Riots to Rights*, 88–98.

90. Resolutions against joining the Common Market came from at least two separate counties in 1971. This was caused by the identification of Europe with Catholicism and an erosion of British sovereignty.

91. CC, 8 Mar. 1971.

92. Walker, *History of the Ulster Unionist Party*, 190–1.
93. *Review Body on Local Government in Northern Ireland* (Belfast: North Ireland Government, 1970), chs. 5 and 7; CAIN events 1970, accessed Dec. 2005.
94. Walker, *History of the Ulster Unionist Party*, 191.
95. GL, June 1971, 16–18.
96. Letter from Roy Bradford, Minister of Development, to Williams, 14 Sept. 1971.
97. Letter from GOLI to Roy Bradford, 1 Feb. 1972.
98. Letter from Rev. Dr James Johnston to Williams, 27 Jan. 1972.
99. CC, 19 Nov. 1971.
100. Letter from W. C. Moody to W. Henry Stothers, 22 Oct. 1971; CC, 17 Apr. 1972.
101. 'Kangaroo Court', *The Protestant* (21 Dec. 1971).
102. For more discussion of this local link, see Christopher Farrington, *Ulster Unionism and the Peace Process in Northern Ireland* (Basingstoke: Palgrave, forthcoming).
103. Unidentified statement from Hutchison in County Armagh Grand Lodge archives, *c.* 1971.
104. CC, 17 Apr. 1972.
105. Bryan, *Orange Parades*, 91.
106. Walker, *History of the Ulster Unionist Party*, 191.
107. CAIN: Sutton Index of Deaths in the Troubles, accessed Dec. 2005.
108. GL, Dec. 1971, 16.
109. CC, 8 Dec. 1971; GL, Dec. 1971, 43.
110. GL, Dec 1971, 40.
111. Cliftonville District 3 Lodge (Belfast) minutes, 26 Aug. 1969.
112. GL, Dec. 1971, 40, emphasis added.
113. CC, Feb. 1972; GL, Sept. 1972, 17.
114. GL, Dec. 1971, 41.
115. Ruth Dudley Edwards, *The Faithful Tribe: An Intimate Portrait of the Loyal Institutions* (London: Harper Collins, 1999).
116. CC, Dec. 1971.
117. GOLI membership returns, 1966–2005.
118. Belfast County initiation forms, 1971.
119. CC, 11 Sept. 1970, 9 June 1971.
120. CC, 20 Dec. 1971.
121. Walker, *History of the Ulster Unionist Party*, 192–3.
122. CC, 25 Feb. 1972; CAIN events 1972, accessed Dec. 2005.
123. Walker, *History of the Ulster Unionist Party*, 194–5; GL, June 1972, 18.
124. CC, 10 Mar. 1972; GL, June 1972, 18–19.
125. Speech by Brian Faulkner to the annual UUC meeting, 3 Mar. 1972.
126. Ibid.
127. CC, 2 Oct. 1964.
128. CC, 10 Dec. 1969, 10 Sept. 1971; GL, Dec. 1972, 11.
129. CC, 10 Mar. 1972.
130. CAIN events 1971, accessed Dec. 2005; Walker, *History of the Ulster Unionist Party*, 193.
131. CC, 25 Feb. 1972; CAIN events 1972.
132. CC, 10 Mar. 1972.

133. Walker, *History of the Ulster Unionist Party*, 195.
134. GL, June 1972, 13, 17.
135. GL, June 1972, 18–19.

Chapter 4

1. CC, 29 Mar. 1972.
2. GL, June 1972, 20.
3. CC, 9 June 1972.
4. GL, June 1972, 21.
5. CC, 9 June 1972.
6. Henry Patterson and Eric Kaufmann, *Unionism and Loyalism in Northern Ireland since 1945* (Manchester; Manchester University Press, forthcoming).
7. GL, June 1972, 22.
8. Graham Walker, *A History of the Ulster Unionist Party: Protest, Pragmatism and Pessimism* (Manchester: Manchester University Press, 2004), 214.
9. CAIN events 1972, accessed 2005.
10. Walker, *History of the Ulster Unionist Party*, 214–15.
11. Letter from LOL 630A secretary J. Rollston to Killylea District Lodge 1 secretary Brown, 17 Apr. 1972.
12. Resolution printed in County Tyrone minutes, 10 May 1972, courtesy of Tyrone Grand Lodge (held by the current secretary).
13. Belfast County initiation forms, 1971.
14. Letter from Lindsay Smith to Grand Secretary Walter Williams, 16 Aug. 1972.
15. 'Formula for Loyalist Unity', LOL 688, presented to Loyalist leaders, July–Aug. 1972.
16. Orange Order statement, 7 Dec. 1972.
17. Form letter from Williams, 10 Aug. 1972.
18. For instance, GOLI was congratulated by Randalstown District 22 Lodge (Antrim) for its actions. Letter from H. Nicholl, Randalstown District secretary, to Grand Lodge, 19 Aug. 1972.
19. Letter from Ian Paisley to Williams, 14 Aug. 1972.
20. GL, Dec. 1972, 36.
21. Letter from Herbert Ditty of Ulster Loyalist Association to Williams, 19 Aug. 1972.
22. Letter from Williams to Paisley, 18 Aug. 1972.
23. Letter from Paisley to Williams, 22 Aug. 1972.
24. Letter from Captain William Johnston, Adjutant, 1st Battalion, UVF, to Williams, 21 Aug. 1972.
25. Letter from Stanley Morgan to Williams, 21 Aug. 1972.
26. *BT* (15 Aug. 1972).
27. Minutes of Unionist Unity Conference, 23 Aug. 1972.
28. Letter from Paisley to Williams, 25 Aug. 1972.
29. Letter from Williams to Paisley, 28 Aug. 1972.
30. CC, 10 Sept. 1971, 8 Dec. 1971.
31. Letter from Scottish Grand Secretary John Adam to Williams, 11 Sept. 1972.
32. Letters from Adam to Williams, 13 Sept. 1972 and 20 Oct. 1972.

33. CC, 27 Oct. 1972.
34. Letter from Williams to Adam, 10 Nov. 1972.
35. GL, Dec. 1972, 38–9.
36. CC, 27 Oct. 1972.
37. CC, 13 Dec. 1972; PREM 15/1013 at Public Record Office website <http://www.nationalarchives.gov.uk/default.htm>, accessed 2005.
38. CC, 13 Dec. 1972; GL, Apr. 1973, 9–14; Walker, *History of the Ulster Unionist Party*, 215–16.
39. CC, 13 Dec. 1972; GL, Dec. 1972, 44; CC, 28 Apr. 1973, special meeting.
40. GL, Apr. 1973, 9–13.
41. County Armagh minutes, 30 Mar. 1973, Orange Museum, Loughgall, County Armagh; letter from Bessbrook District 11 Lodge secretary William Kennedy to Armagh County secretary Adrian Leeman, 21 May 1973; GL, June 1973, 27.
42. CAIN biographies, Martin Smyth, accessed 2005.
43. Walker, *History of the Ulster Unionist Party*, 216–17.
44. CC, 13 June 1972; County Tyrone minutes, 8 Nov. 1973.
45. Letters from UUP treasurer George Hyde to F. C. Armstrong, 1 Jan. 1973 and 23 Mar. 1973; letter from Armagh Grand Secretary A. Leeman to G. Hyde, 11 Jan. 1973.
46. Walker, *History of the Ulster Unionist Party*, 217–18.
47. GL, June 1973, 29–30.
48. Walker, *History of the Ulster Unionist Party*, 218–19; CAIN events 1973, accessed 2005.
49. B. O'Duffy, 'Containment or Regulation? The British Approach to Ethnic Conflict in Northern Ireland', in B. O'Leary and John McGarry, eds., *The Politics of Ethnic Conflict Regulation* (New York and London: Routledge, 1993), 143–4; CAIN events 1974, accessed 2005.
50. GL, June 1973, 40.
51. CC, 7 Dec. 1973.
52. CC, 5 Oct. 1973.
53. GL, Dec. 1973, 19–21.
54. CC, 7 Dec. 1973.
55. Public Affairs Advisory Subcommittee minutes, 7 Dec. 1973; GL, Dec. 1973, 23.
56. GL, Dec. 1973, 16–18.
57. UUUC 'Policy Document', 1974.
58. CAIN events 1974.
59. GL, June 1974, 20.
60. CAIN events 1974, accessed 2005; Walker, *History of the Ulster Unionist Party*, 220.
61. FCO 87/334 at Public Record Office website <http://www.nationalarchives.gov.uk/default.htm>, accessed 2005.
62. CAIN events 1974; Walker, *History of the Ulster Unionist Party*, 220–1.
63. CC, 31 May 1974; GL, June 1974, 20–2; letter from Derryhale LOL 81 to Portadown District Lodge 1 secretary, 16 Jan. 1974.
64. CC, 10 June 1974.
65. CAIN: Sutton Index of Deaths in the Troubles, accessed 2005.
66. Paul Dixon, *Northern Ireland: The Politics of War and Peace* (Basingstoke: Palgrave, 2001), 296.

67. CC, 31 May 1974.
68. CC, 28 Oct. 1974; New Ulster Movement, 'A New Constitution for Northern Ireland', Aug. 1972; GL, Dec. 1974, 35.
69. GL, Dec. 1974, 37.
70. CC, 11 Dec. 1974.
71. CC, 5 Dec. 1975.
72. GL, June 1975, 22–3.
73. GL, June 1976, 11.
74. GL, Dec. 1976, 4–5.
75. CC, 17 Sept. 1976.
76. CAIN events 1975, accessed 2005.
77. GL, June 1975, 17; CC, 5 Dec. 1975.
78. CC, 5 Dec. 1975
79. CC, 10 Dec. 1975.
80. CAIN events 1975; Walker, *History of the Ulster Unionist Party*, 226.
81. Dixon, *Northern Ireland*, 158–61.
82. CC, 25 Feb. 1977.
83. CC, 26 Mar. 1976.
84. CC, 12 Mar. 1976.
85. CC, 30 Apr. 1976.
86. CC, 28 May 1976.
87. GL, June 1976, 9.
88. Ibid.
89. CC, 17 Sept. 1976, 8 Dec. 1976.
90. CC, 5 Oct. 1973.
91. GL, June 1975, 12.
92. CC, 8 June 1977.
93. GL, June 1977, 10.
94. Michael Kerr, *Imposing Power Sharing: Conflict and Coexistence in Northern Ireland and Lebanon* (Dublin: Irish Academic Press, 2005).
95. GL, June 1976, 16.
96. Walker, *History of the Ulster Unionist Party*, 222–6.
97. CC, 12 Mar. 1976.
98. Ibid.
99. CC, 17 Sept. 1976.
100. Ibid.
101. CC, Nov. 1976.
102. CC, 8 Dec. 1976; GL, Dec. 1976, 6.
103. CC, 25 Feb. 1977.
104. CC, 17 Sept. 1976.
105. Walker, *History of the Ulster Unionist Party*, 226.
106. CAIN events 1977, accessed 2005.
107. Walker, *History of the Ulster Unionist Party*, 226.
108. CC, 25 Apr. 1977.
109. CAIN events 1977.
110. CC, 12 Mar. 1976.
111. CC, 25 Feb. 1977.

112. CAIN: Sutton Index of Deaths in the Troubles.
113. CC, 13 June 1979.
114. Ruth Dudley Edwards, *The Faithful Tribe: An Intimate Portrait of the Loyal Institutions* (London: Harper Collins, 1999), 274–5.
115. CC, 25 Feb. 1977.
116. CAIN: abstract on organizations (USC), accessed 2005.
117. CC, 8 June 1977. Douglas drew Central Committee's attention to the fact that the USC men were inconvenienced by having to wait an hour to use Grand Lodge since there was no caretaker on duty.
118. Ibid.
119. GL, June 1977, 8; CC, 8 June 1977.
120. CAIN: Sutton Index of Deaths in the Troubles.
121. CC, 8 June 1977.
122. GL, June 1977, 8.
123. CC, 23 Sept. 1977.
124. CC, 3 Mar. 1978.
125. CC, 28 Sept. 1977.
126. CC, 2 Dec. 1977.
127. This argument has been made by the resource mobilization thesis and used to explain the success of decentralized grassroots organizations. For example, see Z. Munson, 'Islamic Mobilization: Social Movement Theory and the Egyptian Muslim Brotherhood', *Sociological Quarterly*, 42 (2001), 487–510.
128. GL, June 1974, 10–11.
129. CC, 23 Sept. 1977.
130. CAIN events 1977; GL, Dec. 1977, 11–12; CC, 23 Sept. 1977.
131. CC, 13 June 1979.

Chapter 5

1. Henry Patterson and Eric Kaufmann, *Unionism and Orangeism in Northern Ireland since 1945* (Manchester: Manchester University Press, forthcoming).
2. GL, Dec. 1977, 12.
3. Note that this does not necessarily indicate a willingness to support an executive based on proportional representation.
4. Class is measured in this survey by social class of head of household, which may be less accurate than the education measure.
5. It is important to note that education is strongest as an effect on attitudes to power-sharing in greater Belfast and weaker in other urban areas (though still significant), and has no effect in rural areas. Conjugal status is important as a predictor only in 'other urban' areas.
6. Jonathan Tonge and Jocelyn A. J. Evans, 'Eating the Oranges? The Democratic Unionist Party and the Orange Order Vote in Northern Ireland', paper presented at Elections, Public Opinion and Parties annual conference, Oxford University, 10–12 Sept. 2004.
7. Cecil Houston and William J. Smyth, *The Sash Canada Wore: A Historical Geography of the Orange Order in Canada* (Toronto and Buffalo: University of Toronto Press, 1980).

8. LOI Commission report (GOLI, 1997).
9. CC, 2 Mar. 1973, 13 June 1973, 10 Dec. 1975, 17 Sept. 1976, 8 Dec. 1976, 9 June 1978, 11 June 1980, 9 June 1982.
10. GL, June 1977, 7.
11. CC, 31 May 1974, 11 Dec. 1974.
12. Brian Kennaway, *The Orange Order: A Tradition Betrayed* (London: Methuen, 2006).
13. CC, 3 Mar. 1978.
14. CC, 14 June 1978.
15. GL, June 1979, 6.
16. GL, Dec. 1980.
17. CC, 10 Dec. 1980.
18. Kennaway, *The Orange Order*.
19. Z. Munson, 'Islamic Mobilization: Social Movement Theory and the Egyptian Muslim Brotherhood', *Sociological Quarterly*, 42/4 (2001), 487–510.
20. GL, Dec. 1978, 32–3, 38–40.
21. GL, June 1975, 14.
22. CC, 5 Dec. 1980.
23. CC, 7 Sept. 1979.
24. GL, Dec. 1980, 32–3.
25. CC, 15 Mar. 1980.
26. Gordon A. McCracken, 'Scottish Orangeism in the Twentieth Century', paper presented at conference 'Orangeism and Protestant Politics', University of Ulster at Jordanstown, Belfast, 2002; Eric Kaufmann, 'The Dynamics of Orangeism in Scotland: The Social Sources of Political Influence in a Large Fraternal Organization', *Social Science History*, 30/2 (2006), 263–92.
27. GL, Dec. 1977, 11.
28. GL, 13 Dec. 1978.
29. CC, 9 June 1972.
30. CC, 12 Dec. 1979.
31. GL, Dec. 1978, 32.
32. CC, 3 Mar. 1978.
33. CC, 14 June 1978.
34. GL, Dec. 1978, 5.
35. GL, Dec. 1978, 5–7.
36. CAIN elections, accessed 2005; Graham Walker, *A History of the Ulster Unionist Party: Protest, Pragmatism and Pessimism* (Manchester: Manchester University Press, 2004); 228–9. In the system of 'single transferable vote' voters can transfer their votes from less popular candidates who lose in the first round to the more popular figures who survive successive run-offs.
37. CC, 12 Dec. 1979; CAIN biographies: Martin Smyth, accessed 2005.
38. Walker, *History of the Ulster Unionist Party*, 228.
39. Ibid., 248.
40. See, for example, G. H. Mead, *Mind, Self, and Society from the Standpoint of a Social Behaviorist* (Chicago: University of Chicago Press, 1967).
41. Ibid., 229.
42. John Darby, 'Northern Ireland: The Background to the Peace Process', CAIN 2003, accessed 2005.
43. CC, 11 June 1980.
44. GL, June 1980, 20.
45. GL, Dec. 1980, 5.

46. GL, Dec. 1981, 8.
47. CAIN events 1981, accessed 2005.
48. CC, 9 June 1982.
49. Patterson and Kaufmann, *Unionism and Orangeism*.
50. CC, 18 Dec. 1982.
51. GL, June 1984, 22.
52. GL, June 1985, 9.
53. 'Anglo-Irish Agreement—Reaction', CAIN events; CAIN events 1986, accessed 2005.
54. CAIN events 1986; Walker, *History of the Ulster Unionist Party*, 238–40.
55. GL, June 1986, 19–20.
56. Fearghal Cochrane, *Unionist Politics* (Cork: Cork University Press, 2001), 227–30.
57. GL, 1987, 6–7; GOLI 'Policy Statement', 1987.
58. CAIN events 1987, accessed 2005; Walker, *History of the Ulster Unionist Party*, 240.
59. CAIN events 1987.
60. Walker, *History of the Ulster Unionist Party*, 238.
61. *Common Sense: Northern Ireland—An Agreed Process* (New Ulster Political Research Group, 1987, 1993), on CAIN website, accessed 2005.
62. GL, Dec. 1987, 6–7; GOLI 'Policy Statement', 1987.
63. GL, Dec. 1987, 10.
64. GL, 1988, 9.
65. GL, Dec. 1989, 7; June 1990, 4–7; June 1991, 6; Dec. 1992, 8; June 1993, 7–8, 11.
66. GL, June 1991, 7; Dec. 1992, 8; Patterson and Kaufmann, *Unionism and Orangeism*.
67. GL, Dec. 1987, 11.
68. GL, Dec. 1987, 6.
69. GL, 1993, 7–8, 11.
70. GOLI, 'Anglo-Irish Diktat Protest Convention' plans, 13 Nov. 1993.
71. County Fermanagh Grand Lodge minutes, 1994, courtesy of Fermanagh Grand Lodge (held by the current secretary).
72. GL, June 1995, 9.
73. Letter to lodges from Lurgan District 6 Lodge master S. Gardiner, 3 Nov. 1986.
74. GL, June 1993, 6–8; Dec. 1993, 5.
75. CC, 24 Sept. 1982; Kennaway, *The Orange Order*.
76. For more on social capital, see Robert D. Putnam, *Bowling Alone: The Collapse and Revival of American Community* (New York: Simon & Schuster, 2000). Further discussion of membership trends can also be found in Ch. 10 below.
77. GL, June 1993, 18; Dec. 1993, 14; June 1994, 16; GOLI membership returns.
78. Walker, *History of the Ulster Unionist Party*, 244.
79. Ibid, 237–40.
80. Paul Dixon, 'Political Skills or Lying and Manipulation? The Choreography of the Northern Ireland Peace Process', *Political Studies*, 50/3 (autumn 2002); Paul Dixon, *The Northern Ireland Peace Process: Choreography and Theatrical Politics* (London: Routledge, forthcoming).
81. CAIN events 1993–4, accessed 2005; 'The Irish Peace Process—Chronology of Key Events' (April 1993–April 1998), on CAIN website, accessed 2005.
82. GL, June 1995, 5–6.

83. Paul Dixon, *Northern Ireland: The Politics of War and Peace* (Basingstoke: Palgrave, 2001), 252–4.
84. CC, 1972–83.
85. Neil Jarman and D. Bryan, *From Riots to Rights: Nationalist Parades in the North of Ireland* (Coleraine: Centre for the Study of Conflict, University of Ulster, 1998), 68.
86. Letter from Bessbrook District 11 Lodge secretary W. Kennedy to Armagh County Grand Lodge, 10 Nov. 1978; CAIN events 1976, accessed 2005.
87. Brendan Murtagh, *Community and Conflict in Rural Ulster* (Coleraine: Centre for the Study of Conflict, University of Ulster, 1999), 43–5.
88. L. Adams, *Cashel: A Study in Community Harmony* (Cashel: Cashel Community Development Association, 1995).
89. Letter from Loughgall District Lodge 3 secretary Joseph Campbell to Armagh County Grand Lodge, undated, *c.* Apr. 1979.
90. Letter from Kildarton LOL 540 secretary Roy Pillow to Armagh District 5 Lodge, undated.
91. Letter from Armagh County Grand Lodge to Harold McCusker, UUP MP, 2 May 1981.
92. GL, June 1981, 4.
93. GL, Dec. 1981, 3.
94. CC, 13 Dec. 1972, 10 Dec. 1975, 12 Mar. 1976, 23 Feb. 1977, 8 June 1977, 3 Mar. 1978, June 1979, 11 June 1980.
95. CC, 18 Dec. 1982.
96. Ibid.
97. CC, 3 June 1983.
98. CC, 11 June 1980.
99. Tyrone County minutes, 1976, courtesy of Tyrone Grand Lodge (held by the current secretary).
100. Circular from Inver Temperance LOL 920 secretary Thomas Egerton, 26 June 1980.
101. GOLI membership returns.
102. N. Cigar, *Genocide in Bosnia: The Policy of 'Ethnic Cleansing'* (College Station: Texas A & M University Press, 1995).
103. P. Doherty and M. Poole, *Ethnic Residential Segregation in Belfast* (Coleraine: Centre for the Study of Conflict, University of Ulster, 1995).
104. Interview with Henry Reid, 14 Mar. 2000.
105. Murtagh, *Community and Conflict*.
106. Ruth Dudley Edwards, *The Faithful Tribe: An Intimate Portrait of the Loyal Institutions* (London: Harper Collins, 1999), 262–6.
107. Murtagh, *Community and Conflict*, 29,33; Maurice Halbwachs, *The Collective Memory* (1950; New York: Harper & Row, 1980).
108. Interview with Reid, 14 Mar. 2000.
109. Interview with Trevor Geary, 16 Jan. 2003; interview with Noel McIlfettrick, 5 Mar. 2003.
110. Murtagh, *Community and Conflict*, 18–20.
111. GOLI membership returns.
112. Seamus Dunn and Valerie Morgan, *Protestant Alienation in Northern Ireland: A Preliminary Survey* (Coleraine: Centre for the Study of Conflict, University of

Ulster, 1994), 16; Desmond Bell, *Acts of Union: Youth Culture and Sectarianism in Modern Ireland* (London: Macmillan, 1990).

113. T. Kirk, 'The Polarisation of Protestants and Roman Catholics in Rural Northern Ireland: A Case Study of Glenravel Ward, Co. Antrim, 1956–1988', PhD dissertation, Queen's University of Belfast, 1993.

114. Murtagh, *Community and Conflict*, 33, 48–50.

115. Fermanagh County minutes, Dec. 1938, 1951; Northern Ireland Census, 1926–71 (Database of Irish Historical Statistics: Census Material, 1901–71, digital version compiled by M. W. Dowling et al., Colchester: UK Data Archives, SN 3542).

116. Patterson and Kaufmann, *Unionism and Orangeism*.

117. Fermanagh County minutes, 1963.

118. GL, Dec. 1963, 34–5.

119. Fermanagh County minutes, 1960.

120. CC, 24 Sept. 1982; GOLI expulsion forms.

121. GL, June 1964, 17; June 1996, 16.

122. GL, June 1998, 13.

123. Murtagh, *Community and Conflict*, 31–2; P. Devine and L. Dowds, *Northern Ireland Life and Times Survey, 2004* [computer file], Colchester: UK Data Archive, SN 5227 (Oct. 2005).

124. GOLI expulsion forms.

125. GOLI expulsion forms. The province of Newfoundland had a majority favouring a relaxation of the law by the 1970s, but this was resisted by a majority in Ontario into the 1990s. Interview with past Newfoundland Grand Master Ralph Roberts, Cupids, Newfoundland, 19 Aug. 2003.

126. Interview with George Chittick, Belfast, 17 Mar. 2000; Neil Jarman and D. Bryan, *From Riots to Rights: Nationalist Parades in the North of Ireland* (Coleraine: Centre for the Study of Conflict, University of Ulster, 1998), 51.

127. Murtagh, *Community and Conflict*, 27–8.

128. CC, 9 June 1982; GL, June 1982, 13–14; June 1988, 9, 13–14.

129. GL, June 1986, 15.

130. Dominic Bryan, *Orange Parades: The Politics of Ritual, Tradition and Control* (London: Pluto, 2000), 161.

131. CC, 12 Dec. 1979.

132. S. Elliott, J. Ditch, and E. Moxon-Browne, *Northern Ireland General Election and Political Attitudes Survey, 1992* [computer file], Colchester: UK Data Archive, SN 3720 (July 1997).

133. ARK Northern Ireland Elections <http://www.ark.ac.uk/elections/>, accessed 2005.

134. GL, June 1989, 10.

135. Ibid.

136. This was omitted from the initial regression analysis of 1978 views on power-sharing because we were most interested in background variables.

137. Walker, *History of the Ulster Unionist Party*, 232–3.

138. Bell, *Acts of Union*, 13, 55; GOLI membership returns.

139. Dean Godson, *Himself Alone: David Trimble and the Ordeal of Unionism* (London: Harper Perennial, 2004), 296.

Chapter 6

1. Ruth Dudley Edwards, *The Faithful Tribe: An Intimate Portrait of the Loyal Institutions* (London: Harper Collins, 1999), ch. 12.
2. Dominic Bryan, *Orange Parades: The Politics of Ritual, Tradition and Control* (London: Pluto, 2000).
3. Brian Kennaway, *The Orange Order: A Tradition Betrayed* (London: Methuen, 2006).
4. Bryan, *Orange Parades*, 182.
5. Ibid., 125–8.
6. Desmond Bell, *Acts of Union: Youth Culture and Sectarianism in Modern Ireland* (London: Macmillan, 1990), 9–13.
7. Bryan, *Orange Parades*, 87–8.
8. Neil Jarman and D. Bryan, *From Riots to Rights: Nationalist Parades in the North of Ireland* (Coleraine: Centre for the Study of Conflict, (University of Ulster, 1998), p 17
9. P. Doherty and M. Poole, *Ethnic Residential Segregation in Belfast* (Coleraine: Centre for the Study of Conflict, University of Ulster, 1995).
10. Jarman and Bryan, *From Riots to Rights*.
11. Bryan, *Orange Parades*, 182.
12. PC annual report, 2004 (Belfast: Parades Commission, 2004), http:/www.parades-commission.org.
13. This refers to post-1922 Northern Ireland, since bans did occur in 1849–72.
14. Jarman and Bryan, *From Riots to Rights*, 16, 89; PC annual report, 2004.
15. W. H. Wolsey, *Orangeism in Portadown District* (Portadown: Portadown Times, 1935), 2–3; Chris Ryder and Vincent Kearney, *Drumcree: The Orange Order's Last Stand* (London: Methuen, 2001), 7.
16. Ryder and Kearney, *Drumcree*, 7.
17. On the other hand, the general weakness of Orangeism in cities and towns means that, of urban areas, only Enniskillen has as high a proportion in the Order. The presence of almost 1,000 Orangemen, despite the fact that many come in from surrounding parts of the greater Portadown rural belt, makes Portadown a major centre of Orange activity. If we consider that there was nearly twice this number of Orangemen in the city in 1995–7, we can appreciate that Portadown did deserve the title of 'Orange Citadel'.
18. GOLI membership returns, 1991, 2001.
19. GOLI membership returns, 1966–2004; Armagh County reports, 1913–66 (many missing), Orange Museum, Loughgall, County Armagh.
20. Ryder and Kearney, *Drumcree*, 52–5.
21. Ibid., 68–9.
22. Ibid., 80–4.
23. For more on the legality of public order justifications for blocking parades, see Brian Currin's assessment in Ryder and Kearney, *Drumcree*, 352.
24. Ibid., 75–9, 81.
25. Ibid., 79.
26. Circular from United Ulster Loyalist Front, 24 July 1985, Orange Museum, Loughgall, County Armagh.

27. Letter from Portadown Arch Committee members to Armagh County master Norman Hood, 27 June 1986, Orange Museum, Loughgall, County Armagh.
28. Letter from Olive Whitten to Hood, 8 July 1986, Orange Museum, Laoghgall, County Armagh.
29. GOLI press release, 9 July 1986.
30. GL, June 1986, 5–6.
31. GL, June 1987, 4–5.
32. Ryder and Kearney, *Drumcree*, 88–9; CC, 1995–2003.
33. Sandy Row District 3, Belfast, meeting minutes, 25 Nov. 1986.
34. Jarman and Bryan, *From Riots to Rights*, 78.
35. Ryder and Kearney, *Drumcree*, 87–90.
36. Dean Godson, *Himself Alone: David Trimble and the Ordeal of Unionism* (London: Harper Perennial, 2004), 130.
37. Edwards, *The Faithful Tribe*, 288; Jarman and Bryan, *From Riots to Rights*, 81.
38. Edwards, *The Faithful Tribe*, 287–9.
39. GOLI press release, 24 Apr. 1995.
40. *News Letter*, (Belfast, 24 Apr. 1995).
41. GOLI press release, 24 Apr. 1995.
42. GOLI news release, 14 Apr. 1995.
43. Meeting between Secretary of State Patrick Mayhew and Grand Lodge officers, 10 Apr. 1995.
44. Letter from Grand Secretary John McCrea to Mayhew, 21 Apr. 1995.
45. Letter from George Patton to Mayhew, 24 Apr. 1995.
46. Minutes of meeting between RUC and Grand Lodge officers, 19 May 1995, emphasis added.
47. Kennaway, *The Orange Order*.
48. Godson, *Himself Alone*, 133–6.
49. Ibid., 140–1.
50. Ibid., 133.
51. Letter from Portadown District 1 Lodge secretary Robert Wallace to Armagh County secretary Joseph Campbell, 4 Nov. 1995.
52. GL, Dec. 1995, 6.
53. United Prayer Breakfast vision statement; United Prayer Breakfast invitation, 2 Oct. 1995; letter from McCrea to A. H. Wilson, secretary of Lower Iveagh District Lodge 1, County Down, 8 Nov. 1995.
54. GL, Dec. 1995, 15; Steve Bruce, *Comparative Protestant Politics* (Oxford: Oxford University Press, 1998).
55. Letter from Tyrone County secretary Robert Abernethy to McCrea, 20 Nov. 1995.
56. Letter from Ballymarlow LOL 637 to Ballymen a District Lodge 8, undated.
57. Letter from Ballinea True Defenders LOL 1511 secretary Ronnie Carson to Ballycastle District 23 Lodge secretary McKillop, undated.
58. Godson, *Himself Alone*, 108–9, 147; Edwards, *The Faithful Tribe*, 322.
59. Kennaway, *The Orange Order*.
60. BBC News <http://news.bbc.co.uk/1/hi/northern_ireland/687810.stm>, accessed 2005.
61. Kennaway, *The Orange Order*.

62. GL, Dec. 1995, 7.
63. GOLI reports.
64. LOI Commission, 1997.
65. Belfast County application forms, 1961–86.
66. Kennaway, *The Orange Order*.
67. Ryder and Kearney, *Drumcree*, 142.
68. Kennaway, *The Orange Order*.
69. Letter from William Thompson to Walter Millar, undated, *c.* 1995.
70. Ryder and Kearney, *Drumcree*, 131.
71. GL, Dec. 1995, 11.
72. Ibid.
73. GL, Dec. 1995, 12.
74. GL, Dec. 1995, 13–14.
75. Joel Patton et al., 'Spirit of Drumcree' Response to the Rev. Bro. Kennaway's Report on the Ulster Hall Rally', undated; S. Spence, 'Comparison of Report [to Video Evidence]', undated.
76. Steve Bruce, *The Edge of the Union: The Ulster Loyalist Political Vision* (Oxford: Oxford University Press, 1994).
77. Kennaway, *The Orange Order*.
78. Presentation by SOD to GOLI, 28 May 1996.
79. GL, Dec. 1995, 15.
80. Edwards, *The Faithful Tribe*, 324; Kennaway, *The Orange Order*.
81. Ryder and Kearney, *Drumcree*, 1.
82. Letter from Martin Smyth to David Dowey, 4 Mar. 1996.
83. Paul Connolly, 'Orange Chiefs in Showdown with Hardliners', *BT* (28 May 1996).
84. Kennaway, *The Orange Order*.
85. CC, 28 May 1996.
86. Ibid.; Ryder and Kearney, *Drumcree*, 279.
87. CC, 28 May 1996.
88. GL, June 1996, 14–15.
89. GL, June 1996, 10.

Chapter 7

1. Dean Godson, *Himself Alone: David Trimble and the Ordeal of Unionism* (London: Harper Perennial, 2004), 233–8.
2. Chris Ryder and Vincent Kearney, *Drumcree: The Orange Order's Last Stand* (London: Methuen, 2001).
3. Ruth Dudley Edwards, *The Faithful Tribe: An Intimate Portrait of the Loyal Institutions* (London: Harper Collins, 1999), 343–6.
4. Hansard, HC (series 5), vol. 281, col. 558 (11 July 1996).
5. Godson, *Himself Alone*, 238–41.
6. GL, Dec. 1997, 14.
7. Letter from Gary Moore, LOL 1046, to GOLI, 14 Aug. 1996.
8. Hansard, HC (series 5), vol. 281, col. 559 (11 July 1996).
9. CC, 15 Mar. 1997.

10. Letter from William Coulter, Grand Secretary of City of Londonderry Grand Lodge, to GOLI, 30 May 1997.
11. GL, Dec. 1996, 14; Edwards, *The Faithful Tribe*, 395.
12. *Irish News* (23 Apr. 1999); GL, Dec. 1999, 22; CC, 22 Sept. 2000.
13. Interview with Ralph Roberts, Brigus, Newfoundland, 19 Aug. 2003.
14. CC, 22 Sept. 2000.
15. 'Document Reveals Lodge Mediation Deal', *BT* (11 Apr. 1997).
16. Undated statement from Grand Master Robert Saulters to GOLI, *c.* May 1997.
17. GL, June 1997, 11–12. At the time, the Republic of Ireland and Belfast were strongly overrepresented.
18. Letter from William McBride, Sandy Row District Lodge 5, to GOLI, 27 Mar. 1997; letter from secretary W. McCreedy, Whiterock LOL 974, to GOLI, 20 Mar. 1997.
19. Letters from respective lodges to GOLI, 4 May 1997.
20. Edwards, *The Faithful Tribe*, 393–4.
21. CC, 9 May 1997.
22. Letter from Markethill District Lodge 10 to Grand Lodge, 18 Apr. 1997.
23. GL, 11 June 1997, interim report.
24. GL, handwritten minutes, 11 June 1997.
25. Brian Kennaway, *The Orange Order: A Tradition Betrayed* (London: Methuen, 2006).
26. LOI Commission report, 1997.
27. Edwards, *The Faithful Tribe*, 396–7.
28. Ryder and Kearney, *Drumcree*, 209.
29. Dominic Bryan, *Orange Parades: The Politics of Ritual, Tradition and Control* (London: Pluto, 2000), 173.
30. Ryder and Kearney, *Drumcree*, 206.
31. Godson, *Himself Alone*, 286–96; Edwards, *The Faithful Tribe*, 402.
32. Grand Lodge press release, 10 July 1997.
33. Statement by Londonderry City Grand Master Alan Lindsay and Grand Secretary Douglas Caldwell, 12 July 1997; Ryder and Kearney, *Drumcree*, 225.
34. Godson, *Himself Alone*, 280–3.
35. Minutes of meeting between RUC Chief Constable and City of Londonderry Orange Lodge officers, 14 Nov. 1997; Ryder and Kearney, *Drumcree*, 226.
36. Minutes of meeting between RUC Chief Constable and City of Londonderry Orange Lodge officers, 14 Nov. 1997.
37. Recollection of David Wilson, St Michael's College, University of Toronto, Nov. 2005.
38. Ryder and Kearney, *Drumcree*, 195.
39. *Orange Banner* (*c.* late Dec. 1997).
40. GL, June 1976, 7–8.
41. GL, June 1986, 10–11.
42. Godson, *Himself Alone*, 82–3.
43. EC minutes, 3 Mar. 1988, 27 Oct. 1989; GL, June 1990, 8–9.
44. GL, June 1996, 12.
45. EC minutes, 23 May 1997.
46. Letter from Adam Ingram, MP, to Brian Kennaway, 15 Dec. 1998.
47. Trimble, quoted in Godson, *Himself Alone*, 308–9.

48. Kennaway, *The Orange Order*.
49. EC minutes, 12 Sept. 1997.
50. Kennaway, *The Orange Order*.
51. EC minutes of meeting with PC, 12 Sept. 1997.
52. EC minutes, 19 Sept. 1997.
53. Letter from Grand Secretary John McCrea to Saulters, 18 Sept. 1997.
54. Interview with County Tyrone Grand Secretary Perry Reid, 17 Mar. 2004.
55. Letters from lodges to McCrea, 27 Jan 1998, 5 Nov. 1998, 19 Nov. 1998.
56. 'Patton Faces Expulsion', *BT* (19 Nov. 1997).
57. CC, 3 Oct. 1997.
58. Unpublished paper entitled 'Discipline', signed by George Patton, undated.
59. CC, 31 Oct. 1997.
60. 'Orangemen Block Fate of Member', *BT* (3 Dec. 1997).
61. Ryder and Kearney, *Drumcree*, 322.
62. 'Patton Survives Rap from Order', *BT* (5 Dec. 1997).
63. *Orange Banner* (*c.* Jan. 1998).
64. I recall George Patton showing me car parts from previous blasts in a special case at the House of Orange, Dublin Road, in 2000.
65. Kennaway, *The Orange Order*.
66. Ryder and Kearney, *Drumcree*, 322.
67. Ibid.; Kennaway, *The Orange Order*.
68. *Orange Banner* (*c.* Jan. 1998).
69. GL, Dec. 1997, 27.
70. GOLI meeting of trustees, 29 Dec. 1997.
71. Ibid.
72. Kennaway, *The Orange Order*.
73. GOLI meeting of trustees, 29 Dec. 1997.
74. Kennaway, *The Orange Order*.
75. Minutes of meeting between Orange leaders and SOD, 14 Jan. 1998.
76. CC, 16 Jan. 1998.
77. Bryan, *Orange Parades*.
78. Kennaway, *The Orange Order*.
79. Minutes of meeting between Orange leaders and SOD, 2 Feb. 1998.
80. Meeting between McCrea, Denis Watson, and counsel, 21 Jan. 1998.
81. CC, 6 Feb. 1998.
82. Undated Central Committee position paper, *c.* Feb. 1998.
83. Kennaway, *The Orange Order*.
84. Minutes of meeting between Orange leaders and SOD, undated, *c.* Mar. 1998.
85. Interview with George Chittick, 17 Mar. 2000.
86. LOI Commission report, 1997.
87. GL, Dec. 1995, 8. In Smyth's words, '"one man one vote" is a sorry reflection of 1968/9. It was false then. It is falser today.'
88. Submission to LOI Commission from SOD.
89. LOI Commission report, 1997.
90. GL, June 1997, 11–12.
91. LOI Commission report, 1997, 5.

92. LOI Commission report, 1997.
93. Worshipful Masters' conference resolutions, 1997.
94. G. Patton, 'Discussion Document', *c.* early 1998.
95. County Antrim Grand Lodge circular, 30 Jan. 1998.
96. Hereward Senior, *Orangeism: The Canadian Phase* (Toronto and New York: McGraw-Hill Ryerson, 1972).
97. CC, 21 Mar. 1998.
98. Letter regarding proceedings from County Antrim Grand Lodge to GOLI, 6 Apr. 1998.
99. Minutes of special GOLI meeting, 15 Apr. 1998.
100. Letter from LOL 1892 to Belfast District Lodge 3 secretary, 8 Jan. 1998.
101. Letter from LOL 1892 to Belfast District Lodge 3 secretary, 17 July 1998.
102. Letter from Kinnego LOL 5, Loughgall, undated, *c.* mid 1998.
103. Godson, *Himself Alone.*
104. Ryder and Kearney, *Drumcree*, 254–62.
105. Ibid., 274–5.
106. County Tyrone minutes, 10 Nov. 1998, courtesy of Tyrone Grand Lodge (held by the current secretary).
107. Interview with Reid, 17 Mar. 2004.
108. County Tyrone minutes, 28 Aug. 1998.
109. County Tyrone minutes, 10 Nov. 1998; Edwards, *The Faithful Tribe.*
110. County Tyrone minutes, 10 Nov. 1998.
111. Letter from Joel Patton to McCrea, 4 Dec. 1998.
112. Interview with Ruth Dudley Edwards, 17 Nov. 2005.
113. Edwards, *The Faithful Tribe.*

Chapter 8

1. Michael Kerr, *Imposing Power Sharing: Conflict and Coexistence in Northern Ireland and Lebanon* (Dublin: Irish Academic Press, 2005).
2. ARK NI Election Study, 1998 <http://www.ark.ac.uk>, accessed 2005.
3. Dean Godson, *Himself Alone: David Trimble and the Ordeal of Orangeism* (London: Harper Perennial, 2004), 362–3.
4. Ibid., 341–3.
5. Ibid., 359–60; Colin Coulter, 'The Culture of Contentment: The Political Beliefs and Practice of the Unionist Middle Classes', in P. Shirlow and Mark McGovern, eds., *Who Are the People? Unionism, Protestantism and Loyalism in Northern Ireland* (London: Pluto Press, 1997), 129–30.
6. Jonathan Tonge and Jocelyn A. J. Evans, 'Eating the Oranges? The Democratic Unionist Party and the Orange Order Vote in Northern Ireland, paper presented at Elections, Public Opinions and parties annual conference, Oxford University, 10–12 Sept. 2004, 8; Godson, *Himself Alone*, 240.
7. *BT* (2 May 1998).
8. Godson, *Himself Alone*, 362.
9. Millward Brown website <http://www.ums-research.com>, accessed 2005.

10. *BT* (13 Apr. 1998).

11. Godson, *Himself Alone*, 365.

12. GOLI handwritten minutes, 15 Apr. 1998.

13. GL, 15 Apr. 1998, 21.

14. ARK Northern Ireland Life & Times Survey, 1992, 1993 <http://www.ark.ac.uk/nilt/>, accessed 2005.

15. Tonge and Evans, 'Eating the Oranges'.

16. *BT* (7 May 1998).

17. Interview with Trevor Geary and visit to Tullyvallen Orange Hall, 16 Jan. 2003.

18. GOLI press releases, 2 May 1998, 12 May 1998.

19. Letter from York LOL 145 to Belfast District Lodge 3 secretary Denis Blyberg, 27 Sept. 1997.

20. UUC list with pro- and anti-Agreement stances attributed by UUP strategists, *c.* 2003.

21. Tyrone County minutes, 6 May 1998, Courtesy of Tyrone Grand Lodge (held by the current secretary).

22. *BT* (22 May 1998).

23. GL, June 1998, 30.

24. *BT* (7 May 1998).

25. CC, undated, *c.* mid 1998.

26. Interview with Tyrone Grand Secretary Perry Reid, 17 May 2004.

27. ARK NI Election Study, 1998.

28. Brian Kennaway, *The Orange Order: A Tradition Betrayed* (London: Methuen, 2006).

29. EC minutes, 20 Feb. 1998.

30. EC minutes, 23 Oct. 1998.

31. Letters from Nelson McCausland to Brian Kennaway, 20 Oct 1998 and 20 Nov. 1998.

32. Letter from LOL 1422 to John McCrea, 1 Apr. 1998.

33. Kennaway, *The Orange Order*.

34. Letter from Denis Watson to Kennaway, 18 Feb. 1999.

35. Letter from Kennaway to Grand Treasurer Mervyn Bishop, 9 Mar. 1999.

36. Robert Saulters, quoted in Kennaway, *The Orange Order*, 202.

37. EC Investigating Committee minutes, 19 Mar. 1999 and 23 Feb. 1999.

38. GL, June 1999, 9–13.

39. Quoted in Ed Moloney, 'Newshound,' <http://www.nuzhound.com/index.php>, 19 June 2000.

40. *BT* (23 June 2000).

41. Henry Patterson, *Ireland Since 1939* (Oxford and New York: Oxford University Press, 2002), 181–212, 224–32.

42. Jonathan Tonge, *The New Northern Irish Politics* (Basingstoke: Palgrave, 2005), 66–81; Jonathan Tonge and Jocelyn A. J. Evans, 'Faultlines in Unionism: Division

and Dissent within the Ulster Unionist Council', *Irish Political Studies*, 16/3 (2001), 111–31.

43. E. Kaufmann and H. Patterson, 'The Dynamics of Intra-Party Support for the Good Friday Agreement in the Ulster Unionist Party', *Political Studies* (forthcoming, 2006).

44. Jonathan Tonge and Jocelyn A. J. Evans, 'For God and Ulster? Religion, Orangeism and Politics within the Ulster Unionist Council', paper presented to the Political Studies Association of Ireland conference, University of Ulster, Belfast, 2002.

45. Godson, *Himself Alone*, 297.

46. 'Northern Ireland Report', Leverhulme Trust, Nov. 1999 <http://www.ucl.ac.-uk/constitution-unit/publications/devolution-monitoring-reports/index.html>, accessed 2005; Tonge and Evans, 'Faultlines in Unionism', 114.

47. Tonge and Evans, 'Faultlines in Unionism', 118–20; Tonge, *The New Northern Irish Politics*, 72–3.

48. Eric Kaufmann, 'The Orange Order in Ontario, Newfoundland, Scotland and Northern Ireland: A Macro-Social Analysis,' in David A. wilson, ed., *The Orange Order in Canada* (Dublin: Four Courts, forthcoming).

49. Kaufmann and Patterson, 'The Dynamics of Intra-Party Support.'

50. *BT* (27 Mar. 2000).

51. Interview with Reid, 17 Mar. 2004.

52. GL, Mar. 2002, 4.

53. Ibid. 19; Kennaway, *The Orange Order*.

54. Kaufmann and Patterson, 'The Dynamics of Intra-Party Support.'

55. Ibid.; interview with Reid, 17 Mar. 2004.

56. Godson, *Himself Alone*, 182.

57. Minutes of meeting between GOLI officers and UUC officers, 11 Dec. 1995. Cunningham, for instance, served on the Order's Finance Committee. See GL, Dec. 1996, 36.

58. *BT* (3 Aug. 1998).

59. *BT* (8 June 1998).

60. Letter from Josias Cunningham to Grand Secretary Denis Watson, 26 May 1999.

61. Memorandum on Orange–UUP link from Cunningham to Watson, 25 Oct. 1999.

62. Interview with Reid, 17 Mar. 2004.

63. Tonge and Evans, 'Faultlines in Unionism', 121.

64. Circular from Peter Weir, MLA, 17 Apr. 2000.

65. GL, June 1981, 15.

66. LOI Commission report, 1997.

67. GL, June 1996, 5.

68. GL, Dec. 1997, 17.

69. GL, Mar. 1999, 8.

70. Letter from Antrim secretary William Leathem to Watson, 15 Feb. 1999.

71. Interview with Drew Nelson, 27 May 2003.

72. Letter from Dunmurry (Antrim) 'True Blues' LOL 1046 secretary Tom Williams to Derriaghy District (Antrim), 15 Dec. 1999.

73. GL, June 1999, 19; *BT* (28 Apr. 2000).

74. GL, June 2000, 25.

75. Letter from George Patton to Jeffrey Donaldson, MP, 10 May 2000.
76. Letter from J.C. Taylor & Co., solicitors, to GOLI, 17 May 2000.
77. *BT* (15 Apr. 2001).
78. Letter from UUC secretary to G. Patton, 27 Feb. 2002.
79. Letter from David Brewster to G. Patton, 14 Feb. 2002.
80. Letter from Brewster to G. Patton, 8 Mar. 2002.
81. Letters between UUP and Orange Order, Mar.–June 2002.
82. Letter from G. Patton to UUC Executive Committee chairman James Cooper, 11 Sept. 2002.
83. GOLI circular, 4 Nov. 2002.
84. Letter from G. Patton to Cooper, 1 Oct. 2002.
85. GL, June 2002, 19.
86. Speech by Cooper to annual UUP conference, 19 Oct. 2002.
87. Robin Wilson and R. Wilford, UCL Constitution Unit monitoring report, Nov. 2002, at http://www.ucl.ac.uk/constitution-unit/research/devolution/.
88. Graham Walker, *A History of the Ulster Unionist Party: Protest, Pragmatism and Pessimism* (Manchester: Manchester University Press, 2004), 268.
89. Tonge and Evans, 'Eating the Oranges', 5.
90. *BT* (21 Jan. 2003).
91. Circular from G. Patton to Grand Lodge officers, 23 Dec. 2002.
92. Minutes of meeting of Orange UUC delegates, 29 Jan. 2003.
93. GL, May 2004, 35.
94. Eric Kaufmann, 'The Decline of the UUP: An Electoral Analysis', presented at Political Studies Association conference, Lincoln, UK, 6 Apr. 2004. See <http://www.sneps.net/OO/papers.html>, accessed 2005.
95. Interview with Antrim Grand Secretary William Leathem, 30 Oct. 2004.
96. Tonge and Evans, 'Eating the Oranges'.
97. Christopher Farrington, 'The Democratic Unionist Party and the Northern Ireland Peace Process', paper presented at Political Studies Association conference, Lincoln, UK, 6 Apr. 2004, 10.
98. GL, June 2002, 20.
99. Farrington, 'The Democratic Unionist Party', 8–10.
100. CC, 5 Dec. 1975.
101. CC, 12 Mar. 1976.
102. GL, June 1977, 6–7; Belfast County initiation forms, 1961–86.
103. CC, 8 June 1977.
104. GL, June 1977, 6; CC, 8 June 1977.
105. CAIN events 1981, accessed 2005.
106. CC, 9 Dec. 1981; GL, Dec. 1981, 13–14.
107. CC, 2 Feb. 1982; GL, June 1982, 9.
108. GL, Dec. 1983, 39.
109. GL, June 1984, 6; June 1967; Feb. 1968, 10–11. This may have stemmed from overtures by the Antrim Grand Master, the Rev. John Brown, for it was Brown who won Grand Lodge approval to rescind the 1903 law against contact with the IOO so as to preach at an Independent Orange service in 1967.
110. GL, June 1989, 10.

111. Kennaway, *The Orange Order.*
112. GL, June 1993, 5.
113. GL, Dec. 1998, 5–6.
114. GL, Dec. 1999, 7–8.
115. Kennaway, *The Orange Order.*
116. GL, June 2002, 21.
117. GL, Dec. 2002, 22.
118. GL, Mar. 2003, 3.
119. GL, 11 June 2003, 18; June 2004, 16; 25 Sept. 2004, 5; 8 Dec. 2004, 16.
120. GL, Mar. 2005, 11.
121. Interview with unidentified EC members, Armagh city, 16 Jan 2003.
122. GL, Mar. 2004, 4.
123. GL, Mar. 2005, 2–3.
124. Interview with G. Patton, 9 June 2005.
125. GL, June 2005, 13–14.
126. Kennaway, *The Orange Order.*

Chapter 9

1. Interview with Drew Nelson, 6 Mar. 2003.
2. GL, June 1996, 10; GL, Aug. 1998, 24–5.
3. GL, Aug. 1998, 25–7.
4. GL, Aug. 1998, 29–31.
5. GOLI Parades Strategy document, *c.* Aug. 1998.
6. County Fermanagh Grand Lodge resolution, 20 Aug. 1998.
7. Letter from County Fermanagh Grand Secretary G. Dane to Grand Master Robert Saulters, 25 Aug. 1998.
8. Letter from County Cavan Grand Lodge to GOLI, 27 Aug. 1998.
9. County Tyrone reply to Parades Strategy Committee, 26 Aug. 1998.
10. CC, 4–5 Dec. 1998.
11. Letter from R. Givan, Annahoe District Lodge 6 secretary, to Perry Reid, Tyrone Grand Secretary, 17 Aug. 1998.
12. Letter from Castlecaulfield District Lodge 4 to Tyrone Grand Lodge, 20 Aug. 1998.
13. Letter from Strabane District Lodge 2 to Tyrone Grand Lodge, undated.
14. County Tyrone reply to Parades Strategy Committee, 26 Aug. 1998.
15. GOLI Civic Forum meeting minutes, 2 Oct. 1998.
16. Letter from R. Fleming, County Down Grand Lodge, to Saulters, 26 Aug. 1998.
17. Letter from Antrim secretary Drew Davison to Grand Lodge, 29 Aug. 1998.
18. Letter from Belfast Grand Secretary Thomas Haire to Grand Secretary John McCrea, 28 Aug. 1998.
19. Letter from Whitewell Temperance LOL 533, Belfast, to Belfast County Lodge, 27 Sept. 1998.
20. Letter from Londonderry secretary W. Knox to McCrea, 27 Aug. 1998.
21. Letter from Armagh secretary W. McLoughlin to McCrea, 27 Aug. 1998.
22. GOLI Civic Forum meeting minutes, 2 Oct. 1998.

23. CC, 4–5 Dec. 1998; GL, Dec. 1998, 12.
24. GL, Dec. 1997, 6–8.
25. Chris Ryder and Vincent Kearney, *Drumcree: The Orange Order's Last Stand* (London: Methuen, 2001), 286–7.
26. GOLI minutes of meeting with American Consul General, 7 Oct. 1998.
27. CC, 2 Oct. 1998.
28. 'Drumcree Winter Initiative' drafts, 26 Oct. 1998.
29. Ryder and Kearney, *Drumcree*, 290.
30. Minutes of meeting between Orange deputation and Prime Minister Tony Blair, 30 Oct. 1998.
31. G. Patton, 'Telephone Log', 6 Nov. 1998.
32. Ibid., 9–10 Nov. 1998.
33. Ibid., 16 Nov. 1998.
34. Memo from George Patton to GOLI officers, 6 Nov. 1998.
35. GOLI briefing paper for meeting with archbishops Robin Eames and Sean Brady, undated.
36. Minutes of meeting between GOLI officers and church leaders Eames, Brady, Larkin, and Hoey, 20 Nov. 1998.
37. Transcript of meeting between Orange deputation and Blair, 23 Nov. 1998.
38. Fax from David McNarry to David Montgomery, late Nov. 1998.
39. Draft letter from McCrea to Blair, undated.
40. Letter from Blair to McCrea, 8 Dec. 1998.
41. Letter from Grand Secretary Denis Watson to Blair, 16 Dec. 1998.
42. Dean Godson, *Himself Alone: David Trimble and the Ordeal of Unionism* (London: Harper Perennial, 2004), 438–41.
43. Ryder and Kearney, *Drumcree*, 303.
44. GL, June 1999.
45. Ryder and Kearney, *Drumcree*, 319.
46. Ibid., 294–5, 299.
47. Godson, *Himself Alone*, 442–3.
48. GL, Mar. 1999.
49. Ryder and Kearney, *Drumcree*, 297.
50. Meeting between COI leaders and GOLI officers, 21 June 1999.
51. Ryder and Kearney, *Drumcree*, 310.
52. Ibid., 328–32.
53. Letter from Omagh District to Tyrone Grand Lodge, 22 Oct. 2000; letter from P. Reid to Watson, 24 Nov. 2000.
54. GL, Feb. 2001, 4–7.
55. *BT* (12 July 2005, 10 July 2004, 12 Dec. 2003, 13 July 2002, 11 July 2001); interview with County Armagh Grand Secretary Joe Campbell, 5 Mar. 2003.
56. GOLI Parades Forum meeting, 26 May 1999.
57. Ryder and Kearney, *Drumcree*, 319–20.
58. GL, Mar. 2000, 4.
59. GL, June 2000, 22.
60. Ryder and Kearney, *Drumcree*, 320.
61. Ibid., 346–54; GL, Feb. 2001, 3, 8.

62. GL, Sept. 2000, 5.
63. GL, Feb. 2001, 3.
64. Ibid.
65. PC confidential document ref. OH/O/017/03.
66. *BT* (11 July 2001).
67. *BT* (9 July 2001); D. Bryan and N. Jarman, 'Marching to the Beat of Different Traditions', *Irish News* (9 Sept. 1996).
68. CC, 14 Sept. 2001; GL, Sept. 2001, 4.
69. Northern Ireland Executive news release, 9 Oct. 2000, <http://www.nics.gov.uk>.
70. GL, Apr. 2000, 9–11.
71. Letter from David Trimble to Saulters, 19 Jan. 2001.
72. Ibid.
73. Letter from Jim Wilson, MLA, to G. Patton, 22 Jan. 2001.
74. Letter from Ivan Davis to G. Patton, 27 Mar. 2001.
75. GL, Apr. 2001, 9–11. If there was a post-1950 precedent, it is difficult to find in the Orange records. The Order certainly applied pressure to previous Orange legislators, but I could find no evidence of formal letters in the post-1950 period.
76. Letters from Denis Watson to Ian Paisley and Trimble, 14 June 2001; GL, June 2001, 23–4.
77. GL, Sept. 2001, 4.
78. GL, Dec. 2002, 17.
79. GOLI report of meeting with Secretary of State John Reid, 26 Mar. 2001.
80. GL, Feb. 2001, 7–8.
81. Letter from David Brewster to G. Patton, 12 Sept. 2001.
82. Letter from Watson to J. Reid, 25 Oct. 2001.
83. Ibid.; faxed letter from J. Reid to Watson, 28 Nov. 2001.
84. CC, 7 June 2002.
85. PC confidential document ref. OH/O/017/03.
86. Sir John Quigley, *Review of the Parades Commission* (Belfast: Northern Ireland Government, 2002), 126–35.
87. Ibid., 295–302.
88. Ibid., 51–3.
89. GL, Dec. 2002, 16.
90. GL, Dec. 2002, 22.
91. Minutes of GOLI Human Rights Strategy meeting, 13 Feb. 2003.
92. GL, Mar. 2003, 12; minutes of meeting between Loyal Orders, UHRW, and Secretary of State Paul Murphy, 11 Mar. 2003.
93. Memo from GOLI officers to G. Patton, 10 Feb. 2003.
94. GL, June 2003, 27.
95. Minutes of GOLI Republic of Ireland Affairs Committee meeting, 2 Mar. 2002; GL, June 2003, 26.
96. GL, Sept. 2003, 3.
97. GL, Dec. 2003, 13.
98. *BT* (7 Apr. 2004).
99. GL, June 2004, 9–10. The fund was originally designed only to assist individual Orangemen facing court cases for civil disobedience.
100. GL, June 2004, 11.

101. House of Commons Northern Ireland Affairs Committee, The Parades Commission and Public Processions Northern Ireland Act 98, 2nd Report of Session 2004–5, ii, Ev. 65, 67.
102. Ibid., Ev. 66.
103. Ibid., Ev. 68–9.
104. <www.uhrw.org>.
105. House of Commons Northern Ireland Affairs Committee, The Parades Commission and Public Processions Northern Ireland Act 98, 2nd Report of Session 2004–5, ii, Ev. 158–60.
106. Ibid., Ev. 68–9.
107. Quigley, *Review of the Parades Commission.*
108. GL, Dec. 2004, 13.
109. GOLI returns.
110. Parades Commission Annual Report 2003–4 (http://www.paradescommission.org/), 4, accessed 2005.
111. GL, June 2004, 11.
112. GL, 24 June 2004, 25.
113. GOLI resignation forms, 2003.
114. GOLI resignation forms, 2001.
115. GL, 10 Dec. 2003, 11–12; GL special meeting, 24 June 2004, 24–6; Brian Kennaway, *The Orange Order: A Tradition Betrayed* (London: Methuen, 2006).
116. GL, Sept. 2004, 4–5; GOLI memo to private lodges, 28 Sept. 2004.
117. GL, Dec. 2004, 12; GOLI memo to private lodges, 28 Sept. 2004.
118. GL, Dec. 2004, 12, 15.
119. Ibid. 14.
120. Jonathan Tonge and Joceyn A. J. Evans, 'Eating the Oranges? The Democratic Unionist Party and the Orange Order Vote in Northern Ireland', paper presented at Elections, Public Opinion and Parties annual conference, Oxford University, 10–12 Sept. 2004.
121. 'Parades Commission Must Go', *Orange Standard* (Nov. 2005).
122. GL, 26 Feb. 2005, 26; *BT* (22 Feb. 2005).
123. GL, 26 Feb. 2005, 4.
124. *BT* (17 Sept. 2005).
125. Paul Dixon, 'Peter Hain, Secretary of State for Northern Ireland: Valuing the Union?', *Irish Political Studies* (forthcoming).
126. BBC <http://news.bbc.co.uk/>, 22 Dec. 2005.
127. *BT* (1 Dec. 2005).
128. GL, Sept. 2005, 8.

Chapter 10

1. *Orange Banner* (*c.* early 1997).
2. Quoted in Brian Kennaway, *The Orange Order: A Tradition Betrayed* (London: Methuen, 2006).
3. Chris Ryder and Vincent Kearney, *Drumcree: The Orange Order's Last Stand* (London: Methuen, 2001).

4. GOLI resignation forms, 1999.
5. Ibid.
6. Ibid.
7. Ibid.
8. Ibid.
9. Ibid.
10. Ibid.
11. GOLI resignation forms, 2000.
12. GOLI resignation forms, 1998–2003.
13. Ryder and Kearney, *Drumcree*.
14. Interview with Chris McGimpsey, Belfast City Hall, 12 Mar. 2000.
15. Seamus Smyth, 'The Faded Sash: The Decline of the Orange Order in Canada, 1920–2000', in David A. Wilson, ed., *The Orange Order in Canada* (Dublin: Four Courts, forthcoming).
16. GOLI Belfast County reports of proceedings.
17. GOLI suspension forms; GOLI resignation forms.
18. Londonderry City District 1 minute book, 1942–75; Londonderry City county reports; interview with William McClay, Derry, 7 Nov. 2002; occupations for district officers in 1961 and 1971 were attributed by McClay.
19. LOI Commission report, 1997.
20. Seamus Smyth, 'The Faded Sash'; Grand Orange Lodge of Ontario West reports of proceedings, 1921–61.
21. Based on a time-series analysis of thirty variables of annual data, largely from the Northern Ireland Statistical Research Agency (1995–2005), the *Ulster Yearbook* (1959–77), and the *Northern Ireland Annual Abstract of Statistics* (1981–95). The methodology is based on time-series analysis in Stat 7.0 using Prais-Winsten and ARIMA AR(1) modelling, in both regular and first-differenced formulations. In both Prais-Winsten and ARIMA AR(1) time-series models, the first lag of initiates was significant at the $p<.01$ level ($t = 2.34$ and 2.37) while outflows were of borderline significance at the $p<.1$ level ($t = -1.38$ and -1.89).
22. This may have been influenced by a higher average age (25 in 1971 instead of 20 in 1961).
23. Interview with Chris McGimpsey, 12 Mar. 2000.
24. Interview with Drew Nelson, 6 Mar. 2003.
25. Northern Ireland Statistical Research Agency <http://www.nisra.gov.uk/>, Annual Abstract of Statistics.
26. For details of the statistical analysis, see <http://www.sneps.net/Orange/book1-.htm>.
27. Kaufmann, 'The Orange Order in Ontario, Newfoundland, Scotland and Northern Ireland: A Macro-Social Analysis', in Wilson, ed., *The Orange Order in Canada*.
28. Kennaway, *The Orange Order*.
29. Eric Kaufmann, 'Condemned to Rootlessness: The Loyalist Origins of Canada's Identity Crisis', *Nationalism and Ethnic Politics*, 3/1 (1997), 110–35.
30. David Beito, *From Mutual Aid to the Welfare State: Fraternal Societies and Social Services, 1890–1967* (Chapel Hill, NC, and London: University of North Carolina Press, 2000).

31. Robert D. Putnam, *Bowling Alone: The Collapse and Revival of American Community* (New York: Simon & Schuster, 2000).
32. P. Hall, 'Social Capital in Britain,' *British Journal of Political Science*, 29 (1999), 417–61.
33. Paola Grenier and Karen Wright, 'Social Capital in Britain: An Update and Critique of Hall's Analysis', paper presented to American Political Science Association, Washington DC, 2005.
34. John Belton and Kent Henderson, 'Freemasons—an Endangered Species,' *Ars Quatuor Coronatorum: Transactions of Quatuor Coronati Lodge No. 2076*, 113 (2001), 117–18.
35. 'The Way Forward for Orangeism' (Belfast: GOLI, 2003).
36. Duncan Morrow, Derek Birrell, John Greer, and Terry O'Keeffe, *The Churches and Inter-Community Relationships* (Coleraine: Centre for the Study of Conflict, University of Ulster, 1991), 20.
37. Unpublished figures for Orange and Masonic orders in Ontario, 1891–1991, collected by Eric Kaufmann and J. C. Herbert Emery.
38. See detailed statistical analysis on website: <http://www.sneps.net/Orange/book1-.htm>.
39. Peter Day, 'The Orange Order and the July 12th Parade in Liverpool since 1945', MA dissertation, University of Salford, 2005, 32; Elaine McFarland, *Protestants First: Orangeism in Nineteenth Century Scotland* (Edinburgh: Edinburgh University Press, 1990), 214.
40. Kaufmann, 'The Orange Order'.
41. Ibid.
42. This figure subtracts the two districts in the city lodge that are in the Republic of Ireland. I am indebted to David Fitzpatrick for pointing this out at a seminar in Belfast.
43. See also the Provincial [Masonic] Grand Lodge of Londonderry and Donegal website at <http://www.irish-freemasons.org/londonderry.htm>.
44. Social and Community Planning Research, *Northern Ireland Social Attitude Survey, 1989–1991: Cumulative File* [computer file], Colchester: UK Data Archive, SN 3292 (Sept. 1996); P. Devine and L. Dowds, *Northern Ireland Life and Times Survey, 1998* [computer file], Colchester: UK Data Archive, SN 4229 (July 1997); P. Devine and L. Dowds, *Northern Ireland Life and Times Survey, 2004* [computer file], Colchester: UK Data Archive, SN 5227 (Oct. 2005).
45. Jonathan Tonge, *The New Northern Irish Politics* (Basingstoke: Palgrave, 2005), 194.
46. Morrow et al., *The Churches and Inter-Community Relationships*, 20.
47. LOI Commission, 1997.
48. 'The Way Forward for Orangeism', 18 Jan. 2003.
49. Desmond Bell, *Acts of Union: Youth Culture and Sectarianism in Modern Ireland* (London: Macmillan, 1990); Dominic Bryan, *Orange Parades: The Politics of Ritual, Tradition and Control* (London: Pluto, 2000); interview with David Brewster, 17 Jan. 2003, Limavady.
50. In statistical terms, only Troubles-related deaths significantly predict Orange membership density when variables are first-differenced (de-trended) to account for possible non-stationarity.

51. Fermanagh County minutes, 21 May 1942, courtesy of Fermanagh Grand Lodge (held by the current secretary).
52. Ibid., Nov. 1942.
53. GL, Dec. 1981, 37; June 1985, 7; Dec. 1998, 17–18; Dec. 1999, 5.
54. GL, Dec. 1997, 18.
55. GL, June 2000, 19–20.
56. GL, June 2003, 29.
57. GL, June 2004, 10.
58. Letter from Castlewellan District 12 to County Down Grand Lodge, 20 Jan. 2001.
59. 'The Way Forward for Orangeism', 18 Jan. 2003.
60. Devine and Dowds, *Northern Ireland Life and Times Survey, 2004*.
61. Morrow et al., *The Churches and Inter-Community Relationships*, 43–4.
62. CC, 12 Dec. 1951.
63. Cliftonville District 3 minutes, 10 June 1969.
64. GL, June 1975, 10.
65. GL, June 1996, 20.
66. LOI Commission, 1997.
67. GL, June 1997, 20.
68. Kennaway, *The Orange Order*.
69. Ibid.
70. Bryan, *Orange Parades*.
71. GL, Apr. 2001, 10.
72. CC, 9 June 1967.
73. GOLI expulsion forms, 1967; Kennaway, *The Orange Order*.
74. GL, June 1986, 15.
75. Kennaway, *The Orange Order*.
76. GL, Mar. 2003, 13.
77. Kennaway, *The Orange Order*.
78. GL, Dec. 2003, 12.
79. CC, 7 Oct. 1966.
80. CC, 10 Mar. 1972, 14 June 1972.
81. CC, 29 Oct. 1974.
82. CC, 5 Dec. 1975.
83. CC, 17 Sept. 1976, Nov. 1976.
84. GL, June 1977, 18; CC, 8 June 1977.
85. GL, Dec. 1978, 6–7.
86. CC, 9 Dec. 1981.
87. GL, Dec. 1993, 8–9.
88. GL, June 1998, 31.
89. GL, Mar. 1999, 11.
90. GL, June 2001, 31.
91. GL, June 2004, 15.
92. CC, 5 Oct. 1973.
93. CC, 4 Dec. 1981.
94. GL, Dec. 1983, 32.
95. GL, June 1999, 25.

96. GL, June 1977, 8; CC, 8 June 1977.
97. GL, Dec. 2001, 19.
98. Bryan, *Orange Parades*, 85, 88, 90–1.
99. *BT* (2 Nov. 2001).
100. *BT* (9 June 2003).
101. GL, June 2002, 29.
102. Letter from Stena Line to George Patton, 3 Sept. 2001.
103. Letter from Stena Line to G. Patton, 13 Sept. 2002.
104. Letter from G. Patton to W. Leathem, County Antrim Grand Secretary, 3 Oct. 2002.
105. Faxed letter from David Brewster to G. Patton, 5 Nov. 2002.
106. *Report on the 12th July 2002—Ardoyne* (Belfast: GOLI).
107. PC confidential document ref. OH/O/017/03; Grand Lodge memo, 10 Feb. 2003.
108. BBC News <www.bbc.co.uk>, 31 Oct. 2005, 10 Sept. 2005; *BT* (27 Sept. 2005).
109. 'Orangemen Blame Police for Belfast Riots', *Guardian* (14 Sept. 2005).
110. Breaking News.ie Archives <http://archives.tcm.ie/breakingnews/2005>, 14 Sept. 2005.
111. *Lessons to be Learned? The Belfast Riots* (Belfast: GOLI, Sept. 2005).
112. GL, Sept. 2005, 3–5.
113. Jonathan Tonge and Jocelyn A. J. Evans, 'Eating the Oranges? The Democratic Unionist Party and the Orange Order Vote in Northern Ireland', paper presented at Elections, Public Opinion and Parties annual conference, Oxford University, 10–12 Sept. 2004.
114. Ibid.
115. GL, Dec. 1997, 10; LOI Commission report, 1997; GOLI Parades Strategy document, *c.* Aug. 1998; GL, Mar. 1999, p. 6; GOLI resignation forms, 1998–2003; Kennaway, *The Orange Order*; minutes of special meeting between Orange Order and PSNI, 9 May 2005.
116. Neil Jarman and D. Bryan, *From Riots to Rights: Nationalist Parades in the North of Ireland* (Coleraine: Centre for the Study of Conflict, University of Ulster, 1998).
117. Comments from Belfast County Master Dawson Baillie, Nov. 2002.
118. Interview with the Rev. Mervyn Gibson, 17 Sept. 2005; interview with G. Patton, 9 June 2005.
119. Interview with Drew Nelson, 13 July 2004.
120. PC confidential document ref. OH/O/017/03.
121. Interview with Gibson, 17 Sept. 2005.
122. Interview with George Chittick, 17 Mar. 2000.
123. Interview with Gibson, 17 Sept. 2005.
124. E. Kaufmann, 'The New Unionism', *Prospect* (Nov. 2005).
125. GL, Sept. 2000, 6.
126. GL, Sept. 2001, 3; Dec. 2001, 10.
127. GL, Mar. 2002, 6–7, 22–4.
128. CC, 10 Dec. 1969, 10 Sept. 1971, 13 June 1973, 22 Sept. 1978; GL, Dec. 1981, 37.
129. GL, Dec. 1998, 9, 13.
130. Eric Kaufmann, *The Rise and Fall of Anglo-America: The Decline of Dominant Ethnicity in the United States* (Cambridge, MA: Harvard University Press, 2004), 292–6; E. Kaufmann, 'The Decline of the WASP in the United States and Canada', in

E. Kaufmann, ed., *Rethinking Ethnicity: Majority Groups and Dominant Minorities* (London: Routledge, 2004), 61–83.

131. <http://billmon.org/archives/000030.html>, accessed 2005.
132. GL, Dec. 1981, 37–8.
133. GL, Dec. 1982, 5–6.
134. Donald Harman Akenson, *God's Peoples: Covenant and Land in South Africa, Israel, and Ulster* (Ithaca: Cornell University Press, 1992).
135. GL, Dec. 1983, 14.
136. GL, June 1997, 12–14.
137. GL, June 1998, 11.
138. GL, Mar. 1999, 10.
139. GL, Sept. 2000, 11.
140. GL, June 2001, 28; Dec. 2003, 15.
141. GL, Dec. 2004, 19.
142. GL, Mar. 2002, 11.
143. GL, Mar. 2004, 6.
144. GL, Sept. 2005, 28.
145. GL, Mar. 2005, 3–4.
146. GL, Dec. 2004, 23–4; Mar. 2005, 6–7; Sept. 2005, 6.
147. GL, Mar. 2005, 11; Sept. 2005, 7.
148. Interview with Lord Laird of Artigarvan, 17 Nov. 2005.
149. 'Alabama Orangemen Head for Tobermore', GOLI press statement, 4 July 2005 <http://www.grandorange.org.uk/>, accessed 2005.
150. Interview with Brian Kennaway, 16 Mar. 2000.
151. Kaufmann, 'Condemned to Rootlessness'.
152. Interviews with John McGrath, 28 Feb. 2003, 6 Mar. 2003.

Chapter 11

1. Ruth Dudley Edwards, *The Faithful Tribe: An Intimate Protrait of the Loyal Institutions* (London: Harper Collins, 1999).
2. Steve Bruce, *The Edge of the Union: The Ulster Loyalist Political Vision* (Oxford: Oxford University Press, 1994) 32–4
3. 'Apprentice Boys of Derry Parade', Police Service of Northern Ireland website <http://www.psni.police.uk> accessed 2005.
4. Interview with Alex Rough, 28 Sept. 2004, Toronto Orange Centre.
5. Christopher Farrington, 'The Democratic Unionist Party and the Northern Ireland Peace Process', paper presented to the Political Studies Association, Lincoln, UK.
6. D. Horowitz, *Ethnic Groups in Conflict* (Berkeley: University of California Press, 1985), 293–8.
7. Eric Kaufmann, 'The Orange Order in Ontario, Newfoundland, Scotland and Northern Ireland: A Macro-Social Analysis', in David A. Wilson, ed., *The Orange Order in Canada* (Dublin: Four Courts, forthcoming); Eric Kaufmann, 'The Orange Order in Scotland since 1860: A Social Analysis', in M. Mitchell, ed., *The Irish in Scotland* (Edinburgh: Birlinn, forthcoming).

8. For example, see Ian Adamson, *The Ulster People: Ancient, Mediaeval and Modern* (Bangor: Pretani Press, 1991).
9. Paul Dixon, *Northern Ireland: The Politics of War and Peace* (Basingstoke: Palgrave, 2001), 296.
10. E. Kaufmann, 'Liberal Ethnicity: Beyond Liberal Nationalism and Minority Rights', *Ethnic and Racial Studies*, 23/6 (2000), 1086–119.

Index